KB041674

American Bar Exam Review

미국 변호사법 ④

백희영

MEE
기출문제 해설집

박영사

머리말

본 기출문제 해설집은 미국변호사 시험 중 MEE(multistate essay examination)를 위한 것으로서, 2008년부터~2022년까지의 MEE기출문제 15년치에 대한 모범답안 및 그 해설집이다.

출제위원회(NCBE)에서 제공하는 기출문제 해설도 있으나, 그 내용이 너무 길고 복잡하여 수험생이 이를 파악하기에는 시간이 너무 오래 걸리는 단점이 있다. 필자가 항상 강조하듯이 '미국변호사 시험'은 말 그대로 자격증을 획득하기 위한 시험이다. 누구나 짧은 시간 내에 빠르게 합격하면 되고 그 이상의 의미는 없다. 아무리 많은 시간을 투입하여 열심히 공부했어도 합격하지 못하면 아무 의미가 없고 육체적·정신적 피로만 축적될 뿐이다. 미국법에 대한 심도 있는 연구나 그 이상의 의미는 합격한 후에 각자의 전문 영역에서 더 깊이 있게 연구하면 되는 일이다.

따라서 필자는 수험생들이 반드시 써넣어야 할 필수 단어와 논점, 답안 분량을 고려하여 본 서를 집필하였다. 즉 실제 시험장에서 쓸 수 있고 충분히 합격할 수 있는 수준의 답안을 써두었고 그에 적합한 해설을 붙여 두었다. 즉 본 서는 오직 빠른 시험 합격을 목적으로 한 기출문제 해설서이다.

캘리포니아는 MEE가 아닌, CEE를 진행하는 바, 캘리포니아 시험을 준비하는 수험자에게 본 서는 적합하지 않다.

본 서의 특징은 다음과 같다.
1. 심플하며 이해하기 쉽고 현장 실전용이다.
2. 각 문제별로 '난이도'를 표기하였다.
3. MEE에서는 답안이 길다 하더라도, 꼭 필요한 단어가 없으면 합격할 수 없다. 점수에 직결되는 '핵심 단어 및 논점'을 정리해두었다.
4. 각 기출에 대한 지문 요약, 중요 논점, 답안 로직, 고득점 포인트 등을 정리해두었다.
5. 본 서의 '답안요령'은 해당 논점에 대해 반드시 써야 할 키워드들이다.
6. 본 서의 '예상질문'은 해당 기출에 관한 예상 질문과 그에 대한 해설이다.
7. 본 서의 '연도별 기출정리표'는 2008년부터 2024년 2월까지의 기출문제를 과목별로 정리한 것이다.

8. 본 서는 다음과 같은 약자를 사용하였다.
    - Feb: February
    - Sep: September
    - Oct: October
9. 2015년도 시험부터는 시험 범위에서 negotiable instruments가 제외됨에 따라, 이에 대한 해설은 본 서에 싣지 않았다.

끝으로, 이 책이 나올 수 있도록 도와주신 박영사 관계자분들께 감사드린다. 본 해설집과 더불어 나의 강의가 수험생 여러분들의 수험기간을 조금이라도 단축시킬 수 있다면 나로서는 매우 기쁘겠다. 여러분들의 빠른 합격을 기원드린다.

2024년 8월 15일
백희영 씀

차례

1. The will may be invalid in part because of Harriet's undue influence.

A will is invalid if it was executed as a result of undue influence. Undue influence occurs when the wrongdoer exerted influence over testator's free will and caused the testator to make a distribution. The burden of proof is on the contestant, who must show: (1) the testator was susceptible to undue influence, (2) the alleged wrongdoer had the opportunity to exert undue influence upon the testator, (3) the alleged wrongdoer had a disposition to exert undue influence, and (4) the will appears to be the product of undue influence.

Here, it is clear that Harriet had opportunity and disposition to influence Testator. Harriet was a housekeeper of Testator and she limited his contacts with Doris and repeatedly ask him to provide for her in his will. Harriet threatened to quit if Testator did not provide for her in his will and he created will in a short time after the threat. Testator was not susceptible, since he managed all of his own financial affairs and maintained these activities until his death. On the other hand, Testator would be susceptible, since he was increasingly ill and dependent on Harriet.

In most jurisdictions, a presumption of undue influence arises when there is a confidential relationship between the testator and alleged wrongdoer. It is unclear whether the court concludes the confidential relationship between Harriet and Testator. If the court finds the confidential relationship, the burden of proof would shift to Harriet.

A will is invalid in whole or in part if it was executed as the result of undue influence. A portion of will that are infected by undue influence becomes invalid, not the whole will.

Here, it is less clear whether the entire will was infected by undue influence. Testator and Sam had been estranged for several years prior to the time of Testator's death and it is possible that Testator would have left his entire estate to Doris if he had not left a one−half share to Harriet. However, there is no stating that Testator was estranged with Fred, Bob, and Ella. Additionally, there is a possibility that Testator could provide a share to Sam.

In sum, the will may be invalid in part because of Harriet's undue influence.

2. Testator's estate will be pass to Testator's heirs, Doris, Sam, and Fred.

If the will is invalid in whole, Testator's estate will be distributed to his heirs. Testator's heirs would be his two surviving children, Doris and Sam, and his grandchild, Fred who is the representative of Bob. Doris's child, Ella would not take a share, because Doris survived Testator and there is no basis for Ella to represent her mother.

In sum, Testator's estate will be pass to Testator's heirs, Doris, Sam, and Fred.

3. Harriet's one−half share of the estate would pass to Doris entirely under the modern rule, while it would be equally distributed to Testator's heirs under the no residue of a residue rule.

Under the common law no residue of a residue rule, the invalid share passes to the testator's heirs. In modern, the invalid share falls into residuary legatee. This approach is based on the theory that the testator's executed will evidences an intention to benefit the legatees listed in a will.

If the will is invalid in part, the bequest to Harriet is invalidated. Under the common law, Harriet's one−half share of the estate would pass to the testator's heirs equally, Doris, Sam, and Fred. However, Harriet's one−half share would pass to Doris who is the only residuary legatee in the majority of jurisdiction.

In sum, Harriet's one−half share of the estate would pass to Doris entirely under the modern rule, while it would be equally distributed to Testator's heirs under the no residue of a residue rule.

해설

난이도: 하

핵심 단어 및 논점

- validity of will
- undue influence
- intestate succession
- no residue of a residue rule (common law)
- residue of a residue rule (UPC)

본 기출은 undue influence가 will의 '전체'에 영향을 미친 경우(2번 문제)와 '부분적'으로 영향을 미친 경우(3번 문제)로 구분하고 있다.

1. Library cannot be found liable to Paul under a strict liability theory, since it is not a commercial seller.

A commercial seller is subject to strict product liability for physical harm thereby caused, when he sells any defective product that is unreasonably dangerous to the consumer. The commercial seller is defined as one who engaged in the business of selling products for use or consumption.

Here, the chicken salad sandwich was unreasonably dangerous to Paul because it contained salmonella bacteria. If Paul seeks to raise a strict liability action against Library, he does not need to establish Library's negligence. However, Library is not a commercial seller, because it is not engaged in the business of selling the sandwich.

In sum, Library is not subject to strict product liability, since it is not a commercial seller.

2. Supermarket cannot be found liable to Paul under a strict liability theory, since the chicken was not defective.

The term "commercial sellers" include a retailer who has no control over the design and manufacture of a product. Thus, retailers can be subject to strict product liability, if they sell defective products.

Here, Supermarket is a commercial seller, who sold the defective chicken. The fact that Paul is not a direct purchaser of the chicken does not make a different result. This is because the privity of contract is not required in raising strict product liability.

A product is defective when it is unreasonably dangerous. A product could have a manufacturing defect, a design defects, or inadequate warnings.

Here, the chicken was contained in packages labeled with a prominent warning describing the risk of salmonella contamination and the precautions necessary to avoid that risk. Thus, the chicken had adequate warnings. The risk of salmonella contamination is the nature of the chicken, and it is not by defective manufacturing or design. Thus, the chicken is not defective.

In sum, Paul cannot recover damages from Supermarket under a strict liability theory.

3. Ann, Bill, and Chuck cannot be found liable under either a strict liability or negligence theory.

Negligence action can be raised when the defendant failed to exercise reasonable care.

Here, the Health Department determined proper preparation and cooking can ensure that the chicken is safe for eating. It shows that one of Ann, Bill, and Chuck was negligent.

Under the res ipsa loquitur doctrine, jury can infer negligence when (1) the event is of a kind which ordinarily does not occur in the absence of negligence, (2) the negligence is within the scope of the defendant's duty to the plaintiff, and (3) the defendant was exclusive to the control.

Here, Ann, Bill, and Chuck had a duty to exercise reasonable care (proper preparation and cooking) for Paul who was a lunch patron and who was foreseeable to consume the chicken salad. However, Paul cannot establish the exact person who was negligent. Thus, Paul cannot recover the damage under the res ipsa loquitur doctrine.

Under the alternative liability doctrine, jury can find two defendants liable when each was negligent and either individual could have caused the plaintiff's injuries. Here, Paul cannot show that any of the defendants were negligent.

Under the joint venture doctrine, the jury imputes one defendant's negligence to other defendants who are engaged in a common project. Here, the fact shows that Ann, Bill, and Chuck independently volunteered to make the chicken salad. Thus, they did not engaged in a common project and therefore the joint venture doctrine is inapplicable in this case.

Regarding strict product liability, Ann, Bill, and Chuck are not commercial sellers. Thus, Paul cannot recover from any of them by raising a strict product liability claim. In sum, Ann, Bill, and Chuck cannot be found liable under either a strict liability or negligence theory.

해설

난이도: 1번 문제: 하
1번 문제: 하
3번 문제: 중

핵심 단어 및 논점

- strict liability
- commercial seller
- defective product (warning)
- res ipsa loquitur doctrine

- alternative liability doctrine
- joint venture doctrine
- strict product liability

1번, 2번 문제

- 본 기출문제의 1번 문제는 "commercial seller" 정의에 중점을 두고, 2번 문제는 "defective" 여부에 중점을 두고 있다.

- 'Strict liability를 입증하는데 있어 피고의 negligence 유무는 무관하다'는 점을 명시하는 것이 고득점 포인트다. 이는 products liability뿐만 아니라 일반적인 strict liability에 관해 논하는 경우에도 그러하다.

2008Feb Family Law

1. The court did not err in refusing a dissolution of Husband's dissolution of his adoption.

An adoption order is the final and complete transfer of parental rights and responsibilities. It is difficult to seek a dissolution of stepparent adoption compared to stranger adoptions. Regarding dissolution claims, courts typically consider the length of the relationship, the child's needs, and the parents' motives. Here, Amy and Bert was Wife's two children and Husband adopted them, thus Husband is stepparent. Husband adopted them 10 years ago and neither Amy nor Bert has ever had a relationship with their biological father. Amy, age 6, is minor and she needs Husband's support. Additionally, Husband's dissolution petition is seemed only for financial reasons. The financial reason is not adequate reason for dissolution of adoption.

In sum, the court did not err in refusing dissolution of Husband's dissolution of his adoption.

2. The court did not err in refusing to retroactive downward modification and in refusing to modify future support obligation.

The interstate enforcement and modification of child support are governed by the UIFSA. Retroactive modification of child support obligations is completely forbidden. Thus, the court did not err in refusing to retroactive downward modification.

Modification of future child support order is typically available only when the petitioner can show a substantial change in circumstances. A significant decrease in income is a substantial change. However, when a parent wants to modify a child support obligation because he has voluntarily reduced his income, courts use different approaches. Some courts use good faith approach and permit downward modification only if a petitioner has acted in good faith. Some courts refuse to modify whenever the income shift was voluntary. Many courts balance the interests of both parent and child under a multifactor approach. They consider many factors, such as impact of such a shift on the child, duration of petitioner's income loss, the likelihood of a promotion that would ultimately be beneficial to child, and modification of child custody order.

Here, Husband reduced working hours to finish writing a novel and the income shift is voluntary. There is no obvious end point and it is not a valid basis for modification. Additionally, Wife worked full time at the job she has held since her marriage, but has been borrowing money to meet the family's expenses. By contrast, Husband can easily give up his plan to write a novel. The timing of Husband's decision to reduce the working hour is similar with the time that he wanted to stop supporting. It shows that Husband's income reduction is made in bad faith.

In conclusion, the court did not err in refusing to retroactive downward modification and in refusing to modify future support obligation.

3. The court erred in denying Husband's petition, since Bert is employable and Husband's commands are reasonable.

Generally, a divorced parent is required to provide educational support for a child over the age of majority. However, parents may terminate support to employable children who disobey reasonable parental opinion.

Here, Husband commands Bert not to join a rock band and requested Bert that he leaves the band and devotes more time to study. Bert's college grades have slipped from A's to C's, and he has been arrested for driving while intoxicated. Husband's commands are reasonable and Bert ages 19 who is employable.

In sum, the court erred in denying Husband's petition.

해설

난이도: 하

핵심 단어 및 논점

- dissolution of adoption order
- modification of child support order
- substantial change in circumstances
- employable children

<u>1. The trial court did not err in admitting into evidence the hospital record, since it falls within hearsay exception even if it is double hearsay. The first level falls within the business records exception, and the second level falls within the medical treatment exception.</u>

Hearsay is an out-of-court statement offered in evidence to prove the truth of the matter asserted.

Here, the hospital record containing Victor's statement is double hearsay. The record is an out-of-court statement and the prosecutor is offering it to prove the truth of the matter asserted, Victor told Nurse that Dan stabbed him. Nurse's statement is also an out-of-court statement and it is to prove the truth that Dan stabbed him. If both levels of hearsay fall within hearsay exceptions, the record is admissible. The record itself is the first level of hearsay. Victor's statement to Nurse is the second level of hearsay.

A record of acts, events, conditions, or diagnoses is admissible hearsay under the business records exception, if: (1) it is made at or near the time of the recorded event by a person who has personal knowledge on the event and (2) the making of the record is the regular practice of the business.

In this case, Nurse's writing in the hospital record falls within the business record exception. Nurse had personal knowledge on the event Victor said and she made the record near the time of the Victor's statement. The fact states that it is the regular practice admitting nurse to record patient's information. Thus, the first level of hearsay is admissible under the business records exception.

If a statement is: (1) regarding medical history, symptoms, or the general character of the cause of the symptoms (2) made by a person who is seeking medical treatment and (3) reasonably relevant to treatment, the statement falls within the hearsay exception.

Here, Victor's statement is regarding cause of the symptoms and he made this statement to seek medical treatment. However, the portion of the Victor's statement regarding the identity of the person who cased the symptom is not relevant to treatment, and it is not admissible. Another portion of the statement falls within the hearsay exception and is admissible.

In sum, the trial court did not err in admitting into evidence the hospital record, since it falls within hearsay exception even if it is double hearsay. The first level falls within the business records exception, and the second level falls within the medical treatment exception.

2. The trial court erred in sustaining Wife's claim of privilege, since the statement is not the one against Victor and the statement is not confidential.

There are two privileges in the marital relationship. A witness privilege applies when a witness—spouse has the right not to testify against an accused spouse in a criminal case.

Here, Wife's statement regarding the identity of Victor's assailant is not the one against Victor, and witness privilege cannot be applied.

Confidential communication privilege can be hold by both spouses if statements (1) were in private and (2) both spouses do not reveal the communication to anyone. Here, there is no fact stating the communication between Wife and Victor was not in private, and Wife can raise the privilege. However, Wife told Friend that Dan is not assailant. The part of the communication is revealed to a third party and it is not confidential. The privilege cannot apply here.

In sum, the trial court erred in sustaining Wife's claim of privilege, since the statement is not the one against Victor and the statement is not confidential.

3. The trial court did err in sustaining the prosecutor's hearsay objection, when Victor's statement to wife is used to impeach Victor's credibility.

Victor's statement to Wife that Dan was not his assailant is hearsay, if it was made out of court and it is used to prove the truth of the matter asserted. However, Victor's statement to wife is admissible if it is used to impeach his credibility. Additionally, any inconsistent statement can be used to attack the credibility of declarant.

Here, if the hospital record is admitted prove that Victor identified Dan as his assailant, Victor's statement to Wife is admissible to attack Victor's credibility.

In sum, the trial court did err in sustaining the prosecutor's hearsay objection, when Victor's statement to wife is used to impeach Victor's credibility.

해설

난이도: 하

핵심 단어 및 논점

- hearsay
- double hearsay
- hearsay exception
  - business record exception
  - medical treatment exception
- privilege for confidential marital communication
- hearsay v. impeachment

1번 문제

| 답안요령 |

> 1. Analysis(해당 증거의 relevance에 대한)
> 2. Hearsay 정의
>   + analysis
> 3. Double hearsay exception rule
>   + analysis
> 4. 1st level이 해당하는 exception rule
>   + analysis
> 5. 2nd level이 해당하는 exception rule
>   + analysis
> 6. 결론

| TIP | Double hearsay인 경우, 바깥에 있는 hearsay(first level)부터 analysis한다.

2번 문제

배우자 관계에서 인정되는 privileges에 대해 논할 때, spousal immunity와 confidential communication privilege를 구분하여 각 privilege에 대해 analysis하는 것이 고득점 포인트다.

1. Cal violated the duty of loyalty to Prime, since he has benefit personally from the contract made between Prime and Smart.

Each boarder has duty of loyalty to the corporation. Duty of loyalty includes duty to refrain from competing with the company, not to have a conflicting interest personally, and to account to the company and to hold as trustee for the company any benefit derived by the member in the conduct of the company's activities.

Here, Cal is the CEO and chairman of the board of Prime and therefore he has a fiduciary duty of loyalty of Prime. When Smart was hired by Prime, Cal had benefits personally because Cal had a 25% partnership interest in Smart. Even if he stated that he would not be involved in any work to be performed by Smart for Prime and he did not participate in the vote, he is entitled to a share of benefits from Smart's work for Prime.

In sum, Cal violated the duty of loyalty to Prime.

2. Cal have no defense to liability, since he did not fully informed disinterested boarders and it is hard to say that the transaction is fair.

Safe harbor rule protects a director who breaches his duty of loyalty. First of all, a director's conflicting interest transaction is protected under the safe harbor, when: (1) there is an approval by disinterested directors or shareholders, (2) a director fully disclosed all relevant information, and (3) a director played no part in the disinterested directors' vote directly or indirectly.

In this case, Cal breached his duty of loyalty through the conflicting interest transaction. This transaction was approved by the Board who is disinterested with it and Cal played no part in the vote. However, Cal did not fully disclose all relevant information that Smart's proposed fee for the consulting assignment was substantially higher than it normally charged for comparable work.

Thus, Cal could not be protected from his violation of duty of loyalty.

Secondly, when a director establishes that conflicting interest transaction was fair to the corporation, a director could be protected.

In this case, it seems hard to say that the contract with Smart was fair, since Smart's proposed fee was substantially higher than normal fee.

In sum, Cal could not be protected through fairness.

3. The directors of Prime, other than Cal, violated their duty of care, since they were not in an informed manner.

Under the business judgment rule, it is presumed that a member makes a decision (1) in a good faith, (2) in an informed manner, (3) based on a rational basis, and (4) for the best interest of the corporation. If a member does not qualify this presumption, he violated his duty of care.

Here, there is no fact showing eight members of the Board were acting in bad faith. However, those members did not make a decision not in an informed manner, since they did not ask about the basis for Smart's proposed fee. Reasonable members would ask more about Smart's fee. Additionally, they discussed the relative merits of the two proposals only for 10 minutes, and it is too short to discuss.

In sum, the directors of Prime, other than Cal, violated their duty of care.

해설

난이도: 하

핵심 단어 및 논점

- corporation
- fiduciary duty
- conflicting interest transaction
- business judgment rule (BJR)

2번 문제

Directors가 행한 특정 행위에 대해 책임을 져야 하는지 그 여부를 판단하는 문제로서, 다음과 같은 logic을 가진다.

BJR에 따르면 director의 행위는 보호되는 바, 책임을 지지 않는다.

→ Director가 한 특정 행위는 BJR과 연관이 있다.

→ 다만, 주주(director에게 책임을 묻고자 하는 자)는 director의 행위가 not good faith임을 증명할 것이다.

→ 주주의 증명으로서 BJR이 적용될 수 없는 바, director는 그 행위에 대해 책임이 있다.

답안요령

1. Duty of loyalty (conflicting interest transaction)
   + analysis
2. Safe harbor rule
   + analysis
3. Fairness
   + analysis

TIP1 Conflicting interest transaction에 관한 case의 경우, safe harbor rule을 우선 적용하고, safe harbor rule의 요건을 만족하지 못한 경우 fairness에 대해 추가적으로 analysis한다.

TIP2 1번: Conflicting interest transaction 용어가 modern과 CL에서 차이가 있다는 점을 서술하는 것이 고득점 포인트다.

TIP3 3번: Fairness 여부를 판단해야 할 행위가 어떤 유형의 행위인지 그 여부에 따라 entire fairness review(fair price와 fair dealing)의 적용여부가 다르다.

1. The Corporation's motion for a post−judgment JMOL was procedurally improper, since it made JMOL at the close of Plaintiff's evidence.

A party may make a motion for judgment notwithstanding the verdict (JNOV) when: (1) the party makes the motion no later than 28 days after the entry of judgment and (2) the party previously made JMOL at the close of all the evidence.

First, the Corporation moved for a post−judgment JMOL eight days after the entry of judgment. Second, the moving party must make the motion at the close of the record or it loses its right to renew the motion after the entry of judgment. Even if the Corporation moved for JMOL motion after the close of Plaintiff's evidence, it was not at the close of all the evidence.

When a party moved for JNOV but moved for JMOL at the close of the plaintiff's case, federal courts are divided in treating the party. Some federal courts require strict compliance and held that it is insufficient for JNOV motion.

In some other federal courts, moving for JMOL at the close of all evidences is not a substantially important for JNOV motion, if the evidence introduced by the defendant was brief and could not have possibly changed the court's decision on the earlier motion. However, the evidence Corporation submitted was substantial and could have changed the court's view, if it made the motion at the close of all evidence.

In sum, the Corporation's motion for a post−judgment JMOL was procedurally improper, since it made JMOL at the close of Plaintiff's evidence.

2. The trial court should not grant Corporation's motion for a post—judgment JMOL, because Corporation's argument does not justify the motion for JNOV.

A motion for JMOL at the close of all evidence or JNOV can be granted, if a reasonable jury would not have a legally sufficient basis to find for the nonmoving party.

Here, the Corporation argues that its evidence was more persuasive and more credible than Plaintiff's evidence, but it cannot be a basis for overturning the jury's verdict. This is because it is regarding factual determination, and even if the evidence was more persuasive and more credible, it does not mean that jury acted unreasonably. The fact that the trial judge believes that Corporation's information and its witness is credible does not make a different result, because the credibility of witness is the core function of jury.

In sum, the trial court should not grant Corporation's motion for a post—judgment JMOL, because Corporation's argument does not justify the motion for JNOV.

3. The trial court should not grant Coporation's motion for a new trial because of the Corporation's more persuasive evidence, since there is no fact to show miscarriage of justice.

The motion for a new trial should be filed within 28 days of the entry of judgment. In general, the grounds for a new trial are that: (1) the verdict is against the weight of the evidence, that the damages are excessive, or (2) the trial was not fair.

The trial judge must respect the collective wisdom of the jury. It is not proper for a court to grant a new trial on the ground that the verdict is against the weight of the evidence unless the record shows that the jury's verdict resulted in a miscarriage of justice.

Here, Corporation's first ground for the motion for a new trial is that its evidence was more persuasive and more credible than Plaintiff's evidence. Because the court is not required to weigh the evidence in light most favorable to the verdict winner, it would support the motion for a new trial. However, the facts were highly disputed at trial. Notwithstanding the fact that the court may believe that Corporation's evidence was more persuasive, it would be improper for the court to grant Corporation's motion for a new trial on this basis.

In sum, the trial court should not grant Corporation's motion for a new trial.

4. The trial court should grant Corporation's motion for a new trial because of the jury's conduct, because it made the trial unfair.

Even though motions for a new trial based on juror's nondisclosures during voir dire are usually unsuccessful, a new trial should be granted if the withheld information would have justified a disqualification.

Here, Corporation's second ground for a new trial was juror's improper nondisclosure of the information that the juror would bias against Corporation. If the Corporation known of juror's nondisclosed information, it surely would have moved that the potential juror be struck. The bias should be actual biases. The fact shows that the jury had actual bias even before the trial began. Thus, the court could find that the jury's foreperson's bias against Corporation fundamentally undermines the fairness of the trial.

In sum, the trial court should grant Corporation's motion for a new trial.

해설

난이도: 상

핵심 단어 및 논점

- judgment notwithstanding the verdict (JNOV)
- new trial
- juror's nondisclosures during voir dire

1. State Bank has superior claim to DC's checking account at State Bank, since it has a perfected security interest in the deposit account.

A security interests is enforceable when: (1) debtor signed a security agreement. (2) debtor has rights in the collateral, and (3) secured party gave money to secured party.

Here, the checking account is deposit account for the security interest purpose. Both State Bank and Frist Bank made effective security interests in the account, because all requirements are satisfied: DC's president signed security agreements, DC has rights in the account, and each bank gave DC a loan.

A security interest in a deposit account is perfected only when: (1) secured party is the bank with which the deposit account is maintained, (2) the bank where the account is held has agreed in writing to follow the instructions of the secured party, or (3) the secured party becomes the bank's customer as to the account.

Here, even though First Bank filed the financing statement, its security interest was not perfected. First, the demand account is maintained with State Bank, rather than First Bank. Second, there is no such agreement in this case. Third, there is no fact that First Bank became State Bank's customer. By contrast, State Bank has a perfected security interest in the deposit account, because it is the bank with which the account is maintained.

Between an unperfected secured creditor and a perfected secured creditor, a perfected secured creditor has superior claim to the collateral.

In conclusion, State Bank has superior claim to DC's checking account at State Bank, since it has a perfected security interest in the deposit account.

2(a). First Bank has a superior claim to DC's officer equipment, since it perfected the security by filing.

A security interest in equipment is perfected when an effective financing statement is filed. A financing statement is effective when it contain: (1) the name of the debtor, (2) the name of the secured party, and (3) an indication of the collateral. Here, First Bank filed its financing statement in the correct filing office in State A. In the statement, the name of debtor was wrongly stated.

Regarding the name of a registered corporation, a financing statement must states the name of the organization that is indicated on the public record. However, minor errors do not make a financing statement ineffective, unless those errors make the financing statement seriously misleading.

Here, First Bank's financial statement incorrectly listed the name of the debtor as "Dart Incorporated," which is different from the name reflected on other public records. However, a search under the wrongful name would turn up the financing statement listing "Dart Incorporated" as the debtor. In short, incorrectly stated name is not seriously misleading in this case and, therefore, First Bank's security is perfected.

In conclusion, First Bank has a superior claim to DC's officer equipment, since it perfected the security by filing.

2(b). First Bank has a superior claim to DC's office equipment, since First Bank perfected its security interest before State Bank becomes a lien creditor.

A judgment lien creditor takes priority over a security interest only when the creditor became a lien creditor before the conflicting security interest is perfected. A judgment lien creditor becomes a lien creditor when the sheriff levied.

Here, First Bank is a perfected secured creditor and State Bank is a judgment lien creditor. State Bank became a lien creditor on January 3 of the following year and First Bank's security interest is perfected on December 23.

In sum, First Bank has a superior claim to DC's office equipment, since First Bank perfected its security interest before State Bank becomes a lien creditor.

해설

난이도: 하

핵심 단어 및 논점

- enforceability of security interests
- deposit account (perfection)
- filing mistakes
- judgment lien

1. Student's statement should not be suppressed, since there were no unreasonable seizure.

Under the Fourth Amendment, the person has the right to be free from unreasonable seizure by the lawful enforcement. If the seizure violated individual's Fourth Amendment rights, then Student's statement is invalid because those are the fruit of the poisonous tree.

A person has been seized, if a reasonable person would have believed that he was not free to leave. Here, Student was seized, because he was called to the manager's office and stayed there for 20 minutes. There were two police officers, one sat behind the manager's desk and the other sat near the door with his revolver visible. Under these circumstances, reasonable person would believe that he is not free to leave.

Although the police did not have probable cause (PC) to arrest Student for the armed robbery, the Fourth Amendment permits detention of an individual for a brief period of time, if the police have a reasonable articulable suspicion.

Here, the police officers did not have probable cause, because an anonymous caller, the principal, and teacher stated that it could be or might be Student. These information is insufficient to create PC to arrest Student, but sufficient to create reasonable articulable suspicion for the police officers. The fact that an anonymous caller made a statement of identification does not make a different result, because officers corroborated it with the principal and teacher's identification.

In sum, Student's Fourth Amendment right was not violated and therefore his statement should not be suppressed.

2. Student's statements should not be suppressed, since Student was not in custody.

Law enforcement officers are required to read Miranda warnings to a suspect when the suspect is subjected to an in-custody interrogation. The interrogation is defined not only as questioning initiated by law enforcement, but also as any words that the police should know those words are likely to elicit an incriminating response from the suspect.

Custody is defined as either a formal arrest or restraint on freedom of movement. In determining whether there is custody, the court considers how reasonable perceive the circumstances and objective factors about interrogation.

Here, when Student was in the manager's office, he was with two police officers. He was outnumbered two to one. Police officer had visible firearm and did not tell him that he is free to leave. However, the officer told Student that "We would like to talk to you" and he did not inform him he is under arrest for the robbery. Reasonable person could not believe that he is under arrest or is in restraint on freedom. In sum, Student would not be subject to an in custody interrogation. Thus, there was no violation of Student's Miranda rights.

In sum, Student's statements should not be suppressed, since Student was not in custody.

3. Student's confession should not be confessed, since there was no coercive conduct and the police's conduct was not sufficient to overcome Student's will.

The confession is not voluntary when: (1) the police subjected the suspect to coercive conduct and (2) the conduct was sufficient to overcome the will of the suspect.

First, Student could argue that there were police's coercive conducts, because the police interviewed Student in a small and closed room with visible firearm. Police lied that three people positively identified Student as the robber. However, trickery and deceit are insufficient to make a confession inadmissible. Thus, there were no coercive conducts of the police.

Second, in determining whether the conduct was sufficient to overcome the will of the suspect, the court considers subject factors, such as suspect's age, experience, education, and familiarity with the criminal justice system. Here, Student is an adult of intelligence and had been delinquently in juvenile court for auto theft and had been placed on supervision for one year. Student was much familiar with the criminal justice. Additionally, only the police's deceit regarding the strength of the evidence does not make the confession involuntary and the police's general description of prison was not a threat but a statement of fact. Thus, there was no conduct sufficient to overcome the will of the suspect, and the Student's confession was voluntary.

In sum, Student's confession should not be confessed, since there was no coercive conduct and the police's conduct was not sufficient to overcome Student's will.

해설

난이도: 상

핵심 단어 및 논점

- Fourth Amendment
- seizure
- fruit of the poisonous tree doctrine
- detention
- Miranda warnings
- in−custody interrogation
- confession (voluntariness)
- trickery and deceit

1번 문제

답안요령

1. 4th Amendment + Fruit of the poisonous tree doctrine★
2. Seizure/Search 정의
    + analysis
3. PC/RS
    + analysis

3번 문제

1. Voluntarily
2. Analysis(coercion 존재여부)
3. Analysis(sufficiency to overcome 존재여부)
4. Knowingly
    + analysis

TIP 용의자 진술의 '자발성'에 대해 논하는 경우, 용의자가 진술하는 과정에서의 ①
coercion과 ② sufficiency to overcome 존재여부를 각각 analysis하는 것이 고
득점 포인트다.

1. Friend breached the duty of loyalty by investing the trust assets in a corporation in which Friend had a substantial investment.

A trustee owes trust beneficiaries a duty of loyalty and must administer the trust exclusively in the beneficiaries' interests. Duty of loyalty is breached when there is a transaction involving conflict of interest or self−dealing. An investment in a corporation in which the trustee has an interest that might affect the trustee's best judgment is presumptively a breach of the duty of loyalty.

Here, Friend held 70% of the common stock in A Corp., and he invested in the corporation. There is no fact suggesting fairness of the investment.

In sum, Friend breached the duty of loyalty by investing the trust assets in a corporation in which Friend had a substantial investment.

2. Friend breached the duty to invest prudently by investing the trust assets in the illiquid stocks of cash−poor, closely held corporations without proven products.

A trustee owes trust beneficiaries a duty to invest trust assets prudently. In determining whether trustee breached this duty, courts consider several factors: (1) the distribution requirements of the trust, (2) general economic conditions, (3) the role the investment plays in relationship to the trust's overall investment portfolio, and (4) the trust's need for liquidity.

Here, the investments in A Corp. and B Corp. represented 90% of the trust assets. The investments drastically reduced the liquidity of the trust, and making it impossible to meet the trust's distribution requirements, income distribution to James. Moreover, the technologies that both companies planned to develop were unproven. Working prototypes had not been developed and there was no evidence that such inventions would succeed in the highly competitive cell−phone market.

In sum, Friend breached the duty to invest prudently by investing the trust assets in the illiquid stocks of cash−poor, closely held corporations without proven products.

3. Friend breached the duty to diversify by investing 90% of the trust's assets in two corporations that were involved in the same type of business and subject to the same market risks.

A trustee owes a duty to diversify trust investments unless he reasonably determines that the purposes of the trust are better served without diversifying.

Here, Friend invested most part of the trust's assets, 90%, in A Corp. and B Corp., which were developing competing technologies to make ballpoint pens. Both corporations were involved in the same type of business and the fact finder would determine that the investment is not diverse. Moreover, there is no fact supporting that a lack of diversification was warranted because of special circumstances.

In sum, Friend breached the duty to diversify by investing 90% of the trust's assets in two corporations that were involved in the same type of business and subject to the same market risks.

4. Friend breached the duty of care by investing the trust assets in a manner that precluded administration of the trust in accordance with its terms and purposes.

A trustee owes duty of care that a duty to administer the trust in good faith, in accordance with its terms and purposes and the interests of the beneficiaries.

Here, Settlor gave James the power to annually withdraw up to 5% of trust principal over the first 10 years of the trust. However, Friend made investments, making it impossible to carry out the terms of the trust (providing James with an annual income). The investments prevented James from exercising his withdrawal power and reducing his income from the trust.

In sum, Friend breached the duty of care by investing the trust assets in a manner that precluded administration of the trust in accordance with its terms and purposes.

해설

난이도: 하

핵심 단어 및 논점

- duty of loyalty (self−dealing)
- duty to invest trust assets prudently
- duty to diversify
- duty of care

1. Finance Company has the superior claim to the 25 delivery trucks, since Bank did not note the security interest on the on the certificates of title.

Debtor's fleet of delivery trucks is equipment for UCC9 purpose. Bank has security interest in that equipment. Bank filed its appropriate financing statement, but did not note its security interest on the certificates of title. Under the state statute, Bank's security interest in that equipment is not perfected.

Here, Finance Company perfected its security interest in the 25 trucks following the state statute.

In conclusion, Finance Company has the superior claim to the 25 delivery trucks, since Bank did not note the security interest on the on the certificates of title.

2. Finance Company has the superior claim to the GPS units installed in the 25 delivery trucks, since the units became accessions and Finance Company's interest is perfected under the certificate of title statute.

When goods are physically united with other goods in a same identity of the original goods, the goods become accessions. When a security interest in such goods is created and perfected before the goods become accessions, the security interest continues after the goods become accessions.

When the collateral is united with other collateral, the two items of collateral are regarded as the whole. Whether either creditor has security interest in the whole or has security interest only to its original collateral depends on the security agreement.

Here, once the GPS units were attached to delivery trucks, those became accessions to those trucks. Global perfected security interest in the GPS units and it continued after the attachment. According to each security agreements, Global's security interest does not include the whole, while Finance Company's security interest agreement includes the accessories.

The priority rule about accessions is the same as the rules for other collateral. However, when there is an applicable certificate of title statute, a security interest in an accession is subordinate to a security interest in the whole which is perfected following the certificate of title statute.

Here, Global's security interest in the GPS units installed in the trucks is subordinate to Finance Company's claim, which is perfected in consistent with the certificate of title statute.

In sum, Finance Company has the superior claim to the GPS units installed in the 25 delivery trucks, since the units became accessions and Finance Company's interest is perfected under the certificate of title statute.

3. Global has the superior claim to the remaining 15 GPS units, since Global's interest is purchase money security interest ("PMSI").

Equipment is the goods that are not inventory, farm products, or consumer goods. Here, the GPS units are equipment for UCC9 purpose.

Bank's security agreement includes the after−acquired collateral clause and the clause is valid. Even though Bank's interest in the GPS units were not created or perfected until Debtor acquired rights in them, Bank filed its financing statement and perfected its security interest in them.

A security interest is a purchase money security interest (PMSI), when the collateral secures a purchase money obligation on that collateral. The GPS units secure the Debtor's purchase money obligation, $40,000 here, and it is a purchase money security interest. A purchase money security interest is perfected when a secured interest filed a financing statement as soon as a debtor obtained possession of the collateral. Here, Global's security interest in the GPS units is perfected.

A perfected purchase money security interest prevails over a conflicting perfected interest.

In sum, Global has the superior claim to the remaining 15 GPS units, since Global's interest is purchase money security interest ("PMSI").

해설

난이도: 1번 문제: 하
        2번 문제: 중
        3번 문제: 하

핵심 단어 및 논점

- perfection
- equipment
- certification of title
- accession

- priority
- after-acquired collateral
- equipment
- purchase money security interest (PMSI)

2번 문제

- GPS는 accession이며, truck에 부착되었다 하더라도 GPS상의 secured interest는 소멸되지 않는다(그대로 유지된다). GPS와 truck을 하나(whole)로 취급할 것인지, 각각의 담보물로 취급할 것인지는 채무자·채권자간 체결한 계약 내용에 의거하여 판단한다.

- Accession에도 priority에 관한 일반적인 rules가 동일하게 적용된다. 즉 perfection에 따라 priority가 정해지는데, 본 사안과 같이 perfection에 있어 별도의 조건 (certificate of title)을 요구하는 경우에는 예외의 rule이 적용된다.

1. The First Amendment precludes liability for Star to sue News for libel, since Scoop honestly believed that the woman was Star.

When public officials or public figures seek to recover damages in a defamation action, they must prove that the defendant reporter acted with actual malice. Actual malice is defined as knowledge that the published defamation was false or reckless disregard of whether it was false or not. Public figure is a person who assumes roles of especial prominence in the affairs of society or a person who may voluntarily inject himself into a particular controversy to influence the resolution of the issues involved.

Here, Star is a word—famous actress, and he is a public figure. She can recover only if she proves that News acted with actual malice. News honestly believed that the woman in the photograph was Star. Thus, he did not have knowledge that the published defamation was false. However, the next page of the same edition of News featured a separate story about the premiere of Star's new movie and most people would have been able to tell from the photograph that this was not the case. These facts show that there could be some reckless disregard. It is a close call.

In sum, the First Amendment precludes liability for Star to sue News for libel, since Scoop honestly believed that the woman was Star.

2. The First Amendment does not preclude liability for Scoop's trespass, since the tort law is not for the suppression of free speech.

The First Amendment does not preclude the press's liability that was arises under general law, if the generally applicable law is not for the suppression of free speech. Only the fact that the enforcement of applicable laws result in incidental effects against the rights under the First Amendment does not make the laws unconstitutional.

Here, Scoop broke into the hotel through a back door and it constitutes trespass under generally applicable tort law. The tort law is not for the suppression of free speech, and Scoop is subject to the tort law as a public member. The obstruction to the Scoop's ability to gather and report the news is an incidental effect of the tort law. Thus, Scoop's trespass is subject to tort law.

In sum, the First Amendment does not preclude liability for Scoop's trespass, since the tort law is not for the suppression of free speech.

3. The First Amendment precludes liability, since the picture was lawfully obtained and is involving a matter of public.

When a media defendant has lawfully obtained a private fact and the news story involves a matter of public concern, the First Amendment shields the media from liability. In some jurisdictions, the First Amendment protection is incorporated directly into the tort rule.

Here, Scoop took a photograph of Lex and the young woman, while he was waiting on a public street outside the hotel. Although Lex and the woman were in the private car, passerby could see the kiss. Thus, News and Scoop did not acted unlawfully in obtaining the picture. Therefore, a court would conclude that Lex had no reasonable expectation of privacy. Additionally, the news story is about a matter of public concern. Lex often uses his show as a platform to argue that adultery should be criminalized and therefore a public figure. The picture Scoop obtained is relevant to the argument. Thus, News is not liable for invasion of privacy.

In sum, the First Amendment precludes liability, since the picture was lawfully obtained and is involving a matter of public.

해설

난이도: 하

핵심 단어 및 논점

- freedom of speech (First Amendment)
- defamation
- public figure
- general law
- trespass
- invasion of privacy

3번 문제

General law가 인정되는지 그 여부를 판단할 때, defenses를 analysis하는 것이 고득점 포인트다.

1. Green cannot attach and execute upon the partnership real estate, because Green was partner's individual creditors.

Partners have an equal right to use the partnership property for partnership purposes. This is because partners and a partnership are different and partnership property is owned by partnership. Partners cannot use the partnership property for personal use.

Here, Amy, Beck, and Curt are partners of the partnership. Amy borrowed $25,000 from Green in order to deal with personal financial problems. Thus, Green's judgment against Amy cannot be executed upon the partnership real estate, because Green is Amy's individual creditor.

In sum, Green cannot attach and execute upon the partnership real estate.

2. Red should reduce a claim against Beck to a judgment, or should persuade Beck to assign him Beck's interest in the partnership.

When a partner's individual creditor wants to get a partner's financial interest in the partnership, the creditor must raise a claim against the partner. The partner's financial interest in the partnership is the transferable interest in the partnership, including the partner's share of profits and losses and the right to receive distributions. The creditor can persuade Beck to assign him a partner's interest in the partnership.

Here, Red should reduce a claim against Beck to a judgment and seek a charging order against Beck's financial interest in the partnership. Red can choose to persuade Beck to assign him a partner's interest in the partnership.

3. White does not have a right to inspect partnership books and records and to participate in the management of the partnership, because those rights are not financial interest in the partnership.

Generally, a person can become a partner only with the consent of all partners. A partner can assign only the financial interest of the partner, and the assignee cannot become a partner only with the assignment. The partner's financial interest in the partnership is the transferable interest in the partnership, including the partner's share of profits and losses and the right to receive distributions.

Here, Curt has assigned all of his interest in the partnership to White. White has only the financial interest of the partner. A right to inspect partnership books and records and to participate in the management of the partnership is not the financial interest of the partner.

In sum, White does not have a right to inspect partnership books and records and to participate in the management of the partnership, because those rights are not financial interest in the partnership.

4. White cannot force a dissolution and winding up of the partnership, because the partnership is for a 25-year term.

A assignee of a partner's financial interest in a partnership can enforce dissolution of the partnership if the partnership is a partnership at will or, if a partnership is for a term or a particular undertaking, the term or the undertaking has been completed.

Here, the partnership is a partnership only for a 25-year term, and it is not a partnership at will. Thus, White can enforce dissolution only when the term is expired.

In conclusion, White cannot force a dissolution and winding up of the partnership.

해설

난이도: 하

핵심 단어 및 논점

- transferable interest
- financial interests
- dissolution
- winding up

3번 문제

Partner의 채권자가 '어떤 유형의 자산에 권리를 행사할 수 있는지' 그 여부에 대해 논하는 문제다. 로직은 다음과 같다.

Partner가 되기 위해서는 모든 partner들의 동의가 필요하지만, partner의 채권자는 이 요건을 만족하지 못하였다.

→ 또한 financial interest만이 transferable interest이다. Inspecting 권리는 이에 해당하지 않는다.

→ 따라서 partner의 채권자는 본 권리를 행사하겠다는 주장을 할 수 없다.

1. The oral lease agreement created a month－to－month tenancy.

Under a statute of frauds, more than one year leases must be in writing. However, under the partial performance doctrine, an at－will or periodic tenancy is created when the tenant takes possession and the landlord accepts rent. When rent has been paid for a substantial period of time, it is a periodic tenancy.

Here, Tenant took possession of the office and Landlord accepted the rent. Thus, there is a valid periodic tenancy even though the lease was not in writing.

In sum, a month－to－month tenancy was created.

2. Tenant did not properly terminate the tenancy, since he noticed two weeks before the termination.

A periodic month－to－month tenancy can be terminated by either party with a one－month notice of termination. Under the common law, the oral notice is sufficient, but in modern, the written notice is required.

Here, Tenant gave Landlord a two－week notice of termination. Thus, the notice was ineffective, regardless of the type of notice, since it did not satisfy the one－month notice requirement.

In sum, tenant did not properly terminate the tenancy.

3. Landlord is not entitled to collect $800 from Tenant.

When a periodic tenancy arises, the terms of the unwritten lease, except the provision about the lease term, are enforceable. Generally, a tenant's right is assignable. When an assignment arises, privity of estate arises between the assignee and the landlord and the privity of contract exists between the tenant and the landlord. The tenant is bound to pay rent as a surety. The tenant is liable to the landlord when the assignee fails to pay the rent.

Here, Friend is an assignee of the lease. He sent Landlord the $800 check for the rent, but Landlord refused it. Thus, there is no obligation Friend owes to Landlord.

In sum, Landlord is not entitled to collect $800 from Tenant.

해설

난이도: 하

핵심 단어 및 논점

- statute of frauds (SOF)
- part performance doctrine
- periodic tenancy
- notice of termination
- assignment
- privity of estate
- privity of contract

1. The court should not order the joinder of CreamCorp as an additional defendant, because it is not a compulsory joinder.

Under FRCP, courts can join defendants over the plaintiff's objection only when: (1) the court cannot accord complete relief among existing parties if the absent person is not joined, (2) the absent person claims an interest in the action that would be impaired if that person is not joined, and (3) the person's absence may leave any of the parties subject to a risk of multiple liability.

First, CreamCorp is not necessary for the court to accord complete relief. If Guest got sick because of the oysters, the court can order complete relief between Guest and Ron. If Guest got sick because of the ice cream, the court can afford complete relief that Ron is not liable, and Guest can raise a separate action against CreamCorp. Thus, CreamCorp is not required for complete relief. Second, CreamCorp has an interest in the subject matter of the action, but the existence of the CreamCorp has no impact on the interest. If Guest got sick because of the oyster, the interest of CreamCorp will not be impaired. Even if Ron discovered that Guest was suffered because of CreamCorp, CreamCorp is not bound by it, since CreamCorp is not a party of the action. Third, the absence of CreamCorp does not leave Ron and/or Guest subject to a risk of multiple liabilities. If Ron is held liable to Guest, Ron will pay Guest without other liability on the same claim. Thus, Ron cannot compel Guest to join CreamCorp as an additional defendant.

In sum, the court should not order the joinder of CreamCorp as an additional defendant, because it is not a compulsory joinder.

2. The Federal rules of civil procedure require Ron to join his claim, since it is a compulsory counterclaim.

Counterclaim is a claim that is brought by a defendant against a plaintiff. There are two types of counterclaim: compulsory and permissive.

Defendant brings a compulsory counterclaim against plaintiff if the counterclaim arises out of the same transaction or occurrence as the plaintiff's claim against the defendant. A defendant may bring a permissible counterclaim if there is subject matter jurisdiction.

Here, Ron, a defendant of the claim, is trying to join his claim against Guest for the unpaid $50 to Guest's lawsuit. The claim raised by Ron is a counterclaim. Ron's claim arises out of the same transaction or occurrence as Guest's claim that she became sick because of the meal in the restaurant. Both claims arose out of the meal Ron served Guest. Even if Ron's claim did not arise out of the same transaction as the Guest's claim, it could be joined as a permissive counterclaim.

In sum, the Federal rules of civil procedure require Ron to join his claim, since it is a compulsory counterclaim.

3. The court will exercise supplemental jurisdiction over Ron's counterclaim.

Under the supplemental jurisdiction statute, district courts may hear claims that could not be heard, if those claims that are part of the same or controversy under Article III, if they derive from common nucleus of operative fact.

Here, Ron's counterclaim is a state law claim and there is complete diversity of citizenship between Guest and Ron. However, the amount in controversy is only $50, and therefore the counterclaim cannot be heard in the federal court. Under the supplemental jurisdiction statue, Ron's claim can be heard in federal court, because it arises out of the same transactions or occurrences of Guest's claim. Both claims arose out of the meal Ron served Guest. Thus, the federal court would have the supplemental jurisdiction over the Ron's counterclaim.

The district court has discretion to decline to exercise supplemental jurisdiction in three situations: (1) there are complex issue on state claim, (2) state claim predominates federal claim, (3) federal court dismissed all claims that it had original jurisdiction, or (4) there are other compelling reasons.

Here, the counterclaim does not have complex issue on state claim. The counterclaim for unpaid bill does not predominate the claim about food poisoning. There is no fact showing the federal court dismissed its claims or there are other compelling reasons to decline. Thus, there is no reason for the federal court to decline to exercise supplemental jurisdiction. Ron's counterclaim would be joined under the supplemental jurisdiction statute.

In sum, the court will exercise supplemental jurisdiction over Ron's counterclaim.

해설

난이도: 하

핵심 단어 및 논점

- complusory joinder
- counterclaim (permissive counterclaim)
- supplemental jurisdiction
  - common nucleus of operative fact
  - court's discretion

1. Under UPC, the Amendment to Wife's Trust can apply to the assets distributable to the trust from Husband's probate estate, while the Amendment cannot apply to the assets under the common law incorporation-by-reference doctrine.

Here, Article Five of Wife's Trust provided as: Wife may revoke or amend this trust at anytime prior to her death by a written instrument delivered to Bank. Wife has right to amend and she followed all instructions of the provision. Thus, Wife's amendment is valid.

Under the UPC, a person may bequeath assets to a trust by identifying the trust in the will. The terms of the trust must be executed before or concurrently with the execution of the testator's will. When the trust is amended after testator's will was executed, the amendment applies to the assets passing to the trust from the will.

Here, the trust (Wife's Trust) is created before the wills are created. Thus, the pour-over provisions are valid and the amendments to the trust governs the disposition of his estate.

In common law incorporation-by-reference doctrine, pour-over provision is valid when: (1) testator intended to incorporate, (2) document exists when or before the execution of the will, and (3) the document is substantially identified in the will. When the trust is amended after testator's will was executed, the amendment does not apply to the assets passing to the trust from the will, but the original trust provision applies.

Here, the will stated that "... of Wife's Trust, which was created simultaneously with the execution of my will." It shows that Wife intended to incorporate and the trust is substantially identified in the will. Moreover, the trust exists before the execution of the will. Thus, the pour-over provision in the will is valid. However, the amendment to Wife's Trust cannot apply to the assets from Husband's probate estate. Thus, Son and Grandchild would share equally in

Husband's estate.

In sum, under the UPC, the Amendment to Wife's Trust can apply to the assets distributable to the trust from Husband's probate estate, while the amendment cannot apply to the assets under the common law incorporation−by−reference doctrine.

2. Son could be entitled to a share of the assets of Wife's Trust, according to the interpretation of the amendment to Wife's trust.

The amendment to Wife's Trust is capable of two interpretations. One is that Niece's children must satisfy both the age and survivorship contingencies at Niece's death in order to take. The other one is that the age contingency can be satisfied after Niece's death, following the Wife's intent.

According to the narrower interpretation, Son is not entitled to the share of the assets of Wife's Trust. This is because the trust terminates when Niece's died and at the time of the death of Niece, Son was 20 years old, not satisfying the age contingency.

However, there could be an argument that Wife's purpose of age 21 requirement was to assure that a beneficiary was sufficiently maturity when Son took possession of the property and that Wife never anticipated that Niece would die only five years later.

Bank could easily keep the trust open until it was clear whether the underage child could meet the age contingency.

In sum, Son could be entitled to a share of the assets of Wife's Trust, according to the interpretation of the amendment to Wife's trust.

3. Grandchild is not entitled to a share of the assets, while Grandchild can take a share of the trust following the UPC.

Under the UPC, when a remainder class gift is bequeathed to a class composed of children and a child dies before the even upon which the remainder becomes possessory (Niece's death), a substitute gift is created in the descendants of the deceased child. Grandchild would take as the representative of Daughter.

However in some states, the survivorship contingency contained in the trust amendment could eliminate any subsequent gift to Grandchild.

Under the common law, Grandchild is not a taker under the trust instrument because the gift was limited to Niece's children who survived the trust termination and the word "children" includes the ancestor's immediate offspring, not more remote descendants. Anti—lapse statutes do not apply to trust.

In sum, Grandchild is not entitled to a share of the assets, while Grandchild can take a share of the trust following the UPC.

해설

난이도: 하

핵심 단어 및 논점

- pour—over provision (amendment)
  - UPC
  - incorporation—by—reference doctrine (common law)
- interpretation
- remainder class gift

1번 문제

- "Power to revoke" 논점은 대개 별도의 문제로 출제되나, 본 문제에서는 별도의 언급이 없으므로, 이에 대해 서술하는 것이 고득점포인트다. 본 사안에 명시된 Article Five를 활용하여 analysis한다.

- 본 문제의 핵심 논점은 amendment이나, 관련된 pour—over provision 및 incorporation by reference에 대해 서술해야 한다.

1. State A is more closely related with the matter than State B and UPAA would be applied.

Regarding the enforceability of premarital agreement, courts apply (1) the law of the state where a premarital contract was executed or (2) the law of the state where significant relationship with the matter at issue.

Here, the premarital contract was executed in State A. Thus, if State A adopted first method approach, UPAA should be applied. Regarding significant relationship, Hal and Wendy entered into the agreement in State A and they married in State A. The child was born in State A and they lived there most of their six year marriage. Three months ago, Wendy took Child and moved back to State A. Wendy would argue that State A has significant relationship, since State A is closely related to their contracts and marriages. However, Hal would argue that he lived in State B after Hal and Wendy separated and some marital assets are in State B. Thus, State B also has some relationship with them.

In sum, State A is more closely related with the matter than State B and UPAA would be applied.

2. The waiver−of−property−rights provision is enforceable.

The enforceability of the premarital agreement depends on three factors: voluntariness, fairness, and disclosure. In many states, an agreement is unenforceable if the party against whom enforcement is sought succeeds in showing any one of involuntariness, unfairness, or lack of adequate disclosure. However, under UPAA, an agreement is unenforceable if the party against whom enforcement is sought succeeds in showing (1) involuntariness or (2) unfairness and lack of adequate disclosure.

Here, Wendy cannot show inadequate disclosure or lack of knowledge. Lawyer gave Wendy an accurate list of Hal's assets and a copy of Hal's tax returns for the past three years. Regarding involuntariness, it could be established by fraud, duress, or coercion, and there are many factors to be considered, such as lack of opportunity to talk with independent counsel, other reasons for proceeding with the marriage (pregnancy), financial losses and embarrassment arising from cancellation of the wedding, maturity of parties, prior experience of marriage. Wendy would argue that Hal told Wendy to sign a premarital agreement two weeks before their wedding. However, she was an adult and she had been previously divorced. There is no fact showing the hardship from canceling the wedding of lack of opportunity to take with counsel. Thus, Wendy cannot establish involuntariness.

In sum, the waiver−of−property−rights provision is enforceable.

3. If the court found that the premarital agreement is not in the best interest of child, the agreement is unenforceable.

The orders for a child's support and custody should be in the best interest of the child. Thus, premarital agreement cannot bind the court's support and custody order.

In sum, if the court found that the premarital agreement is not in the best interest of child, the agreement is unenforceable.

4. The profits from Wendy's songs written after she left Hal are subject to division at divorce.

Only marital property is divisible at divorce regardless of the title. By contrast, separate property is not divisible at divorce. The property is marital if it was granted during the marriage by any methods, except for gift, descent, or devise. A separate asset can be transformed into marital property, if marital funds or significant efforts by the owner's spouse enhance its value or build equity during the marriage. In the minority jurisdictions, all assets whenever or however acquired are separate property. When courts decide property division order, only marital property is considered.

In the majority of jurisdictions, marital property continues to accrue until a final divorce decree is entered. In the minority of jurisdictions, marital property stops accruing after the date of permanent separation or the date of filing for a divorce.

Here, Wendy's songs are written after the first five years of the marriage, and the spouses' waive of all claims to property is not applicable on it. Additionally, there is no divorce decree entered, Wendy's songs are marital property. The fact that Wendy had not received profits from the songs does not change the result. This is because contingent expectancies are subject to division at divorce if they were marital property.

In sum, the profits from Wendy's songs written after she left Hal are subject to division at divorce.

해설

난이도: 하

핵심 단어 및 논점

- jurisdiction of enforceability of premarital agreement
- enforceability of premarital agreement 판단 요소
- child support/custody
- best interest of child
- property division order
- marital property
- accrue

2번 문제

답안요령

> 1. In some states
> 2. UPAA
> 3. 각 요소 rule
> 4. Analysis + 결론

1. Rancher is entitled to expectation damages for $500,000 and the waste doctrine is inapplicable in this case.

Nonbreaching party is entitled to expectation damages for breach of contract. The purpose is to put the nonbreaching party in as good a position as if the other party had fully performed. Expectation damage arises when: (1) it is caused by defendant, (2) it was foreseeable, (3) it is reasonably certain, and (4) it is unavoidable. Expectation damage should be reduced by the costs that were avoided by the breach.

Here, Rancher and Gasco made a contract and Gasco was required to restore Ranch to its pre−exploration condition by March 31. However, Gasco failed to do it and it cost $500,000. Where a contractor's performance has been incomplete or defective for a construction contract, the usual measure of damages is the reasonable cost of replacement or completion. Thus, Rancher would be entitled to the cost of restoration, $500,000.

However, when an award for the cost of completion is wasteful, a court may apply the waste doctrine. Under the waste doctrine, the measure of damages becomes the difference in value of the property/land. The waste doctrine will apply if (1) the contractor performs in good faith but defects nevertheless exist and (2) meaning the cost to restore greatly exceeds the difference in value. If the breach is willful and only completion of the contract will enable the nonbreaching party to use the land for its intended purposes, the cost of completion is considered the appropriate damages award.

Here, Gasco willfully chose not to restore Ranch to its pre−exploration condition and Gasco's failure to restore makes the pasture unusable. Rancher had to cancel his plans to conduct roping clinics. Thus, waste doctrine is not applicable in this case and Rancher is entitled to $500,000.

In sum, Rancher is entitled to expectation damages for $500,000 and the waste doctrine is inapplicable in this case.

2. Rancher would be entitled to damage awards less than $300,000.

Consequential damages result from the nonbreaching party's particular circumstances. Usually, consequential damages are lost profits resulting from the breach. These damages may be recovered only if: (1) it was foreseeable that breach of contract would result in damages, (2) the damages can be proved with reasonable certainty, and (3) the damages could not have been avoided through reasonable efforts.

First of all, Gasco would have known that its breach of contract (the failure to restore Ranch) makes Ranch unable to run the roping clinic business. This is because Ranch specified his plan of business to Gasco. Thus, loss profit by the breach of contract was foreseeable. Secondly, the breach of contract resulted with a problem on Rancher's new business. Rancher had experience on roping clinics on the road but no experience on Ranch. Courts are reluctant to recognize lost profits to new businesses, because such profits are too remote and speculative to meet the reasonable certainty requirement. Thus, it is a close call whether there is reasonable certainty to recognize Rancher's lost profits. This is because the lost profits could be reasonable certain by calculating based on the prior similar experience.

Regarding the last factor of consequential damages, mitigation requires the nonbreaching party to take reasonable steps to reduce the damages.

Here, Rancher could have restarted his business on the road before he bought Ranch. However, the alternative may not be substantially different from or inferior to the originally planned business. Thus, it is uncertain whether the business on the road is substantially inferior to one in Ranch. If the court finds that it is similar, then Rancher's consequential damage awards would be reduced by the amount that Rancher could earn from the business on the road.

Additionally, contract damage awards must be reduced by costs that are avoided by the breach.

Here, even if Rancher's damages of $300,000 were foreseeable and reasonably certain, that amount should be reduced by the costs that Rancher avoided by the breach. Thus, Rancher's damages would be less than $300,000.

In sum, Rancher would be entitled to damage awards less than $300,000.

해설

난이도: 상

핵심 단어 및 논점

- expectation damages
- waste doctrine
- consequential damages
- duty to mitigate

2번 문제

답안요령

1. Expectation damages 정의 + 목적★
   + analysis
2. Waste doctrine
   + analysis
3. 결론(damage award $)

1. Hanson's is legally bound to the contract for Boysenberry－granola muffins, because Taster had actual authority.

A principal is liable on a contract made by an agent when the agent has actual or apparent authority. Actual authority exists when a principal makes an agent to believe that the principal wants the agent to act on behalf of principal.

Here, the contract between Hanson's and Taster expressly stated that Taster had authority to buy the recipes for a price not to exceed $5,000. Thus, Taster had actual authority to make the contract.

In sum, Hanson's is legally bound to Boysenberry－granola muffins contract.

2. Hanson's is legally bound to the contract for Almond－pecan tarts, because Taster had apparent authority.

Apparent authority arises when (1) a third party reasonably believes that the actor is authorized, (2) that belief is from the principal's manifestation, and (3) the third party has no notice.

Here, Taster did not have actual authority to make the contract with Bakers Bonanza, because the price exceeds $5,000. However, Hanson's president stated at the annual baking industry trade show that Hanson's would hire a consultant to enter into contracts to buy recipes from other bakers on Hanson's behalf. Additionally, the contract price was within the typical recipes price ranges. Thus, Taster had apparent authority to make the contract.

In sum, Hanson's is legally bound to Almond－pecan tarts contract.

3. Hanson's is not legally bound to the contract for chocolate truffle cake contract, because Taster had neither actual nor apparent authority.

Taster had no actual authority to make the contract exchanging for a copy of Hanson's secret fruitcake recipe. This is because the contract between Hanson's and Taster required Taster to keep Hanson's recipe secret from everyone. Taster also had no apparent authority. Typically, baked—goods recipes are sold for prices between $3,000 and $6,000. There is no suggestion that non—cash consideration is typical. Additionally, Hanson's long history and the fact that the use of secret recipe is closely guarded by the company suggest that it is unreasonable for a third party to believe that Taster has authority.

In sum, Hanson's is not legally bound to the contract for chocolate truffle cake contract, because Taster had neither actual nor apparent authority.

4. Hanson's is not legally bound to the contract for the baking oven, because Taster had neither actual nor apparent authority.

Taster had no actual authority, since he was empowered to purchase baked—goods recipes, not the sophisticated baking oven. Moreover, Taster's act was not necessary or incidental to achieving Hanson's objectives. There is no fact indicating that the act of Hanson's could have caused Ironcast to believe that Taster had authority to buy baking equipment.

In sum, Hanson's is not legally bound to the contract for the baking oven, because Taster had neither actual nor apparent authority.

해설

난이도: 하

핵심 단어 및 논점

- agency
- actual authority
- apparent authority

답안요령

1. General agency rule
2. Principal's liability
   i. Actual authority
      + analysis
   ii. Apparent authority
      + analysis
3. 결론

1. The Court did not err in overruling Defense Counsel's objection to cross examination, since it is relevant and probative of Witness's credibility.

Generally, character evidence is not admissible to prove that a person acted in conformity with the particular character trait. However, a court may, in its discretion, admit a prior bad act evidence for impeachment of a witness's credibility when: (1) it is provided during cross-examination and (2) it is probative of untruthfulness.

Here, Witness's testimony was critical to establish that Plaintiff had removed a safety guard from the table saw. It could devastate the Plaintiff's testimony. Thus, the inquiry about an alleged lie by witness is relevant and probative of Witness's credibility.

In sum, the Court did not err in overruling Defense Counsel's objection to cross examination, since it is relevant and probative of Witness's credibility.

2. Whether the Court should have admitted Exhibit 37 depends on which approach is adopted in this jurisdiction.

Extrinsic evidence of specific conducts of a witness is not allowed for impeachment. Regarding documents, one approach holds that a document is extrinsic evidence while other approach holds that a document is not extrinsic evidence if the witness who is impeached can provide the foundation for admission of the document.

Here, Extrinsic 37 was provided by Plaintiff's counsel, when the witness was impeached and the witness denied the alleged lie. If Extrinsic 37 is an extrinsic document, the court should sustain Defense Counsel's objection. If Extrinsic 37 is not an extrinsic document, the court should overrule Defense Counsel's objection. In sum, whether the Court should have admitted Exhibit 37 depends on which approach is adopted in this jurisdiction.

3. The Court did not err in sustaining Defense Counsel's objection to the introduction of Exhibit 37, since it was provided by Plaintiff's Counsel.

A recorded recollection is a record regarding a matter that the witness knew but now cannot recall enough to testify, and it was made when to refresh the witness's memory. When the document is shown to witness to refresh his recollection, the witness must read it to himself and the document should not be read aloud to the jury. The document is admissible as an exhibit only if it is offered by the lawyer who has not used the exhibit to refresh the recollection of the witness.

Here, Exhibit 37 was used by Plaintiff's Counsel to refresh Witness's recollection and it was re−offered as an exhibit by Plaintiff's Counsel. Thus, it is inadmissible.

In sum, the Court did not err in sustaining Defense Counsel's objection to the introduction of Exhibit 37, since it was provided by Plaintiff's Counsel.

4. The Court did not err in sustaining Defense Counsel's objection, since it is an extrinsic evidence.

The testimony regarding 12 years of construction experience during his job interview is relevant only to the witness's credibility and it constitutes extrinsic evidence.

In sum, the Court did not err in sustaining Defense Counsel's objection, since it is an extrinsic evidence.

해설

난이도: 하

핵심 단어 및 논점

- character evidence v. impeachment
- bad act
  - character evidence
  - impeachment
- extrinsic evidence (document)
  Bad act를 이용한 impeachment에서 extrinsic evidence는 제출할 수 없다.
- exhibit (recorded recollection)

1번 문제

Bad acts는 substantive evidence 또는 impeachment 목적으로 제출가능한 증거이다. Substantive evidence로서 제출된다면 character evidence의 admissibility에 관한 rule에 부합해야 할 것이고, impeachment 목적으로 제출된다면 그 방법(extrinsic 또는 intrinsic evidence)에 관한 rule에 부합해야 할 것이다. 문제에서 bad act가 제출된 '목적'이 명시되어 있지 않다면 두 경우를 구분하여 각각 analysis해야 할 것이나, 본 문제에서는 impeachment 목적으로 제출되었다는 점이 명시되어 있는 바, character evidence에 관한 rule을 서술하는 것은 적합하지 않다.

2번 문제

본 문제의 핵심은, extrinsic evidence로서 document를 인정할지에 대한 견해가 나뉜다는 점이다.

3번 문제

답안요령

> 1. Recorded recollection 정의
>   + analysis
> 2. Exhibit 제출 요건
>   + analysis

1. Andy is entitled to 200 shares of XYZ stock under the modern approach, while Andy is entitled only to 100 shares under the common law.

Bequest of stock owned by a testator when the testator's will was signed includes subsequently acquired shares of the same stock as the result of a stock dividend. This is because stock dividends are treated like stock splits. Additional shares of stock from the same company are merely a change in form, not substance. Under the common law, additionally acquired shares of the same stock are substance.

Andy entitled to 200 shares of XYZ stock, including an additional 100 shares as the result of a dividend paid by XYZ to its shareholders. However, under the common law, Andy is entitled to 100 shares of XYZ stock.

In sum, Andy is entitled to 200 shares of XYZ stock under the modern approach, while Andy is entitled only to 100 shares under the common law.

2. The bequest of the home to Ben adeems under the common law and Ed is entitled to the home. However, Ben would be entitled under the UPC.

Under the common law, an ademption occurs when the subject matter of specific devise is not found in the probate estate at the time of the testator's death. In some modern courts, by the intent test, devisee may be entitled to replacement, if the devisee proves that the testator intended the beneficiary to take the replacement.

Here, Testator grants home at 4 Cypress Garden to Ben in the will. However, at the time of the death of Testator, there was a new condominium Testator purchased in 2006. Under the common law, the bequest of the home adeems and therefore, Ben gets nothing and Ed gets a new home as a residuary legatee.

However, testator purchased the condominium as her new home that was specifically bequeathed to Ben. Thus, the new home would be distributed to Ben as the replacement by the intent test.

In sum, the bequest of the home to Ben adeems under the common law and Ed is entitled to the home. However, Ben would be entitled under the UPC.

3. Carrie is entitled to the blue automobile, since the provision includes a generical description of property.

When there is a bequest of generically described property, it applies to property that satisfies the generic description at the testator's death.

Here, testator stated that "I give my automobile to my friend Carrie." The term "my automobile" is a generical description and there was the blue automobile at the testator's death.

In sum, Carrie is entitled to the blue automobile, since the provision includes a generical description of property.

4. The bequest $100,000 to Dona fails because Donna disclaimed it and anti−lapse statute is inapplicable here. The bequest passes to residuary legatee, Ed.

A beneficiary may disclaim any interest. If a beneficiary disclaims a general bequest, the bequest passes as if the disclaimant had predeceased the testator.

Here, Donna made a valid disclaimer. She was not a blood relation to Testator, and there is no issue under the anti−lapse statute.

In sum, the bequest $100,000 to Dona fails because Donna disclaimed it and anti−lapse statute is inapplicable here. The bequest passes to residuary legatee, Ed.

해설

난이도: 하

핵심 단어 및 논점

- stock dividends
- ademption
- general bequest (abatement)
- disclaim

1. It is a close call whether the deed created tenants in common or join tenants.

When a deed includes two or more grantees, it creates a joint tenancy or a tenancy in common. Under the common law four unities test, time, title, interest and possession are required to create a joint tenancy.

Here, Parent's deed to the daughters granted them interest at the same time, and they acquired their interest under the same instrument. They acquired equal interest in the property, and they acquired the right to possession of the property. Thus, four−unities test is satisfied.

In modern, there is a presumption that a conveyance to two or more persons creates tenancy in common. Each states use different ways to rebut the presumption. In some states, term "joint tenancy" and "survivorship" rebut the presumption.

Here, the Parent's deed does not include those terms, and the presumption could not be rebutted. In some state, term "jointly" alone can rebut the presumption. In some other states, term "jointly" shows grantor intended that grantees own together, rather than that they own as joint tenants.

Here, the deed includes the term "jointly" and "equally, to share and share alike." It evidences grantor's intent to give equal shares to two daughters. Thus, in some states, the deed would be interpreted as creating joint tenants with right of survivorship.

The fact that the deed was never recorded has no effect on the formalities of the deed.

In sum, it is a close call whether the deed created tenants in common or join tenants.

2. Jessie's mortgage served the joint tenancy under the title theory. In either theory, Jessie's contract of sale severed the joint tenancy and Karen and Buyer hold the farm as tenants in common. Buyer is subject to the mortgage.

When property is held by two persons in joint tenancy, a conveyance by one joint tenant of her entire ownership interest severs the joint tenancy as to conveyed share. This is because the conveyance severs time and title unities. When a joint tenant transfers mortgage interest, a severance also occurs depending on title theory or lien theory.

Under the title theory, the mortgagee takes title to the property for the duration of the mortgage. Thus, a mortgage severs the joint tenancy and therefore it would convert the joint tenancy into a tenancy in common. Under the lien theory, the mortgagor holds title and the mortgagee takes only a lien on the property.

Here, Jessie borrowed $60,000 from Credit Union. Under the title theory, mortgage severs the joint tenancy. Under the lien theory, Jessie holds title and Credit Union takes only a lien on the property. Thus, joint tenancy severs at the time of the creation of the mortgage. However, under either theory, the result would be same because Jessie made a contract of sale to Buyer. After Jessie entered the contract, Jessie's interest is not same with the Karen's because of the equitable conversion theory. Jessie's interest is subject to Buyer's equitable interest or title. Because the joint tenancy was severed, Karen had no right of survivorship. Thus, Buyer and Karen hold the farm as tenants in common.

Bona fide purchaser takes free of mortgage which was made by the seller. Bona fide purchaser is a person who (1) paid value for an interest and (2) had no notice.

Buyer would argue that he is a bona fide purchaser and is not subject to Credit Union's mortgage. However, Buyer had constructive notice of the mortgage. This is because Credit Union properly and promptly recorded the mortgage before Buyer entered into a contract with Jessie. Constructive notice arises through the recording system. If Buyer made a proper title search by looking in the grantor−grantee index system, he should be able to recognize the existence of the mortgage. Thus, he is not a bona fide purchaser and he is subject to the mortgage.

In sum, Jessie's mortgage served the joint tenancy under the title theory. In either theory, Jessie's contract of sale severed the joint tenancy and Karen and Buyer hold the farm as tenants in common. Buyer is subject to the mortgage.

3. Buyer is subject to the mortgage and Legatee is entitled to the balance of the purchase price.

Under the doctrine of equitable conversion, the seller's legal title is considered personal property and the buyer's equitable title is considered real property, when the contract of sale is signed.

Here, at the time of signing the contract, seller, Jessie holds title as personal property and Buyer holds the title as real property. Thus, the balance of the purchase price should be passed to Legatee, following the Jessie's will.

In sum, Buyer is subject to the mortgage and Legatee is entitled to the balance of the purchase price.

해설

난이도: 하

핵심 단어 및 논점

- tenancy in common
- four unities test
- severance
- mortgage
- title theory v. lien theory
- bona fide purchaser (BFP)
- doctrine of equitable conversion

1. The email service would be consistent with the Federal Rules of Civil Procedure and the U.S. Constitution.

Service of process upon a corporation outside the United States is authorized in any manner except personal delivery. There are many ways of service and the federal court has broad discretion to direct service by any means that are not prohibited by international agreement.

There are no international agreements that affect the court's resolution of the issues in this case. Thus, the federal court has broad discretion to authorize any means of service, including e—mail like in this case. Email is seems like the best way of service. This is because the defendant, Copyco sells only on the Internet. Its website does not list any information, except for the email address and an internet address. It seems that Copyco prefers email as a contact method. Additionally, email does not put burden on the plaintiff, Bearco.

In sum, email service would be permitted.

Even if the service is permitted by the Federal Rules of Civil Procedure, the service must be consistent with the U.S. Constitution. Under the due process clause, the service must be reasonably calculated to afford the interested parties an opportunity to present their objections.

Here, Copyco's website does not list any information, except for the email address and an internet address. Email was the service that is reasonably calculated to reach Copyco. Thus, service by email does not violate the due process clause.

In sum, the email service is consistent with the Federal Rules of Civil Procedure and the U.S. Constitution.

2. State A's unfair competition law should apply to resolve Bearco's claim, following the most significant relationship approach of the Second Restatement of Conflict of Laws.

The Erie doctrine requires a federal court to apply the substantive law of the state where it sits, if the federal court hears the case based on the diversity jurisdiction. Choice of law rule is the substantive law.

Here, The Bearco's claim was held in the U.S. District Court for State A, and State A follows the most significant relationship approach.

Under the most significant relationship approach, there are several factors to be considered: (1) the place where the injury occurred, (2) the place where the conduct causing the injury occurred, (3) the place of incorporation and place of business of the parties, and (4) the place where the relationship between the parties is centered.

First, Bearco's injury is the loss of customers who bought Copyco's Griz bears, and the injury would occur in all states throughout the U.S. This is because Copyco sells its bears to consumers throughout the U.S. The most of the injury would be in State A where Bearco is incorporated and State B where Bearco's factories are located. Second, Copyco's conduct occurred both in Country X and in all U.S. states. Third, Bearco is incorporated in State A and Copyco is incorporated in Country X.

In tort cases, when the contacts split among many jurisdictions, courts put emphasis on the purpose of the laws that is the basis of the claim. Here, the claim raised under the unfair competition. The purpose of the unfair competition is to protect business from the economic harm caused by unfair competition. On Bearco's behalf, the injury would be centered in State A, where it is incorporated, and State A has an interest in seeking the law. By contrast, on Copyco's behalf, Country X would be interested to protect Copyco by seeking the law.

When local and foreign law fit under the law and both conflicts, local law is typically applied, unless there is a strong reason not to do so. Here, Copyco would foresee that it could be subject to State A. Thus, State A's unfair competition law would apply in this case.

In sum, State A's unfair competition law should apply to resolve Bearco's claim, following the most significant relationship approach of the Second Restatement of Conflict of Laws.

해설

난이도: 하

핵심 단어 및 논점

- service of process
- Erie doctrine
  - most significant relationship approach

1. The jury may award Nephew damages from Tenant.

In negligence action, a plaintiff must show that the defendant owed the plaintiff a duty to conform his conduct to a standard necessary to avoid a foreseeable unreasonable risk of harm of others, that the defendant breached the duty, and that the defendant's conduct was both the cause in fact and the proximate cause of the plaintiff's injuries. In determining whether the actions are reasonable, jury would consider appropriate precautions to avoid foreseeable risks. Jury may consider the likelihood that the risk will eventuate and the burden of taking precautions against such foreseeable risk.

Here, Nephew was a guest and his presence was known to Tenant, so Tenant has duty to Nephew to prevent foreseeable risk of harm. Carrying a pot of boiling water clearly has foreseeable risk of serious burn. A jury might also conclude that it was foreseeable that someone could come out of bedroom quickly and collide with the boiling water. To take precautions, Tenant could speak loudly that he is coming with hot water or Tenant could close the bedroom door.

Nephew also has a duty to prevent foreseeable risks to him and others. In determining whether minor exercised reasonable care, the jury would compare the minor's actions against that of a minor of like age, intelligence, and experience.

Here, Nephew was age eight. An adult could conclude that Nephew's action of chasing a ball into the hall without looking or calling out would create foreseeable risk. A normal toddler does not foresee risks, but a normal adolescent does foresee such risks. Nephew is between a toddler and an adolescent. Thus, it is a close call.

Under the common law contributory negligence approach, the plaintiff could not recover from the defendant if the jury found that the plaintiff's negligence was actual and proximate cause of his injuries. Under the comparative negligence approach, the jury apportions fault between parties, if the jury finds that two or more parties are negligent. The plaintiff's total damages awarded by jury would be reduced by his fault.

Even if jury found Nephew was negligent, Nephew's total damages would be reduced by his fault under the comparative negligence approach and it does not eliminate Tenant's negligence liability under the comparative negligence approach. In sum, the jury may award Nephew damages from Tenant.

2. Nephew's damages award from Landlord is depending on whether Landlord's action is proximate cause of Nephew's injury.

(1) If an actor violates a statute that is designed to protect against the type of accident the actor's conduct causes and (2) if the accident victim is within the class of persons the statute is designed to protect, the actor is negligent per se.

Here, a state statute provides that every apartment building and every part thereof shall be kept in good repair. Landlord violated the statute, since he did not take steps to correct the malfunctioned problem permanently. Nephew is within the class of persons the statute is designed to protect. However, it is unclear whether the accident is the type of accident that the statute is designed to protect against. Thus, the jury may conclude that Landlord is not negligent per se.

In a negligence action, a defendant is liable only if his action was the proximate cause of the plaintiff's injury. Intervening actors that are difficult to be anticipated may break the chain of causation, and a court conclude that the defendant's acts are not proximate cause of the plaintiff's injuries. Foreseeability and the degree of dependence on the defendant's negligence are considered to decide whether intervening acts break the chain of causation.

Here, Landlord did not permanently fixed the furnace and cause loss of hot water. The jury could find that the collision was foreseeable result of loss of hot water. Thus, Landlord's action could be determined as the proximate cause of Nephew's injury. By contrast, the jury could find that the landlord's negligence in failing to repair timely is too remote from burn injuries. Thus, Landlord's action could not be determined as the proximate cause. It is a close call.

In conclusion, if the jury concludes that landlord's action was a proximate cause, Nephew could get damages award against Landlord. By contrast, if the jury concludes that landlord's action was not a proximate cause, Nephew could not get damage award against Landlord.

해설

난이도: 하

핵심 단어 및 논점

- negligence
- reasonability
- foreseeable risk
- child (standard of care)

- comparative negligence
- negligence per se
- proximate cause

1번 문제

- 본 답안의 핵심은 두 요소를 비교형량하여 reasonability를 판단하는 것이다. ① Risk 가 foreseeable했었는지 그 여부와 ② precaution을 취하는 것이 reasonable했었는지 그 여부가 그것이다.
- 본 답안은 '보편적인' negligence에 대해 논했으나, 그보다 더 narrow한 negligence 를 논하더라도 로직한 답안이 될 수 있다. 예컨대, Nephew가 invitee이고 Tenant가 landowner라는 점을 근거로, Tenant는 Nephew에게 foreseeable risk에 대한 적절한 precaution을 취할 의무가 있다고 작성할 수 있다.

> **답안요령**
>
> 1. Negligence에 대한 general rule
> 2. Foreseeable ris
> 4. Reasonability
>   + analysis

2009Feb Family Law

1. The court's assertion of personal jurisdiction over Dad was consistent with due process requirement.

The interstate enforcement and modification of child support are governed by the UIFSA. In determining the personal jurisdiction over a nonresident defendant, long–arm statute is adopted and the court use minimum contacts test as due process requirement. Due process requires that defendant's acts be a purposeful activity and it was foreseeable that he will be in the forum state.

Here, Dad's vacation in State A was his voluntary conduct, and the child's birth was foreseeable and the state has strong interest in ensuring the child's support. Dad can argue that due process is violated, because his vacation was more than 14 years ago and he has never met child. However, Dad's visitation and the sexual activity are directly related to the basis for jurisdiction. Additionally, Dad continues to have a support obligation to Child.

In sum, State A has personal jurisdiction over Dad.

2. Child support and custody order should be in the best interest of child, and the liberal visitation order would be granted to Dad.

The orders for a child's support and custody should be in the best interest of the child.

Here, Mom and Dan made agreement to waive Dad's right to establish his paternity of Child and Dad's all child support obligations. This agreement eliminates the relationship between Dad and Child, and it would conflict with the child's interest to have two parents supporting and caring him. Thus, the agreement between Mom and Dan when Child was born is ineffective.

When courts make child support order, they must consider all earnings and income of the noncustodial parent. Sate public assistance benefit levels are not considered.

Here, the State A court should order the value of Dad's child support obligation based on his earnings and income, not based on the state public assistance benefit levels.

Child custody order (or visitation) is based on the best interest of child. Many factors are considered.

Here, Dad had never visited State A and never met Child more than 14 years. However, it does not mean that Dad's visitation would endanger Child's well−being. Thus, the court would not deny Dad's petition for visitation. Child is already 14 years old, and Child's opinion should be considered but it is not determinative.

In sum, child support and custody order should be decided in the best interest of child, and the liberal visitation order would be granted to Dad.

해설

난이도: 하

핵심 단어 및 논점

- jurisdiction of child support order
- long−arm statute
- due process
- minimum contact test
- purposeful availment
- child support
- child custody
- visitation
- best interest of child

2번 문제
피고의 '자발성' 그리고 피고의 행위와 청구취지 간의 '연관성'에 초점을 두고 서술한다.

1. The directors will not be protected from liability, since they failed to be fully informed.

Directors owe a duty of loyalty and a duty of care. Duty of loyalty includes duty to refrain from competing with the company, not to have a conflicting interest personally, and to account to the company and to hold as trustee for the company any benefit derived by the member in the conduct of the company's activities. Duty of care requires directors to act as a prudent person with reasonable care.

The breach of duty of care is protected under the business judgment rule (BJR). Under BJR, there is a presumption that a board makes a decision (1) in a good faith, (2) in an informed manner, (3) based on a rational basis, and (4) for the best interest of the corporation.

Here, the directors, except for Major, had no conflicting interest against the company and they did not breach duty of loyalty. However, they breached their duty of care, since they failed to be informed when they approve the purchase of a number of valuable items of Major's personal property. The directors approved the purchase without a rational basis. They just relied on Major's statement that he has investigated the value of his property to be purchased by Corporation. The statement of Major lacks enough substance to be relied, since the boarders knew that Major was interested in the transaction and it is unwarranted knowledge. Thus, there was a breach of duty of care and it could not be protected under BJR.

In sum, the directors will not be protected from liability, since they failed to be fully informed.

2. Major will not be protected from liability, since Major involved in an conflicting interest transaction.

BJR is not applicable when there is fraud, illegality, or conflict of interest.

Here, Major has benefits from the transaction with the company and it is a conflict of interest and BJR is inapplicable. However, Major can be protected from liability by establishing fairness of the transaction.

Thus, Major will not be protected from liability by BJR.

3. Major will not be protected from liability, since Major failed to fully provide information to disinterested directors.

As mentioned above, BJR is not applicable to Major, since there was a conflict of interest against the company.

Safe harbor rule protects a director who breaches his duty of loyalty. First of all, a director's conflicting interest transaction is protected under the safe harbor, when: (1) there is an approval by disinterested directors or shareholders, (2) a director fully disclosed all relevant information, and (3) a director played no part in the disinterested directors' vote directly or indirectly.

Here, the transaction was approved by another member of Board who has no interest in the transaction. However, Major did not fully inform them. Major misrepresented them that it is fair market value without further inquiry.

In sum, Major is not protected from liability by the approval of disinterested directors.

4. The directors will be protected from liability by the exculpatory provision in the articles of incorporation.

An exculpatory provision is a provision that exculpates the directors from liability for breach of care. Exculpatory provision does not protect directors for actions done in bad faith or for the breach of the duty of loyalty. While negligence does not establish bad faith, gross negligence may constitutes an action in bad faith.

Here, directors breached their duty of care by approving the transaction with unwarranted information. Although relying on Major's statement is foolish, it is not gross negligence. Additionally, directors had no interest from the transaction and they did not breach their duty of loyalty. Thus, the exculpatory provision will protect the directors.

In sum, the directors will be protected from liability by the exculpatory provision in the articles of incorporation.

5. Major will not be protected from liability, since Major breached his duty of loyalty and he did in bad faith.

As mentioned above, exculpatory provision does not protect directors for actions done in bad faith or for the breach of the duty of loyalty.

Here, Major made misrepresentation and it is an action done in bad faith. Major breached his breach of duty of loyalty, since there is a conflict of interest and no fairness to the corporation.

In sum, Major will not be protected from liability, since Major breached his duty of loyalty and he did in bad faith.

해설

난이도: 상

핵심 단어 및 논점

- corporation
- fiduciary duty
- business judgment rule (BJR)
- conflicting interest transaction
- safe harbor rule
- fairness
- exculpatory provision

3번 문제

답안요령

> 1. Duty of loyalty (conflicting interest transaction)
>   + analysis
> 2. Safe harbor rule
>   + analysis
> 3. Fairness
>   + analysis

TIP1 Safe harbor rule을 우선 적용하고, safe harbor rule의 요건을 만족하지 못한 경우에는 fairness에 대해 추가적으로 analysis한다.

TIP2 1번: Conflicting interest transaction 용어가 modern과 CL에서 차이가 있다는 점을 서술하는 것이 고득점 포인트다.

TIP3 3번: Fairness 여부를 판단해야 할 행위가 '어떤 유형의 행위'인지 그 여부에 따라 entire fairness review(fair price와 fair dealing)의 적용여부가 다르다.

1. Trustee breached his fiduciary duty, since he abused discretion even if there are absolute and uncontrolled discretions.

A trustee has a fiduciary duty to follow the trust made by the settlor, and it is a breach of trust if a trustee fails to do so. The court will not ordinarily question a trustee's exercise of a discretionary power, particularly when the trustee is granted absolute and uncontrolled discretion. Trustees' actions may be reviewed if there is abuse of discretion. When the trustee's decision is unrelated to the settlor's goals, the trustee's decision is abuse of discretion.

In this case, Trustee may distribute trust income to either David or Edna with his absolute and uncontrolled discretion according to the Settlor's terms of the trust. Trustee distributed all trust income only to David, solely because of the personal disagreement with Edna's political opinions.

For these reasons, trustee's decision is an abuse of discretion and a breach of the duty to carry out the terms of the trust.

In sum, trustee breached his fiduciary duty, since he abused discretion even if there are absolute and uncontrolled discretions.

2. Trustee must return to the trust the profit, because she breached the duty of loyalty.

Trustees have a duty of loyalty to beneficiaries, such as the duty not to do self–dealing. Self–dealing includes the purchase of trust assets by the trustee in his individual capacity. The fair and reasonable price cannot be the reason of the self–dealing. Additionally, under the no further inquiry rule, there is no need to inquire into the motivation for the self–dealing transaction or even its fairness.

Here, Trustee breached her duty of loyalty to the trust beneficiaries by buying trust assets in her personal capacity. Saving sales commission does not change the result under the no further inquiry rule.

In sum, Trustee must return to the trust the profit, because she breached the duty of loyalty.

3. The distribution of the trust property would be distributed depends on the Settlor's charitable intent under the cy pres doctrine.

Under the cy pres doctrine, when the trust property for a charitable purpose could not be distributed as the trust, it would be distributed according to the settlor's intention. If settlor has a specific charitable intention, the property reverts to the settlor.

Under the common law (and the Restatement Third of Trust), testator's general charitable intention is presumed. However, under UTC it is a conclusive presumption of general charitable intention. If a particular charitable purpose becomes unlawful, impracticable, the court may apply cy pres to modify the trust.

In this case, the Settlor wanted to distribute his trust property to his alma mater, Business College, with the charitable intent. Under the common law (and the Restatement Third of Trust), Settlor stated that the distribution is for "long-standing interest in the area of education," and it evidences general intention. Additionally, there is no evidence that testator viewed Business College as a sole mean to complete the goal.

Under UTC, the trust terms expressed nothing and cy pres doctrine is mandatory, and the court must reform the court.

In this case, there is no statement regarding the distribution in the situation practice is impossible. For these reasons, the court must authorize Trustee to distribute trust property.

In sum, the distribution of the trust property would be distributed depends on the Settlor's charitable intent under the cy pres doctrine.

해설

난이도: 하

핵심 단어 및 논점

- abuse of discretion (fiduciary duty)
- duty of loyalty (self−dealing)
- no further inquiry rule
- cy pres doctrine

2번 문제

> **답안요령**

```
1. Self−dealing
   + analysis
2. No further inquiry rule★
   + analysis
2. Beneficiary's remed
   + analysis
```

TIP Self−dealing에 관한 답안 작성 시, no further inquiry rule과 이에 대한 analysis가 고득점 포인트다.

1. Anti—Tax could argue that his statement was not for an imminent lawbreaking. However, Anti—Tax could be convicted because he urged viewers "to make Tax pay up."

The First Amendment does not shield the conviction of individuals who incite or advocate breaking the law, when: (1) there is advocacy of illegal conduct and not just an abstract expression of ideas, (2) the advocacy calls for imminent law—breaking, or (3) the law—breaking is likely to occur. The statute should distinguish between abstract expression of ideas and such advocacy.

Here, Anti—Tax said he call on viewers "to make Tax pay up" and "show him what a taking really means." He is advocating nonpayment of the proposed tax increase. His advocate of nonpayment of tax does not calls imminent law—breaking, since the legislation about tax increase has not been enacted yet. There are no clear facts that anyone will take seriously Anti—Tax's suggestion. It is unclear whether "make Tax pay up" constitutes imminent law—breaking. However, Anti—Tax provided Tax's address and urged the viewers to take which means a theft. There is a circumstantial evidence that one of viewers acted, since two days after Anti—Tax's remarks the crime occurred. Thus, it is uncertain whether the Anti—Tax's statement calls for imminent law—breaking.

The Sedition Statute applies only to advocacy of imminent law—breaking, thus there is no overbreadth of the statute. Additionally, the statute does not put barrier on speech before it occurs and, therefore, there is no prior restraint.

In sum, Anti—Tax could argue that his statement was not for an imminent law—breaking.

2. Anti-Tax's conviction could not be permitted, since the Abusive Words Statute is overbroad that offends the First Amendment.

When there are fighting words, the First Amendment protection is excluded. Fighting words are defined as words which by their very utterance inflict injury or tend to incite an immediate breach of the peace. When a speech is likely to cause a violent reaction from others, it is under the fighting-words doctrine.

Here, Anti-Tax's statement that urges viewers to "make Tax pay up" was likely to cause a violent reaction, and therefore it would be under the fighting-words doctrine.

When a statute is overbroad, a statute is unconstitutional.

Here, the Abusive Words Statute provides that it punishes directing "any abusive word," and it is clearly overbroad. The First Amendment provides the highest level of protection on commentary on public matters, and its protection extends to sharp attacks on government and public officials. Anti-Tax's statement that "You're a dishonest imbecile" is a typical example abusive statement that is protected under the First Amendment. Thus, the Statute is overbroad.

In sum, Anti-Tax's conviction could not be permitted, since the Abusive Words Statute is overbroad that offends the First Amendment.

해설

난이도: 하

핵심 단어 및 논점

- freedom of speech (First Amendment)
- unprotected speech
- words advocating breaking law
- fighting words
- overbroad and vague

Anti−Tax가 기소된 근거는 Sedition Statute와 Abusive Words Statute, 이 두 state laws 이다. 첫 번째 문제는 'Sedition Statute를 근거로 할 때 against convicting을 주장할 수 있는가'를 판단하는 문제이다. 다시 말해, Sedition Statute의 위헌성을 주장할 근거를 찾는 문제이다. TV program에서 언급한 speech로 인해 conviction이 이루어졌으므로, ① speech(freedom of speech)에 대한 제재, ② statute 자체의 헌법적 문제, 이 두 가지를 판단해야 한다. ①의 경우, 해당 statute의 제한 기준(content−based 또는 content−neutral), speech가 이루어진 장소(public forum, designated public forum 또는 nonpublic forum), 적용되는 test(SS, IR 또는 RR test) 등을 판단한다. ②의 경우, overbroad/vague 판단, prior restraint를 판단한다. 두 번째 문제는 'Abusive Words Statute를 근거로 할 때 against convicting을 주장할 수 있는가'를 판단하는 문제로서, 첫 번째 문제와 동일한 logic을 바탕으로 서술하면 된다.

답안요령

1. 해당되는 unprotected speech 정의
   + analysis
2. overbroad/vague 판단★
   + analysis
2. Prior restraint★
   + analysis

TIP1 표현행위에 관한 법률조항의 위헌성 여부를 판단하는 경우, 별도의 문제가 출제되지 않더라도 overbroad / vague 여부와 prior restraint에 대해 analysis하는 것이 고득점 포인트다.

TIP2 본래 freedom of speech 침해여부는 ① 해당 statute의 제한 기준(content-based 또는 content-neutral), ② speech가 이루어진 장소(public forum, designated public forum 또는 nonpublic forum), ③ 적용되는 test(SS, IR 또는 RR test), 이 세 기준을 통해 판단하는 것이 원칙이다. 그러나 본 문제에서는 Anti-Tax의 statement가 unprotected speech에 해당하는지 그 여부를 판단하는 것에 초점을 두고 있는 바, 위 답안요령 내용만으로도 충분하다.

2009July Family Law

1. State B court should enforce the State A child support order.

The interstate enforcement and modification of child support are governed by the UIFSA. Under UIFSA two−state procedure, a child support order registered in another state is enforceable in the adopting state, as the order was issued by the adopting state.

Here, there was a child support order against Husband registered in State A. It is enforceable in the same manner and procedures in the State B, as the order was issued by State B. Thus, the fact that State has no personal jurisdiction over Husband does not change the result. This is because UIFSA adopts two states procedure. In conclusion, Husband did not follow the order issued in State A and the support order is enforceable, and State B should enforce the State A child support order.

In sum, State B court should enforce the State A child support order.

2. The State B should not modify the State A custody order.

As to custody−modification, UCCJEA and PKPA adopt same standards. Original court has exclusive and continuing jurisdiction to modify custody order when: (1) either parent or the child continue to live in the state and (2) the original courts do not decline to exercise jurisdiction. Under the UCCJEA, a significant connection between the child and the person remaining in the original state is required instead of nonexistence of the original court's decline.

Here, Husband remains State A. Husband and Son kept contact until two months ago, and Son and Husband had significant connection. Thus, the original issuing state, State A has exclusive and continuing jurisdiction to modify the order.

In sum, the State B should not modify the State A custody order.

3. Husband would obtain modification of the custody, since there are many factors favor to Husband.

Courts permit modification of the child's custody order when there is a substantial change in circumstances. The modification of the child's custody order should be in the best interest of the child. There are several factors to be considered, such as stability and finality.

In some states, the relocating custodial parent has the burden of proof and the parent needs to show that the move is for the child's best interests. In some states, the relocating custodial parent additionally needs to show that the move is for a proper purpose and it is reasonable method. In other states, objecting parent has the burden of proof and the parent needs to show that the move is not for the child' best interests.

After relocation, Husband can spend time only for six weeks during the summer. It has large impact and reduces Husband's residential time with the child. Husband could argue that good promotion is not a necessary for moving. While Son has lived in State A, he has already established school and social relationships. Additionally, Wife notified Husband about the move after she already moved. These things support Husband. By contrast, there are some factors favor to Wife. Higher income in new job and better access to grandparents will be provided. Additionally, the relocation was motivated by vindictiveness.

In sum, Husband would obtain modification of the custody.

4. Under UIFSA, State A court should not modify retroactively, but whether to modify the support order prospectively depends on whether Husband obtained modification on the custody order.

Under UIFSA, an issuing state has continuing and exclusive jurisdiction to modify a support order when: (1) the child or any party continues to live in the state and (2) there is any party that does not consent to the jurisdiction of another forum.

Here, Husband continues to reside in State A and there is no fact showing any party consented to the jurisdiction of another forum. In sum, State A has jurisdiction to modify the support order.

Retroactive modification of child support obligations is completely forbidden. Thus, State A should not modify the support order retroactively.

By contrast, courts permit prospective modification of the support order when there is a substantial change in circumstances. Prospective modification of the support order is closely related to the custody order.

If Husband obtains modification of the custody order, State A court might order to reduce prospectively on Husband's support order. This is because the custody order would reduce Wife's residential time with Son for only eight weeks per year and it is a substantial change. Additionally, Wife's net income increased by $1,000 per month. By contrast, if Husband failed to obtain modification of the custody order, State A court might not order to reduce prospectively on Husband's support order. Public policy favors to maintain legal support obligations. Wife's move would increase her residential time with Son and it would cause higher spending for child raising.

In sum, under UIFSA, State A court should not modify retroactively, but whether to modify the support order prospectively depends on whether Husband obtained modification on the custody order.

해설

난이도: 하

핵심 단어 및 논점

- child support order
- enforcement order
- two-state procedure
- jurisdiction of child support order
- child custody order
- modification of child custody order
- jurisdiction of child custody order
- substantial change in circumstances
- best interest of child

4번 문제

논점: Child support order의 modification order

1. UIFSA 적용
   + analysis
3. PJ와 무관함★
   + analysis

TIP 생각 route ①

Child support order에 대해 UIFSA가 적용된다. → 두 요건을 모두 충족하므
로 original court, 즉 State A 법원이 재판권을 가진다. → State B 법원은 재
판권이 없다. → State B 법원이 피고에 대해 personal jurisdiction을 가지나
이것으로는 not enough하다.

생각 route ②

State B 법원은 피고에 대해 personal jurisdiction을 가지나 이것으로는 not
enough하다. → Child support order에 대해 UIFSA가 적용된다. → 두 요건
이 모두 충족되지 못하였으므로 original court, 즉 State A 법원은 재판권을
가지지 못한다. → State B 법원이 재판권을 가진다.

1. Leaseco's interest in the printing press is security interest, rather than lease interest, according to the economic realities of the transaction.

Whether a transaction in the lease form creates a true lease or a security interest depends on the economic realities of the transaction.

Here, under the agreement between Leaseco and Printco, Printco is required to pay Leaseco full cost of the press and ensured Leaseco annual return of about 10%. Printco cannot terminate the agreement. If Printco complies with the agreement, it could keep the printing press. If Printco does not comply with the agreement, Leaseco could recover the printing press. In short, in the economic realities of the transaction, it is equivalent with the installment sale of the press and secures Printco's payment obligation. The fact that the agreement specified title to remain is provided to Leaseco does not make a different result.

In sum, Leaseco's interest in the printing press is security interest, rather than lease interest, according to the economic realities of the transaction.

2. Bank had a right to repossess and sell the printing press, since it perfected its security interest on it.

A security interest is created and attaches to the collateral only if the debtor has rights in the collateral.

In a signed agreement, Bank has a security interest in "all Printco's equipment, whether now owned or hereafter acquired." In other words, Bank advanced value to Printco. Printco acquired rights in the printing press and therefore Bank's security interest attached to the press. Bank filed a financial statement covering Printco's equipment, and therefore Bank's security interest is perfected.

Following a debtor's default, a secured party may repossess and sell any collateral that secures its debt. Here, Printco defaulted and therefore Bank had a right to repossess and sell the printing press.

In sum, Bank had a right to repossess and sell the printing press, since it perfected its security interest on it.

3. Bank has a superior interest in the proceeds of the sale of the printing press, since the proceeds of the disposition is insufficient to satisfy Bank and Leaseco.

Between an unperfected secured creditor and a perfected secured creditor, a perfected secured creditor has superior claim to the collateral. Here, Bank has priority over the collateral, since it perfected the security interest and Leaseco did not.

When a secured party with priority disposes of collateral, the proceeds of that disposition are distributed in the following order: (1) the expenses of the disposition, (2) satisfaction of the obligation owed to the disposing secured party, and (3) satisfaction of any obligation secured by a subordinate interest.

Here, Bank sold all of Printco's equipment at a public auction for a total of $75,000. The amount owed to Bank was $150,000, which is the amount that cannot fully satisfy interests of both Bank and Leaseco. Thus, Bank is entitled to $150,000 and Leaseco is entitled to nothing.

In sum, Bank has a superior interest in the proceeds of the sale of the printing press, since the proceeds of the disposition is insufficient to satisfy Bank and Leaseco.

4. Leaseco has no right to recover the printing press from Purchase, since Bank's sale of the press discharged Leaseco's security interest.

When a secured party disposes of collateral, it transfers the debtor's rights in the collateral to any transferee for value, and discharges the secured party's interest in the collateral and any subordinate security interest.

Here, Bank sold the printing press to Purchase for $50,000. The buyer purchased it in good faith and he is a transferee for value.

In sum, Leaseco has no right to recover the printing press from Purchase, since Bank's sale of the press discharged Leaseco's security interest.

해설

난이도: 하

핵심 단어 및 논점

- perfection
- debtor's default
- disposition of the collateral

2009July Contracts

1. Sam cannot recover, since it was not bargained for exchange.

Generally, a promise is enforceable when it is supported by consideration, and there is consideration if it is bargained for in exchange for a return promise or performance. The promisor must have sought and received something of legal value in exchange for the promise.

Here, Sam rescued Resident's dog and Resident promised to afford the cost of the program. However, the promise was not exchange for Sam's rescue of the dog, but it was made in recognition of the prior action. Resident's promise was not for in exchange for Sam's promise to apply for paramedic training. Thus, there is no consideration on Sam's promise.

In sum, Sam cannot recover, since it was not bargained for exchange.

2. Under the material benefit rule, Sam could recover less than $1,000.

Under the material benefit rule, a promise that is not supported by consideration may be enforceable, if it is made in knowing a benefit that is received before by the promisor from the promise. This rule recognizes moral consideration. However, this rule does not apply, if the promisee provided the benefit as a gift, or to the extent that the promise value is disproportionate to the benefit.

Here, Resident promised to give Sam $1,000 in recognition of Sam's rescue of Resident's dog. The promise for $1,000 is made in knowing a prior Sam's benefit. Thus, the material benefit rule is applicable. However, it is unclear whether Sam intended to provide the benefit as a gift when he rescued the dog. Sam may rescue the dog with selflessness or with the belief to be heroic for financial reward. If the court finds Sam provided the benefit as a gift, Resident is bound by the promise.

However, even if Resident is bound by the promise, Sam could be entitled to the amount less than $1,000 if the court finds $1,000 is disproportionate to the value of the rescue of the dog.

In sum, Sam could recover less than $1,000.

3. Under the doctrine of promissory estoppel, Sam could recover portion of all of the $1,000.

To establish a promissory estoppel claim, (1) the promisor should have reasonably expected that the promisee would change his position in reliance on the promise when the promise is made, (2) the promise changed position in reliance on the promise, and (3) the promisee's detriment and injustice can be avoided only by enforcing the promise. Damages under a promissory estoppel claim is limited as just requires.

Here, Sam changed his position in reliance on Resident's promise by registering the cosmetology training program. Resident could argue that he did not reasonably expected that Sam would change the program. However, Resident stated that "I want to compensate you for your heroism," and it shows that the promise was not supported by the condition of specific program, the paramedic training program. Thus, Sam could recover that portion of $1,000 that is determined to avoid injustice.

In sum, under the doctrine of promissory estoppel, Sam could recover portion of all of the $1,000.

해설

난이도: 중

핵심 단어 및 논점

- consideration
- material benefit rule
- promissory estoppel doctrine

1. GlassCo begins with a filing of a notice of removal in the federal district court. The notice should be received by state court and all parties.

A defendant removes a civil action from state court to federal court if the federal courts have original jurisdiction over the action. Procedually, as a first step for removal, the defendant files a notice of removal in the federal district court for the district where the state action is pending. The notice must be filed within 30 days of the defendant's receipt of such initial pleading, or within 30 days after the service of summons, whichever period is shorter. The notice of removal must be signed and must include a statement of the basis for federal jurisdiction. A copy of the materials from the state court proceeding must also be filed. After filing the notice of removal, the defendant must serve notice of the filing on all adverse parties and file a copy of the notice of removal with the state court.

Removal is "automatic," therefore, once the state court received a copy of the notice of removal, the case is removed and the state court can take no further action in the case.

In sum, GlassCo begins with a filing of a notice of removal in the federal district court. The notice should be received by state court and all parties.

2. The Federal Rules of Civil Procedure permits the separate claims of Ann and Bill to remain joined in a single lawsuit.

Two or more plaintiffs can join their claims in a single lawsuit, if the plaintiffs raise any right to relief that arises out of the same transaction or occurrence and there are any questions of law or fact common to all plaintiffs.

Here, Ann and Bill are raising claims that arose out of the accident of the falling glass. Additionally, those claims raise common questions of fact, whether the glass accident was caused by negligence by employees. There is also a common question of law, because both claims are governed by State X statutes.

The fact that Ann and Bill are asserting separate rights for relief does not make a different result. Thus, the claims of Ann and Bill can be joined in a single lawsuit.

In sum, the Federal Rules of Civil Procedure permits the separate claims of Ann and Bill to remain joined in a single lawsuit.

3. The federal court has supplemental subject matter jurisdiction.

Removal of a case from state court to federal court is proper only when the removed civil action is within the original jurisdiction of the federal court.

Here, Ann's claim against GlassCo is within the original diversity jurisdiction of the federal court, since Ann and GlassCo are citizens of different states, and Ann's amount in controversy exceeds $75,000. Bill's claim against GlassCo is not within the diversity jurisdiction, since the amount in controversy ($5,000) does not exceed $75,000.

However, district courts may have supplemental jurisdiction if those claims arise out of the same transactions or occurrences of the primary claims under Article III. Commonly, common nucleus of operative fact test is used.

As mentioned above, Bill's claim and Ann's claim arise out of the same transaction, the accident of glass falling. Both claims have common questions of fact and law. Additionally, there is no situation in which the court may deny to exercise supplemental jurisdiction.

In sum, the federal court has supplemental subject matter jurisdiction.

해설

난이도: 하

핵심 단어 및 논점

- removal (process)
- joinder
- supplemental jurisdiction

1번 문제
논점: Removal의 process

3번 문제
논점: Jurisdiction 중 SPJ

답안요령

1. SPJ에 대한 기본 rule
2. Considering factors (×4)
   + analysis
3. Court's discretion (×3)
   + analysis
4. 결론

1. The trial court did not err in denying John's motion to suppress, since John lacks a reasonable expectation of privacy in the home and the bag's contents.

A lawful enforcement officer can search without warrant, when he has voluntary consent to do so. Here, the police did not have warrant, but Crystal's mother consented to search of her home.

Only a person can allege Fourth Amendment violation only when he has standing to challenge it. A person has standing when he has a reasonable expectation of privacy in an object or premises.

Here, John could argue that the consent of Crystal's mother was coerced or involuntary. However, he had no reasonable expectation of privacy in Crystal's home. As to the leather bag, John gave Crystal the bag with the gun after they had left the Minit Mart and told her to get rid of it. In short, he surrendered reasonable expectation of privacy in the bag to challenge the search on it and he cannot control the bag anymore.Thus, John cannot challenge the search on Crystal's home and the leather bag.

In sum, the trial court did not err in denying John's motion to suppress, since John lacks a reasonable expectation of privacy in the home and the bag's contents.

2. The trial court did not err in denying John's motion for judgment of acquittal, since there are sufficient evidence for a reasonable jury to find the commission of John's attempted armed robbery.

A motion for judgment of acquittal should be granted, only if the prosecution has failed to present sufficient evidence for a reasonable jury to find that the defendant committed each element of the charged offense beyond a reasonable doubt. Here, the prosecutor needs to present sufficient evidence for attempted armed robbery. The prosecutor needs to prove that (1) John intended to commit an armed robbery and (2) John's actions constitute attempt to commit the crime.

First, there are many facts to show John's intent to commit the armed robbery: the statement of the store clerk, the printouts of e-mails from John, and taking a weapon when he walked into the Mart to threat the store clerk.

Second, an actual attempt exists when John's actions went beyond mere preparation. In determining whether the defendant's conduct constitutes attempt, there are many approaches. In some states, the actor's conduct must be proximate to the crime. In some states, the actor's conduct must be dangerously proximate to the crime. Under the Model Penal Code, a defendant's conduct must be a substantial step toward commission of the crime. In some states, defendant's conduct must unambiguously manifest the criminal intent.

Here, John loaded a gun, put it in his bag before he entered the Mart, and his had was with the gun for the entire time that he were in the Mart. It may satisfy the proximate test. He entered the store with an intention to rob by force. He failed to commit the crime just because Crystal cried and left the store. Thus, most states would find that his conducts are actual attempt.

In sum, there are many evidences that show John's commitment.

3. The trial court did not err in failing to instruct the jury on the defense of abandonment, since his abandonment was involuntary.

In most jurisdictions, voluntary abandonment is not a defense to the crime of attempt once the actor's conduct has gone beyond mere preparation. In minority jurisdiction, the abandonment of an attempt before the crime is completed is an affirmative defense, but the abandonment must be utterly voluntary.

Here, John left the store before he complete his crime, but left the store after his conduct has gone beyond mere preparation. Additionally, his abandonment was taken as a response to Crystal. An abandonment based on any extrinsic factor is not voluntary. Thus, his abandonment was involuntary.

In sum, the trial court did not err in failing to instruct the jury on the defense of abandonment, since his abandonment was involuntary.

해설

난이도: 하

핵심 단어 및 논점

- search without warrant
- voluntary consent
- reasonable expectation of privacy
- judgment of acquittal
- attempted armed robbery
- beyond mere preparation (attempt)
- voluntary abandonment (defense to attempt)

1번 문제

답안요령

> 1. Consent → Warrantless search 가능
>   + analysis
> 2. 4조 주장 가능여부★
> 3. Analysis (E.P. in 물건)
> 4. Analysis (E.P. in 장소)

TIP1 Search의 합헌성 여부를 논하는 경우, 자신의 헌법적 권리가 침해되었다고 주장하는 자(원고)에게 해당 주장을 할 수 있는 권리가 있는지, 즉 경찰이 search한 장소 또는 물건에 대해 권리를 가진 자인지 그 여부를 논하는 것이 고득점 포인트다.

TIP2 Search 논점에서 E.P. 유무여부를 판단하는 경우, 장소에 대한 E.P.와 그 물건에 대한 E.P.를 구별해서 서술하는 것이 고득점 포인트다.

1. The Metropolitan Limited Partnership is a general partnership.

To be a limited partnership, it must include a general partner who signed the initial Certificate of Limited Partnership, and the certificate must be filed with the state.

Here, there is a general partner, Warren, but Warren did not signed the agreement. Additionally, there is no certificate that is initially filed.

A general partnership is the association of two or more persons to carry out on as co-owners a business for profit forms a partnership, whether or not the persons intent to form a partnership. Mere a common property or part ownership is not enough to establish a partnership. Establishing a partnership requires more than co-ownership.

Here, Andy, Ben, and Carol provided contribution $500,000 to the venture. Additionally, they hired a marketing company to develop a campaign to resell the land. Thus, they acted as co-owners. Even though they did not intend to form a partnership, MLP is a general partnership.

In sum, the Metropolitan Limited Partnership is a general partnership.

2. Marketing must obtain a judgment against partners individually and against the partnership and levy execution against the partnership's asset.

Under the UPA 1997, partners in a general partnership are jointly and severally liable for obligations of the partnership. A partnership creditor can collect the full amount of the debt from any one of the partners. However, the creditor must first exhaust partnership's assets before seeking payment on partner's individual property.

When partnership's creditor tries to collect from partners personally, the creditor must obtain a judgment against partners individually and against the partnership and levy execution against the partnership's asset. This is because a judgment against a partnership is not a judgment against a partner.

Here, Marketing would follow these steps and if MLP's assets fail to satisfy Marketing's judgment, then Marketing may recover from Andy, Ben, and Carol individually.

In sum, Marketing must obtain a judgment against partners individually and against the partnership and levy execution against the partnership's asset.

3. Andy, Ben, and Carol are personally liable for the claim and Zen must follow the steps that Marketing must follow.

Partners in a general partnership are jointly and severally liable for obligations of the partnership. Even though partners in a limited partnership (LP) are not jointly and severally liable for partnership's obligations, the debt on Zen's claim is created before the partnership becomes LP. Thus, limited liability protection does not apply to the debts.

In sum, Andy, Ben, and Carol are personally liable for the claim and Zen's step would be same as Marketing as mentioned above.

해설

난이도: 하

핵심 단어 및 논점

- formalities of GP
- partnership creditors and partners
- limited liability protection

1번 문제

- 두 명 이상이 이익을 위해 회사를 운영하는 경우 GP가 설립된다는 점, 별도의 formalities 가 필요하지 않다는 점을 서술한다.
- 본문에 partner가 partnership의 이익(share of profits)을 나누어 받았다는 사실이 명시되어 있는 경우, partner와 creditor를 구분하는 것이 고득점 포인트다.
- GP 외에 다른 유형의 회사, 예컨대 LP, LLP 등이 특정 formalities를 만족하지 못한 경우, "해당 formalities를 만족하지 못하였으나 별도의 formalities가 필요하지 않은 GP에 해당한다."는 점을 서술한다.

3번 문제

논점: LP로 변경된 '전' 발생한 partnership debt에 대한 partner's 책임

로직은 다음과 같다.

GP에서 partner는 jointly and severally liable하다(personally liable하다).

→ Entity theory에 의거하여 partnership debt의 성격은 GP에서 발생한 partnership debt의 성격을 띤다.

→ 따라서 limited liability protection 적용되지 않는다.

→ Partner는 해당 partnership debt에 대해 personally liable하다.

2009July Decedents' Estates and Trusts

1. Testator's will is not invalid on the basis of undue influence, since susceptibility is not recognized in this case.

A will is invalid if it was executed as the result of undue influence. Undue influence occurs when the wrongdoer exerted influence over testator's free will and caused the testator to make a distribution. The burden of proof is on the contestant, who must show: (1) the testator was susceptible to undue influence, (2) the alleged wrongdoer had the opportunity to exert undue influence upon the testator, (3) the alleged wrongdoer had a disposition to exert undue influence, and (4) the will appears to be the product of undue influence.

Here, Friend had both the opportunity and disposition to exert undue influence upon the testator. Friend and Testator were together over two year period. Friend told Testator to be generous by leaving her everything. However, susceptibility is typically based on age, personality, physical and mental health, and ability to handle business affairs. Friend was 70 but was a successful businessman. There is no evidence that she was physically or mentally in poor condition. Additionally, Friend and Brother tried to make a share by misrepresenting on the will, rather than directly persuading the testator.

In sum, Testator's will is not invalid on the basis of undue influence, since susceptibility is not recognized in this case.

2. Testator's will is invalid in whole or in part on the basis of fraud.

A will executed by fraud is invalid. Fraud occurs when a testator is deceived by a misrepresentation and it led to execute a will. Fraud in the inducement occurs when a person misrepresents facts. Fraud in the execution occurs when a person misrepresents the character or contents of the instrument signed by the testator.

Here, Brother told the testator that he drafted the will in accordance with testator's instructions. However, the will gave Friend a general power of appointment over trust assets. Friend promised Brother that she would be very generous to him if Testator left her everything. It shows their intent to getting everything. Thus, they intended to deceive testator. In sum, Testator's will is invalid on the basis of undue fraud.

If the will is invalid by undue influence or fraud, it may be invalid entirely or only for the portions that is infected by the fraud or undue influence.

Here, there is no fact that Friend played a role in the selection of Charity as taker in default. Therefore, a court might invalidate only the part of the general power and leaves Charity as the residuary taker.

In sum, Testator's will is invalid in whole or in part on the basis of fraud.

3. Testator's estate should be distributed to Charity or Sister, depending on the approach regarding a general power of appointment.

Whether a general power of appointment is effectively exercised depends on the donee's intent and any formalities required by the donor.

Here, there are no formalities required by Testator. However, donee of the power, Friend did not specifically refer the power, it is unclear whether she intended to exercise the power. Under the majority approach, a residuary clause in a donee's will without reference of the power is not an effective exercise of a general power. Under this approach, Charity, the taker in default of appointment, would take Testator's estate. However, under the minority approach, general residuary clause is an effective exercise of a power. Thus, under this approach, Sister would take Testator's estate.

In sum, Testator's estate should be distributed to Charity or Sister, depending on the approach regarding a general power of appointment.

4. Testator's estate should be distributed to Niece under the parentalic method or to Niece and Uncle equally under the parentalic method.

If Testator's will is invalid, his estate will be distributed based on state rules of intestate succession.

First of all, the accident was occurred before Testator marries Friend and therefore Friend has no inheritance right on Testator's estate.

Under the parentalic method, the issue of an intestate's parents take to the exclusion of any issue of the intestate's grandparents. Here, Niece is a grandchild of Testator's parents and Uncle is a child of Testator's grandparents. Thus, Niece takes to the exclusion of Uncle.

Under the consanguity method, people in the same degree of consanguinity to testator share equally. Here, Niece and Uncle would share equally, because they are in the third degree of consanguinity to Testator.

In sum, Testator's estate should be distributed to Niece under the parentalic method or to Niece and Uncle equally under the parentalic method.

해설

난이도: 하

핵심 단어 및 논점

- undue influence (validity of will)
- fraud (validity of will)
- general power of appointment
- intestate succession
  - parentalic method
  - consanguity method

1번 문제

논점: Undue influence

2번 문제

논점: Invalidate partially or entirely

활용하기 좋은 문장: If the will was tainted by [fraud], it may invalidate the entire will or only for the portions that is infected by the [fraud].

1. Bank has the superior claim to the first ton of copper sheet.

Inventory is defined as raw materials, work in process, or materials used or consumed in debtor's business. Here, the copper sheet is inventory of Kitchenware, because Kitchenware use the copper sheet to produce cookware.

Reservation of title by a seller of goods notwithstanding delivery to the buyer is not effective is limited to a reservation of security interest in effect.

Here, the sales contract between Copperco and Kitchenware indicates that Copperco would retain title to all copper sheet until it received full payment for it. The first ton of copper sheet was delivered to Kitchenware, but Copperco was not paid for it. However, Copperco has reservation of security interest, regardless of the contract provision. Copperco did not file a financing statement with respect to it, and therefore the security interest is not perfected.

A security interest is created and attaches to the collateral only if the debtor has rights in the collateral. Here, a security agreement granted Bank a security interest in "all inventory that Kitchenware now owns…or acquires in the future." Once Kitchenware received the copper sheet, Kitchenware holds the title of the sheet and Bank's security interest attaches. Bank filed a financial statement, so its security interest in the copper sheet is perfected.

Between an unperfected secured creditor and a perfected secured creditor, a perfected secured creditor has superior claim to the collateral. Here, Both Copperco and Bank has security interest in the copper sheet. Copperco's security interest is unperfected, while Bank's security interest is perfected.

In sum, Bank has the superior claim to the first ton of copper sheet.

2. Copperco has the superior claim to the second ton of copper sheet, because Bank's security interest in the sheet did not attach.

A security interest is created and attaches to the collateral only if the debtor has rights in the collateral.

Here, the second ton of copper sheet was hold by Copperco and was not delivered to Kitchenware. Under the contract between Copperco and Kitchenware, Copperco has security interest in the second ton and Kitchenware has not right on it. Therefore, Bank's security interest in the second ton did not attach.

In sum, Copperco has the superior claim to the second ton of copper sheet.

해설

난이도: 하

핵심 단어 및 논점

- inventory
- perfection
- enforceability of security interest

1. Bob took the land subject to the power−line easement, since he has inquiry notice on it.

The state statues provided that "A conveyance of real property is not valid against any subsequent purchaser who, without notice, purchases real property in good faith and for valuable consideration." Notice may be actual, constructive, or inquiry. Constructive notice arises from the recording system. Inquiry notice arises from visual inspection.

Here, Abe is a subsequent purchaser of Owen, and Bob is the subsequent purchaser of Abe. When Abe purchased the property, Abe had inquiry notice on the power−line easement. Even though Owen did not mention the easement, the power lines were erected over the land and the power lines remained on the land. Thus, Abe's interest in the property was subject to the power−line easement.

In sum, Bob's title on the land is subject to the power−line easement.

2. Bob took the land subject to the gas−line easement, under the shelter doctrine.

Under the "shelter doctrine," when a bona fide purchaser acquires title free of a prior encumbrance, he can convey that title to a subsequent purchaser free of that encumbrance. Bona fide purchaser is a person who (1) paid value for an interest and (2) had no notice.

Here, when Abe purchases the land from Owen, the gas−line easement was never recorded and it could not be discovered though visual inspection because the pipes were restored under the surface of the land. Thus, Abe was a bona fide purchaser, since she paid value for the land and had no notice on the easement. By contrast, Bob had actual notice on the gas line because he had helped dig the trenches on the land. However, under the shelter doctrine, he took the title on the land free of the gas—line easement. This is because he purchased the land from Abe, a bona fide purchaser.

In sum, Bob's title is free from the gas—line easement.

3. Bob cannot obtain damages from Owen under the common law. However, Bob could obtain in some jurisdictions.

A full covenant includes a covenant against encumbrances, which warrants that there are no outstanding third—party rights that negate the title of the property. Under the common law, the covenant against encumbrances are present covenant and it is breached at the time of the conveyance if there is an encumbrances. Furthermore, the covenant does not run with the land.

Here, Owen conveyed the land to Abe by a full covenant and warranty deed. There was power—line easement and the covenant against encumbrances was breached at the time of the conveyance. However, Bob is a remote grantee of Owen, thus he cannot obtain damages from Owen.

In some jurisdictions, a remote grantee can sue based on the covenant against encumbrances. However, a remote grantee with notice of the easement may not sue when the grantee, with the notice, (1) never relied on the covenant or (2) bargained for a reduction in the purchase price because of the easement. In some cases, unrecorded easement which was recognized through visual inspection breaches the covenant against encumbrances.

Here, Bob, a remote grantee, recognized the power—line easement through visual inspection and the gas—line easement through actual notice. There are no facts showing that Bob never relied on the covenant or purchased the land for a reduced price.

In sum, Bob cannot obtain damages from Owen under the common law. However, Bob could obtain in some jurisdictions.

해설

난이도: 하

핵심 단어 및 논점

- conveyance
- priority
- recording statute
- inquiry notice
- easement

- shelter doctrine
- bona fide purchaser (BFP)
- covenants of title
- covenant against encumbrances
- remote grantee

1. The agreement regarding Harry's law degree is effective, while the agreement regarding alimony is ineffective.

In majority of jurisdictions, a settlement agreement, in whole or portion, is invalid when it is made by fraud, overreaching, unfairness, or duress. In minority of jurisdictions, a settlement agreement is ineffective when one spouse is not represented by counsel.

Here, Wendy was not represented by counsel and Harry, an attorney, failed to tell Wendy to be represented. Additionally, Harry told Wendy that a divorce court would definitely not impose any further obligations on him, and it was untrue. Thus, the settlement agreement was made by fraud. The agreement regarding Harry's law degree is not unfair and it is effective. By contrast, the agreement regarding alimony is unfair and it is ineffective.

In sum, the agreement regarding Harry's law degree is effective, while the agreement regarding alimony is ineffective.

2. There would be no advantage to Wendy of obtaining a divorce based on Harry's adultery.

In many states, there is no fault−based divorce, and spouse cannot obtain a divorce on grounds of adultery. In these states, Wendy has no advantages to obtain a divorce based on Harry's adultery.

In many states, financial misconduct is considered for the property division or alimony decision, and marital misconduct is considered only when it is serious. In some states, marital misconduct is considered in alimony decision. In some other states, it is not considered in alimony decision.

In sum, in most states, Harry's adultery would not be considered either for property distribution or for alimony award. However, in some states, it would be considered.

3(a). Wendy cannot obtain a cash award representing her share of the value of Harry's law license.

A professional degree or license is a property that is not subject to division at divorce.

Thus, Harry's law license is not divisible and therefore Wendy cannot obtain a cash award representing her share of the value of Harry's law license.

3(b). Wendy would obtain short−term rehabilitative alimony.

If the settlement agreement between Harry and Wendy is invalid, Wendy can obtain alimony.

There are many types of alimony: permanent, rehabilitative, lump sum, and reimbursement. Permanent or long−term alimony is rarely available and there should be a long marriage and a significant and long−term gap between husband's and wife's economic prospects. Regarding rehabilitative alimony, a spouse must establish that (1) she has no sufficient property to provide for his reasonable needs and (2) she has no ability for self−support. In modern, courts consider the ability for self−support as one typical factor for granting rehabilitative alimony, but several factors are considered.

Here, her marriage year is very short, only 3 years. Additionally, Wendy could find a career of which income is similar or even higher than Harry's, since she is young and has no child. Thus, Wendy could not obtain permanent and long−term alimony. Regarding rehabilitative alimony, even though state law does not authorize reimbursement alimony, Wendy can seek short−term rehabilitative alimony. Wendy cannot get reimbursement alimony. This is because she can find a career and she can self−support, even though she has not property. In modern, Wendy's ability for self−support would be considered, but other many factors, such as Wendy's young age, Wendy's contribution to Harry's law license, Harry's salary, and the short marriage period.

In sum, the court would grant short−term rehabilitative alimony to Wendy.

해설

난이도: 하

핵심 단어 및 논점

- settlement agreement
- fault—based divorce
- adultery
- property division order
- professional license
- spousal support order

3번 문제

Alimony에 관한 판결은 법원의 재량(discretion)이 넓게 인정되는 영역이므로, 구체적인 alimony type과 amount를 정하는 것보다는 열린 결말로 서술한다.

2010Feb Torts

1(a). Penny has no battery claim against Dennis, because Dennis did not have intent to bring harmful or offensive contact to the plaintiff's person.

In a battery action, the plaintiff must prove: (1) the defendant's act brought harmful or offensive contact to the plaintiff's person, (2) defendant had intent to bring harmful or offensive contact to the plaintiff's person, and (3) causation. The intent can be established through either motivation or knowledge.

Here, Dennis did not have intent to bring harmful or offensive contact. He did not desire to bring about the harmful contact between the baseball and Penny. He also did not know that his action could cause the harmful contact, because the Fernbury Flies is located in the Park.

In sum, Penny has viable tort claim against Dennis.

1(b). Penny has negligence claim against Dennis, because the burden of precaution taking substantially outweighs the risk.

In negligence action, a plaintiff must show that the defendant owed the plaintiff a duty to conform his conduct to a standard necessary to avoid a foreseeable unreasonable risk of harm of others, that the defendant breached the duty, and that the defendant's conduct was both the cause in fact and the proximate cause of the plaintiff's injuries. In determining whether the actions are reasonable, jury would consider appropriate precautions to avoid foreseeable risks. Jury may consider the likelihood that the risk will eventuate and the burden of taking precautions against such foreseeable risk.

Here, Denny's burden of taking precaution is very high. The precaution that could be taken by Denny to prevent the risk of hitting passerby is not hitting the baseball at all or without maximum force. Denny is a professional minor league baseball member and taking precaution is inconsistent with Denny's job.

Additionally, the risk is relatively low, based on the Flies' records stating only 20 balls had previously been hit over the Park fence adjoining Oak Street. In short, the burden of precaution taking substantially outweighs the risk.

In sum, Penny has negligence claim against Dennis, because the burden of precaution taking substantially outweighs the risk.

2(a). Penny has no claim against the Fernbury Flies for Denny's actions for vicarious liability, because Dennis was not liable for his actions.

Under the doctrine of vicarious liability, employers are liable for the actions of an employee when the employee is acting within the scope of his employment.

Here, Dennis was within the scope of his employment when he hit the baseball, because he acted as a baseball player. However, Dennis had no liability for his actions.

In sum, Penny has no claim against the Fernbury Flies for Denny's actions for vicarious liability.

2(b). Penny has negligence claim against the Fernbury Flies.

In a negligence claim, custom is relevant, but it is not determinative.

Even if Fernbury Flies' conduct conformed to the industry standard, Penny would be successful in his negligence claim, if he establishes that the cost of adding netting to the fence was relatively fair compared to the risk of injuries from balls. The Fernbury Flies maintained the 10−foot−high fence surrounding the Park. However, in Japan, where ballparks are often located in congested urban neighborhoods, netting is typically attached to ballpark fences. The fact that half of the balls hit out of the Park onto Oak Street occurred during the past decade would also support Penny's negligence claim.

In sum, Penny has negligence claim against the Fernbury Flies.

2(c). Penny could recover for harm caused by adverse reaction to the medication, under the eggshell skull doctrine.

Under the eggshell skull doctrine, a plaintiff can recover for the full extent of his injuries which is greatly in excess of those that a normal victim would suffer.

Even though Penny's neurological damage was resulted by adverse reaction to the medication, rather than the Fernbury Flies' action, Penny could recover for harm caused by adverse reaction to the medication as well as concussion if he successes in negligence claim.

해설

난이도: 하

핵심 단어 및 논점

- battery
- harmful or offensive contact
- foreseeable risk
- reasonability

- vicarious liability
- custom
- eggshell skull doctrine

1(b)번 문제

① Risk가 발생할 확률(the likelihood that the risk will eventuate)과 ② 예방의 부담(the burden of taking precautions against such foreseeable risk), 이 두 요소를 비교형량하여 analysis하는 것이 고득점 포인트다.

1. Smith has a right to inspect Omega's corporate books and records, since there is a proper purpose.

A shareholder has a right to inspect corporate books and records for a proper purpose. A proper purpose is a purpose reasonably related to a person's interest as a shareholder. The shareholder needs to express an inspection purpose to address economic risks of the corporation to request the inspection.

Here, Smith asked to inspect Omega's corporate books and records in order to determine the value of his shares. The purpose is related to the shareholder's interest. Additionally, Omega, Inc. is a closely held corporation which has no market that continuously values its shares. In a closely held corporation, the appropriate books and records would be the only way to examining the values of shares.

In sum, Smith's purpose is proper and Smith has a right to inspect.

2. Smith does not need to first make a demand on the corporation, since it is a direct suit.

There are two types of suits that shareholders could bring against the company: derivative and direct suit. In determining whether the suit is derivative or direct suit, it depends on how the shareholders frame it.

A derivative suit is one regarding fiduciary breach by directors or challenging allegedly illegal action by management. If a claim is for shareholder's rights, it is a direct suit. If a transaction could be challenged either by derivative or direct suit, court permits a direct suit. While derivative proceeding requires prior demand to company, direct suit does not requires it.

In this case, Smith is going to bring a suit to compel the payment of a dividend, which is for the right of shareholders. It is not to challenge actions by

management or for the interest of corporation. Thus, it is a direct suit.
In conclusion, Smith does not need to first make a demand on the corporation.

3. The suit is not likely to be successful, since the decision not to pay a dividend is not made in bad faith.

Under business judgment rule, there is a presumption that a board makes a decision (1) in a good faith, (2)in an informed manner, (3) based on a rational basis, and (4) for the best interest of the corporation. In sum, BJR is not applicable when there is fraud, illegality, or conflict of interest. Any actions by directors regarding the business judgment are under BJR. In this case, the decision not to pay a dividend is regarding business judgment of directors.

To prevail in a suit, a shareholder, Smith in this case must prove that the decision is made by directors in bad faith. Bad faith can be found by determining whether the decision of the directors is for their personal interests rather than the corporate benefits. Bad faith is usually proved through various earmarks of it, such as intense hostility against the minority and high salaries or bonuses. Here, there was some hostility of directors (Baker and Jones). They told Smith that he should go away and let them run the show and they refused to reveal the amounts of their salaries in response to an inquiry from Smith. However, these hostilities were not the basis of the boarder's decision, not to pay a dividend. Thus, Smith can success in a suit only by finding that the decision is for the boarder's benefit themselves rather than corporate's benefit, even if funds are legally available to pay dividends.

In sum, the suit is not likely to be successful, since the decision not to pay a dividend is not made in bad faith.

해설

난이도: 하

핵심 단어 및 논점

- corporation
- right to inspect
- derivative suit v. direct suit
- business judgment rule

1번 문제

논점: Shareholder's right to inspect 중 proper purpose

주주의 right to inspect에 관한 문제는, 크게 ① 주주가 해당 요청에 대해 권한을 가지는지 그 여부를 판단하는 문제와 ② 해당 요청 과정의 적합성을 판단하는 문제로 구분된다. 따라서 출제의도를 정확히 파악하는 것이 중요하다. 본 문제는 ①유형에 해당하나, 사안에서 서류의 구체적 묘사 없이 "corporate books and records"라는 표현을 사용하였으므로, proper purpose가 핵심 논점이다.

> **답안요령**
>
> 1. Right to inspect
> 2. "For proper purpose"
>   + analysis
> 3. "Corporate books and records"
> 4. Procedural requirements
>   + analysis

3번 문제

논점: Director's duty of care & BJR, Directors가 행한 특정 행위에 대해 책임을 져야
     하는지 그 여부

로직은 다음과 같다.

BJR에 따르면 director의 행위는 보호되는 바, 책임을 지지 않는다.

→ Director가 한 특정 행위는 BJR과 연관이 있다.

→ 다만, 주주(director에게 책임을 묻고자 하는 자)는 director의 행위가 not good faith임

을 증명할 것이다.

→ 주주의 증명으로서 BJR이 적용될 수 없는 바, director는 그 행위에 대해 책임이
있다.

답안요령

1. BJR
   + analysis
2. S/H's rebutting
   + analysis
3. 결론

1. The federal district court has subject matter jurisdiction.

Federal courts have original jurisdiction over civil actions when the plaintiff and defendants are citizens of different States and the amount in controversy excesses $75,000. The diversity must be complete.

Here, Plaintiff Surrogate is a citizen of State B, because she is domiciled in State B. Defendant Husband is a citizen of State A. Thus, there is complete diversity of citizenship between Surrogate and Husband. Regarding corporations' citizenship, the citizenship can be dual. A corporation is a citizen of States in which the corporation has been incorporated and it has principal place of business. Thus, Insureco is a citizen of State A and State C. Therefore, there is complete diversity of citizenship between Insureco and Surrogate. An alien who is admitted to US for permanent residence is deemed a citizen of the State where the alien is domiciled. Thus, Wife, who is not a U.S. citizen, is a citizen of State A. Therefore, she is also diverse from Surrogate.

Regarding amounts in controversy, Surrogate seeks to compel any or all of the defendants to pay the $500,000 and it exceeds $75,000.

In sum, the federal district court has subject matter jurisdiction.

2. The federal district court should not dismiss the action, since domestic relations exception does on apply in this case.

The federal courts have declined to exercise jurisdiction over domestic relations issues. However, the mere fact that a case involves domestic relations does not mean that the federal courts have no jurisdiction over the case. Domestic relations exception applies only to cases that are primarily marital disputes, such as the issuance of a divorce, alimony, or child custody decree.

Here, Surrogate's claim against the defendants is related to the issue whether

Surrogate is a natural child. However, the issue whether Surrogate is a natural child is to determination of the breach of contract and the breach of the insurance policy. There was no issue regarding divorce, alimony, or child custody. Thus, domestic relations exception does on apply here.

In sum, the federal district court should not dismiss the action, since domestic relations exception does on apply in this case.

3. Surrogate properly joined three defendants in a single action.

The Federal Rules of Civil Procedure permits the plaintiff to join multiple defendants when: (1) any right to relief is asserted against the defendants jointly, severally, or arising out of the same transaction or occurrence, and (2) there are common questions of fact or law for all defendants.

When courts determines whether the claims arises out of the same transaction or occurrence, they considers many factors, such as: (1) whether the issues of fact and law in the claims are same, (2) whether the same evidence would support or refute the claims, (3) whether there is a logical relationship between those claims, and (4) whether res judicata would bar a subsequent suit on the cross—claim.

Here, Surrogate's claims against three defendants arise out of the baby's birth and hospitalization. There are common questions to the claims, such as the circumstances of birth, the term of the surrogacy agreement. Thus, joinder is appropriate in this case.

In sum, Surrogate properly joined three defendants in a single action.

해설

난이도: 하

핵심 단어 및 논점

- jurisdiction (DCJ)
- corporation's citizenship
- domestic relations issues
- permissive joinder
- supplemental jurisdiction

3번 문제

적합한 joinder인지 그 여부를 판단하는 문제로, SPJ를 판단해야 한다.

답안요령

> 1. SPJ에 대한 기본 rule
> 2. Considering factors (×4)
>   + analysis
> 3. Court's discretion (×3)
>   + analysis
> 4. 결론

1. Witness's opinion should not be excluded, since it is an opinion of lay witness.

The opinion that Driver was speeding is relevant to prove whether Driver is negligent. Lay witness opinion is admissible if: (1) the opinion is rationally based on the witness's perception, (2) the opinion held to determine a fact in issue, and (3) the opinion is not based on scientific, technical, or other specialized knowledge. In this case, Witness perceived that car was moving faster than surrounding cars. These perceptions provide a rational and logical basis for his opinion that the car was speeding. The fact states that Witness has no specialized training, experience, or education which means it is commonsense conclusion.

In sum, Witness's opinion should not be excluded, since it is an opinion of lay witness.

2. Spouse's testimony should be excluded, since it is character evidence.

Generally, character evidence is not admissible to prove that a person acted in conformity with the particular character trait, except for some situations in criminal cases.

In this case, Spouse's proposed testimony is relevant to prove whether Pedestrian is negligent. However, Spouse's proposed testimony that Pedestrian is very cautious and risk−averse is about Pedestrian's character. The purpose of the proposed testimony is to prove that Pedestrian would have acted consistently at the time of the accident.

In sum, spouse's testimony should be excluded, since it is character evidence.

3. The evidence of Pedestrian's cell phone use at any time should not be excluded, since it is a habit.

Pedestrian's cell phone use is relevant to Pedestrian's negligence. To contrast to the character evidence, habit evidence is admissible to prove that a person acted in conformity with that habit.

In this case, Pedestrian would state that he invariably ends a call or lowers the cell phone when preparing to cross a street and Pedestrian would claim that he acted in conformity with it at the time of the accident.

In sum, the evidence of Pedestrian's cell phone use at any time should not be excluded, since it is a habit.

4. Pedestrian's memory loss is admissible, while evidence of Pedestrian's other injuries is inadmissible.

Under the Federal rules of evidence Rule 403, if a probative value is substantially outweighed by the danger of prejudice, confusion, or misleading the jury, the relevant evidence is not admissible.

In this case, Pedestrian's memory loss is relevant in determining who is liable for the accident. Additionally, it is relevant to suggest that Pedestrian's testimony regarding the accident is less reliable, and there is no danger of prejudice. Thus, Pedestrian's memory loss is admissible.

Regarding Pedestrian's painful fractures, it is not relevant to prove who caused the collision. It could be relevant, if it is used to determine the value of damage after the determination of Dan's negligence. Therefore, Pedestrian's other injuries would be waste of time and unfair prejudice. Thus, Pedestrian's painful fractures violate the Rule 403 and inadmissible.

In sum, Pedestrian's memory loss is admissible, while evidence of Pedestrian's other injuries is inadmissible.

해설

난이도: 하

핵심 단어 및 논점

- opinion testimony
- character evidence
- habit
- FRE 403

<u>1(a). Doris is entitled to share in the trust, because Doris became the member of class of Settlor's surviving children before the class close.</u>

Under the rule of convenience, the class closes when the named person dies or the gift becomes possessory.

Here, there is a class gift of "Settlor's surviving children," and Doris was adopted before Settlor dies.

In sum, Doris is entitled to share in the trust, because Doris became the member of class of Settlor's surviving children before the class close.

<u>1(b). Whether to whom Alan's share pass depends on which approach is adopted in this jurisdiction.</u>

When a remainderman predeceases the life tenant, the trust assets are distributed based on the directives stated in the trust instrument. If there is a class gift, a deceased child's descendants take the deceased child's share by representation.

Here, Alan is a remainderman and predeceased Settlor. The trust instrument indicates that trust assets would be distributed to Settlor's surviving children. Thus, Alan's share would be distributed to Ben, Claire, and Doris. Alan's share would be distributed to his child.

In sum, whether to whom Alan's share pass depends on which approach is adopted in this jurisdiction.

<u>1(c). Claire's disclaimer is effective and she is deemed to have predeceased Settlor. Her share in the trust would be distributed to Ben and Doris, or to Claire's child.</u>

In most states, a disclaimer is effective when it is in writing and is made, for a testamentary transfer, within nine months of the decedent's death or, for a future interest in a nontestamentary transfer, within nine months of the future interest would become indefeasibly vested. Under UPC, a disclaimer is effective when it is made at any time prior to acceptance of the interest. Here, Clair's disclaim met both requirements and it is effective.

When the future interest holder effectively made a disclaimer, the disclaimant is deemed to have predeceased the life tenant.

Here, Claire is deemed to have predeceased Settlor. Under the common law, Claire's share in the trust would be distributed to Ben and Doris, the surviving class members. Under UPC, Claire's share in the trust would be distributed to her child, regardless of the surviving contingency.

In sum, Claire's disclaimer is effective and she is deemed to have predeceased Settlor. Her share in the trust would be distributed to Ben and Doris, or to Claire's child.

2. Bank is not liable for losses on the investment in XYZ stock, since it followed Settlor's direction.

A trustee has a duty of care, which requires a trustee to administer the trust as a prudent person with reasonable care. A trustee is under a duty to invest and manage trust assets as an ordinary invest would. However, if the trust is revocable, a trustee's duties are owed exclusively to the settlor. When Settlor is only one income beneficiary and Settlor holds the power to revoke the trust, Settlor could be treated as the effective owner.

Here, if the trust was irrevocable, where are many facts to show Bank's breach of duty of care: investing 90% of the trust assets in one stock and retaining the investment in XYZ declining stocks. There were no income beneficiaries other than Settlor and the trust was a revocable.

In sum, Bank is not liable for losses on the investment in XYZ stock, since it followed Settlor's direction.

해설

난이도: 하

핵심 단어 및 논점

- rule of convenience
- substitute gift
- disclaimer
- duty of care
- duty to invest and manage (prudent investor rule)

1. Fran and Gina are partners, but Hank is a creditor of Petals.

A general partnership arises when two or more persons do a business for profit as co-owenrs. No formalities and no intent are required to form it.

Here, when Gina joined with Fran to run the business a partnership is created. Because there was no formalities to form the partnership, it is a general partnership.

When a person receives a share of the net profits of partnership, it is presumed that a person is a partner in the partnership. However, this presumption is inapplicable when those profits are received as payment of a debts by installment or otherwise.

Here, Gina received her share of the net profits for as long as Petals remains in business. Additionally, Gina worked at the shop and helped Fran with business planning for Petals. Gina also agreed to share losses with Fran. Thus, Gina is a partner of Petals. Hank receives a share of the net profits of Petals, but the memo line of the check stated that "loan to Petals." The presumption that Hank is a partner of Petals is inapplicable and therefore Hank is not a partner, but is a creditor.

In sum, Fran and Gina are partners, but Hank is a creditor of Petals.

2. Ivan is entitled to Gina's share, since he is a transferee.

The partner's financial interest in the partnership is the transferable interest in the partnership, including the partner's share of profits and losses and the right to receive distributions. The transfer is effective when the transferor gives notice on the transfer to partnership.

Here, Gina assigned to Ivan, as a gift, all of her interest in Petals. Gina's share of the monthly net profits of Petals is transferable financial interest. Gina gave

Fran a copy of the letter and it constitutes notice to partnership.

In sum, Ivan is entitled to Gina's share, since he is a transferee.

3. Ivan is not entitled to inspect the books and records.

Generally, a person can become a partner only with the consent of all partners. A partner can assign only the financial interest of the partner, and the assignee cannot become a partner only with the assignment. The partner's financial interest in the partnership is the transferable interest in the partnership, including the partner's share of profits and losses and the right to receive distributions.

Here, the right to inspect the books and records of Petals is not transferable financial interest. Additionally, Fran stated that he don't want anything to do with Ivan and there is no consent of all partners.

In sum, Ivan is not entitled to inspect the books and records.

4. Fran is not entitled to use the delivery truck on Sundays to take her children, since she used partnership property for her personal use.

Partners have an equal right to use the partnership property for partnership purposes. This is because partners and a partnership are different and partnership property is owned by partnership, not by the partners. Partners cannot use the partnership property for personal use.

Here, the delivery truck was purchased in the name of Petals and therefore it is a partnership property. Fran is not entitled to use the truck for personal purpose, such as taking her children to their soccer games.

In sum, Fran is not entitled to use the delivery for taking her children.

해설

난이도: 하

핵심 단어 및 논점

- formalities of GP
- partner's interests: partner가 partnership에 대해 가지고 있는 권리를 partner의 채권자에게 이전할 수 있는지 그 여부를 판단한다.
- partnership property
- dissolution

1번 문제

논점: Partner와 creditor 구분

- 지문에 partner가 partnership의 이익(share of profits)을 나누어 받았다는 사실이 명시되어 있으므로, 핵심 논점은 partner와 creditor 구분이다.
- GP 정의 및 특징에 대해 서술한다.

1. Under UCC2, Buyer can revoke the acceptance and recover purchase price and additional damages. Under the common law, Buyer can rescind the contract and he is entitled to restitution and additional damages.

A contract for the sale of goods is governed by UCC2. Here, a contract between Buyer and Seller is to sell the car and it is governed by UCC2. The basic laws about fraud and misrepresentation are applicable to the contracts of UCC2.

Under UCC2, the seller creates express warranties when he makes affirmation of fact about the goods that are part of the bargain and the affirmation warrants that the goods will be same as those affirmations and descriptions.

Here, seller said that the brakes and clutch were replaced in the last six months. It is an affirmation of fact about the car and it creates express warranties. The statement regarding beautiful shape for a vehicle of this age is mere an opinion and it does not create express warranties.

Under the common law, a misrepresentation is any statement that is not same with the facts. A misrepresentation is material when it induced assent to the contract. A misrepresentation is fraudulent when a speaker knew that is it false.

Here, Seller made a misrepresentation about the brakes and the clutch and this statement induced the buyer to enter the contract. The statement is material misrepresentation. Additionally, Seller knew that the brakes and the clutch are not new ones and statement is fraudulent misrepresentation.

A buyer can rescind a contract if his assent was induced by fraudulent or material misrepresentation and he was justified in relying on those misrepresentations.

Here, Buyer tried to let his mechanic to look at the car and make it sure that the car is as Seller represented it. However, Seller stated that the car is exactly as he described it. Thus, Buyer's relying on Seller's misrepresentation is justified and therefore he can rescind the contract.

When the buyer spent reasonable period of time for inspection, it is same is the failure to reject the goods and it is acceptance. Once the buyer accepted goods, he cannot reject them. However, the buyer can revoke the acceptance if: (1) the goods do not conform to the contract, (2) the nonconformity substantially impairs the value of the goods to the buyer, and (3) the buyer accepted the goods either on the reasonable assumption that a nonconformity would be cured or without discovery of a nonconformity if acceptance was induced by either difficulty of discovery before acceptance or the seller's assurance.

Here, the car did not conform to the contract and the brakes and clutch were not new. These old brakes and clutch impairs the value of the car. They buyer accepted the car without discovery of the facts regarding old brakes and clutch because of the seller's assurance. Thus, Buyer's revocation is effective.

When the buyer's revocation of acceptance is effective, the buyer is entitled to the purchase price that he had already paid to seller. Here, Buyer is entitled to recover $5,000 from Seller.

Under UCC, buyer is entitled to the difference between the market price of a car conforming to the contract and the contract price, plus incidental and consequential damages. Alternatively, buyer may cover by buying a car in substitution for the car bought from the seller. Covering purchase must be commercially reasonable. If buyer makes a covering purchase, buyer may recover the excess of the cover price over the contract price, plus incidental and consequential damages. These remedies are also available to misrepresentation claim.

Here, under the market price method, Buyer would recover only to any incidental and consequential damages. If Buyer finds substitute and cover the car, Buyer is entitled to the covering price in excess of $5,000 plus incidental and consequential damages.

In sum, under UCC2, Buyer can revoke the acceptance and recover purchase price and additional damages. Under the common law, Buyer can rescind the contract and he is entitled to restitution and additional damages.

해설

난이도: 상

핵심 단어 및 논점

- express warranty (UCC2)
- misrepresentation (CL)
- rescind
- revocation of acceptance
- cover damages

본 기출문제의 1번 문제는 contracts, 2번 문제는 negotiable instruments에 관한 것이다. Netorigable instruments는 2015Feb부터 시험범위에서 제외된 과목으로, 2번에 대한 답안은 본 서에 싣지 않았다.

1(a). The testator's will is valid, since it was properly signed under the doctrine of integration.

Under the state statue, no will or codicil is valid unless signed the testator and two attesting witnesses. Under the doctrine of integration, a multi−page will is valid even if only the last page is executed when: (1) the supporter of the will can establish that all pages were physically exist together when the testator and witnesses signed the last page of the will and (2) the testator intended that each page to be part of his will. There is a presumption that all pages of the will were present together when the last page was signed, if the pages began to mention the distribution orderly when those are read together.

Here, Testator, in the presence of two witnesses, read the three pages and signed it on the line provided on page 3. All three pages were together when the last page was signed by the testator and two witnessed. The attorney said to Testator "Please sign your will" and Testator did so. It shows that Testator intended the document to be his will. Additionally, page 1 of the will included introductory clauses and two bequests, and page 2 and 3 of the will contained clauses relating to the responsibilities of the executor. Thus, the supporter of the will would rely on a presumption that all pages physically existed together when the testator and witnesses signed the last page of the will.

In sum, the testator's will is valid, since it was properly signed under the doctrine of integration.

1(b). Even though the handwritten codicil is invalid, the revocation of bequest of $20,000 is invalid under DRR.

Under the state law, no will or codicil thereto is valid unless signed by the testator and two attesting witnesses. Here, Testator tried to change the bequest of

$20,000 by crossing out the bequest. It was neither signed nor attested. Thus, the handwritten codicil (crossing out the bequest) is invalid.

However, under the dependent relative revocation (DRR), if a testator revokes a will or codicil based on a mistaken understanding, the revocation is ineffective if the testator would not have revoked without the mistake.

Here, Testator tried to revoke the bequest of $20,000 to Sister with the phrases, "I give $40,000 to Sister." Even if the revocation is invalid under the state law, it seems that Testator's revocation was to give Sister more money. If he knew that his cancellation is invalid and Sister gets nothing, he would not want the cancellation. Under DRR, testator's revocation is invalid and the bequest of $20,000 to Sister is valid.

In sum, even though the handwritten codicil is invalid, the revocation of bequest of $20,000 is invalid under DRR.

2. Abby and Bruce are clearly entitled to the Testator's estate, but the share of Carl and Don are unclear.

Biological children and adopted children are equally entitled to take in intestate succession. Regarding nonmarital children, they are included in the term "children" only if paternity is established.

In most of the jurisdictions, paternity may be established by clear and convincing evidences, such as evidence of subsequent marriage of the parents, by acknowledgment by the father, or by an adjudication of paternity during the life of the father. Here, there are no clear and convincing evidences on Testator's paternity. Thus, it is unclear whether Don will be included in the bequest of "children."

In the majority of jurisdictions, extrinsic evidence is inadmissible to make a difference on the written words in a will. Under this approach, the only way to ascertain the intent of the testator is the written words. In the minority jurisdictions, a will could be changed based on the clear and convincing of (1) a mistake of facts or law or (2) the donor's intention.

Here, Testator told his attorney that he had two children, Abby and Bruce and he did not tell the attorney that he had adopted his stepchild. Testator stated "my children" in his will, which is ambiguous. Under the majority approach, attorney cannot testify that Testator told him only two children, Abby and Bruce. Under the minority approach, the attorney could testify to show that Testator used "my children" based on the mistake of law or to show Testator's intent. However, it is unclear whether the attorney's testimony is unclear whether it is clear and convincing.

In sum, Abby and Bruce are clearly entitled to the Testator's estate. However, Carl and Don are unclear.

해설

난이도: 하

핵심 단어 및 논점

- handwritten codicil
- validity of will (codicil)
- doctrine of integration
- dependent relative revocation (DRR)
- children (term 해석)
- extrinsic evidence

1. The First Amendment precludes Homestead's enforcement of its anti−leafleting ordinance against Chapter.

The First Amendment applies to the state through incorporation in the Fourteenth Amendment. Here, the Homestead's enforcement of anti−leafleting ordinance is a state action.

When a governmental regulation of speech is not content−neutral, the regulation must meet the strict scrutiny. When a governmental regulation of speech imposes only reasonable restrictions on the time, place, or manner of speech in public forums, the regulations must (1) be content neutral, (2) meet the requirements of intermediate scrutiny, and (3) open alternative opportunities to engage in speech. To meet intermediate scrutiny requirement, the regulation must be narrowly tailored to serve an important governmental interest. Public forum includes a public street or sidewalk.

Here, Homestead's anti−leafleting ordinance is content neutral, since it forbids one means of communication, regardless of the content of the speech. Thus, the ordinance must pass the intermediate scrutiny. However, Homestead did not open alternative opportunities to engage in speech. It is not regulating time, place, or manner of speech, but it is restricting the leafleting entirely. Additionally, the fact that Homestead employees spent several hours cleaning up the discarded leaflets does not serve an important governmental interest. The purpose to keep the streets clean is insufficient to justify an anti−leafleting ordinance and any burden imposed upon the city in cleaning and caring for the streets is for the constitutional protection of freedom of speech and press. Thus, the anti−leafleting ordinance of Homestead is unconstitutional under the First Amendment.

In sum, the First Amendment precludes Homestead's enforcement of its anti−leafleting ordinance against Chapter.

2. The First Amendment precludes Principal's denial of Church Club's request to use classroom space for its meetings, because it does not violate the Establishment Clause and Free Exercise Clause.

A designated public forum is created when a governmental entity opens a location to speech even though it could close the location. All the rules applicable to a traditional public forum apply to a designated public forum. Here, High School opened its classrooms after scheduled classes to student groups to meet, and it creates a designated public forum. Thus, the High School should not discriminate among speakers based on the contents of the speech.

The content neutral access does not change when the case involves religious issues. In a public forum, religious speech stands on an equal footing with nonreligious speech, and content—neutral access rules do not violate the Establishment Clause.

Here, the classrooms are open to student groups and content neutral regardless whether the student groups use classrooms for religious reasons. Thus, when the Principal denies Church Club officers to use classrooms, it does not violate the Establishment Clause and Free Exercise Clause.

In conclusion, the First Amendment precludes Principal's denial of Church Club's request to use classroom space for its meetings, because it does not violate the Establishment Clause and Free Exercise Clause.

3. The First Amendment does not provide grounds to vacate Father's trespass conviction.

Father's trespass could be interpreted as two ways: a physical conduct or a conduct with communicative value.

The government can regulate conduct that has no communicative value.

Here, the father's marching into Principal's office might have no communicative value and it simply was a conduct. Thus, the First Amendment does not protect the father's trespass conviction.

The father's entrance into Principal's office could be treated as a conduct having communicative value, since father entered to express his opinion. A government regulation on speech related conduct must serves an important governmental interest and the interest is not to suppress expression, and the interest is no greater than necessary to serve the state's interest.

Here, Principal's office was not a public forum, because the door was closed with a sign reading "No admittance without an appointment." The Principal was meeting with another parent. School has an important interest in prohibiting trespassers from entering Principal's office where private communications may be taken. The interest is not related to suppress the expression. Additionally, the means of protecting the interest are closely related to advancement of High School's interest. Thus, the trespass conviction would be upheld.

In conclusion, the First Amendment does not provide grounds to vacate Father's trespass conviction.

해설

난이도: 상

핵심 단어 및 논점

- freedom of speech (the First Amendment)
- content—neutral restriction
- public forum
- designated public forum
- Establishment Clause
- communicative value

2번 문제

답안요령

> 종교단체의 speech가 제한된 경우
> 1. Freedom of speech에 관한 rules
>   + analysis
> 2. Freedom of religion에 관한 rules★
>   + analysis

TIP '종교'에 관한 speech가 제한된 경우, 별도의 문제가 출제되지 않더라도 freedom of religion에 대해 analysis하는 것이 고득점포인트다.

3번 문제

답안요령

> 1. Conduct without communicative value
>   + analysis
> 2. Conduct with communicative value
>   + analysis(표현행위가 이루어진 forum에 대한)
>   + analysis(판단기준이 되는 rule에 대한)

TIP 특정 conduct를 규제하는 법의 위헌여부를 판단할 경우, 그 행동이 '단순한 행위'를 의미하는 경우와 '의미를 전달하려는' 행위인 경우로 구분하여 analysis하는 것이 고득점 포인트다.

2010July Real Property

1. The terms could be interpreted variously, depending on the court's interpretation and implication of the power of termination.

If the Owner−to−School deed conveyed a fee simple determinable to School, then Owner retained a possibility of reverter, which became possessory immediately upon the happening of the event written in the instrument. If the Owner−to−School deed conveyed a fee simple condition subsequent, Owner may or may not have a power of termination or right of entry for condition broken, depending on whether the court would be willing to imply a forfeiture provision when there is no expressed statement.

To create a fee simple determinable, the typical formulation would be "so long as," while to create a fee simple on condition subsequent, the typical formulation would be "but if." When the terms of the deed are ambiguous, the courts try to find the grantor's intention and they typically prefer for the fee simple on condition subsequent.

Here, the words in the Owner−to−School deed are ambiguous. The term "if" is not enough to create either a fee simple on condition subsequent or a fee simple determinable. If the court implies a forfeiture provision in the deed, the result will be same whether it is a fee simple determinable or a fee simple subject to the condition subsequent. The fee simple determinable requires Owner or his successors to make a demand, while the fee simple subject to the condition subsequent does not. If the court implies no power of termination, School has a fee simple absolute and therefore School holds the title on the land even if it does not use it to teach children aged 5 to 13.

In sum, the terms could be interpreted variously, depending on the court's interpretation and implication of the power of termination.

2. Daughter brought an action against School within the statute of limitation.

The state law provides that actions to recover the possession of real property shall be brought within 10 years after the cause of action accrues.

Here, Owner—to—School deed indicated that School must use Blackacre only to teach children aged 5 to 13. However, School built a new classroom building in other premises and build administrative offices in Blackacre. School's use of Blackacre was beyond the intended purpose. Thus, Owner's successor, Daughter must bring an action against School within 10 years, if the deed created fee simple determinable to School. Here, the school changed its use only three years ago.

Thus, the statute of limitations has not run on the interest.

In sum, Daughter brought an action against School within the statute of limitation.

3. Ann's interest depends on what types Owner created interest to School. Mary's interest depends on the approach the state adopts.

If Owner retained a future interest in Blackacre, Owner's bequest to Daughter upon his death is valid, since the state law provides that all future interests are alienable, devisable, and descendible. Daughter conveyed a deed to Husband for life, with the remainder to "my surviving children."

The term "surviving" can be interpreted in many ways. In majority jurisdictions, a survivorship contingency should be satisfied at the termination of the interests that precede distribution of the remainder. Here, Daughter's children's survivorship contingency must be satisfied at the time of Husband's death. Bill predeceased Husband, and therefore Mary has no interest in Blackacre. However, in other jurisdictions, a survivorship contingency must be satisfied when the testator died. Here, the testator is Daughter and her children, Ann and Bill, were survived testator. Thus, Bill and Ann are entitled to Blackacre and Bill's share will pass to Mary.

In sum, if Owner bequeathed a fee simple determinable, Ann (and Mary) is immediately entitled to Blackacre. If Owner bequeathed a fee simple subject to condition subsequent with the power of termination, Ann (and Mary) becomes possessory until the power of termination was exercised.

해설

난이도: 하

핵심 단어 및 논점

- fee simple determinable
- possibility of reverter
- power of termination
- fee simple condition subsequent
- statute of limitations (SOL)
- term 해석
- survivorship contingency

2010July Family Law

1. The premarital agreement is enforceable under the UPAA. In some states not adopting UPAA, the enforceability of the agreement depends on the state's approach.

The enforceability of the premarital agreement depends on three factors: voluntariness, fairness, and disclosure. In many states, an agreement is unenforceable if the party against whom enforcement is sought succeeds in showing any one of involuntariness, unfairness, or lack of adequate disclosure. However, under UPAA, an agreement is unenforceable if the party against whom enforcement is sought succeeds in showing (1) involuntariness or (2) unfairness and lack of adequate disclosure.

Here, Husband and Wife both disclosed their assets to each other and Wife and both had enough opportunity to talk with attorney. There is no fact showing Husband's or Wife's involuntariness. Thus, under the UPAA, the agreement is unenforceable.

In the states that do not adopt UPAA, the agreement could be unenforceable even if there is an adequate disclosure. Regarding unfairness, in some state, it is determined at the time of signing of the premarital agreement. In some states, it is determined at the time of divorce, and in some other state, it is determined at either point in time or the court invalidates an agreement whenever the agreement is unfair. In some states, it is ineffective if it includes spousal support waivers.

Here, the agreement stated that Wife would pay all Husband's premarital debts and therefore, at the time of divorce, the agreement is fair. At the time of divorce, the agreement would be unfair, since Wife would be entitled to all marital assets and Husband's real estate inherited by Husband during the marriage and titled in his name. Additionally, Husband was injured in a car accident and

he claimed he was disabled and ceased working altogether. In some states, the agreement would be ineffective because of the spousal support waive provision.

In sum, the premarital agreement is enforceable under the UPAA. In some states not adopting UPAA, the enforceability of the agreement depends on the state's approach.

2. Wife's pension and a share in the marital home are divisible.

Marital property is divisible at divorce regardless of the title. By contrast, separate property is not divisible at divorce. The property is marital if it was granted during the marriage by any methods, except for gift, descent, or devise. A separate asset can be transformed into marital property, if marital funds or significant efforts by the owner's spouse enhance its value or build equity during the marriage. When courts decide property division order, only marital property is considered.

Here, Husband's real estate is separate property, since it was inherited. The marital home is marital property, since it was purchased during marriage. Wife's pension would be partially separate and partially marital, because Wife's pension reflects both working prior to marriage and working after marriage.

In sum, Wife's pension and a share in the marital home are divisible.

3. Husband would not be entitled to alimony.

There are many types of alimony: permanent, rehabilitative, lump sum, and reimbursement. When courts consider the alimony award, they consider: parties' financial resources and needs, their marital contributions, and the marital duration. Some states consider spousal misconduct. Regarding the party's needs, courts consider: the standard of living enjoyed during the marriage, the ability of economical self—support, and health. Regarding marital contribution, courts consider both negative and positive actions, such as failure to make economic or noneconomic contributions and misuse or marital funds.

Here, both Husband and Wife had high school education and they had 15 year marriage time. The marital standard of living was not very high and Wife made great contribution in contrast to Husband. Even though Husband was injured in a car accident five years ago, he worked at part—time odd jobs and he never tried to find work as a pilot before he became injured. There was no Husband's economic contribution. Additionally, Wife's salary is not high to pay alimony and Husband's inherited property could be used for his self-supporting.

However, if Husband could show his disability for self-support, the court would determine that his current need outweighs his lack of economic contributions. The Husband would be entitled to alimony from Wife.

In sum, Husband would not be entitled to alimony.

해설

난이도: 하

핵심 단어 및 논점

- premarital agreement
- enforceability of premarital agreement 판단 요소
- property division order
- marital property
- separate property
- spousal support order

1번 문제

논점: Enforceability of premarital agreement

> **답안요령**
>
> 1. In some states (or)
> 2. UPAA (and)
> 3. 각 요소 rule
> 4. Analysis★ + 결론

TIP1 Enforceability와 관련하여 적용되는 두 개의 rule이 있으며, 하나는 요건 중 하나(or)만 만족하면 되고, 다른 하나는 모든 요건을 모두(and) 만족해야 한다는 점에 유의한다.

TIP2 UPAA가 적용되고 부부간 full disclosure가 존재하는 경우, unconscionability에 대한 analysis를 생략하고 바로 involuntariness에 대한 analysis를 하는 것이 좋다. Full disclosure가 존재한다면 unconscionability 존재여부와 무관하

게 UPAA의 premarital agreement's enforceability 두 번째 요건을 만족하지 못하기 때문이다.

TIP3 각 state마다 unconscionability를 판단하는 '기준시점'이 다르므로, 다양한 기준에 입각하여 analysis하는 것이 고득점 포인트다.

3번 문제

Alimony에 관한 판결은 법원의 재량(discretion)이 넓게 인정되는 영역이므로, 구체적인 alimony type과 amount를 정하는 것보다는 열린 결말로 서술한다.

1. The U.S. District Court for the District of State B may exercise personal jurisdiction over Credit Union.

Federal district courts exercise personal jurisdiction to the same extent as the courts of general jurisdiction of the state where the district court sits. Here, State B's long−arm statute extends personal jurisdiction as far as the Constitution allows.

Under the Due Process Clause of the Fourteenth Amendment, a state court has personal jurisdiction over a nonresident defendant who established minimum contacts with the state. Even if the contacts in State B is not continuous and systematic required to establish general jurisdiction, a nonresident defendant is subject to specific jurisdiction when his contacts with the forum state demonstrate purposeful availment of the benefits of the forum state, and it was foreseeable that the defendant may be hauled into the forum state's courts.

Here, Paul's claim is related to the loan agreement with Credit Union. The loan paperwork lists Paul's State B address and Credit Union sends a loan statement and payment coupon to Paul's State B address each month. Additionally, the claim is raised because of the mailing to the State B, incorrect address. Although these contacts were not continuous and systematic contacts for general jurisdiction, Credit Union's contacts were purposefully availed itself of the benefits of State B and it could foresee that it would be hauled into the State B's courts if its conducts are wrongful. Credit Union could argue that sending the paperwork to an incorrect address does not demonstrate purposeful availment. However, it entered into the agreement with the knowledge that Paul is living in State B and it would perform its duty in State B. Thus, there were Credit Union's minimum contacts in State B.

Even though there is minimum contact between the defendant and the forum state, the court cannot exercise PJ when the defendant proves it is unfair.

Here, Credit Union would have a burden to participate in the claim in State B, since it is domiciled in State A. However, the modern transportation would reduce its burden. Thus, there will be no unfairness.

In sum, the U.S. District Court for the District of State B may exercise personal jurisdiction over Credit Union.

2. Whether the court has diversity jurisdiction over the case depends on the citizenship of Paul, since the intent of Paul is unclear.

The district courts have original jurisdiction over the civil actions when there is complete diversity of citizenship between the parties and the amount in controversy exceeds $75,000.

Regarding corporations' citizenship, the citizenship can be dual. A corporation is a citizen of the state where the corporation has been incorporated and it has principal place of business. The principal place of business is the corporation's nerve center where the corporation maintains its headquarters. Here, Credit Union is incorporated in State A and its headquarters are in State A. Thus, the citizenship of Credit Union is State A.

State citizenship for individual U.S. citizens is determined by their domicile, the home where the individual intends to return. To change the domicile, the individual should physically present in the new state and have intent to remain in the state. Here, Paul's domicile was in State A, but he moved to State B without determination to remain in State B. It is unclear whether he had intent to remain in State B, since he took a job and accepted a position as a permanent employee at a law firm, but he bought a vacation home in State A and visits there once a month for two or three days. It is unclear whether Paul has intent to return to State A or to remain in State B.

Regarding the amount in controversy, the amounts must be based on plaintiff's good−faith allegations without a legal certainty that the plaintiff cannot recover the amount alleged. Here, there is no legal certainty that Paul cannot recover $240,000. The difference between the damage alleged by Plaintiff and the actual loss does not make a change.

In sum, if the court decides that Paul had intent to return to State A and Paul is a citizen of State A, then the court has no diversity jurisdiction over the case. By contrast, if the court decides that Paul had intent to remain in State B and Paul is a citizen of State B, then the court has diversity jurisdiction over the case.

3. The court has no federal-question jurisdiction over the case, since it violated well-pleaded complaint rule.

Federal courts have original jurisdiction over all civil actions arising under the federal laws or Constitution. Under the well-pleaded rule, plaintiff's complaint must state that his own cause of action is based upon federal laws or the Constitution. Merely mentioning of the federal statute to rebut an anticipated defense or to deny the applicability of the law does not establish federal-question jurisdiction.

Here, Paul is a plaintiff in this case, and he mentioned on the federal statute just to rebut an anticipated defense. He did not have a claim related to the federal statute. Thus, the court has no federal-question jurisdiction over the case.

In sum, the court has no federal-question jurisdiction over the case, since it violated well-pleaded complaint rule.

해설

난이도: 하

핵심 단어 및 논점

- personal jurisdiction (PJ)
- minimum contacts
- DCJ
- corporation's citizenship
- individual's citizenship
- amount in controversy (AIC)
- well-pleaded rule (FQJ)

1번 문제

답안요령

> 1. (Federal PJ = state)
> 2. △ = nonresident (long-arm & due process)
> 3. DP (minimum contact & notice)
> 4. "Minimum contact"
> 5. Analysis (stream of commerce theory)
> 6. Fairness

3번 문제

답안요령

> 1. FQJ
> 2. Well-pleaded doctrine★

2010July Criminal Law

Larceny by trick is a type of theft offense. To establish larceny by trick, actus reus elements are: (1) a false representation of material fact (2) that causes another person to transfer title to property to the defendant. The required mens rea elements are: (1) knowledge that the representation of fact is false and (2) intent to defraud.

1. Owner's statement regarding the new hard drives satisfies actus reus elements of larceny by false pretenses.

A false representation should be about fact, not about opinion. Commercial puffery is not generally considered false pretenses.

Here, Owner's statement that "We have the best refurbished computers in town" is an opinion. However, Owner's statement that a computer technician always installs new hard drives and replaces any defective parts is a statement of fact and it was false. By this false statement, Owner succeeds to make Customer to transfer $250 cash to him. Owner could argue that Customer would have another reason for purchasing the computer in addition to his false statement. However, Owner's statement was enough to contribute to Customer's purchasing. Thus, there is a causal link between the false representation and the purchase.

In conclusion, Owner's statement regarding the new hard drives satisfies actus reus element of larceny by false pretenses.

2. Owner acted with the knowledge that the statement is false and with the intent to defraud Customer, satisfying mens rea elements.

Under the majority of jurisdictions, courts adopt willful blindness standard. The defendant satisfies knowledge mens rea element, when the defendant is aware of a high probability of the fact's existence and deliberately avoids learning the truth. Under the minority of jurisdictions, required knowledge element is satisfied when defendant had actual knowledge.

Here, Owner had never raised the issue with the technician because the technician offered much faster service and lower rates than those of any other technician in the area. From the faster service and lower rates, Owner should have known that the technician does not install new hard drives. Thus, under the willful blindness standard, Owner satisfies knowledge element.

The intent to fraud is established when the defendant intents that the person to whom the false representation is made will rely on it. Here, the Owner made the statement about the new hard drives to persuade Customer to buy a computer. Thus, Owner had intent to defraud.

In sum, Owner's act satisfies all elements to be guilty of larceny by false pretenses.

해설

난이도: 하

핵심 단어 및 논점

- larceny by trick
- false representation
- commercial puffery
- willful blindness (knowledge)

1. Shareholders listed in the record on the record date are entitled to vote at an annual shareholders' meeting.

Shareholders listed on the record are registered as shareholder on a record date is entitled to vote at a particular shareholder meeting.

In this case, the record date was December 30th, and Amy was the owner of the 50 shares, not Zach. Zach was not listed in the record on the record date and it is not entitled to vote at the meeting.

Thus, Ame has the vote power at the meeting.

2. A shareholder proxy is revocable.

A shareholder is not required to physically attend the meeting by the use of proxy. A valid proxy must be written and signed. Shareholder proxies generally are revocable, unless the proxy is irrevocable because it is related with an interest or legal right. Any action revokes that proxy when the action is taken in contrast to a proxy.

In this case, Brian gave Dell a proxy to vote Brian's shares. Brain's proxy is not related with an interest or legal right of Dell and it is irrevocable. Brain attended at the shareholder's meeting and his voting was inconsistent with the grant of a proxy to Dell.

Thus, Brian revoked the proxy and Brian's vote of 25 against proposal should be counted and Dell's vote should not be counted.

3. A shareholder of record may attend and vote at an annual shareholders' meeting.

A shareholder of record is entitled to attend and vote at an annual shareholders' meeting.

Here, on the record date, December 30, Carter was listed on the record.

Thus, Carter's vote is proper and it should be counted.

4. Treasury shares should not be counted.

Treasury shares are shares that are required by a corporation, and these are considered authorized but not outstanding. Shares that are not outstanding do not count.

Here, X Corporation has 50 shares that it repurchased from Amy which are treasury shares.

Thus, the 50 shares should not be counted.

5. The shareholder proposal is approved, since the articles of incorporation prevail over the bylaws.

When a corporation's articles of incorporation conflicts with its bylaws, the articles of incorporation preempts the bylaws.

Here, X Corporation's articles of incorporation require an affirmative vote by the holders of two—thirds of the shares entitled to be voted to approve any proposal at a shareholders' meeting, and the bylaw conflicts with it. Thus, the counting of shares should follow the articles of incorporation. Amy's 50 votes and Brain's 25 votes are counted in favor of the proposal. Carter's 25 votes are counted against the proposal.

Thus, the voting satisfies the approval requirement and the proposal should be passed.

해설

난이도: 하

핵심 단어 및 논점

- shareholder of record
- record date
- proxy
- treasury shares

1. Ron's friend was not entitled to any of the trust income, because Trustee has uncontrolled discretion.

When a trustee has uncontrolled discretion, beneficiaries can compel distribution only when there is abuse of discretion. There is no abuse of discretion, if the trustee acts honestly and in a state of mind contemplated by the testator.

Here, under the Testator's duly probated will, Trustee has uncontrolled discretion. Thus, Ron, beneficiary of the trust, can compel payments only when Ron could establish that there was abuse of discretion. There is no fact to show trustee's abuse of discretion.

Creditor has no greater rights in the trust than beneficiary has. In some states, a creditor cannot assert the beneficiary's right to complain of abuse of discretion.

The friend has no greater rights in the trust than beneficiary has, and the friend could not compel payment as Ron could not. Even if the friend could show trustee's abuse of discretion, it could not be the reason for compelling.

In sum, Ron's friend was not entitled to any of the trust income, because Trustee has uncontrolled discretion.

2. If the state follows the common law, the trust principal would be distributed to Carol and Ginny. By contrast, if the state follows UPC, the trust principal would be distributed only to Carol.

An adopted individual is the child of his adopting parents.

Here, Carol would be treated same as a Ron's biological child. Even if Carol was adopted by Ron after the creation of the trust, Carol is still entitled to a share of the remainder allocated to "grandchildren." This is because the class gift closes when one person becomes entitled to possession of the remainder interest. There was no person who became entitled to the possession before Ron's death.

A class gift closes when at least one class member is entitled to distribution.

Here, the distribution to Testator's grandchildren occurs at the time of Ron's death. So, the class gift of Testator's grandchildren is closed at Ron's death.

Under the common law, when the trust creates a vested remainder in a person or member of class and then provides that the remainder should pass to that person's child if the remainder person predeceases the life tenant, the remainder is divested only if the deceased remainder person has a child. If the remainder person dies childless, the remainder is not divested and passes to the remainder person's estate.

Here, Peter's remainder would be distributed to his survived child. However, Peter survived with no child, so his share would be vested in his estate. According to Peter's will, his share would be distributed to his wife, Ginny.

Under the UPC, future interest is contingent on the beneficiary's surviving to the distribution date.

Here, Peter predeceased Ron, so he had no interest to pass to Ginny.

In conclusion, if the state follows the common law, the trust principal would be distributed to Carol and Ginny. By contrast, if the state follows UPC, the trust principal would be distributed only to Carol.

해설

난이도: 하

핵심 단어 및 논점

- uncontrolled discretion
- creditor's right
- adopted child
- rule of convenience
- substitute gift

1. The judge should have permitted Prosecutor to question Witness about the written statement and admitted the copy of the statement, since a prior inconsistent statement and extrinsic evidence of it are admissible for impeachment.

It is permissible for a lawyer to impeach the credibility of any witness, including a witness called by the lawyer. Prior inconsistent statement made by a witness is admissible to impeach the credibility of the witness, when the witness was given an opportunity to explain or deny the statement.

In this case, witness testified that she had no memory of the incident, and judge may find that this testimony is inconsistent with the out of court statement regarding same issue. Additionally, the copy of the statement is an extrinsic evidence regarding the statement made in police headquarters. If the witness has been given an opportunity to explain or deny all or part of it, the statement should be admitted for impeachment purpose. There is no hearsay issue here, since those statements were not used to prove the truth, rather than to impeach the credibility.

In sum, the judge should have permitted Prosecutor to question Witness about the written statement and admitted the copy of the statement, since a prior inconsistent statement and extrinsic evidence of it are admissible for impeachment.

2. The part of Witness's written statement regarding Defendant's identification is admissible, while the other part of the statement is inadmissible. This is because prior identification statement is officially non−hearsay.

Prior identification statement is officially non−hearsay, if: (1) the witness stands at trial and (2) the witness is subject to cross−examination. Even if the witness is unable to remember the identity at trial, he would be subject to cross–examination, and the prior identification statement is admissible.

In this case, the part of Witness's statement, "I was walking in City Park on May 5, at 2 p.m., when I saw Defendant. I know Defendant from the neighborhood and recognized Defendant as suspect number 1 on the 12–person photograph display shown to me today by Police Officer," is regarding the identity of Defendant. The witness stranded at trial and was subject to cross–examination. The fact that witness did not confirm the identity at trial by suggesting he had no memory of the incident does not make a different result. Thus, part of witness's statement is admissible as prior identification statement.

Regarding the remainder of the witness's statement, it is not admissible. To be admissible prior inconsistent statement for the purpose of proving the truth, the statement must be made under oath and subject to the penalty of perjury.

In sum, the part of Witness's written statement regarding Defendant's identification is admissible, while the other part of the statement is inadmissible. This is because prior identification statement is officially non–hearsay.

3. Buddy's testimony should not be admitted to prove Defendant's character, since it is not proper reputation or opinion.

Character evidence is generally not admissible to prove that a person acted in conformity with the particular character trait. However, in criminal cases, defendant could open the door by bring his relevant character evidence to prove that the defendant did not commit the charged offense. The character evidence is limited in reputation or opinion methods. Reputation methods should use reputation in the community, which means the circles of associates where one lives or works.

In this case, defendant is charged for robbery and assault and he called Buddy to let him testify that defendant is honest and gentle. If honesty is used as truth–telling, it is irrelevant with robbery and assault. However, honesty can be used, since the theft is dishonest as well as gentleness. Buddy testified his friends' opinion, not his own opinion. Buddy's friends' opinion is not proper reputation, since they met Defendant recently and only a few times.

In sum, Buddy's testimony should not be admitted to prove Defendant's character, since it is not proper reputation or opinion.

해설

난이도: 하

핵심 단어 및 논점

- prior inconsistent statement (impeachment)
- prior identification statement (officially non-hearsay)
- character evidence (admissibility)

3번 문제

논점: Character evidence의 admissibility

답안요령

1. Character evidence 기본 rule: not admissible
2. 그러나 in criminal case 가능
3. Limitation (R/O)
4. Analysis

1. Bank has no security interest in the telescope against Smith, since Smith is a buyer in ordinary course of business.

A security interests is enforceable when: (1) debtor signed a security agreement. (2) debtor has rights in the collateral, and (3) secured party gave money to secured party.

Here, Bank has security interest in Astronomy's telescope, because telescope is inventory. Astronomy authenticated a security agreement, Astronomy has rights in the telescope, and Bank loaned money to Astronomy. To perfect a nonpossessory security interest in goods, a financing statement must be filed. Thus, Bank's security interest in the telescope attached. Bank filed a financing statement, and its security interest is perfected.

Generally, a security interest continues after sale of the collateral. However, a buyer in ordinary course of business (BIOCOB), the buyer takes free of security interest which was created by the buyer's seller. BIOCOB is a buyer who (1) buys goods in good faith, (2) without knowledge that the sale violates the rights of another, (3) from a person in the business of selling goods of the kind in the ordinary course of the seller's business.

Here, Johnson is a BIOCOB. First, there is no fact to show Johnson's bad faith and he was unaware of the financial arrangement between Astronomy and Bank. Second, he purchased the telescope from Astronomy, who is in the business of selling goods of the kind in the ordinary course of its business. Because Johnson is a BIOCOB, he took the telescope free of Bank's security interest that was made by Astronomy.

In sum, Bank has no security interest in the telescope against Smith, since Smith is a buyer in ordinary course of business.

2. Astronomy has no security interest in the telescope against Smith, Smith satisfied all factors to be free of Astronomy's security interest.

Under the security agreement between Astronomy and Johnson, Astronomy has security interest in the telescope purchased by Johnson. The security interest is effective and attached, because Johnson signed in the agreement, Johnson has rights in the telescope, and Astronomy gave Johnson value, the telescope here.

When the collateral is a consumer goods and it secures a purchase money obligation on that collateral, the security interest is a purchase money security interest (PMSI) in consumer goods. A PMSI is automatically perfected upon attachment. Consumer goods is a goods that is purchased for personal, family, or household purposes.

Here, Astronomy has a security interest in the telescope to secure Johnson's obligation to pay the balance of the purchase price. The telescope is purchased by Johnson for his personal use, and therefore it is a consumer goods. In short, Astronomy's security interest is a PMSI in consumer goods and is perfected, even though it did not file the financial statement.

A buyer of consumer goods takes free of a security interest in those goods, if the buyer (1) buys without knowledge of the security interest, (2) gives value, (3) purchases the goods for personal, family, or household use, and (4) receives the goods before the filing of any financing statement covering them.

Smith is not a BIOCOB, since he did not purchase the telescope from someone who is in the business of selling goods of the kind. However, he took the telescope free of Astronomy's security interest. First, Smith purchased the telescope from Johnson without knowledge of any interest of Bank or Astronomy in it. Second, Smith purchased it for $27,000. Third, Smith purchased it for personal use. Fourth, he received the goods and at that time there was no filing of any financing statement covering the telescope because Astronomy's security interest was automatically perfected upon attachment.

In short, Astronomy has no security interest in the telescope against Smith, Smith satisfied all factors to be free of Astronomy's security interest.

해설

난이도: 하

1(a). Claimant can establish a prima facie case of battery against Metro for the use of the stun device.

In a battery action, the plaintiff must prove: (1) the defendant's act brought harmful or offensive bodily contact to the plaintiff, (2) defendant had intent to bring harmful or offensive contact to the plaintiff's person, and (3) causation. The intent can be established when the defendant desired to cause the consequences of his act or when he knows that the consequences are certain.

First, the use of the stun device is to incapacitate target and causes the target to suffer paid. Both constitute bodily harm. Second, Metro employee used the stun device with the purpose of physically impairing Claimant. Claimant could reasonably aware that the stun device causes pain.

In sum, Claimant can establish a prima facie case of battery.

1(b). Claimant could not establish a prima facie case of battery against Metro for frisk, since Claimant would not be able to show the frisk was offensive.

A bodily contact is offensive, when it offends a reasonable sense of personal dignity.

Here, Claimant could argue that the contact was offensive. Metro had instructed its employees to ask permission before frisking patrons, so frisking without permission is offensive. However, the frisk without permission was not offensive. The frisk was routine practice in screening process, so the frisk does not offend reasonable sense of personal dignity. The frisk is not offensive.

Regarding intent, there is no fact to show Metro employee had purpose to cause causing offense or Metro employee knew he would cause offense by frisking Claimant. Battery is a protection of dignity against intentional invasion, not against the action that involves a risk of causing an offensive contact. Thus, the fact that Metro employee may have been aware of a risk that some patrons would be offended by a frisk does not make a different result. However, because asking permission before frisking patrons are required to Metro employees, the employee were substantial certain that the frisk without permission would be offense to Claimant. In short, Metro employee had intent for the prima facie case of battery purpose.

In conclusion, if the jury concludes that the frisk was offensive, Claimant could establish battery claim. If the jury concludes that the frisk was not offensive, Claimant could not establish battery claim.

2. Metro has a consent defense to battery for the frisk. By contrast, Metro has no consent defense to battery for the use of the stun device.

Consent is a defense to battery. Consent may be manifested by action or inaction and if words or conduct are reasonably understood by another as consent, they constitute consent and are effective defense.

Here, Claimant told Friend, "I'm certainly not going to allow anyone to touch me," and told Inspector, "leave me alone!" Additionally, the employee is required to ask patrons for permission to frisk. Thus, it is hard to say that Claimant consented to being frisked. However, Claimant saw the posted sign that all entrants are screened and may be searched. Even after she saw the warning sign, she entered and walked through the metal detector. Claimant's conduct constitutes consent to being frisked. Thus, a court may conclude that there was Claimant's consent to being frisked.

Claimant did not consent to being shocked with a stun device. Claimant did not see the warning about the use of stun device.

In conclusion, Metro has a consent defense to battery for the frisk. By contrast, Metro has no consent defense to battery for the use of the stun device.

3. Claimant can establish the prima facie of a strict products liability claim agasint Alertco.

To establish strict products liability: (1) the defendant is a commercial supplier, (2) the defendant produced or sold a defective product, (3) the defective product was the actual and proximate cause of the plaintiff's injury, and (4) the plaintiff suffered damages to person or property. There is a manufacturing defect when a product failed to meet customer's specifications and the defect occurred during the products' manufacture.

Here, Alertco is a commercial supplier. It manufactured the stun device and the defects were occurred during its manufacturing. Thus, all elements to establish strict products liability are satisfied. Whether there was negligence does not change the result.

In sum, Claimant can establish the prima facie of a strict products liability claim against Alertco.

4. Alertco is liable both for Claimant's physical and psychological injuries, under the eggshell skull doctrine.

Under the eggshell skull doctrine, a plaintiff can recover for the full extent of his injuries which is greatly in excess of those that a normal victim would suffer.

Here, Claimant had a history of depression and depressive reaction was caused by the shock.

In sum, Alertco is liable both for Claimant's physical and psychological injuries.

해설

난이도: 하

핵심 단어 및 논점

- battery
- offensive contact
- consent (defense)
- strict products liability
- eggshell skull doctrine

1번, 2번 문제

1번 문제 논점: Battery 성립요소 중 'offensive contact'

2번 문제 논점: Battery에 대한 defense(아래 답안요령 3번)

본 기출은 각 문제가 '한 개' 논점에 대한 것으로, 난이도가 낮은 문제다. 그러나 최근 기출은 'battery에 해당하는가'와 같이 broad한 문제를 출제하고 이에 '관한' 모든 논점을 수험자가 스스로 파악할 것을 요구한다. 따라서 intentional torts에 대한 답안에는 반드시 defenses를 서술해야 한다.

> **답안요령**
>
> 1. 문제에 해당하는 intentional tort's 요소
> 2. Intent
>   + analysis★
> 3. Defenses★
> 4. 기타(vicarious liability 등)

3번 문제

논점: Products liability based on strict liability

답안요령

1. Strict products liability 정의
2. NG proof 필요 없음★
3. "Commercial seller"
   + analysis
4. "Defective" product(manufacturing/design defect)
5. Causation
6. Analysis

TIP　Strict liability를 입증하는데 있어 피고의 negligence 유무는 무관하다는 점을 명시하는 것이 고득점 포인트다. 이는 products liability뿐만 아니라 일반적인 strict liability에 관해 논하는 경우에도 그러하다.

1. The portion regarding child support obligation would be invalidated and the remaining agreement would be valid.

Separation agreement, in whole or portion, is invalid when there is fraud or unfairness.

Here, there are three parts in the separation agreement: property division, spouse support obligation, and child support obligation. Each spouse was represented by their respective attorneys and they revealed full information on assets. Husband could argue that his assets and Wife's assets are not equal. However, the courts at divorce divide assets equitably, not equally. Wife has sole custody of Child and Husband needs to pay $900 per month in child support and spouse support. This amount is not too high compared to his income. Thus, there is neither misrepresentation nor unfairness, regarding property division and spouse support.

Regarding child support provision, Husband is not Child's biological parent. In some states, the fact that Wife did not tell Husband the possibility constitutes misrepresentation. If the state adopts this approach, the portion of the agreement regarding child support obligation is invalid.

In sum, the portion regarding child support obligation would be invalidated and the remaining agreement would be valid.

2(a). A property division award cannot be modified.

A property division cannot be modified after a divorce decree has been entered, because a property division award divides assets based on the equities at the time of divorce and it reflects the past. By contrast, support obligation reflects future and it could be modified if there is substantial change in circumstances.

In sum, a property division award cannot be modified.

2(b). Spouse support cannot be modified, since there is no substantial change of circumstances.

As mentioned above, a spousal support award can be modified when there is a substantial change in circumstances. It is a substantial change, when a spouse has legal obligation to a new spouse and/or child. However, if a spouse has new obligation to stepchild, it is not a substantial change. A situation that could easily be anticipated is not substantial change.

Here, Husband was living with Fiancee at the time he signed the separation agreement. Fiancee had two teenage children, who are stepchildren of Husband. Additionally, Husband's planned marriage to Fiancee was the primary reason for Husband's willingness to sign the separation agreement. Husband could easily anticipate his obligation to support his stepchildren after divorce action.

In sum, Spouse support cannot be modified.

2(c). child support obligation could be modified based on the approach which the court adopts.

Traditionally, courts are very reluctant to terminate parent—child relationship that is already established. There were many bases to bar nonpaternity evidence, such as res judicata or collateral estoppel principles, equitable doctrines of estoppel, and best interest of child. Here, the Child is only 10 years old and he recognizes only Husband as his father. Thus, father—child relationship has already been established.

However, in modern, In modern, courts focus on the interests of erroneously identified fathers. The blood tests can be offered and support obligation may be terminated, regardless of the child's interests.

Here, Husband discovered that he is not Child's biological parent as a result of blood tests. The blood test may be offered and support order may be terminated.

In sum, child support obligation could be modified based on the approach which the court adopts.

해설

난이도: 2(c)번 문제: 중
　　　 그 외 문제: 하

핵심 단어 및 논점

- separation agreement
- property division order
- spousal support order
- modification of spousal support order
- substantial change in circumstances
- child support order
- nonpaternity

2011Feb Contracts

1. Retailer is liable for breach of contract.

Designer's statement when he called Retailer was an offer to enter into a new and modified contract. However, Retailer responded that "I'll do it if I can get a loan." This statement makes Retailer under the obligation with condition of getting a loan. The acceptance contained additional terms and it is a counteroffer. Following Retailer's countoffer, Designer's response, "That will be great" is an acceptance.

It could be arguable that Retailer did not explicitly state that his obligation is conditioned upon a getting a loan. However, Retailer's statement is enough to make it clear that his obligation could be performed only by getting a loan.

When an obligation is subject to a condition precedent, there is an implied obligation to make good faith efforts to satisfy the condition. Here, Retailer's obligation is subject to condition precedent, getting a loan. Thus, Retailer has implied obligation to make a good faith effort to get a loan. However, Retailer did not take other action to obtain a loan after he visited two banks and picked up loan applications. Thus, Retailer violated an implied obligation.

In sum, Retailer breached the contract.

2. Designer can recover his actual damages.

Nonbreaching party is entitled to expectation damages for breach of contract. The purpose is to put the nonbreaching party in as good a position as if the other party had fully performed. Expectation damages arises when: (1) it is caused by defendant, (2) it was foreseeable, (3) it is reasonably certain, and (4) it is unavoidable. Expectation damages should be reduced by the costs that was avoided by the breach.

First of all, the breach was caused by defendant, Retailer, here. Secondly,

Designer specified that he needs cash quickly to make an investment and therefore Retailer could reasonably foresee that his breach would cause the damage to Designer. Secondly, Designer specified that his investment will enable him to make a $35,000 profit and it is enough to make damages reasonably certain. There are no facts showing that there is alternatives to avoid the damages and that there are costs that was avoided by the breach.

In sum, Designer is entitled to recover his actual damages from Retailer.

3. Designer cannot recover punitive damages.

Punitive damages are not recoverable in breach of contract.

Here, there is no fact showing that the breach of contract is a tort.

In sum, Designer cannot recover punitive damages.

해설

난이도: 중

핵심 단어 및 논점

- counteroffer
- condition precedent
- good faith effort
- expectation damages
- punitive damages

1. Delta's corporate existence began on November 15, in which Adam filed Delta's articles of incorporation.

Corporate existence begins when the articles of incorporation are filed. This rule is applicable even if the articles specify an effective date prior to the date of filing.

In this case, Delta's articles of incorporation states that existence would begin on September 1. However, Adam filed the articles of incorporation on November 15, in which later date of September 1.

In sum, Delta's corporate existence began on November 15.

2. Adam is personally liable on the Mega contract, since she acted on behalf of Delta and knew that no incorporation exists.

When all persons acted on behalf of a corporation, knowing that no incorporation exists, they are jointly and severally liable for pre-incorporation transactions.

In this case, regarding Mega contract, Adam acted on behalf of Delta and knew that no incorporation exists, since she did not filed the articles of corporation. However, Baker and Clark did not act on behalf of Delta regarding the Mega contract and they did not know that no incorporation exists, since Adam agreed to file the articles of incorporation.

In sum, Adam is personally liable on the Mega contract.

3. Adam and Baker are personally liable on the Sole contract, since they satisfies the participation and knowledge requirements.

As mentioned above, persons are jointly and severally liable if they satisfy the participation and knowledge requirements for pre−incorporation transactions. When a person erroneously but in good faith believes that the necessary documents have been filed, a person is protected from the liability.

Here, the Sole contract was made on November 1 and at that time Baker knew that no incorporation exists, since he learned that the necessary documents have been filed. Delta's articles of incorporation had not been filed on October 15. There was no good faith belief of Baker that Baker participated in the Sole contract, since he helped Adam negotiate the contract with Sole. Baker was a participant, rather than a prospective shareholder. As mentioned above, Adam knew that articles of incorporation have not been filed. Adam participated in the Sole contract.

In sum, Adam and Baker are personally liale on the Sole contract.

해설

난이도: 하

핵심 단어 및 논점

- corporation
- formalities
- date of filing rule
- de facto corporation
- pre−incorporation transactions

1. The court properly denied Bartender's motion to dismiss, since the defense was not raised when Bartender made the motion to dismiss.

When a party initially makes motion to dismiss under the Rule 12(b), the party must join all other motions permitted by Rule 12 with the motion which are available to the party. If a party fails to join available motions, the party cannot raise those motions later.

Here, Bartender made a timely motion to dismiss Plaintiff's complaint for failure to state a cause of action. It was an initial motion to dismiss under the Rule 12 (b). He also had a motion to dismiss for insufficiency of service of process that was available at that time. However, he did not join the motion to dismiss for insufficiency of service of process, and therefore he cannot raise defenses or objections regarding it. Thus, the court should not allow Bartender's motion to dismiss for insufficiency of service of process after he raised the first motion to dismiss.

In sum, the court properly denied Bartender's motion to dismiss, since the defense was not raised when Bartender made the motion to dismiss.

2. The federal rules of civil procedure permit Bartender to join a claim for battery against Dave, since it is a cross−claim arises out of the same transaction or occurrence.

There is a cross−claim when a defendant's answer states a claim against co−defendant which arises out of the same transaction or occurrence that is the subject matter of the original action. Here, Bartender's answer to the Plaintiff's complaint states a claim against Dave, who is a co−defendant in the action. Thus, Bartender's claim against Dave is a cross−claim.

When courts determine whether the claims arise out of the same transaction or occurrence, they considers many factors, such as: (1) whether the issues of fact and law in the claims are same, (2) whether the same evidence would support or refute the claims, (3) whether there is a logical relationship between those claims, and (4) whether res judicata would bar a subsequent suit on the cross−claim.

First, Both Plaintiff's claim and Bartender's claim are claims for battery which will be governed by State A statute. Both claims have factual questions about the cause and course of the fight that Plaintiff, Bartender, and Dave involved. Even though the factual questions are not exactly same, those are substantial overlap. Thus, there are same issues of fact and law. Second, two claims would require same witness who was in the O.K. Bar. Thus, there will be same evidence in two claims. Third, Bartender's attempts to stop the attack made Dave to injure him. There was a causal link and there is a logical relationship between Bartender's cross−claim and Plaintiff's claim against Bartender and Dave. Fourth, the judgment on Plaintiff's claim would bind Bartender, but he is not in privity with either Dave or Plaintiff. Bartender can bring a claim against Dave in future. Thus, even though Bartender's claim would not be barred under res judicata, other factors strongly suggest that the court should allow his claim to be joined as a cross−claim.

In sum, the federal rules of civil procedure permit Bartender to join a claim for battery against Dave, since it is a cross−claim arises out of the same transaction or occurrence.

3. The court has supplemental subject matter jurisdiction, since Bartender's claim arises out of the same transaction or occurrences of the Plaintiff's claim.

To be heard in federal court, the claim must arise out of the federal laws, or satisfies diversity jurisdiction requirements. Here, the Bartender's claim against Dave does not arise under the federal laws. Bartender and Dave are citizens of State A, and therefore there is no diversity jurisdiction over the claim.

Under the supplemental jurisdiction statute, district courts can hear claims if those claims arise out of the same transactions or occurrences of the primary claims under Article III.

As mentioned above, Bartender's cross−claim and Plaintiff's claim against Bartender and Dave arise out of the same transactions, since they have logical relationship and substantial overlap in factual and legal issues. Thus, the court may exercise supplemental subject matter jurisdiction.

In sum, the court has supplemental subject matter jurisdiction, since Bartender's claim arises out of the same transaction or occurrences of the Plaintiff's claim.

해설

난이도: 하

핵심 단어 및 논점
- Rule 12(b) motion to dissmiss
- cross−claim
- supplemental jurisdiction (SPJ)

2번 문제
논점: Cross−claim

답안요령1

1. Cross−claim
2. "=T/O"
   + analysis
3. Court's discretion★
   + analysis
4. SMJ? (FQJ/DCJ/SPJ)

3번 문제
논점: Jurisdiction(SPJ)에 대한 것으로, 위 답안요령의 4번이 별도의 문제로 출제된 것이다.

답안요령2

1. SPJ에 대한 기본 rule
2. Considering factors (×4)
   + analysis
3. Court's discretion (×3)
   + analysis
4. 결론

1. Testator's will is valid, since it is complied with the statutory requirements.

A holographic will is an unwitnessed will in a testator's handwriting. A holographic is valid if it is complied with the statutory requirement.

Here, the state law disallows all holographic wills but testator's will is not a holographic will, since it was witnessed. The will was witnessed by testator's three friends and immediately thereafter, they signed their names below Testator's name. The testator acknowledged the instrument when she stated "This is my will." Thus, all facts comply with the requirement for a valid will under the state law.

In sum, Testator's will is valid, since it is complied with the statutory requirements.

2(a). Niece is entitled to life insurance policy as she is named in the insurance, because Testator did not comply with the insurance policy.

If there is an effective life insurance when testator died, the policy proceeds are payable to the named beneficiary. Although the owner of the insurance policy can change the named beneficiary without obtaining beneficiary's consent, the owner must change it in accordance with the life insurance contract. However, a beneficiary change that does not comply with the insurance contract is valid, if the insurance owner has "substantially complied" with the contract by taking all reasonable steps to make the change in accordance with the contract terms. In the minority of jurisdictions, the owner can change the beneficiary by his will.

Here, Testator attempted to change the beneficiary of his life insurance and the policy of the life insurance requires Testator to submit the change on the insurer's change−of−beneficiary form to the insurance company. However,

Testator did not submit the form and he just specified that he gives his life insurance proceeds to Cousin in his will. There are no facts showing Testator tried to follow the contract terms.

In sum, Niece is entitled to life insurance policy as she is named in the insurance, because Testator did not comply with the insurance policy.

2(b). Niece is entitled to take Testator's jewelry under the incorporation by reference doctrine.

Under the incorporation by reference doctrine, only a document can be incorporated into a will if: (1) it exists when or before the will was signed and (2) it is sufficiently identified in a will. However, in some states, document that exists when, before, or even after the will was signed can be incorporated by reference, if the will evidences an disposal intent.

Here, a memorandum found in testator's safe—deposit box was signed and dated by Testator the day before she signed her will. Thus, it can be incorporated in the will and therefore Niece will take the jewelry.

In sum, Niece is entitled to take Testator's jewelry under the incorporation by reference doctrine.

2(c). Testator's bank account ($6,000) will be distributed to Church, Library, and School equally through abatement.

Under the common law, lapse occurred whenever a beneficiary predeceased the testator and the testator specified otherwise. A lapsed bequest passes into the residue of the testator's estate. However, under the anti—lapse statutes, the bequest is saved from lapse and deceased beneficiary's issue takes it when: (1) deceased beneficiary is blood relation with the testator and (2) deceased beneficiary has issue and the issue survived the testator.

Here, Testator bequeathed $40,000 to Husband. However, Husband died six months before Testator. He is not related with the testator in blood relationship and therefore, the bequest to him lapses and passes to the residuary estate.

In sum, Husband is not entitled to $40,000.

Abatement of the bequest occurs when the assets of a testator's estate are insufficient to pay all of the bequest under the testator's will. Unless the will specifies otherwise, testamentary bequests abate in the following order: residuary bequests, general bequests, and specific bequests. Abatement within each category is in pro rata.

Here, Testator's probate asset is insufficient to pay all bequests under the will and therefore the bequests should abate. The residuary bequest to Son abates first, and Son receives nothing. The general bequests to Church, Library, and School abate next in pro rata and therefore, they receive $20,000 equally. The specific bequest to Niece has no change. Additionally, under the majority approach, the life insurance is a nonprobate asset and there is no abate.

In sum, Testator's bank account ($6,000) will be distributed to Church, Library, and School equally through abatement.

해설

난이도: 하

핵심 단어 및 논점

- validity of will
- holographic will
- life insurance
- incorporation by reference doctrine
- lapse
- anti−lapse statutes
- abatement
- in pro rata

2011July
2011July Secured Transactions

1. Lender has a superior interest in the clocks.

Inventory is defined as raw materials, work in process, or materials used or consumed in debtor's business. Here, the decorative clocks are inventory of Decorator, because Decorator purchased them for resale to its customers. Under the security agreement, Lender has security interest in Decorator's all present and future inventories, the clocks. The security interest is effective and attaches, when: (1) debtor signed a security agreement, (2) debtor has rights in the collateral, and (3) secured party gave money to secured party. Decorator signed the agreement, it has rights in the clocks, and Lender loaned money to Decorator. Lender perfected its security interest by filing a financing statement. Thus, Lender has perfected security interest in the 25 decorative clocks.

Under UCC9, the substance of a transaction controls, rather than its form given by the parties. Reservation of title by a seller of goods notwithstanding delivery to the buyer is not effective, but the seller has reservation of security interest.

Here, the agreement between Clockwork and Decorator specifies that Clockwork reserves the title on the 25 clocks until the payment. However, Clockwork's interest is to secure Decorator's payment obligation and therefore it has reservation of security interest. The security interest is effective and attaches, because Decorator signed the agreement, Decorator has right on the clocks, and Clockwork gave clocks to Decorator. To perfect the security interest in possessory goods, a secured interest must either possess the goods or file a financing statement. Clockwork did not possess the clocks and did not file the financing statement. Thus, Clockwork has unperfected security interest in the clocks.

Between an unperfected secured creditor and a perfected secured creditor, a perfected secured creditor has superior claim to the collateral.

Here, both Clockwork and Lender have security interest in the clocks. However, Clockwork's security interest is unperfected, while Lender's is perfected.

In conclusion, Lender has a superior interest in the clocks.

2. Lender has a superior interest in the vacuum cleaner.

Equipment is the goods that are not inventory, farm products, or consumer. Under the security agreement, Lender has security interest in Decorator's all present and future equipment. The vacuum cleaner is equipment, since Decorator leased it for use in its business. Thus, the security interest in the vacuum cleaner is effective and attaches, because Decorator signed the agreement, Decorator has rights in the cleaner, and Lender loaned money to Decorator. Lender perfected the security interest by filing the financial statement.

Whether a transaction in the lease form creates a true lease or a security interest depends on the economic realities of the transaction.

Here, the agreement between Vac and Decorator is presented as a lease. However, Decorator will automatically become the owner of the vacuum cleaner if it complies with the agreement. Thus, Vac's interest is a security interest and the transaction is governed by UCC9. The security interest in the vacuum cleaner is effective and attaches, because Decorator signed the agreement, Decorator has right on the cleaner, and Vac gave value to Decorator. However, Vac did not perfect its security interest in the cleaner, since he neither possesses it nor files a financial statement. In short, Vac has unperfected security interest in the vacuum cleaner.

Between Vac and Lender, Lender is a perfected secured creditor and Vac is an unperfected secured creditor.

In conclusion, Lender has superior claim to the collateral.

해설

난이도: 하

핵심 단어 및 논점

- inventory
- enforceability of security interest
- perfection
- equipment

1. The traffic stop and subsequent arrest did not violate Suspect's constitutional rights, because Officer had probable cause that seat belt law violation has occurred.

Under the Fourth Amendment, the police may stop an automobile when the police have probable cause that a traffic violation has occurred. The probable cause that an individual committed minor offense does not violate the Fourth Amendment.

Here, Officer's stop does not violate Suspect's constitutional right. Officer stopped the car because of his violation of the state seat belt law. The fact that Officer had never stopped a driver merely for violating the seat belt law indicates that the violation of the state seat belt law is minor offense, but it does not make a different result. Even if Officer stopped the car as a pretext and he hoped to uncover evidence of a more serious crime, the stop was constitutional.

In sum, the traffic stop and subsequent arrest did not violate Suspect's constitutional rights.

2. Officer's seizure of evidence from Suspect's car did not violate Suspect's constitutional rights, since the evidence was obtained through plain view.

Under the Fourth Amendment, a police officer can lawfully seize evidence when he has a warrant. However, if the evidence is found in plain view, the police officer can lawfully seize evidence without warrant. The plain view doctrine applies, if: (1) the police was lawfully present in a position, (2) the evidence shows incriminating character apparently, and (3) the police has lawful right of access to the object.

First, Officer had probable cause to stop Suspect's vehicle and he lawfully arrested him under the state law. Following the stop, Officer is permitted to look into the car window. Second, Officer had probable cause to believe that white powder contained in a clear plastic bag is an illegal drug. This is because Officer knew that Suspect was a reputed drug dealer and Suspect's statement "that cocaine isn't mine" suggest Officer's probable cause. Even if the statement violated Miranda rights, the violation does not prevent Officer to establish probable cause. Third, Officer has lawful right of access, because the vehicle was parked.

In short, the evidence is admissible under the plain view doctrine.

3. Officer's questioning of Suspect violated Suspect's Miranda rights, since Suspect was subject to in−custody interrogation.

Law enforcement officers are required to read Miranda Warnings to a suspect when the suspect is subject to an in−custody interrogation. There is custody when reasonable person under similar circumstances would believe she was not free to leave. There is interrogation when police either expresses questioning or elicit an incriminating response from the suspect.

Here, Suspect was arrested when Officer asked Suspect, "Are those drugs yours?" Officer's statement was questioning without Miranda Warnings.

In sum, Officer's questioning of Suspect violated Suspect's Miranda rights, since Suspect was subject to in−custody interrogation.

4. Suspect's confession should not be suppressed, since prior violation of Miranda rights does not have impact on the confession and Suspect did not made unambiguous invocation of the right to counsel.

Since a violation of Miranda is a violation of a constitutional rule, Miranda violations do not taint derivative evidence and the fruit of the poisonous tree doctrine does not apply. If there was a violation of Miranda, a subsequent confession by the suspect may nonetheless be admitted if the subsequent interrogation is not be seen as party of a single unwarned sequence of questioning and the suspect waived his Miranda rights voluntary and knowingly.

Here, Officer interrogated Suspect when he arrested Suspect and found a clear plastic bag at first. Officer initiated custodial interrogation again in the police station. The subsequent custodial interrogation is not seemed as part of the prior interrogation, because it occurred in different place and different time. Thus, the violation of Miranda right in prior interrogation does not have impact on the subsequent custodial interrogation.

A suspect must unambiguously invoke his right to counsel which means that a reasonable officer would understand the statement to be a request for counsel.

Here, Detective read Suspect his Miranda rights. According to Suspect's statement, "Maybe I need a lawyer," a reasonable police would understand that the suspect might invoke his right to counsel. Additionally, the fact Suspect understood his Miranda rights shows that the waiver of right was knowing.

In conclusion, Suspect's confession should not be suppressed.

해설

난이도: 하

핵심 단어 및 논점

- Fourth Amendment
- automobile stop
- seizure
- plain view (search without warrant)
- Miranda warnings (Fifth Amendment)
- fruit of the poisonous tree doctrine
- unambiguously (right to counsel)

4번 문제

답안요령

1. Violation of Miranda ≠ Fruit of poisonous tree★
2. Requirements
   + analysis
3. (Defendant invoked the right to counsel)
   + analysis
4. 결론

| TIP1 | 2번: 독립된 '장소'이면서 독립된 '시간'에 이루어진 interrogation임을 analysis 한다. |

| TIP2 | 3번: 미란다 고지를 받은 후 피고인이 진술할 때, 'knowing and voluntary했음'을 서술한다. |

2011July Trusts

1. The terms of Testator's testamentary trust can be reformed to permit the sale of the home.

Under the equitable deviation doctrine, equitable deviation from administrative provision is allowed when an unanticipated change in circumstances would substantially impair the accomplishment of the purposes of the trust. An administrative provision of a trust is one as to the management of trust property.

In this case, the trust provision directing trustee to retain the home and not to sell it is administrative. The character of the neighborhood where the home is located has changed dramatically and it was unanticipated change to the Testator. There are lots of apartment buildings and shopping malls. Thus equitable deviation doctrine is applicable in this case.

Under the UTC, administration provision can also be modified if continuation of the trust terms would be impracticable or wasteful or impair the trust's administration. In this case, the purpose of the retention of the home was to provide Daughter a comfortable residence throughout her life. However, the changed circumstance would impair it, since there are lots of noisy factors in the neighborhood.

In sum, the terms of Testator's testamentary trust can be reformed to permit the sale of the home.

2. Under the common law, the trsutee could not obtain authorization. However, under UTC, the trsutee could obtain authorization, since it is dispositive provision.

Under the common law, the equitable deviation doctrine applies only to administrative provisions of a trust. However, under UTC, the court may modify the dispositive terms of a trust based on the settlor's probable intention if there is an anticipated circumstances. A dispositive provision of a trust is one relating to the allocation of trust property. When the trustee transforms the dispositive provision, trustee should consider the settlor's intention.

In this case, the trust provision "After Daughter's death, I direct the trustee to sell the home and to distribute the sale proceeds to Charity" is dispositive, since it is relating to the allocation of the home. It is hard to say that Testator hoped that his Daughter has a comfortable residence even in an unanticipatedly changed circumstance. For these reasons, a court could allow the trustee to use the sale proceeds and the earnings to pay Daughter's rent.

However, the modification of the provision could result in the complete loss of the reminder interest, Charity. Daughter is a life interest in the home and $24,000 would be expended annually from $300,000 trust. On the other hand, the trustee could be authorized to purchase a new residence with the proceeds from the home's sale in favor of both remainderman and Daughter.

In sum, under the common law, the trsutee could not obtain authorization. However, under UTC, the trsutee could obtain authorization, since it is dispositive provision.

3. Under the cy pres doctrine, the trust assets will not pass to Testator's estate.

Under the cy pres doctrine, when the trust property for a charitable purpose could not be distributed as the trust, it would be distributed according to the settlor's intention. If settlor has a specific charitable intention, the property reverts to the settlor.

Under the common law and the Restatement Third of Trust, testator's general charitable intention is presumed. However, under UTC, it is a conclusive presumption of general charitable intention. If a particular charitable purpose becomes unlawful, impracticable, the court may apply cy pres to modify the trust.

In this case, the Settlor wanted to distribute the sale proceeds to Charity. Under the common law and the Restatement Third of Trust, there is no evidence that testator viewed Charity in Capital City as a sole mean to complete the goal. Thus, the sale proceeds would not be passed to Testator's estate with the presumption of general charitable intent.

Under UTC, cy pres doctrine is mandatory with the conclusive presumption of the general charitable intention if the charitable purpose becomes impossible. In this case, Charity no longer exists and there is no statement of the distribution in this situation.

In sum, the trust assets should not be passed to Testator's estate under cy pres doctrine.

해설

난이도: 하

핵심 단어 및 논점

- equitable deviation doctrine
- administrative provision
- cy pres doctrine

1. Railroad's easement was not abandoned.

Easement can be distinguished by many ways, such as unity of ownership, abandonment, and condemnation. Regarding abandonment, there must be a stop using with the evidence of the user's intent to abandon the easement.

Here, Railroad had an easement on the Sam's land. The fact that no trains have operated over them since 2000 does not mean abandonment. There is no Railroad's intent to abandon its easement, such as removing its tracks.

In sum, Railroad's easement was not abandoned.

2. The state adopts notice—type recording statute, and it protects a subsequent purchaser only when the purchaser was under required circumstances.

Under the common law first—in—time, first—in—right principle, a priority is established by priority of time. Here, Sam's conveyance to Daughter was prior to the conveyance by the executor of Oscar's estate to Purchaser, and therefore Daughter will have priority over Purchaser.

However, if there is a state recording statute protects, Purchaser could be protected under the statue.

Here, the state adopts notice—type recording statute. Under a notice—type recording statute, a subsequent purchaser can prevail against prior purchaser only if: (1) the prior conveyances were unrecorded, (2) a subsequent purchaser paid value for the land, and (3) a subsequent purchaser had no notice. Here, Purchaser paid value for the land and the prior conveyances (easement to Railroad and title to Daughter) were unrecorded.

In sum, the state adopts notice—type recording statute, and it protects a subsequent purchaser only when the purchaser was under required circumstances.

3. Purchaser was not a bona fide purchaser, since he had inquiry notice.

Constructive notice arises from the recording system.

Here, the state uses a grantor–grantee indexing system. However, Purchaser could not recognize both Railroad's easement and Daughter's title. This is because both interests were wild deeds, which means that interests were recorded outside the chain of title. The public record would show that Oscar had not conveyed his land to anyone. Thus, there was no contructive notice to Purchaser.

Inquiry notice arises when the buyer gets knowledge from facts and circumstances about the existence of a prior conveyance that could be recognized by exercising reasonable diligence. In some states, a purchaser by quitclaim deed is presumed to have notice of any interests. However, in the majority states, Purchaser would not have inquiry notice from the quitclaim deed alone. Inquiry notice also arises from visual inspection.

Here, the existence of railroad tracks could be recognized through a visual inspection. If Purchaser exercised reasonable diligence, Purchaser would find the easement even though it was outside the chain of title. Regarding the title that was conveyed to Daughter from Sam, Purchaser could have discovered that the easement was conveyed from Sam, as he found the easement by visual inspection. Sam's name in the grantor–grantee indexing system would reveal the conveyance to Daughter.

In sum, the visual inspection of the easement would discover the conveyance to Daughter.

In conclusion, Purchaser is not protected under the recording statute, and therefore Daughter has priority over Purchaser.

해설

핵심 단어 및 논점

- easement
- abandonment (termination of easement)
- notice—type recording statute

- bona fide purchaser (BFP)
- notice
- inquiry notice and quitclaim deed

2번, 3번 문제

답안요령

1. CL (first—in—time, first—in—right principle)
2. In modern(해당 recording statute)
3. Constructive notice
   + analysis
4. Inquiry notice
   + analysis
5. 결론

1. BritCo can immediately appeal the district court's order, since the judge specified that there was no just reason for delay.

Under the final judgment rule, litigants may appeal only from final judgments. A final judgment is one that ends the litigation on the merits and leaves only execution of the judgment for the court to do.

Under the default rule, when there is more than one claim for relief, a grant of judgment on one claim is not a final judgment and litigants cannot move for immediate appeal. However, litigants can move for immediate appeal if the court expressly determines that there is no just reason for delay.

Here, there are multiple claims raised by the parties: Office Equip sued for breach of contract and BritCo sued for breach of a contractual covenant not to compete with BritCo. When the court made judgment on BritCo's counterclaim, it specified that there was no reason for delay. Thus, the decision on the counterclaim constitutes a final judgment. In sum, the judgment on the counterclaim is appealable.

In sum, BritCo can immediately appeal the distric court's order, since the judge specified that there was no just reason for delay.

2. BritCo cannot immediately appeal the district court's order, since the order is not a final judgment and there are no exceptions applicable in this case.

Under the final judgment rule, the district court's refusal to enforce the forum-selection clause is not an appealable interlocutory order, since it is far from ending the litigation on the merits.

However, there are some exceptions to the final judgment rule: collateral order doctrine, mandamus or prohibition, and the doctrine of pendent appellate jurisdiction.

Under the collateral–order doctrine, an immediate appeal may be taken from an interlocutory order that conclusively determines an important issue in a case if: (1) that issue is independent (collateral to) the merits of the action and (2) if a delay in appellate review would effectively preclude the losing party from an opportunity to vindicate its rights on appeal. Here, BritCo's contractual right can be vindicated on an appeal and therefore the judgment on the forum selection clause is not appealable.

An immediate appeal may be taken from an interlocutory order when the litigant seeks mandamus or prohibition (extraordinary writ) from the appellate court that reverses the trial court's ruling. However, the possibility of a successful appeal is very low. Thus, it is highly unlikely that an appellate court would grant a writ.

Under the doctrine of pendent appellate jurisdiction, the jurisdictions of the appellate courts are limited to final decisions, and reasons of judicial economy alone would not justify a court in expanding its jurisdiction to cover nonfinal orders. The party seeking review of a nonfinal order on the ground that it is pendent to an appealable order would need to show inextricably intertwined or meaningful review of the ruling.

Here, the forum selection ruling and the ruling denying BritCo's counterclaim are not inextricably intertwined. Meaningful review of the counterclaim issue is possible without any consideration of the forum selection question. Thus, doctrine of pendent appellate jurisdiction is inapplicable in this case.

In sum, BritCo cannot immediately appeal the district court's order, since the order is not a final judgment and there are no exceptions applicable in this case.

해설

난이도: 1번 문제: 하
　　　　 2번 문제: 상

핵심 단어 및 논점

- final judgment rule
- default rule
- collateral–order doctrine
- doctrine of pendent appellate jurisdiction

1. State B will recognize a common law marriage under the full faith and credit clause.

Under the full faith and credit clause, a valid marriage is valid anywhere, unless it violates public policy of another state.

Here, if Dave and Meg entered into a common law marriage in State A, the marriage is also valid in State B.

2. Dave and Meg did not enter into a common law marriage in State A.

To establish a valid common law marriage, it requires that the spouses: (1) cohabitated, (2) made present agreement to be married, and (3) held themselves out to others as a married couple.

Here, Dave and Meg cohabitated. However, there was no present agreement and holding out. When Dave and Meg discussed marriage, Meg told Dave that "we can't afford that now." Meg did tell her family and friends that Dave is her fiance. Fiance is not meaning a married spouse, but is an intended spouse.

In sum, Dave and Meg did not enter into a common law marriage in State A.

3. State B cannot constitutionally grant Meg and Husband's adoption petition.

When an unmarried father shows full responsibilities of parenthood by participating in the upbringing of his child, his interest to contact with his child is protected under the Fourteenth Amendment Due Process Clause. A father is entitled to a hearing to demonstrate his parental fitness before his parental rights may be terminated if he lived with his children and their mother and held the children out as his own. Father's right is also protected under the Equal

Protection Clause. The state must give a father the opportunity to veto his child's adoption when state law grants an unmarried mother a veto similarly.

Here, Dave agreed that Child's birth certificate would identify Dave as Child's father. Dave held the child as his own to his friends and relatives. Additionally, he lived with Meg and Child and supported them by taking on a second job. Thus, Dave's right to contact with Child is protected under the Fourteenth Amendment Due Process Clause. Dave recognized the petition to terminate Dave's parental rights and authorize Husband's adoption of Child by hiring a private investigator. It was not through notice of the petition. Although the notice and hearing of the petition is based on the name of putative father registry, Dave is faultless not to list his name on it because State B does not have a putative father registry. Dave had no way to get notice of the petition. Additionally, the State B statute that permits a veto power only to a mother or a married father is unconstitutional under the Equal Protection Clause.

Under the adoption consent statutes, a father who has done everything in his capacity to establish a full relationship with his child has a veto right.

Here, Dave did not satisfy the state B statute which requires him to consistently support the child. This was because Meg took Child and abruptly left Dave. Thus, he has no fault for his failure to satisfy the statutory veto requirements. The State B statute that permits an unmarried father to veto the adoption of his child with requirements is unconstitutional.

In sum, State B cannot constitutionally grant Meg and Husband's adoption petition.

4. The UCCJEA does not permit State B to terminate Dave's parental rights or issue an order awarding custody to Meg.

A child's home state has exclusive jurisdiction to issue an initial custody degree. Under UCCJEA, a home state is a state where the child has lived with a parent, for at least six consecutive months immediately before the commencement of a child-custody proceeding. Child custody proceeding includes a proceeding for termination of parent's rights.

Here, Meg took Child from State A only five months ago and Dave still lives in State A. Thus, State A is child's home state in which has exclusive jurisdiction to terminate parent's rights.

In sum, the UCCJEA does not permit State B to terminate Dave's parental rights or issue an custody award to Meg.

해설

난이도: 중

핵심 단어 및 논점

- common law marriage
- conflict of laws
- requirements of common law marriage
- adoption
- unmarried father

- Due Process Clause
- Equal Protection Clause
- adoption consent statute
- jurisdiction of child custody order
- home state

1. Private does not violated the man's rights under the Equal Protection Clause, since there were no state actions.

Under the Fourteenth Amendment, no state shall deny to any person within its jurisdiction the equal protection of the laws. Private parties constitute state action when: (1) they performed a traditional public function, (2) there is judicial enforcement of certain private contracts, (3) there is joint action between a state and private actor, or (4) there is state encouragement of private discrimination.

First, Private did not perform public function. Second, there is no judicial enforcement of private contract. Third, the fact that the State A Board of Education regulates the curriculum of nursing schools could not make a conclusion that there was a joint action between a state and Private. Fourth, there is no state's direct encouragement on Private's discrimination.

In sum, Private's actions do not constitute state action, and therefore Private is not under the Equal Protection Clause.

2. Public has violated the man's rights under the Equal Protection Clause, since it is not substantially related to curing the historical discrimination, and the Male Nursing Opportunity Program is not substantially equivalent with the female programs.

State laws can make discrimination based on gender, only when the laws serve important governmental goals and the discrimination means are substantially related to the achievement of those goals. The burden of justification is entirely on the state.

Here, Public is an agency of the state government and all its faculty and staff are state employees. Thus, the action of Public is state action. The man was denied admission to Public solely because of the gender. The letter from Public suggests the discrimination based on gender, stating "your grades and test scores would have been sufficient to admit you if you were female." Thus, the discrimination would be constitutional, only when the law serves important governmental objectives.

The letter said that the discrimination was to remedy the historical discrimination and provide opportunities for women. However, 95 percent of State A nurses have been female and it suggests that State A is reinforcing outdated stereotypes of women as nurses. Additionally, if the goal is to end the discrimination against women in the health care field, it is not clear how the law advances the goal. Thus, Public's discrimination does not serve important governmental goals and therefore Public violated the man's rights under the Equal Protection Clause.

A state can treat men and women differently and provide separate facilities for each gender, guaranteeing the equal protection. The state has the burden to show: (1) the exceedingly persuasive justification for the separate treatment and (2) the separate facilities are substantially equivalent.

Here, there is the Male Nursing Opportunity Program that allows male residents of State A to become nurses. However, the Male Nursing Opportunity Program facilities are not modern as those at Public, the faculty is not as experienced, and graduates do not enjoy the same employment opportunities as graduates of either Public or Private. In short, the program is substantially inferior to the female Public program.

In sum, the Male Nursing Opportunity Program violates the man's right under the Equal Protection Clause.

해설

난이도: 하

핵심 단어 및 논점

- state action
- Equal Protection Clause
- IR test (gender)

논점: 'Gender를 차별'하는 법의 위헌성 여부

답안요령

---

1. 법을 제정한 주체(state 또는 federal)
2. 차별한 근거(gender) → IR test
   + analysis
3. 예외: 남녀에게 다른 facility를 제공하였으나 차별은 아닌 경우★

1번 문제

- 행위자가 private individual/entity이나, 그 성격이 주(州)와 다름없어 state action으로 인정됨을 서술한다.
- EP의 합헌성 판단기준은 'class 분류기준'이고, DP의 합헌성 판단기준은 '박탈된 권리의 유형'이다.

2번 문제

별도의 문제가 출제되지 않았더라도 '예외 rules'에 대해 analysis하는 것이 고득점 포인트다.

2011July Agency and Partnership

1(a). Adam's dissociation is effective, but he cannot participate in the winding up and he is liable for any damages caused by his wrongful dissociation.

A partner can dissociate from the partnership at any time by giving notice to the partnership. The partner's right to dissociate cannot be changed by a partnership agreement. Thus, even if the dissociation is wrongful, it is effective.

Here, the PSS partnership agreement states that any partner can withdraw from the partnership upon giving six months' written notice. Adam provided notice but it did not satisfy the time limit. Thus, the dissociation is effective but is wrongful. Because the dissociation is wrongful, Adam is liable to Beth, Chris, and the partnership for any damages caused by his dissociation.

Regardless of whether dissociation is wrongful, dissociation results in dissolution. However, if dissociation is wrongful, a dissociating partner is liable to the damage for the breach of the partnership agreement and he cannot participate in the winding up process.

Here, Adam's dissociation results in PSS's dissolution and Adam is liable to any damages for the breach of the partnership agreement. Additionally, he cannot participate in the winding up of the partnership.

In sum, Adam's wrongful but effective dissociation results in dissolution.

1(b). Since the dissociation is wrongful, Beth and Chris may chose whether to wind up the business or not.

The results of wrongful dissociation are different under the UPA 1997 and UPA 1914.

Under the UPA 1997, When there is a partner's wrongful dissociation, it does not result in partnership dissolution if the remaining partners waive the right to make the partnership end and its wound up. Here, Adam's dissociation was wrongful and it would not result in partnership dissolution if Beth and Chris waive the right. If Beth and Chris waive the right, the partnership needs to purchase Adam's interest for a buyout price. If they did not waive the right and decided to wind up the business, Adam could not participate in the winding up process. However, Beth and Chris could choose to continue PSS's business for a reasonable time.

Under the UPA 1914, a dissociation results in the dissolution of the partnership. However, if the Beth and Chris want to continue business, Adam will receive the value of his interest less the damages caused by wrongful dissolution. If the Beth and Chris does not want to continue the business, the Adam has the same rights to the partnership property as the remaining partners.

2(a). Adam's dissociation is not wrongful, and therefore he can participate in winding up process.

As mentioned above, if Adam's dissociation is not wrongful, the results under UPA 1997 and UPA 1914 would be same.

Adam would not liable for any damages to the partnership or Beth and Chris. His dissociation results in dissolution and the business is to be wound up. Adam is entitled to participate in the winding up process, and he can force the cessation of operations of PSS and the sale of its assets.

2(b). The partnership will be dissolved and wound up, and all partners will participate in the winding up process.

The results under UPA 1997 and UPA 1914 would be same.

As mentioned above, PSS will be dissolved and wound up. All partners including Adam will participate in the process and they vote for an immediate winding up and sale of assets.

3. Adam will be liable for partnership debts.

If a partner's act was proper to the winding up process, the partnership is bound for a partner's act. Each partner is jointly and severally liable for the partnership's liability under the UPA 1997 and jointly liable under the UPA 1914.

Here, even though Adam is a wrongful dissociating partner, he is liable for the partnership debts because it is caused during the winding up process.

In sum, Adam will be liable for partnership debts.

해설

난이도: 하

핵심 단어 및 논점

- dissolution
- wrongful v. rightful dissolution
- winding up

2012Feb
2012Feb Evidence

1. The hospital's motion to exclude evidence of its new policy should be sustained, since the evidence was used to prove hospital's negligence and it violates public policy.

Evidence is relevant if it has tendency to make a fact more or less probable than it would be without the evidence. However, evidence of subsequent measures is not admissible to prove negligence under the public policy.

In this case, the hospital's new policy is relevant to prove whether the hospital is negligent. The policy change is a subsequent measure to make a better hospital service than the original policy. Woman wishes to use the new policy to prove that the hospital is negligent at the time of her visitation of the hospital, but it is inadmissible because of public policy.

In sum, the hospital's motion to exclude evidence of its new policy should be sustained, since the evidence was used to prove hospital's negligence and it violates public policy.

2. The hospital's motion to exclude evidence of its offer to settle should be excluded, because of the public policy.

The evidence of hospital's offer to settle with the woman is relevant to prove whether the hospital is negligent. However, under the federal rule of evidence, evidence of settlement offers and statement during settlement negotiation should be excluded, if the settlement is made when claim was disputed. This is because public policy encourages people to compromise and settle down the disputes.

In this case, the hospital offered woman to settle down the claim and it was made when claim is disputed. Woman wanted to provide the evidence of hospital's settlement to prove its negligence.

In sum, the hospital's motion to exclude evidence of its offer to settle should be excluded, because of the public policy.

3(a). The man's motion to exclude evidence of his offer for $10,000 should not be excluded, since it was not made when the claim is disputed.

Evidence of man's offer to woman to provide $10,000 is relevant to prove whether man is negligent. However, evidence of offering medical expense or promising to pay should be excluded, if it is used to prove offeror's negligence. The offering should be made when the claim is disputed.

In this case, man's offer is a promise to pay woman $10,000 and woman wishes to provide it to prove liability for the injury. However, man's offer is made four months before woman filed the suit. Disputed claim requirement does not require a filed lawsuit, but man's offer before the woman had made no contact is much lass a disputed claim.

In sum, man's motion to exclude evidence of his offer for $10,000 should not be excluded, since it was not made when the claim is disputed.

3(b) The man's motion to exclude evidence of his offer to provide medical expenses should be excluded, because of the public policy.

Evidence of man's offer to provide woman medical expenses are relevant to prove man is liable for physical injuries. However, the evidence should be excluded under the public policy. The offer to pay medical expenses should be made when the claim is disputed.

In this case, man's offer was made after woman filed a civil action against the man and it satisfies the disputed claim requirement.

In sum, man's motion to exclude evidence of his offer to provide medical expenses should be excluded, because of the public policy.

4. The man's motion to admit evidence that the woman had sexual relations with another student should not be excluded, since its probative value substantially outweighs the danger of harm to victim.

Under the rape shield rule, evidence offered to prove that a victim engaged in other sexual behavior is inadmissible in any civil or criminal sexual misconduct proceeding. However, in civil cases, evidence of alleged victim's other sexual behavior is admissible if its probative value substantially outweighs the danger of harm to victim.

In this case, evidence of the woman's past sexual behavior with another student has substantial probative value, since the woman she alleged that psychological injuries were traumatic because of her belief in sexual abstinence and her lack of prior sexual experience. Woman's prior sexual experience has probative value.

In sum, the man's motion to admit evidence that the woman had sexual relations with another student should not be excluded, since its probative value substantially outweighs the danger of harm to victim.

해설

난이도: 하

핵심 단어 및 논점

- public policy
  - subsequent measures
  - settlement offers
  - medical expense
- rape shield rule

1, 2, 3번 문제

답안요령

1. Relevance 정의
   + analysis
2. Public policy exception(해당 내용 작성)
3. Analysis

1. RepairCo breached the contract, since it did not substantially perform its contractual obligations.

Because the contract was for repairing service, it is governed by the common law. Under the common law, nonbreaching party can recover when there is material breach. A material breach occurs when a party does not provide substantial performance. Whether there is a material breach considers several factors: (1) the extent to which nonbreaching party will lose the reasonably expected benefit the party, (2) the extent to which nonbreaching party will be compensated for the part of benefit that the party will lose, (3) the extent to which breaching party will suffer forfeiture, (4) the possibility that the breaching party will cure his failure, and (5) the extent to which the breaching party acted in good faith and fair dealing.

Here, regarding the first factor, RepairCo repaired only 6 of the 10 vehicles and therefore, GreenCar lose its material portion of expected benefit, repaired 10 vehicles. Secondly, RepairCo can compensate in damages for harm caused by the failure of the parade, but it cannot compensate for reputation lose. Thirdly, RepairCo will not suffer forfeiture, because it does not need to undo its work already done and it will recover restitution. Fourth, RepairCo cannot deliever four cars on April 21. Finally, RepairCo's failure to perform the contract was not in good faith. RepairCo workers had walked off the job when salary negotiations broke down. It states that it planned to raise salary, but wanted "to teach them a lesson." It shows that RepairCo could resolve the problem, but it did not. Thus, RepairCo breached materially by not providing substantial performance.

In sum, RepairCo breached the contract, since it did not substantially perform its contractual obligations.

2. If the contract is divisible, RepairCo might be entitled to recover $6,000.

A contract is divisible if the performances can be divided into part performances and a court will treat the elements of each part as equivalents.

Here, RepairCo could argue that the contract is divisible. Although the contract price is total price for $10,000, it can be divided per each car, $1,000. The RepairCo's obligation under the contract was to repair 10 green cars and it can be divided into 10 performances, since repairing similar cars requires similar working. RepairCo could argue the performance is divisible and therefore it is entitled to the repairing service for six cars, $6,000.

However, GreenCar could argue that the contract is not divisible. GreenCar needed "all" 10 of its cars to fulfill a contract to provide 10 identical green cars to carry dignitaries and all of its cars required to be repaird to be operable for the parade on specific date, April 22. Thus, GreenCar could argue the performance is not divisible.

In sum, if the contract is divisible as RepairCo argues, it is entitled to recover $6,000.

3. Even if the contract is not divisible, RepairCo is entitled to restitution.

A party is entitled to restitution for any benefit that he has provided through part performance over the loss that he has caused by his own breach. This is to bar the nonbreaching party's unjust enrichment.

Here, even if the contract is not divisible and RepairCo cannot recover on the contract, RepairCo may be entitled to some recovery from GreenCar as restitution. The restitution is for part performance of RepairCo, repairing service for six cars and delivery on April 21. Thus, RepairCo is entitled to restitution for the work done on six cars less any incidental or consequential losses resulting from its breach of contract, the failure to repair the remaining four cars on April 21.

In sum, RepairCo is entitled to restitution for work done on six cars.

해설

난이도: 1번 문제: 중
       2번 문제: 하
       3번 문제: 하

핵심 단어 및 논점

- material breach (substantial performance)
- divisible contract
- restitution

Damages에 관한 모든 답안에는 purpose of remedy에 대해 서술하는 것이 고득점 포인트다. 본 답안 1번에 서술했으므로, 2번, 3번 문제에서는 생략하였다.

2번, 3번 문제

> **답안요령**

> 1. Divisible contract 정의
>   + analysis
> 2. Analysis(divisible이라고 주장하는 측 의견)
> 3. Analysis(indivisible이라고 주장하는 측 의견)
> 4. 결론

> **TIP** 동일한 arguable point에 대해 divisible이라고 주장하는 측과 indivisible이라고 주장하는 측의 의견으로 구분하여 analysis하는 것이 고득점 포인트다.

1. Funworld falsely imprisoned Paul.

An actor is liable to another for false imprisonment if: (1) he acts intending to confine the other, (2) his act confines the plaintiff to a bounded area, and (3) causation. Confinement needs not be physical and it needs not be stationary. The intent to confine can be established through either motivation or knowledge.

Here, Employee confined Paul by stopping the Ferris wheel, because Paul was unable to leave the car without danger. Employee knew that his stopping would make Paul unable to leave the car. Thus, Paul can establish a prima facie case of false imprisonment.

Defendant's action would be privileged, if his action was necessary in order to protect some actor's or public interest that is so important to justify the harm caused by defendant's action. Here, Employee did not have any intent to protect some interest not to announce explanation to restart the Ferris wheel.

Employee's action was actual and proximate causation of Paul's injury. Because Employee was acting within the scope of his employment, Funworld is vicariously liable for his conduct.

In sum, Funworld is liable for falsely imprisonment.

2. Funworld was negligent for failing to take any action to stop the boys from rocking their car.

In negligence action, a plaintiff must show that the defendant owed the plaintiff a duty to conform his conduct to a standard necessary to avoid a foreseeable unreasonable risk of harm of others, that the defendant breached the duty, and that the defendant's conduct was both the cause in fact and the proximate cause of the plaintiff's injuries. In determining whether the defendant breached the duty, jury considers the conduct of reasonable person under similar circumstances.

Here, Employee was acting within the scope of his employment, and Funworld is vicariously liable for his conduct. Paul is a business visitor, and Funworld owed Paul a duty of reasonable care to avoid foreseeable risks. If two boys were rocking their car vigorously, the reasonable person in the like situation would take action to stop them to prevent foreseeable risk. Even if the foreseeable risk could be small, Employee's failure to stop them breached his duty.

In sum, Funworld was vicariously negligent for failing to take any action to stop the two boys from rocking the Ferris wheel car.

3. Mom is not entitled to damages for her emotional distress and resulting miscarriage, since she was not within the zone of danger and her shock was not caused by sensory and contemporaneous observance.

A plaintiff (1) is within the zone of danger created by the defendant and (2) suffers a physical manifestation of emotional distress occasioned by a threatened injury may recover from the defendant. Even though the plaintiff was not within the zone of danger, plaintiff can recover from the defendant, in most states, when the plaintiff: (1) was closely related to the victim, (2) was located near the scene of accident, and (3) suffered shock caused by sensory and contemporaneous observance of the accident

Here, Mom was some 100 yards away and her shock was caused by wrongful news relating to the accident from a bystander. Thus, she was not within the zone of danger. Even though she was located near the scene of the accident, she did not have sensory observation, because she did not see or hear the accident.

In sum, Mom is not entitled to damages for her emotional distress and resulting miscarriage, since she was not within the zone of danger and her shock was not caused by sensory and contemporaneous observance.

해설

난이도: 하

핵심 단어 및 논점

- false imprisonment
- necessity (defense)
- negligence
- vicarious liability
- scope of his employment
- negligent infliction of emotional distress (NIED)
- zone of danger

1번 문제

답안요령

1. 문제에 해당하는 intentional tort's 요소
2. Intent
   + analysis★
3. Defenses★
4. 기타(vicarious liability 등)

3번 문제

답안요령

1. NIED general rule (요건×2)
2. Bystander인 경우 적용되는 rule (요건×3)
   + analysis

1. Testator's codicil did not republished "Last Will and Testament" under either common law or UPC.

A codicil that refers to an earlier will is said to republish that will. When there are republications, the republished will is deemed to be executed on the same day as the codicil. Republication can cure defects that might affect the validity of bequests made under a will. Under the republication by codicil doctrine, only a valid will can be republished by codicil. However, under UPC, a will that is not validly executed can be republished in a codicil if there is evidence that is clear and convincing that the testator intended the document to be a will.

Here, the document captioned "last Will and Testament" is not a valid will because Testator did not sign it or have it witnessed. A document sent by the attorney sent Testator is a valid partial will, codicil. Thus, the conflicting portion of the codicil will preempt the portion of the first document: 400 shares of XYZ Corporation common stock to Aunt and testator's home to Cousin. Under the republication by codicil doctrine, Nephew gets nothing. Under UPC, Nephew would get nothing. This is because it is hard to say that the statement "I republish my will" is sufficiently refer the first document captioned "Last Will and Testament" with reasonable certainty. Additionally, there is no clear evidence that Testator intended the first document to be republished in her will.

In sum, testator's codicil did not republished "Last Will and Testament" under either common law or UPC.

2. Daughter is not barred from inheriting from Testator by a slayer statute.

Slayer statute provides that no person shall share in the estate of a decedent when he or she intentionally caused the decedent's death.

Here, because Testator's valid will did not dispose of Testator's entire estate as mentioned above, the remaining assets will pass to Testator's heirs. Daughter would be Testator's only heir. Although Daughter was convicted for murdering her father (Testator's husband), her father's estate is not at issue. Thus, she is entitled to Testator.

In sum, Daughter is not barred from inheriting from Testator by a slayer statute.

3. Cousin's share will be adeems under the common law. Under the intent test, cousin could not get the new house, since there is no Testator's intent to grant Cousin the new house.

Under the common law, an ademption occurs when the subject matter of specific devise is not found in the probate estate at the time of the testator's death. In some modern courts, by the intent test, devisee may be entitled to replacement, if the devisee proves that the testator intended the beneficiary to take the replacement.

Here, the codicil includes a specific devise of her home, located at 340 Green Avenue, Springfield, State A to Cousin. However, Testator sold the house during her life and there was a two−bedroom house located at 12 Elm St. in Springfield. Under the common law, Cousin's share fails. Under the intent test, Cousin could not get a two−bedroom house. This is because Testator called her attorney and said Cousin has a large family. Testator intended to provide a large house to serve Cousin's large family, but a two−bedroom house is too small to serve his family.

In sum, Cousin's share will be adeems under the common law. Under the intent test, cousin could not get the new house, since there is no Testator's intent to grant Cousin the new house.

4. Aunt is entitled to 600 shares of XYZ Corporation under the modern rule, while she is entitled only to 400 shares under the common law.

Today, bequest of stock owned by a testator when the testator's will was signed includes subsequently acquired shares of the same stock as the result of a stock dividend. This is because stock dividends are treated like stock splits. Additional shares of stock from the same company are merely a change in form, not substance. Under the common law, additional acquired shares of the same stock are substance.

Here, three years ago, Testator had 400 shares of XYZ Corporation common sock. Two years ago, Testator received 200 shares of XYZ common stock from XYZ Corporation in the form of the dividend paid in stock.

In sum, Aunt is entitled to 600 shares of XYZ Corporation under the modern rule, while she is entitled only to 400 shares under the common law.

해설

난이도: 1번 문제: 중
　　　　그 외 문제: 하

핵심 단어 및 논점

- codicil
- republication by codicil doctrine
- slayer statute
- ademption
- stock bequest

1번 문제

| 답안요령 |

| --- |
| 1. General rule (republication 정의, 효과, 역할)
2. Republication by codicil doctrine
　　+ analysis
3. UPC
　　+ analysis |

1. Garden LLP is liable for the $500,000 judgment.

Under the entity theory of partnership, when a partnership changed its form to LLP, the LLP is the same entity with the partnership that existed earlier.

Here, the form of Garden Partnership was changed into a limited liability partnership, renamed "Garden LLP." Garden LLP is the same entity with the Garden Partnership. Thus, Garden LLP owes judgment liability for the customer that was created when Garden Partnership exists.

In sum, Garden LLP is liable for the $500,000 judgment.

2. The man and woman are jointly and severally liable to the customer for the $500,000, since limited liability protection does not apply in this case.

Generally, the partners in a general partnership are jointly and severally liable for all obligations of the partnership.

Even though partners in a limited liability partnership (LLP) are not jointly and severally liable for partnership's obligations, the debt of $500,000 is created before the partnership becomes LLP. Thus, limited liability protection does not apply to the debts.

In sum, the man and woman are jointly and severally liable as partners in a general partnership.

3. The investor is not personally liable to the customer, since he joined as a partner after the obligation was created.

A partner is not personally liable for any partnership obligation which was created before his admission to the partnership.

Here, the injury to the customer was occurred before the investor admitted in the partnership as a partner.

Although the investor did not become personally liable, he will lose his investment in the partnership is at risk for the satisfaction of existing partnership debt.

In sum, the investor is not liable to the customer.

해설

난이도: 하

핵심 단어 및 논점

- entity theory
- limited liability protection
- jointly and severally liable

1번 문제

논점: LLP로 변경되기 '전' 발생한 partnership debt에 대한 partnership's 책임

본 문제에서는 "the man and woman took the necessary steps to qualify Garden Partnership as a limited liability partnership"라는 문구를 통해 LLP가 올바르게 설립되었음을 명시하였다. GP가 LLP로 전환되는 과정보다는 entity theory에 대한 analysis에 초점을 둔 문제라고 할 수 있으므로, 본 답안에는 'LLP의 formalities' 내용을 생략하였다.

2번 문제

논점: LLP로 변경된 '전' 발생한 partnership debt에 대한 partner's 책임

GP에서 LLP로 변경된 case에서 analysis의 로직은 다음과 같다.

GP에서 partner는 jointly and severally liable하다(personally liable하다).

→ Entity theory에 의거하여 partnership debt의 성격은 GP에서 발생한 partnership debt의 성격을 띤다.

→ 따라서 limited liability protection 적용되지 않는다.

→ Partner는 해당 partnership debt에 대해 personally liable하다.

3번 문제

논점: New partner and partnership

답안요령

1. Partner가 된 시기에 관해 analysis
2. General rule(prior debt에 대해 책임이 없다.)
   + analysis
3. New partner's contribution★

TIP General rule과 무관하게 새로운 partner의 contribution은 회사채무를 위해 사용될 수 있다는 점을 명시하는 것이 고득점 포인트다.

1. The federal court has removal jurisdiction over the case, since the court has diversity jurisdiction over the case.

Removal of a case from state court to federal court is proper only when the removed civil action is within the original jurisdiction of the federal court. The district courts have original jurisdiction over the civil actions when there is complete diversity of citizenship between the parties and the amount in controversy exceeds $75,000. The amount must be based on plaintiff's good−faith allegations without a legal certainty that the plaintiff cannot recover the amount alleged.

Here, the owner is a citizen of State A and the restorer is a citizen of State B. The amount in controversy is the full contract price, $100,000 that exceeds $75,000. There is no fact showing the owner had bad faith determining the amount in controversy.

In sum, the federal court has removal jurisdiction over the case, since the court has diversity jurisdiction over the case.

2. The change of venue motion should be granted, based on the forum− selection clause in the contract.

Regarding motion for a change of venue, for the convenience of parties and witnesses, in the interest of justice, a district court may transfer any civil action to any other district or division where it could have been brought.

Here, the action originally could have been held in federal court in State B, because a State B federal court has diversity jurisdiction over the case and has a proper venue for the case. When a federal court has diversity jurisdiction, venue is proper in a judicial district where: (1) any defendant resides if all defendants are residents of the forum state, (2) a substantial part of the events which is the basis of the claim occurred, or (3) (if none of the above apply,) any defendant is subject to the court's personal jurisdiction. First, the restorer is a citizen of State. Second, the claim against the restorer was based on the contract and the restorer's repairing work, which were signed and occurred in State B. Thus, the action could originally have been held in State B.

Regarding the convenience and the interest of justice, most of the evidence and witnesses in this case would be found in State B. This is because the restorer performed its duty under the contract in State B and the contract was signed in State B. However, the owner is resided in State A, and therefore holding the case in State B could be inconvenient on the owner's behalf. When the facts regarding convenience and interest of justice are divided, judges usually permit a plaintiff's original venue choice. Then the district court in State A satisfies the convenience and the interest of justice requirements.

However, the existence of a forum−selection clause changes the analysis. A forum−selection clause is a relevant factor that favors change of venue motion, even if the clause is unenforceable under the state law. Here, the contract between the owner and the restorer has a forum−selection clause that states any litigation must be commenced in State B. Thus, the court in State B satisfies the convenience and the interest of justice requirements.

In sum, State B is a proper venue and therefore the State A federal court should grant the motion for change of venue.

3. The change of venue does not affect the law to be applied in resolving the rescission issue.

Under the Erie doctrine, a federal court applies the substantive law of the forum state when it has diversity jurisdiction.

Here, the federal court in State A hears the case based on the diversity jurisdiction. Under the Erie doctrine, the federal court is required to apply the conflict−of−laws rules of State A where the federal court sits, because the choice of law is substantive.

When the venue is changed, the transferee court must apply the same law to the case as the transferor court applies. Here, the venue was changed into State B, the transferee court, and therefore it must apply the same law that State A applies.

In sum, the change of venue does not affect the law to be applied in resolving the rescission issue.

해설

난이도: 1번 문제: 하

　　　　 2번 문제: 중

　　　　 3번 문제: 중

핵심 단어 및 논점

- removal
- complete diversity of citizenship (DCJ)
- change of venue
  - convenience
  - interest of justice
  - forum-selection clause
- Erie doctrine

1번 문제

논점: Removal 요건 중 jurisdiction

Removal에 관한 문제의 경우, 이송받는 federal court의 SMJ 유무여부와 removal 과정 중 어느 것에 초점이 맞춰져 있는지 파악하는 것이 중요하다. 본 기출의 1번 문제는 jurisdiction에 관한 것이다.

1. Sue did not have an easement over Blackacre, since the easement was extinguished by merge.

Easement can be distinguished by many ways, such as unity of ownership, abandonment, and condemnation.

Here, Tom sold to Sue an easement over Blackacre and Blackacre was serviant estate and Whiteacre was the dominant estate. When Sue, an owner of dominant estate, became an owner of serviant estate, the easement was distinguished by unity of ownership.

In sum, Sue did not have an easement over Blackacre.

2. Dan had an easement implied from prior use over Blackacre.

An easement implied from prior use aises when: (1) two parcels of land are in common ownership, (2) one of the parcels are conveyed to grantee, (3) conveyed parcel is dominant parcel, (4) the usage is reasonably necessary, and (5) the usage is apparent.

Here, Sue sold the Whiteacre to Dan when she also owns Blackacre. When Dan purchased the Whiteacre, both Blackacre and Whiteacre were in common ownership. One of the parcels, Whiteacre, was conveyed to Dan and it had been receiving a benefit from Blackacre. The reasonably necessary use means that the easement is important to the enjoyment of the conveyed land or the easement is highly convenient. Here, the use of Blackacre was for more easily access the four—lane highway. Thus, the usage was reasonably necessary. The usage is apparent when the usage is visible. Here, the private gravel road was open and obvious. Additionally, Dan was aware that Sue had used the road without any mention on it. Thus, the usage was apparent.

In sum, Dan had an easement implied from prior use over Blackacre.

3. The proceeds from the sale of Whiteacre must be distributed to Bank, since Bank's loan was an obligatory future advances mortgage.

The typical construction loan is a future advance mortgage. The lender will advance funds to the borrower over a fixed period. The lender secures a mortgage on the property for the entire amount of the money, including future advances. There are two types of future advances mortgage: obligatory advances and optional advances.

If payments under a future-advances mortgage are obligatory, then the junior lender's lien is junior regardless of the time when the junior lien was recorded. If a future-advances mortgage are optional, the junior lender has a priority as to the amounts that junior lender transferred to the mortgagee and recorded it.

Here, Bank's loan was an obligatory future advances mortgage, and Bank recorded its mortgage before Finance Company did so. Thus, Bank is the senior lender for the full value of its loan to Dan, $1,500,000, and it is entitled to all of the foreclosure sales proceeds. Finance Company is entitled to nothing.

In sum, the proceeds from the sale of Whiteacre must be distributed to Bank, since Bank's loan was an obligatory future advances mortgage.

해설

난이도: 하

핵심 단어 및 논점

- easement
- abandonment (termination of easement)
- easement implied from prior use
- future advance mortgage

3번 문제

> 답안요령

> 1. Future-advances mortgage 정의
> 2. Optional v. Obligatory
> 3. Analysis + 결론

1. The directors, except for Claire, received proper notice of the special meeting of the board of directors.

Notice of a special meeting of a board of directors must be provided at least two days prior to the meeting date. The notice must include information regarding the time, location, and the meeting date but it does not need to include the purpose of the meeting.

Here, the secretary prepared a notice of the special meeting and sent it to six of the seven directors. Those six directors received on March 2, 29 days before the meeting. The notice stated that a special meeting would be held on March 31 at 10 a.m.

In sum, the six directors received proper notice.

2. Clarie did not receive proper notice, but she waived it.

A director who did not receive proper notice can waive such notice unless the director objects to the holding of the meeting and does not vote at the meeting.

Here, Alan called Claire and informed her about a special meeting on March 30. Calling could be notice, but it was too late to satisfy 2 days requirement. Thus, Clarie did not receive proper notice of the special meeting. However, Claire attended and voted at the meeting on March 31.

In sum, Claire waived improper notice.

3. The board of directors did not properly approve the purchase.

An action which was taken at a special meeting is proper only when a quorum is present at the meeting. When a corporation has a fixed number of directors, a quorum consists of a majority of that fixed number. With the present quorum, a majority of the quorum is the act of the board of directors.

Here, the corporation's articles of incorporation mandate a seven-member board of directors. Thus, a quorum consists of four directors. Alan and Barb were not present at the meeting, since they could not hear each other. Participation by telephone is valid only if all directors participating may simultaneously hear each other during the meeting. Thus, only five of directors were present at the special meeting and the votes of Alan and Barb should not be counted. Therefore, there were two votes in favor and three votes against the purchase and the purchase of the asset was not approved by the board of directors.

In sum, the board of directors did not properly approve the purchase.

해설

난이도: 하

핵심 단어 및 논점

- corporation
- special meeting of a board of directors
- quorum

1. Trust could be terminated if a court finds that there is no material purpose, while trust could not be terminated if a court finds that there is material purpose and adopts balancing approach.

Generally, an irrevocable trust can be terminated before all income beneficiaries dies, if both the income beneficiaries and the remaindermen unanimously consent. However, if there is a material purpose of the trust, the unanimous consent cannot terminate the trust. Even if the court finds that the settlor had material purpose, it may approve trust termination if the reason for termination or modification outweighs the material purposes.

In this case, the trust provision, "Husband's income interest would terminate if Husband remarried after Settlor's death" demonstrates that a material purpose of the trust is to bar benefit of Husband's second wife. A material purpose should not be inferred from the mere fact that the settlor created a trust for successive beneficiaries.

However, the court could adopt balancing approach by balancing the reason for trust termination and the material purpose. The reason for trust termination is to provide Husband with cash for a retirement home. Without knowing more about Husband's finances, it is impossible to assess how Husband's goal compares to Settlor's goal of ensuring that no future spouse of Husband receives benefits traceable to trust assets. Thus, trust could be terminated if a court finds that there is no material purpose. However, trust could not be terminated if a court finds that there is material purpose and adopt balancing approach. If the court finds that the Husband's need of cash does not outweigh the Settlor's purpose of the trust, the trust could not be terminated.

In sum, trust could be terminated if a court finds that there is no material purpose, while trust could not be terminated if a court finds that there is material purpose and adopts balancing approach.

2. Under the common law, the consent of the four children and Husband could terminate the trust. Under UPC, the consent of the issue of deceased child is also needed.

Under the common law, when a class gift is made to a group (1) who are equally related to a common ancestor and (2) the gift is not expressly subject to a condition of survivorship, the gift is not impliedly subject to such a condition. If a member of such a class fails to survive until the time of distribution, that member's share passes to his or her estate.

In this case, the remainder is a class of "Settlor's children." All class member has a common ancestor (Settlor) and there is no statement regarding a condition of survivorship, and the gift is not subject to condition. Thus, each child is vested and the child's death before the distribution date does not make a different result.

Under UPC, when a beneficiary does not survive to the distribution date, the beneficiary's interest passes to his/her issue (unless the trust instrument specifies an alternate disposition). Here, deceased child's issue would receive benefits in the trust and participate in any termination process unless their interest could be represented by another.

Under the UTC, one group of remaindermen can represent another group of remaindermen in the absence of a conflict of interest. Here, the four children and their issue would have a conflict regarding the distribution, proposed distribution that would exclude the issue from potentially sharing in any trust assets. Thus, the trust could not be terminated merely with the consent of Husband and the four children.

In sum, under the common law, the consent of the four children and Husband could terminate the trust. Under UPC, the consent of the issue of deceased child is also needed.

해설

난이도: 상

핵심 단어 및 논점

- irrevocable trust
- trust termination
- class gift

<u>1(a). Adam would be guilty of involuntary manslaughter, if his conduct satisfies required mens rea element, which is differently defined in each states.</u>

A defendant is guilty of involuntary manslaughter, when the defendant's act creates an unreasonable risk of death or serious bodily injury and causes the death of another human being.

Regarding mens rea, there are different approaches. In some jurisdictions, defendant must have acted recklessly to be convicted of involuntary manslaughter. Recklessness is typically defined as conscious disregard of a known risk of death or serious bodily injury that his conduct created.

Here, Adam stated that "When cars come by, they'll slip on the marbles," "I'll bet they'll have trouble; maybe there will even be a crash." These statements support Adam's recklessness, because he recognized the risk could be created by his conduct and the risk could cause serious bodily injury. However, Adam could argue that he did not act recklessly. First, he did not recognized that his conduct would cause death of others or serious bodily injury. His statement, "they'll get really mad," supports his argument. Second, Adam could argue that he could not anticipate the risk of crash of the two cars at 2 a.m. However, jury could conclude that a reasonable person knows car crash can cause death or serious bodily injury. In short, if the jury concludes that Adam acted recklessly, Adam would be guilty of involuntary manslaughter.

In other jurisdictions, the defendant is guilty when he acted with criminal negligence, which is defined as negligence greater than ordinary negligence. Even if the defendant was unaware of the risk, the defendant could be guilty if an ordinary person in the defendant's situation would have been aware that her conduct created an unreasonable risk of death or serious bodily injury.

Here, the jury is likely to conclude that ordinary person in Adam's situation would have been aware that the marbles could create car accident and death or serious bodily injury. In sum, Adam would be guilty of involuntary manslaughter. In conclusion, mens rea element required for involuntary manslaughter is different among states.

2(b). Adam's conduct was both actual causation and proximate causation of the child's death.

Causation requires both actual causation and proximate causation.

A defendant's action is actual causation if the result would not have occurred but for the defendant's action. Here, the child's death would not have occurred if Adam did not dumped his marbles at a nearby intersection. Thus, Adam's action is actual causation.

Proximate cause is centered to foreseeability. When there is an unforeseeable intervening cause between the result and a defendant's conduct, it is treated as a supervening cause and cut off the defendant's liability. Here, the man would argue that the child's death would not have occurred, if the man properly secured the child's seat belt. It is true that the man's failure to secure was an intervening cause, but it was not unforeseeable. Reasonable person could anticipate that some people or children ride in cars without a seat belts or child restraints, even when that is required under the state law. The man's negligence was combined with Adam's marble dumping, but it was foreseeable and therefore Adam could be guilty of involuntary manslaughter.

2. To be guilty of involuntary manslaughter as an accomplice, Bob must have dual intentions and the intent is defined differently among the jurisdictions.

To be guilty of involuntary manslaughter as an accomplice, a defendant must have dual intentions: (1) intent to assist the primary party and (2) intent that the primary party commits the offense charged. Under the most jurisdictions, the second intent requirement is satisfied when a defendant assisted the primary party with the intent that is required for the primary party's charged offense.

First, even a small amount of assistance can be sufficient to create accomplice liability. Bob had intent to assist Adam, since he drove Adam to the intersection with the knowledge on Adam's plan. Bod had no other purpose to drive to the intersection.

Second, in most states, recklessness is required for involuntary manslaughter. Here, Bob could argue that he stated "That's a stupid idea" and it supports that he did not know the risk. By contrast, the prosecutor could argue that he knew about the risk, since Adam told him about it.

In some states, gross negligence or criminal negligence is required. Here, if a jury concludes that ordinary person in Bob's circumstance could anticipate that the risk of 2,000 dumped marbles could cause accident and serious bodily injury or death, Bob can be convicted.

In a few states, accomplice cannot be convicted for involuntary manslaughter as a matter of law, since the crime requires negligence or recklessness. Here, Bob cannot be convicted in these jurisdictions.

In sum, to be guilty of involuntary manslaughter as an accomplice, Bob must have dual intentions and the intent is defined differently among the jurisdictions.

해설

난이도: 하

핵심 단어 및 논점

- involuntary manslaughter
- recklessness (intent)
- criminal negligence (intent)
- proximate causation (foreseeability)
- accomplice
- dual intentions

1. The Act is a valid exercise of Congress's power to regulate interstate commerce, because the Act regulates an economic activity that has substantial effect on interstate commerce.

Congress may regulates (1) the channels of interstate commerce, (2) the people and instrumentalities that work and travel in the channels of interstate commerce, or (3) economic activities that, in the aggregate, have substantial effect on interstate commerce.

First, the Act does not regulate the channels of interstate commerce, such as pathways. Second, the Act applies to all employees, not only employees who work in the channels of interstate commerce. Regarding the third type of regulation, the regulated activity must be economic or commercial in nature. If Congress had a rational basis for concluding that the class of activities subject to regulation, in the aggregate, has a substantial effect on interstate commerce, the regulation is constitutional.

In Morrison case, the Court held that Congress exceeded its commerce power by enacting a statute giving a cause of action to the victims of gender−motivated violence. However, this case is distinguishable because the statute is limited to violence in the workplace. The workplace is an economic environment and workplace violence directly impedes productivity of the workplace. Therefore, the statute is within the commerce power of Congress.

In sum, the Act is a valid exercise of Congress's power.

2. The Act may be constitutionally applied to state agencies as employers, because the Act regulates both public and private employers on the same terms.

Congress may regulate the states on the same terms as private actors. Congress may not command the states to regulate private conduct.

Here, the Act does not command the state to regulate private conduct. It is merely requires both public and private employers to obey the same federal requirement, to address workplace violence under the threat of civil liability. According to the past case, the federal law that mandates state individual to alter their own activities is not unconstitutional commandeering. Thus, the Act is constitutional.

In sum, the Act may be constitutionally applied to state agencies as employers, because the Act regulates both public and private employers on the same terms.

3. The Eleventh Amendment bars the employee's federal court lawsuit against the state, because the Act did not validly abrogate the state immunity.

The Eleventh Amendment bars lawsuits between a state and one of its citizens, even if lawsuits arise under federal law. This immunity also applies to state agencies. A federal statute abrogates Eleventh Amendment immunity if: (1) the statute unambiguously asserts that it does so and (2) Congress enacted the statute under a power that may abrogate Eleventh Amendment state immunity.

Here, employers may raise lawsuit against state agencies in federal court, only when the Act validly abrogates the state's immunity. The Act specified that any defense of immunity under the Eleventh Amendment to the U.S. Constitution is abrogated. However, there is no fact to show that the Congress had enacted the statute abrogating state immunity. Thus, the federal court must dismiss the employee's lawsuit against the state agency.

In sum, the Eleventh Amendment bars the employee's federal court lawsuit against the state, because the Act did not validly abrogates the state immunity.

해설

난이도: 하

핵심 단어 및 논점

- Commerce Clause
- Morrison case
- federalism principle
- dual sovereignty (Tenth Amendment)
- state immunity
- sovereign immunity (the Eleventh Amendment)

1번 문제

논점: Commerce Clause

답안요령

> 1. Commerce Clause
> 2. Analysis(1, 2번 type이 아니라는 것에 대한 설명)
> 3. 3번 type
> 4. Morrison case와 비교★
>   + analysis

TIP '세 번째' 유형의 regulation의 위헌성 여부를 판단하는 경우, 주어진 case와 Morrison 판례를 비교분석하는 것이 고득점 포인트다.

2번 문제

답안요령

> 1. Tenth Amendment (dual sovereignty)
> 2. Federalism principle
> 3. Analysis + 결론

3번 문제

[비교]

① The Eleventh Amendment: '타 주민(洲民)이나 외국인'이 주 정부를 상대로 손배청구한 소송은 '연방법원'에서 진행할 수 없다.

② The Tenth Amendment: Congress는 주 정부에게 주 주민들을 통치하는 방법에 대해 강요하여서는 아니된다.

③ State sovereignty: '당해 주 주민'이 자신의 주 정부를 상대로 '주 법원'에 손해배상을 청구하는 소는 금지된다.

1. State A has jurisdiction to award custody of Daughter to Grandparents.

A child's home state has exclusive jurisdiction to issue an initial custody order. Under UCCJEA, a home state is a state where the child has lived with a parent, for at least six consecutive months immediately before the commencement of a child−custody proceeding. The home state rule is also applicable when: (1) the child is absent from the home state, (2) no more than six months has passed since the child's departure from the jurisdiction, and (3) a parent continues to live in the home state.

Here, Daughter moved to State B four months before the commencement of the custody proceeding. Thus, State B is not Daughter's home state. However, State A is not a home state either. This is because Mom is living in State B and Daughter is not absent from State A.

When there is no home state, a court may exercise jurisdiction over a child custody determination when: (1) the child and at least one parent have a significant connection with the state and (2) substantial evidence is available in the state regarding the child's care, protection, training, and personal relationships. Here, Mom was married in State A and gave birth to Daughter there. Daughter and Mom lived in State A until four months ago. Additionally, Daughter and Grandparents are in State A now, and Daughter's schooling, friendships, and other personal relationships is available in State A. Thus, child's care, training, and personal relationships are available in State A and therefore State A has jurisdiction over child custody.

In sum, State A has jurisdiction to award custody of Daughter to Grandparents.

2. Even if the child's preference is specially weighted generally, the court could deny Grandparents' custody petition if it does not serve the best interest of the child.

When a child is mature enough to form and express a preference, the courts consider such child's wishes in determining a custody order. Generally, the child's wishes are typically given substantial weight. However, child's preference could be disregarded if it does not serve the best interest of the child.

Here, the custody contest is between Mom and Grandparent, nonparent. Thus, it is not certain that Daughter's preference would be followed.

In sum, even if the child's preference is specially weighted generally, the court could deny Grandparents' custody petition if it does not serve the best interest of the child

3. The State A statute is not constitutional.

Any person can petition for visitation at any time and the person should be given the visitation right whenever the court determines that it serves the best interest of the child. However, parents have constitutional right protected under the Constitution in the care, custody, and control of their child, and even the visitation of the child. Thus, the visitation award which is pursuant to the statute that gave no weight to the parent's determination is unconstitutional.

Here, State A statute authorizes the award of child custody to a grandparent without giving weight on the parent's determination. Additionally, State A statute is to grant custody to a nonparent and it permits larger intrusion, compared to the statute in Troxel case that was to grand nonparent visitation.

In sum, the State A statute is not constitutional.

해설

난이도: 1번 문제: 중
　　　　 2번 문제: 하
　　　　 3번 문제: 하

핵심 단어 및 논점

- child custody order
- jurisdiction of child custody order
- home state
- best interest of child
- visitation order
- parent's constitutional right
- Troxel case

3번 문제

논점: Custody order

　　　답안요령

> 1. General rule (best interest test)
> 2. Parent's constitutional right
> 3. Analysis(Troxel case와 비교)★

　TIP　Custody order에 대한 합헌성은 Troxel case와 비교분석하는 것이 고득점 포인트다. 비교분석 시, ① 제3자에게 주어진 권리(visitation/custody)와 ② 친부모로서의 헌법적 권리에 중점을 둔다.

1. Consumer is free of the bank's security interest, since Consumer is a buyer in ordinary course of business (BIOCOB).

Generally, a security interest continues after sale of the collateral. However, a buyer in ordinary course of business (BIOCOB), the buyer takes free of security interest which was created by the buyer's seller. BIOCOB is a buyer who (1) buys goods in good faith, (2) without knowledge that the sale violates the rights of another, (3) from a person in the business of selling goods of the kind in the ordinary course of the seller's business.

Here, Recycled sold the bicycle to Consumer and Consumer is a BIOCOB. Frist, Consumer purchased the bicycle from Recycled in accordance with reasonable commercial standards of fair dealing without knowledge of the financial relationship between Recycled and Bank. Second, Recycled is in the business of selling bicycles in the ordinary course of its business.

In sum, Consumer is free of the bank's security interest.

2. Bank has a superior claim to the used computer.

A security interest in collateral extends to identifiable proceeds of that collateral. "Proceeds" of collateral is defined as one that was acquired upon the exchange of collateral.

Here, under the security agreement between Bank and Recycled, Bank has security interest in all the inventory of Recycled, whether now owned or hereafter acquired. Inventory is defined as raw materials, work in process, or materials used or consumed in debtor's business. The used computer is not inventory, but it is proceeds of the bicycle. This is because Recycled traded a used bicycle to Student for a used computer.

The security interest in the collateral as proceeds is perfected when the security interest in the original collateral was perfected by the filing of a financing statement in the same office in which a financing statement would be filed in order to perfect a security interest in the collateral as proceeds. Here, the Recycled filed a financing statement in the appropriate state office.

A judgment lien creditor takes priority over a security interest only when the creditor became a lien creditor before the conflicting security interest is perfected. Here, Utility is a judgment lien creditor and Bank has perfected security interest in the used computer.

In conclusion, Bank has a superior claim to the used computer.

3. Bank has a superior claim to the 100 bicycle helmets.

Under the contract between Manufacturer and Recycled, Manufacturer retains title to the helmets until Recycled pays for them. However, Manufacturer's reservation is limited to a reservation of security interest. Manufacturer failed to file a financing statement, so it has unperfected security interest in the 100 bicycle helmets.

Bank has a security interest in the Recycled's inventory, and the bicycle helmets are inventory, since Recycled purchased it for sale. Bank perfected its security interest by filing a financing statement.

Between an unperfected secured creditor and a perfected secured creditor, a perfected secured creditor has superior claim to the collateral. Thus, Bank's security interest is superior to the Manufacture's security interest.

In conclusion, Bank's perfected security interest in the bicycle helmets has priority over Utility's later judgment lien. However, Utility's judgment lien has priority over Manufacturer's unperfected security interest in the bicycle helmets.

해설

난이도: 하

핵심 단어 및 논점

- buyer in ordinary course of business (BIOCOB)
- inventory
- proceeds
- judgment lien (lien creditor)
- perfection

1번 문제

답안요령

> 1. Security interest 기본 rule(collateral에 지속된다)★
> 2. 그러나 BIOCOB인 경우 예외 rule 적용
>   + analysis
> 3. Shelter rule★
>   + analysis

TIP 본 문제는 bank와 consumer 간의 security interest에 대한 문제로서, 'shelter rule'(위 3번)은 서술하지 않는다.

1(a). Susan may recover damages from University, since Susan was injured by foreseeable attack.

In modern, landowner has duty to take reasonable precautions to protect tenants against foreseeable attacks.

Here, University had duty to take reasonable precautions to protect its dormitory residents against foreseeable attacks. Ann's attack was foreseeable, because most of apartments or dormitories lock their doors to protect intrusion by criminals. In other words, the possibility that unauthorized person enters to the dormitory and commits crime was very high. This is why University made entry to the dormitory be controlled by key cards. Additionally, University had sufficient time to repair the broken lock, because it was broken four days before. The University's burden of taking such precautions seems small compared with the possibility that the risk will eventuate.

The jury would find that University's failure to repair the broken door was actual and proximate causation of the Susan's physical damage, because Ann entered through the broken rear entrance. Thus, University was negligent.

In sum, Susan may recover damages from University, since Susan was injured by foreseeable attack.

1(b). Susan may not recover damages for physical injuries from Jim, because his action did not increase Susan's injury and Susan did not rely on Jim's help.

Generally, there is no duty to come to the aid of another. However, once an actor renders services to reduce the risk of harm to another, the actor owes a duty of reasonable care to the other person if: (1) an actor increases the risk of harm compared to the risk without the undertaking or (2) the person who received the services relies on the actor's exercising reasonable care in the undertaking.

Here, Jim's action is arguably negligent. Jim closed the library door and it may make a less possibility for other people to help Susan. However, there is no fact to show the closing and the delay treatment Jim's action caused increased Susan's injury. Moreover, Susan got up and walked to the University hospital and received immediate treatment for her injuries, and it shows Susan did not rely on Jim's action. Thus, jury would find that Jin was not negligent and therefore Susan cannot recover from him.

In sum, Susan may not recover damages for physical injuries from Jim, because his action did not increase Susan's injury and Susan did not rely on Jim's help.

1(c). Susan may not recover damages from Ann's Psychiatrist, because Ann did not ascertained Susan and it is reasonable for the psychiatrist not to warn Susan based on history.

A psychotherapist has a duty to warn persons threatened by the patient. In the most states, victim can recover from a psychotherapist only when: (1) the patient posed a real risk to the specified victim or (2) when the therapist negligently failed to take the threat seriously. In other courts, a psychotherapist has duty to warn to victims who are readily ascertainable and subject to a serious threat of physical violence. In some courts, a psychotherapist has duty when a defendant directly facilitated the patient's attack. However, in some courts, the warnings should be made to broad population and it would be general.

Here, the psychotherapist did not negligently fail to take the threat seriously. Ann's Psychiatrist and Ann have therapy relationship because they met weekly for several months. Psychiatrist's failure to warn was reasonable, because Ann had no history of violent behavior. Moreover, the statement, "was going to make sure," was not specifying a victim. Additionally, Ann did not specified Susan, but she merely stated former University classmates who were cheaters. Thus, the victim was not readily ascertainable. Thus, Psychiatrist is liable to Susan.

In sum, Susan may not recover damages from Ann's Psychiatrist, because Ann did not ascertained Susan and it is reasonable for the psychiatrist not to warn Susan based on history.

2. Susan may also recover damages from University for the PTSD symptoms under the eggshell skull doctrine.

Under the eggshell skull doctrine, a plaintiff can recover for the full extent of his injuries which is greatly in excess of those that a normal victim would suffer.

Here, Ann's attack directly caused Susan's minor physical injuries, but Susan also suffered from PTSD symptoms. Under the eggshell skull doctrine, Susan can recover damages for PTSD symptoms as well as the physical injuries. However, in some states, courts are reluctant to grant tort plaintiffs damage award when mental distress was unaccompanied with any physical injuries. Susan suffered physical injuries by Ann's attack and the attack triggered physical symptoms as PTSD symptoms, such as insomnia, anxiety, and rapid breathing.

In conclusion, Susan may also recover damages from University for the PTSD symptoms.

해설

난이도: 하

핵심 단어 및 논점

- negligence
- reasonability (precaution)
- foreseeable risk
- duty to aid
- duty to warn (psychotherapist's duty)
- eggshell skull doctrine

1번 문제

Susan은 invitee, University는 landowner라는 점을 근거로 University가 Susan에게 foreseeable risk에 대한 적절한 precaution을 취해야 한다고 작성해도 된다. 다만, 그 내용은 risk가 'foreseeable했다'는 점, precaution을 취하는 것이 'reasonable'했다는 점 (두 요건을 비교형량하여)에 중점을 두고 작성해야 한다.

> **답안요령**

> 1. Negligence에 대한 general rule
> 2. Foreseeable risk
> 3. Reasonability
>   + analysis

> **TIP**   3번: ① Risk가 발생할 확률(the likelihood that the risk will eventuate)과 ② 예방의 부담(the burden of taking precautions against such foreseeable risk), 이 두 요소를 비교형량하여 analysis하는 것이 고득점 포인트다.

2번 문제

> **답안요령**

> 1. No duty to aid
> 2. Exception(duty가 인정되는 경우)
> 3. Analysis (요건 i)
> 4. Analysis (요건 ii)

1. The trial court properly permitted Defendant to amend its answer, because it would not result in a form of injustice.

Defendant has a burden of pleading all affirmative defenses. When Defendant failed to raise a potentially valid affirmative defense in its answer, he can later seek to amend. The amendment is permitted when it must not result in injustice. Injustice is defined as undue delay, bad faith, or undue prejudice. There should not be both injustice to defendant and plaintiff.

Here, Plaintiff might argue that she is prejudiced by adding the defense after the close of discovery. However, it is difficult to say that there was prejudice to Plaintiff. This is because the defense was supported by plaintiff's testimony in deposition. Plaintiff's counsel should anticipate well−established affirmative defense. Even if Plaintiff needs more time for discovery because of the amendment of the defense, it is insufficient ground to deny the motion to amend the defense. Thus, justice seems better served by allowing the amendment.

In sum, the trial court properly permitted Defendant to amend its answer, because it would not result in a form of injustice.

2. The court erred in granting summary judgment, since there is genuine issue on defendant's affirmative answer.

A summary judgment motion may be granted only if there is no genuine issue about any material fact and the movant is entitled to judgment as a matter of law. An issue is genuine, if a reasonable jury could return a verdict for a nonmoving party, based on the evidence presented by the nonmoving party. A fact is material, if it is relevant to an element of a claim or defense and its existence would affect the outcome of the case under the governing law. When a court determines whether there is a genuine issue as to material fact, it should consider the depositions, documents, or other materials.

Here, Defendant moved for summary judgment, and therefore he has the burden to provide credible evidence to support its affirmative defense. Defendant tried to establish facts supporting the affirmative defense by relying on Plaintiff's deposition testimony. Thus, if Plaintiff's testimony in the deposition has no genuine issue as to any material fact relating to Defendant's affirmative defense and that, accordingly, Defendant should be granted judgment as a matter of law, Defendant should be granted summary judgment.

Plaintiff admitted the existence of the company procedures that employees could use to complain about perceived discrimination, and it could support the second affirmative defense. However, jury could reasonably find that this was not a reasonable enforcement action for women in workplace, since Plaintiff had not seen any effort. Plaintiff also said that she was afraid that she would suffer retaliation and jury could reasonably find that her fear was reasonable for her failure to use the process. In short, there is a genuine issue as to the reasonableness of employer's care and the reasonableness of the plaintiff's failure to take any preventive opportunities. Thus, without a resolution of those factual issues, summary judgment should not have been granted.

In sum, the court erred in granting summary judgment, since there is genuine issue on defendant's affirmative answer.

해설

난이도: 1번 문제: 하
        2번 문제: 상

핵심 단어 및 논점

- amendment
- summary judgment
  - genuine issue

2번 문제

답안요령

> 1. General rule
> 2. Burden of proof
> 3. Analysis(moving party's evidence에 대해)
> 4. Analysis(주어진 증거를 most favoring the non-moving party하도록)
> 5. 결론

1. Acme has fiduciary obligations both to the LLC and Brown.

In a member—managed limited liability company (LLC), each member has management powers and has fiduciary duties both to the corporation and other members. These fiduciary duties include duty of care and duty of loyalty. Duty of loyalty includes the duty to account to the company and to hold as trustee for the company any benefit derived by the member in the conduct of the company's activities.

Here, Acme refused to bring a claim against Acme, as the manager of A—B LLC. Acme got benefit from this improper action, and it holds improper benefit. Holding an improper benefit is a breach of duty of loyalty.

Under the business judgment rule, there is a presumption that a member makes a decision (1) in a good faith, (2) in an informed manner, (3) based on a rational basis, and (4) for the best interest of the corporation. However, in this case, it is hard to see that Acme acted for the best interest for the LLC. Additionally, Acme is self—interested, and BJR is not applicable.

In sum, Acme has fiduciary obligations both to the LLC and Brown.

2. Brown cannot bring a direct claim against Acme, but Brown can bring a derivative claim against Acme, since it is a claim of the LLC as an entity.

A member of LLC may bring a derivative claim if: (1) a demand is on the other member to bring an action and the member fails to do so or (2) such demand would be futile.

Here, Brown is a member of the LLC and it demanded Acme to bring a claim against Acme. Acme failed to do so and Brown may bring a derivative action against Acme.

Brown individually cannot bring a direct claim against Acme. This is because an

LLC is different from its members. The claim against Acme is a claim of the LLC, not a claim of the members.

In sum, Brown cannot bring a direct claim against Acme, but Brown can bring a derivative claim against Acme, since it is a claim of the LLC as an entity.

3. Brown has sufficient grounds for the judicial dissolution of the LLC, since Acme's action was oppressive.

There are two types of dissolution: voluntary and involuntary. There could be an involuntary dissolution, when a member's action is oppressive and directly harmful to other members. Under the oppression doctrine, courts can order to close corporation when actions by controlling shareholders violate the reasonable expectations of noncontrolling shareholders.

Here, Acme's action was oppressive, since it violated reasonable expectation of Brown that Acme would not violate its fiduciary duties. Additionally, Acme's refusal to bring a derivative suit violated Brown's reasonable expectation that Acme would manage the LLC in the best interests of the LLC. Finally, Brown will suffer reputational harm by the accident caused by Acme's defective concrete. Thus, Acme's action was oppressive.

In sum, Brown has sufficient grounds for the judicial dissolution of the LLC, since Acme's action was oppressive.

4. The losses should not be allocated to Acme and Brown, since LLC's member has a limited liability for company's liability.

An LLC is a form of business association that combines the features of corporations and partnerships. Like corporations, LLC's members have limited liability for company's debts. Thus, generally, a member in a limited liability corporation is not liable for corporation's debts just because he is a member. A member can become liable based on doctrine of piercing the LLC's veil or member's direct liability. There is some basis to pierce the LLC's veil: undercapitalization of the business, failure to follow formalities, fraud, and commingling of assets.

Here, the losses arising from the judgment obtained by the plaintiffs is against LLC, not against its individual members. Thus, LLC's liability to the plaintiffs could not be a liability of its members, Acme and Brown. Additionally, there is no fact supporting the basis to pierce the LLC's veil.

The homeowners may raise a direct claim against Acme for supplying defective concrete, but the homeowners did not bring the claim in this case.

In conclusion, the losses should not be allocated to Acme and Brown.

해설

난이도: 하

핵심 단어 및 논점

- limited liability company (LLC)
- fiduciary duty
- business judgment rule (BJR)
- derivative suit
- direct suit
- oppression doctrine
- involuntary dissolution (judicial dissolution)

1. The house and saving account at a bank is governed by the State A statutes and the farm is governed by the State B.

The law of the state where the real property is located governs the disposition of real property. The law of the state where the decedent was domiciled at his death governs the disposition of personal property.

Here, Zach's probate assets include a house located in State A, a farm located in State B, and a saving account. Because Zach is domiciled at State A, a saving account is governed by State A status.

In sum, the house and saving account at a bank is governed by the State A statutes and the farm is governed by the State B.

2. All assets should be distributed intestate, since Zach's will is not a valid will under either State A or State B law.

Zach's will is a handwritten document and is unwitnessed. Thus, it is a holographic will and it is invalid under either State A or State B law. State A requires that a will must be signed and Zach's will did not satisfy it. The house and the saving account pass to intestate succession in accordance of State A law. Zach's will was not witnessed and State B law does not recognize it as a valid will. Thus, the farm passes to intestate succession in accordance of State B law.

In sum, all assets should be distributed intestate, since Zach's will is not a valid will under either State A or State B law.

3. Alex is entitled to share in the house, the farm, and the saving account.

According to both states' law, Zach's probate assets pass to his surviving children, since Zach's wife predeceased him. Alex is the biological child of Zach and his deceased wife, and he is included in "surviving children" without any arguments. Thus, Alex is entitled to share in the house, the farm, and the saving account.

4. Brian's inheritance right on the house and the saving account depends on how the court interpret the law and he has the right on the farm.

Under the common law, only blood relations could be entitled to share of intestate decedent. Under UPC, adopted children have inheritance rights only when there is an explicit statutory provision. Otherwise, there are some cases that adopted children have same inheritance rights with biological children.

Here, under State A law, it is silent on adopted children. Under the common law, Brain does not have inheritance right, because he is a blood relation with Zach. Under UPC, Brain does not have inheritance right, because State A law does not include an explicit statutory provision. Otherwise, Brain would have same inheritance rights with biological children. Thus, Brian's inheritance right on the house and the saving account depends on how the court interprets the law.

Under State B law, Brain takes inheritance right as specifically mentioned in the law. Thus, Brian has inheritance right on the farm.

In sum, Brian's inheritance right on the house and the saving account depends on how the court interpret the law and he has the right on the farm.

5. Carrie has inheritance rights as a child of Zach.

Under the common law, a nonmarital child could not inherit from either parent. However, in modern, children have rights to inherit from their mothers and to inherit from their fathers, when at least one has established paternity. A statute that disallows nonmarital child's inheritance right when the father's paternity has been adjudicated during his lifetime is unconstitutional.

In this case, because there was adjudication during Zach's lifetime, Carrie would be entitled to a share of Zach's estate despite the provision of the State A. Thus, she has the right on the house and the saving account.

In State B law, Carrie is a biological child and she is entitled to the farm.

In sum, Carrie has inheritance rights as a child of Zach.

해설

난이도: 하

핵심 단어 및 논점

- conflict of laws
- validity of will
- holographic will
- intestate succession
- adopted children
- paternity

1. The tenant was not constructively evicted, because the landlord had no duty to repair the commercial premises.

A term−of−years lease specifies both a beginning and an ending date. Under a term−of−years normally cannot be terminated by the tenant prior to the end of the term, unless the tenant was constructively evicted.

In order to establish a constructive eviction, the tenant must prove that the landlord breached a duty to the tenant, such as a duty to repair, that the landlord's breach caused a loss of the substantial use and enjoyment of the premises. The tenant must also show that he gave the landlord notice adequate to permit the landlord to meet his duty to the tenant.

There was no implied duty on the part of a landlord to repair leased premises under the common law. However, in modern, courts have generally implied a duty to repair in residential leases based on an implied warranty of habitability. Courts have been reluctant to imply a duty to repair in commercial leases. Courts implies a duty to repair in a commercial lease, only when: (1) the repair has been mandated by public authorities, (2) it involves work so substantial that it would not ordinarily fall within the tenant's common law repair duty, and/or (3) the value of the repair would primarily inure to the landlord's reversionary interest.

Here, the tenant is the owner of a valuable manufacturing operation. There are no public authorities requiring the air−conditioning. The repair for the air−conditioning is not structural. The repair involves a feature of the building and it would have not reversionary interest on the landlord.

In sum, the tenant was not constructively evicted, because the landlord had no duty to repair the commercial premises.

2. The landlord did not accept the tenant's surrender of the lease.

When a tenant wrongfully moves from leased premises with the intent to terminate the lease, the landlord may either accept the tenant's surrender of the premises and terminate the lease or hold the tenant to the terms of the lease. Landlord's retention of keys delivered by a tenant constitutes acceptance of surrender only when there is other evidence showing that the landlord intended to accept the surrender.

Here, the landlord put the keys into her desk when the tenant sent the key. However, the landlord's note saying "I repeat, the air−conditioning is not my problem. You have leased the building, and you should fix it," strongly suggests that the landlord did not intend to accept the tenant's surrender.

The tenant might argue that the landlord's failure to make a similar statement when the keys were sent to her a second time. However, the landlord can say that his retention of the keys represented a decision to safeguard the keys, not to accept the tenant's surrender.

In sum, the landlord did not accept the tenant's surrender of the lease.

3. Under the common law, the landlord is entitled to $5,000. In some jurisdictions, the landlord could sue the tenant for damages equal to the difference between $175,000 and the property's fair rental value for the balance of the term.

Under the common law, a landlord had no duty to mitigate damages resulting from a tenant's wrongful termination of a lease. A landlord could recover the full value of rents that were due and unpaid at the time of the suit. A landlord could not sue a tenant for rents due in the future.

Thus, under the common law, on November 1, the landlord could only recover the full value of the two months' rent actually due and unpaid ($5,000 for September and October).

Some courts rejected the no−mitigation−of−damages rule. These courts allow landlords to sue tenants who have wrongfully terminated a lease for damages equal to the difference between the unpaid rend due under the lease and the property's fair market rental value.

Other courts have abandoned the no−recovery−for−future−rent rule. These courts allow a landlord to collect damages equal to the value of rent over the entire lease term minus the property's fair rental value when a tenant has wrongfully terminated a lease and unequivocally shown an intention not to return to the premises or pay future rent.

Here, the tenant returned the keys to the landlord and said, "I will not be returning to the building or making further rent payments," showing abandonment and an intention not to return. The landlord might recover damages in the amount of $5,000 plus the present value of $175,000 minus the fair market rental value of the property over the remaining months of the lease.

In sum, under the common law, the landlord is entitled to $5,000. In some jurisdictions, the landlord could sue the tenant for damages equal to the difference between $175,000 and the property's fair rental value for the balance of the term.

해설

난이도: 하

핵심 단어 및 논점

- constructive eviction (landlord and tenant)
- duty to repair
- implied warranty of habitability
- commercial lease
- surrender
- duty to mitigate
- damages

1. Sailor's October 13 letter to the builder was seeking assurance of the builder's performance under the contract.

Contract parties can take steps to assure due performance of contractual obligations. Under the UCC 2, when there are reasonable grounds for insecurity about the performance of either party, the other may demand adequate assurance of due performance in writing. If the demand for assurance is justified, the other party is required to provide assurance within 30 days and, if not, it is a repudiation of the contract.

Here, the sailor read a news report about the builder's workers' strike and it is a reasonable ground for insecurity about the builder's performance, sending to the sailor a specially manufactured boat on time. Thus, the sailor's demand of the assurance was adequate.

In sum, Sailor's October 13 letter to the builder was seeking assurance of the builder's performance under the contract.

2. The builder's November 25 response to the sailor's letter is a repudiation of the contract, since it did not provide assurance of due performance.

If the demand for assurance is justified, the other party is required to provide assurance within 30 days and if not, it be held as a repudiation of the contract.

Here, Sailor's demand for assurance was justified on October 31. The builder responded to the letter on Nevemer 25, within 30 days. However, the builder stated "I hope we settle it soon so that we can get back to work" and it is not providing assurance of due performance.

In sum, the builder's response is a repudiation of the contract.

3. The sailor's refusal to take and pay for the boat is a breach of the contract, since the builder retracted the repudiation.

The repudiating party can retract the repudiation until the performance is due, when nonbreaching party, because of the repudiation, (1) cancelled, (2) materially changed his position, or (3) otherwise indicated that he considers the repudiation final.

Here, the builder's failure to provide assurance constitutes repudiation. However, he called the sailor on December 3, in which was before the due date, and said he will deliver a boat by December 15. The facts show that the sailor did nothing. Thus, a retraction of the repudiation occurred and the sailor has no right to buy his boat from a shipyard.

In sum, the sailor's refusal is a breach of contract.

해설

난이도: 하

핵심 단어 및 논점

- assurance
- repudiation
- demand for assurance
- repudiation

1. The son's expulsion from the school violated the First Amendment, because AutoCo's actions constitute state action and the school compelled political belief.

The individual rights are protected under the Constitution only when there is state action. State action is defined as an action: (1) directed by the government, or (2) by a private party that is fairly attributable to the government. Private parties can constitute state action when: (1) they performed a traditional public function, (2) there is judicial enforcement of certain private contracts, (3) there is joint action between a state and private actor, or (4) there is state encouragement of private discrimination.

Here, AutoCo is a privately owned corporation. However, it owns and operates a commercial district with shops and streets open to the general public. It provides security, fire protection, sanitation services, and school for residents. The corporation operates "company town" and it does more than own the town. Thus, the actions of AutoCo constitute state action and therefore are governed by the Fourteenth Amendment.

Even though schools have great discretion to regulate the speech of students and teachers, public schools may not force their students to participate in a flag salute ceremony when it offends the political or religious beliefs of the students or their families. In short, schools cannot compel the student specific political belief.

Here, the school constitutes state action, as mentioned above. The son had been expelled from the school with the reason that he refused to recite the Pledge. His refuse was based on his own political beliefs and the political beliefs of his family. Thus, expulsion violates the son's First Amendment right.

In sum, the son's expulsion from the school violated the First Amendment, because AutoCo's actions constitute state action and the school compelled political belief.

2. The father's arrest violates the First Amendment, since the father distributed leaflets in a public forum.

Oakwood's commercial district is treated as government owned property, and the leafleting is subject to the First Amendment because it is an expressive activity. Government regulation of the expression is governed by the public forum doctrine.

When a state tries to regulate expressive activity based on the content in a public forum, its regulation should be narrowly tailored to achieve a compelling governmental interest. When a state tries to regulate expressive activity based on content neutral ground, intermediate scrutiny applies. Under the intermediate scrutiny, the purpose of the regulation may not be the suppression of ideas, the regulation must be narrowly tailored to achieve an important governmental interest, and it must leave open ample alternative channels for expressive activity. Here, AutoCo is regulating the father's expressive activity on the content neutral ground, littering on the grounds. Keeping the streets clean is insufficient governmental interest to ban leafleting in the public streets. The rule is not narrowly tailored to protect expression. Additionally, the rule is likely to ban all leafleting, eliminating an entire class of means of expression.

In sum, the father's arrest violates the father's right under the First Amendment.

해설

핵심 단어 및 논점

- freedom of speech (the First Amendment)
- state action
- content–neutral restriction
- public forum
- IR test

본 사안은 time, place, manner restriction(T/P/M restriction)에 해당하지 않는다. 본 사안의 anti–litter rule은 leaflet 행위를 하는데 있어 시간, 장소, 방법을 제한하는 것이 아니고, 'entirely' 제한하기 때문이다. 대부분의 leaflet distribution은 lettering^{흐트러져 어지럽히다} 결과를 초래하는 바, littering하는 leaflet distribution을 금하는 것은 leaflet distribution을 'entirely' 제한한다고 볼 수 있다.

2번 문제
논점: Public forum에서의 speech를 제한하는 statute의 합헌성

답안요령

> 1. Freedom of speech
> 2. Applicable rule (수정헌법 5조 또는 수정헌법 14조)
>   + analysis (statute를 제정한 주체: state 또는 federal)
> 3. Speech
>   + analysis (제한받은 행위가 speech에 해당하는지)
> 4. Public forum 정의
>   + analysis
> 5. Public forum doctrine
> 6. 주어진 규정의 제한기준(content–based 또는 content–neutral restriction)
>   + analysis★
> 7. 적용되는 test(SS 또는 IR test)
>   + analysis★

TIP1 6번: ① 주어진 statute가 항상 content−based 또는 content−neutral restriction으로 명확히 구분된다는 편견을 버리는 것이 중요하다. 보는 관점에 따라 동일한 statute가 content−based restriction으로도, content−neutral restriction으로도 해석될 수 있다. 이런 경우에는 각 경우를 모두 analysis하는 것이 고득점 포인트다.

② Reed 판례와 비교분석하는 것이 고득점 포인트다.

TIP2 7번: SS test와 IR test에서의 "narrowly tailored"요건 기준이 다름에 유념한다.

1. The buyer took the bicycle free of the retailer's security interest.

The security interest is effective and attaches, when: (1) debtor signed a security agreement containing a description of the collateral, (2) debtor has rights in the collateral, and (3) secured party gave money to secured party.

Here, the retailer's security interest attached, because the man signed a security agreement, he purchased the bicycle, and the retailer sold the bicycle on credit.

When the collateral is a consumer goods and it secures a purchase money obligation on that collateral, the security interest is a purchase money security interest (PMSI) in consumer goods. A purchase money security interest is automatically perfected upon attachment. Consumer goods is a goods that is purchased for personal, family, or household purposes.

Here, the man has obligation to the retailer to purchase the bicycles, so the security interest is PMSI. The man purchased the bicycles to use on vacation, and they are consumer goods. In sum, even though the retailer failed to file a financial statement, retailer's security interest was perfected.

Generally, a security interest continues after sale of the collateral. However, a buyer in ordinary course of business (BIOCOB), the buyer is free from the security interest which was created by the buyer's seller. BIOCOB is a buyer who (1) buys goods in good faith, (2) without knowledge that the sale violates the rights of another, (3) from a person in the business of selling goods of the kind in the ordinary course of the seller's business.

Here, the retailer's security interest was perfected when the buyer purchased the bicycle. Thus, the buyer is not free of the retailer's security interest. Additionally, the BIOCOB exception is inapplicable in this case. Even though buyer purchased the bicycle in good faith without knowledge, but the man was not a person who is in the business of selling bicycles.

However, there is another exception that is applicable here. A buyer of consumer goods takes free of a security interest in those goods, if the buyer (1) buys without knowledge of the security interest, (2) gives value, (3) purchases the goods for personal, family, or household use, and (4) receives the goods before the filing of any financing statement covering them.

First, the buyer had no knowledge of the retailer's security interest. Second, the buyer paid the man $400. Third, the buyer bought the bicycle to ride for weekend recreation. Fourth, no financing statement had been filed.

In sum, the buyer took the bicycle free of the retailer's security interest.

2. The friend did not own the bicycle free of the retailer's security interest.

As mentioned above, the retailer did not authorize the man to dispose of the bicycle. Thus, the retailer's security interest continued in the bicycle even after it was transferred to the man's friend.

There is no any exception applicable for the friend. The friend did not a buyer of the bicycle, because the man gave him the bicycle as a birthday present.

In sum, the friend did not own the bicycle free of the retailer's security interest.

해설

난이도: 1번 문제: 하
　　　　　2번 문제: 중

핵심 단어 및 논점

- PMSI in consumer goods
- buyer in ordinary course of business (BIOCOB)
- perfection
- gift

1번 문제

> **답안요령**

> 1. Security interest 기본 rule(collateral에 지속된다)★
> 2. 그러나 BIOCOB인 경우 예외 rule 적용
>   + analysis
> 3. Shelter rule★
>   + analysis

> **TIP** 본 문제는 retailer와 man 간의 security interest에 대한 문제로서, 'shelter rule(위 3번)'은 서술하지 않는다.

2번 문제

원칙적으로 담보물에 대한 security interest는 해당 담보물에 대한 소유권 및 점유권이 변경된다 하더라도 그대로 유지된다. 그러나 채권자가 security interest에 대해 free함을 authorize하거나 다른 예외의 경우에 해당하면 security interest는 유지되지 못한다. 본 사안에서 buyer는 friend에게 security interest가 있는 담보물(bicycle)을 '선물'로 주었으므로, friend는 bicycle을 구매한 자가 아니다. 이는 어떠한 예외의 경우에도 해당되지 않는 바, security interest가 그대로 유지된다. 다시 말해, UCC9은 담보물 점유자(friend)가 해당 담보물에 대해 value를 지불한 경우에 한해 그를 security interest로부터 보호한다.

2013Feb Federal Civil Procedure

1. Mother's claim against Driver is not barred, since Mother was not a party of the prior lawsuit.

Under the doctrine of claim preclusion, the claimant is barred from asserting the cause of action in a later lawsuit when: (1) earlier judgment is a final judgment on the merits, (2) claimant and defendant in the judgment are same with the earlier judgment, and (3) the claimant asserts the same cause of action with the earlier judgment.

First, the judge entered a judgment in favor of Son against Driver, and Driver did not appeal. Thus, the earlier judgment is a final judgment. Second, Mom was not a party in the case between Son and Driver, and therefore she is not bound by the earlier judgment.

There are some exceptions that nonparty is bound by the judgment. First, a person who is not a party to an action is bound by a judgment when he is represented by a party. However, close family relationships are not sufficient to constitute privity. Thus, Mom would not be bound by the judgment against Driver because she has a family relationship with Son. Second, a person who is not a party to an action is bound a judgment when he consents to be bound. Third, when a nonparty assumed control of the prior lawsuit, a nonparty is bound by the earlier judgment. Here, there are no facts to show applicable exceptions.

In sum, Mother's claim against Driver is not barred, because the claim preclusion doctrine is inapplicable.

2. Under the issue preclusion doctrine, the jury's conclusion does not preclude Mother from litigating that issue, because the issue was not essential to earlier judgment.

Issue preclusion arises when: (1) the same issue is involved in both actions, (2) the issue was actually litigated in the first action, (3) the issue was essential in the earlier judgment, and (4) the earlier judgment is final judgment.

Here, the issue that Mother had negligently failed to maintain the brake lights on her car was involved in both actions. This issue was actually litigated in the first action and there is no fact indicating that there was no opportunity to litigate. The earlier judgment was final. However, the issue was not essential in the earlier judgment against Driver. There is nothing to show that the issue had impact on the judgment. Additionally, Mother was not a party to the first action and Mother and Son were not in privity. Thus, the issue preclusion does not arise, and therefore Mother can litigate that issue in the later lawsuit.

Thus, under the issue preclusion doctrine, the jury's conclusion does not preclude Mother from litigating that issue, because the issue was not essential to earlier judgment.

3. The jury's conclusion does not preclude Driver from litigating Driver's negligent, since Mother was a wait−and−see plaintiff.

As mentioned above, there are some factors to establish issue preclusion.

First, the issue that Driver was negligent was the same issue involved in both actions. Second, the issue was actually litigated and there was sufficient opportunity to litigate. Third, the issue was essential in the judgment against Driver, because Son alleged Driver's negligence and sought damages for his personal injuries. Additionally Driver was a party in earlier judgment, so she is bound by the judgment.

However, when there is nonmutual offensive collateral estoppel (a plaintiff who was not a party in earlier judgment raise issue preclusion against Defendant who was a party in earlier judgment) and a plaintiff was easy to join in the earlier judgment, the plaintiff cannot raise issue preclusion.

Here, Mother could easily have joined in the earlier action. Mother and Son both reside in State A. They have family relationship and Son drove Mother's car at the accident. There is no fact to show that there is reason not to join together. Thus, Mother could easily have joined in the earlier action. Additionally, joinder is authorized when claims arose from same transaction or occurrence and raised a common question of law or fact. In short, Mother is a wait−and−see plaintiff. Thus, a court might disallow her use of non−mutual issue preclusion.

In sum, the jury's conclusion does not preclude Driver from litigating Driver's negligent, since Mother was a wait−and−see plaintiff.

해설

난이도: 하

핵심 단어 및 논점

- claim preclusion
- issue preclusion
- wait-and-see plaintiff

1. Only the agent is the liable to the basket manufacturer for breach of the contract.

A principal is liable on a contract made by an agent when the agent has actual or apparent authority. Actual authority exists when a principal makes an agent to believe that the principal wants the agent to act on behalf of principal. Apparent authority arises when (1) a third party reasonably believes that the actor is authorized, (2) that belief is from the principal's manifestation, and (3) the third party has no notice.

Here, the owner authorized the agent to buy only baskets made of woven wicker, not aluminum. Thus, the agent had no actual authority to make the contract with the basket manufacturer to purchase four aluminum baskets. The owner recently notified basket manufacturer that she or her agent might be contacting them to purchase baskets, but it did not specify name of the agent. Additionally, the manufacturer had no prior dealings with either the owner or the agent. Thus, the manufacturer cannot reasonably believe that the actor is authorized to act on behalf of principal and therefore agent had no apparent authority on the contract.

When there is an undisclosed principal, the opposing party assumes that the party with whom it contracts will be bound by the contract. Thus, when the contract is breached, the agent acted on undisclosed principal's behalf is liable for the breach of contract. Here, the agent never told the manufacturer that he represented the owner or any other principal. Even though the delivery address was the owner's address, the agent did not indicate that the address was that of the owner. Hence, the principal was an undisclosed principal and therefore the agent is liable for the breach of the contract.

In sum, only the agent is the liable to the basket manufacturer for breach of the contract.

2. Both agent and the owner are liable for breach of the contract.

The agent had no actual authority to make the contract with the burner manufacturer, since the owner retained an agent to acquire burners that use a unique whisper technology.

Regarding apparent authority, the manufacturer would argue that the agent had apparent authority. The agent told the manufacturer that the agent represented a well-known hot-air balloon operator, but he did not disclose the owner's name. Thus, the owner is partially disclosed principal under the Second Restatement or unidentified principal under the Third Restatement. Additionally, the owner told the manufacturer that the agent might be contacting them. The manufacturers regularly receive such notices. The agent told him he represented a principal. Based on these things, the manufacturer would argue that it is reasonable to believe that the agent was authorized and the belief is traceable to the principal's manifestation. If the agent was authorized, the owner is liable for the breach of the contract.

When the third party reasonably believed that the opposing party of the contract is an agent who is acting on other person's behalf, the agent is liable for breach of the contract. This is because the agent breached third party's expectation.

In sum, both the agent and the owner are liable for breach of the contract.

3. Only the agent is liable under the Second Restatement of Agency. Both the and the owner are liable for breach of the contract under the Third Restatement.

Under the Second Restatement, the principal cannot ratify an unauthorized transaction with a third person. However, under the Third Restatement, a person may ratify an act if the actor acted as an agent on the principal's behalf.

Here, the agent had no actual authority, since he purchased solar cells, not propane fuel tanks. The solar cell manufacturer had no notice from the owner and the owner did not tell the manufacturer that he was acting on behalf of any other person. Thus, there is no apparent authority, since there is no principal's manifestation. Additionally, the cells were delivered to the agent. The manufacturer cannot reasonably believe that the agent is acting on behalf of the owner.

The owner is not liable to the solar cell manufacturer, since the agent had neither actual nor apparent authority. However, the owner decided to keep the solar cells. Under the Second Restatement, the owner cannot ratify the contract made by the agent with the solar cell manufacturer. However, under the Third Restatement, the owner ratified the transaction. Because the agent acted on the owner's behalf and the owner's using the solar cells manifests assent to the agent's acts.

Under the Second Restatement, when there is an undisclosed principal, the opposing party assumes that the party with whom it contracts will be bound by the contract. Thus, when the contract is breached, the agent acted on undisclosed principal's behalf is liable for the breach of contract. Here, the principal was undisclosed principal and the agent was not authorized. Thus, the agent is liable to the manufacturer. Under the Third Restatement, ratification relates back to the time of the transaction. However, the relating back does not relieve the agent's liability to the third party on the transaction.

In conclusion, only the agent is liable under the Second Restatement of Agency. Both the and the owner are liable for breach of the contract under the Third Restatement.

해설

난이도: 하

핵심 단어 및 논점

- undisclosed principal
- partially disclosed principal
- unidentified principal
- ratification

1, 2번 문제
논점: Principal 및 agent의 책임유무

> 답안요령

1. General agency rule
2. Principal's liability
   i. Actual authority

+ analysis
　　ii. Apparent authority
　　　+ analysis
　3. Agent's liability
　　i. Principal status(해당하는 status)★
　　ii. Reasoning
　4. Analysis + 결론

3번 문제

답안요령

1. Ratify하기 전 principal's liability(agent의 authority 유무)
　i. Actual authority
　　+ analysis
　ii. Apparent authority
　　+ analysis
　iii. 결론(Principal is not bound.)
2. 2nd Restatement에 따른 ratification
　i. Actual authority
　　+ analysis + 결론(Principal is not liable.)
3. 3rd Restatement에 따른 ratification
　　+ analysis + 결론
4. Agent's liability(principal status를 기준으로)
　i. 2nd Restatement
　　+ analysis
　ii. 3rd Restatement
　　+ analysis

TIP　　Ratification에 관한 답안은 Second Restatement가 적용되는 경우와 Third Restatement가 적용되는 경우를 구별하여 analysis하는 것이 고득점 포인트다.

2013Feb Evidence

1. The mechanic's text message is relevant and it is admissible, since it falls within the hearsay exception for present sense impression or the business records.

Evidence is relevant if it has tendency to make a fact more or less probable than it would be without the evidence.

In this case, the mechanic's text message to the woman is relevant. It has tendency to make it more probable that the brakes were defective and to make it more probable that woman was negligent in riding the scooter knowing that it required repair. Thus, mechanic's text message is relevant.

Hearsay is an out−of−court statement to prove the truth of the matter asserted. In this case, the mechanic's text message could be hearsay if it is used to prove whether brakes needed repair. However, present sense impressions exception exists when there is a statement describing an event or condition made while or immediately after the declaration after the declarant perceived it. Here, the text message was written by the mechanic just after he perceived that the mechanic requires repair. Thus, it is present sense impression.

A record of acts, events, conditions, or diagnoses is admissible hearsay under the business records exception, if: (1) it is made at or near the time of the recorded event by a person who has personal knowledge on the event and (2) the making of the record is the regular practice of the business. Here, the mechanic had personal knowledge on the fact of defective brakes and it is in ordinary course of business. Thus, it fits business records exception.

If the text message is not hearsay if it is used to prove whether woman knew defective brakes, her state of mind.

In conclusion, the mechanic's text message is relevant and it is admissible, since it falls within the hearsay exception for present sense impression or the business records.

2. The woman's testimony is relevant and admissible.

The woman's testimony asking the mechanic is relevant, since it has tendency to make it more probable that woman was not negligent.

Hearsay is an out−of−court statement to prove the truth of the matter asserted. Assertion means saying something is so. Here, the woman's questioning can be used to prove whether the scooter was safe to ride for a while. However, Questioning is not an assertion. Thus, the woman's testimony is not hearsay.

In conclusion, the woman's testimony is relevant and admissible.

3. If the mechanic's thumbs−up is used to prove the negligence, it is admissible and relevant. If the gesture is to prove whether the scooter's defective, it is hearsay and inadmissible.

The mechanic's gesture is relevant to prove that the woman was not negligent because she had no knowledge on defective brakes.

Hearsay is a statement, which is defined as a person's oral assertion, written assertion, or nonverbal conduct. Here, the mechanic thumbed up, answering the woman's question. This action is a nonverbal conduct meaning that the scooter was safe to ride. However, there is no hearsay issue, since it is not to prove the truth of matter asserted, but is to show the woman's belief. Thus, if the mechanic's thumbs−up is used to prove the negligence, it is admissible and relevant.

The gesture is relevant to prove whether the scooter's defective, but it is hearsay if it is used to prove that the scooter was safe to ride for a child. Thus, if the gesture is used to prove the scooter's defective, it is not admissible.

In sum, if the mechanic's thumbs−up is used to prove the negligence, it is admissible and relevant. If the gesture is to prove whether the scooter's defective, it is hearsay and inadmissible.

해설

난이도: 상

핵심 단어 및 논점

- hearsay 정의
  - assertion
  - to prove the truth
- business records exception (hearsay exception)

답안요령

> 1. Relevance★
>   + analysis
> 2. Hearsay 기본 rule: 정의 + inadmissible
>   + analysis (hearsay에 해당한다)
> 3. However, [business record] exception + rule
>   + analysis

2013Feb Trusts and Future Interests

1(a). Settlor's amendment of the inter vivos trust is valid, since he has the right to amend the trust.

A power to revoke includes the power to amend.

In this case, the trust instrument expressly specified that the trust was revocable, and the Settlor reserves the right to amend the trust. Thus, the Settlor's amendment of the inter vivos trust is valid.

In sum, Settlor's amendment of the inter vivos trust is valid, since he has the right to amend the trust.

1(b). Settlor's amendment is valid regardless of the failure to have signature to the trust amendment witnessed.

Both trust instrument and amendment to a trust instrument is no needed to follow the formalities requirements of the will to be executed. The only requirement of the execution of an inter vivos trust is intent, the specification of beneficiaries, and the designation of a trustee.

Here, the amendment meets the requirements and the Settlor's unwitnessed signature does not make the amendment invalid.

In sum, Settlor's amendment is valid regardless of the failure to have signature to the trust amendment witnessed.

2. The provisions of the amended trust apply to Settlor's probate assets under UPC, while they do not apply to the assets in common law.

Under UPC, pour-over provision is valid when: (1) trust is in writing; (2) trust is identified in the will; and (3) the trust must exist before or when or even after the execution of the will. When the trust is amended after testator's will was executed, the amendment applies to the assets passing to the trust from the will.

First, the trust is in writing. Second, Settlor executed a will leaving her entire estate to Bank to hold in accordance with the terms of the trust. Third, the will which was created immediately after creating the trust. Thus, the pour−over provision is valid. and the amended trust will apply to the trust assets.

In common law, pour−over provision is valid when: (1) testator intended to incorporate, (2) document exists when or before the execution of the will, and (3) the document is substantially identified in the will. However, even if the provision is valid, the trust amendment does not apply to the probate assets and the original trust applies.

Here, the fact that Settlor signed the amendment shows that the first requirement is satisfied. The trust exists before the execution of the will. The provision in the will specified "the terms of the trust." Thus, pour−over provision is valid. However, the trust assets shall be distributed following the original terms of the trust.

In sum, the provisions of the amended trust apply to Settlor's probate assets under UPC, while they do not apply to the assets in common law.

3. The trust assets should go to University under UPC, while the trust assets should be distributed following the original terms of the trust in common law.

Under UPC, the trust assets should go to University. However, in common law, all trust assets should be distributed following the original terms of the trust even if the amendment was valid.

In sum, the trust assets should go to University under UPC, while the trust assets should be distributed following the original terms of the trust in common law.

4. Trust assets should be distributed Settlor's then−living great−grandchildren at the time to be vested since the provisions in the original trust do not violate the rule against perpetuities (RAP).

Under the common law RAP, no interest is valid, unless it must vest, if at all, within 21 years of one or more lives in being at the time of its creation.

Because the original trust instrument is revocable, the period began to run from the date of Settlor's death. Under the RAP, Settlor's trust is valid. At the time of Settlor's death, there was one granddaughter. Settlor cannot have more children after her death, and the only income beneficiary of the trust is Settlor's surviving granddaughter. This granddaughter is the only person who can produce great—grandchildren. Thus, all great—grandchildren must be born during granddaughter's lifetime, which is the life being for RAP purpose. Grandchild is vested at Settlor's death and great—grandchildren is vested at granddaughter's death. Thus, there is no need time beyond 21 years and the trust instrument is valid under the RAP.

In sum, trust assets should be distributed Settlor's then—living great—grandchildren at the time to be vested since the provisions in the original trust do not violate the rule against perpetuities (RAP).

해설

난이도: 4번 문제: 상
         그 외 문제: 중

핵심 단어 및 논점

- power to revoke
- power to amend
- inter vivos trust
- validity of trust amendment
- pour−over provision (amendment)
- rule against perpetuities (RAP)

본 기출은 pour−over provisions에 관한 논점들이 작은 문제들로 나누어져 출제된 바, 각 문제가 어떤 논점에 중점을 두고 있는지 파악하는 것이 가장 중요하다.

1번 문제
논점: Pour−over provisions 중 power to revoke/amend

2번 문제
논점: Pour−over provisions 중 validity of pour−over provision과 Amendment of provision

3번 문제
논점: 1번 문제와 2번 문제를 종합적으로 판단하여 최종적으로 trust assets가 어떻게 분배되는지 판단

4번 문제

답안요령

> 1. RAP 기본 rule
> 2. RAP시기 계산 기준 (revocable/irrevocable trust)
> 3. Life in being 파악하기
> 4. 해당 life in being이 사망 후 21년 이내에 future interest가 be vested되는지 확인(Be vested되는 경우 해당 양도는 유효하다).

1. The court should not grant the motion to dismiss for lack of subject-matter jurisdiction, since the court has diversity jurisdiction in this case.

The district courts have original jurisdiction when there is complete diversity of citizenship between the parties and the amount in controversy exceeds $75,000.

As to the corporations' citizenship, the citizenship can be dual. A corporation is a citizen of the state where the corporation has been incorporated and it has principal place of business. The principal place of business is the corporation's nerve center where the corporation maintains its headquarters. Here, the food distributor is a State C corporation and its corporate headquarters are in State B. Its top corporate officers have their offices and staff in State B and its decisions are made there. Thus, the citizenship of the distributor is in State B and State B.

State citizenship for individual U.S. citizens is determined by their domicile, the home where the individual intends to return. To change the domicile, the individual should physically present in the new state and have intent to remain in the state. Here, the woman was domiciled in State A, but there are several facts that show she intended to move to State B. She purchased a farmhouse in State B and moved many of her personal belongings to the farmhouse. She is working and living in State B and pays income taxes in State B. However, it is unclear that she intended to remain in State B, since she had not completely cut her ties with State A. She still has personal relationship in State A and refers to the city in State A as home. It is unclear but she intended to remain in State B, since she still remained her social life in State A and therefore she is domiciled in State A.

As to the amount in controversy, the amounts must be based on plaintiff's good-faith allegations without a legal certainty that the plaintiff cannot recover the amount alleged. Here, the woman seeks $400,000 which exceeds $75,000 and there is no fact showing the woman's bad faith. Thus, the amount in controversy requirement was satisfied.

In sum, the court should not grant the motion to dismiss for lack of subject—matter jurisdiction, since the court has diversity jurisdiction in this case.

2. The court should not grant the motion to dismiss for improper venue, since State A could assert personal jurisdiction over the distributor at the commencement of the action.

When a federal court has diversity jurisdiction, venue is proper in a judicial district where: (1) any defendant resides if all defendants are residents of the forum state, (2) a substantial part of the events which is the basis of the claim occurred, or (3) (if none of the above apply,) any defendant is subject to the court's personal jurisdiction.

A corporation resides where it is subject to personal jurisdiction when the action is commenced. Under the Due Process Clause of the Fourteenth Amendment, a state court can have personal jurisdiction over a nonresident defendant who established minimum contacts with the state. The nature of the contacts depends on the defendant's contacts with the forum state. Here, the distributor's food processing, warehousing, and distribution facilities are all located in State A, and it is a continuous and systematic contacts with State A for general jurisdiction.

Even though there are defendant's minimum contacts with the state, the exercise of personal jurisdiction over the nonresident may offend due process if it is unfair. The defendant has the burden of proof to show that the fairness considerations outweigh the existence of minimum contacts. There are many factors to be considered: the burden on the defendant, the plaintiff's interest, the state's interest, and the interests of the interstate judicial system. Here, the distributor's burden to defend in State A would be reduced with the modern transportation. Additionally, even though the woman lives in State B for most of the year, the State A federal court is located close to her home in the city and she maintains an active social life there. Many evidences or witnesses could be in State B, but the fact alone is not enough to defeat State A's jurisdiction over the case. Thus, State A has personal jurisdiction over the distributor at the commencement of the action, and therefore the District of State A is a proper venue.

In sum, the court should not grant the motion to dismiss for improper venue, since State A could assert personal jurisdiction over the distributor at the commencement of the action.

해설

핵심 단어 및 논점

- complete diversity of citizenship (DCJ)
- corporation's citizenship
- individual's citizenship
- venue
- personal jurisdiction (PJ)
- long-arm statutes

2번 문제

답안요령

1. (Federal PJ = state)
2. Defendant = nonresident (long-arm & due process)
3. DP (minimum contact & notice)
4. "Minimum contact"
5. Analysis (stream of commerce theory)
6. Fairness

1. The telephone's company employee's acts were not outside the scope of his employment, since his motive was to help the company.

Under the doctrine of vicarious liability, employers are liable for the actions of an employee when the employee is acting within the scope of his employment. An employee was acting within the scope of his employment if: (1) the act is of kind that the employee is employed to perform, (2) it occurs substantially within the authorized time and space limits, and (3) it is motivated to serve the employer.

Here, the employee had responsibilities to cable damages calls, assessing damage, and reporting back to the telephone company so that a repair unit could be dispatched. Letting the foreman to lift the cable off the highway was to serve the employer (the telephone company).

In sum, even if the employee's act was not expressly authorized, it was not outside of the scope of his employment.

2. Under an apparent authority theory, the telephone company could be liable to the foreman.

A principal can be liable for torts by its agents when: (1) conditions of vicarious liability are satisfied, (2) the principal was negligent or reckless in the selection of the agent, (3) the principal has a special relationship with the injured person to protect the person from harm caused by the agent, or (4) the agent had apparent authority.

Apparent authority arises when (1) a third party reasonably believes that the actor is authorized, (2) that belief is from the principal's manifestation, and (3) the third party has no notice.

Here, the telephone company made manifestations to the foreman about the employee's authority when it sent its employee to the job site in a company vehicle. The foreman would have a basis to believe that the employee was acting on behalf of the company, and he raised the cable as the employee directed him.

In conclusion, under an apparent authority theory, the telephone company could be liable to the foreman.

3. The employee's act was the proximate cause of the foreman's injuries.

In a negligence action, a defendant is liable only if his action was the actual and proximate cause of the plaintiff's injury. Intervening actors that are difficult to be anticipated may break the chain of causation and a court conclude that the defendant's acts are not proximate cause of the plaintiff's injuries. Foreseeability and the degree of dependence on the defendant's negligence are considered to decide whether intervening acts break the chain of causation.

Here, a bus hit the cable and it caused the cable to strike an oncoming car. The oncoming car hit a truck and the foreman was injured. All these accidents are caused by the employee's negligent and were foreseeable. Although the foreman's injuries would not normally anticipate from the fall of a cable, the foreman was within the zone of foreseeable risk.

In sum, the employee's act were the proximate cause of the foreman's injuries.

해설

난이도: 하

핵심 단어 및 논점

- vicarious liability
- doctrine of respondeat superior
- apparent authority theory
- negligence
- proximate causation

<u>1(a). The father or the agency cannot obtain an order enjoining the mother from making contributions, because it does not endanger the daughter's well−being.</u>

Under the common law, a married woman could not own property. Under a statute enacted by the Congress, the wife has full rights to her own earnings. However, based on the mutual support obligation, a creditor sues the spouse of the purchaser, when the creditor provided necessaries to a husband or wife. This rule is applicable only when a creditor already provided goods or services.

Here, the contributions from mother's future paychecks to the religious group are future spending. Thus, there is no mutual support obligation to the mother. The mother has full right to use her own earnings.

Additionally, a state child welfare agency may treat a family decision only when the decision at issue endangers the child's well−being. Here, the mother's decision to donate a portion of her earnings to the religious group does not endanger her daughter.

In sum, the father or the agency cannot obtain an order enjoining the mother from kaing contributions.

<u>1(b). The father or the agency cannot obtain an order requiring the mother to take the daughter to skating lessons, since it is intact family issue.</u>

Generally, American courts do not treat disputes of intact families' private matters, unless disputes are incident to break home.

Here, all family members continued to live together and they are intact family. The issue regarding whether to take the daughter to staking lessons is private matters. It is not incident to break home.

In conclusion, the father or the agency cannot obtain an order requiring the mother to take the daughter to skating lessons, since it is intact family issue.

1(c). The father or the agency can obtain an order to cooperate in giving the daughter her prescribed medications.

Although courts will not treat disputes of intact families' private matters, the state makes an overruling a parental decision and orders appropriate services, whenever the parental decisions endanger the child. The free exercise claim does not make different claim. This is because the power of the parent is subject to limitation, if parental decisions will endanger the child's well—being.

Here, the mother said she wants to stop giving their daughter her prescribed asthma medications. The daughter has severe asthma, and the daughter's physician has said that regular medication use is the only way to prevent asthma attacks, which can be life—threatening. Thus, the mother's decision endangers the health of daughter.

In sum, the father or the agency can obtain an order to cooperate in giving the daughter her prescribed medications.

2. A court would deny the mother's custody and permit the father the custody, because mother's religious decision endangers daughter's well—being.

A child custody contest between parents is decided on the basis of the child's best interests. The court considers various factors, including parent's religion. Under the Establishment Clause, a court should not consider parent's religion, but should consider when parent's religion endangers the child's well—being.

Here, the failure to take asthma medication is life—threatening and it endangers the child's well—being. Daughter is only seven years old and needs parent's good custody.

In sum, a court would deny the mother's custody and permit the father the custody.

해설

난이도: 하

핵심 단어 및 논점

- child custody order
- best interest of child (best interest test)
- religion
- Establishment Clause

1. The caller's statement is admissible, since it falls within the hearsay exception, present sense impressions, and excited utterance.

Hearsay is out−of−court statement to prove the truth of matter asserted. However, there are hearsay exception for present sense impressions and excited−utterance exception. Present sense impressions exception exists when there is a statement describing an event or condition made while or immediately after the declaration after the declarant perceived it. Excited utterance is a statement relating to a startling event or condition, made while the declarant was under the stress or excitement that it causes.

In this case, the caller's statement is hearsay, if it is to prove the truth the caller stated to police (her sister's boyfriend was out of control, he threw a broken beer bottle at her sister, and her sister was bleeding). However, it is present sense impressions, since the caller made the statement, perceiving the accident. It also fits excited utterance exception, since the accident is enough stressful and the caller was stating to police under the stress.

In sum, the caller's statement is admissible as hearsay exceptions.

2. The admission of the caller's statement did not violate the boyfriend's right, since it is not testimonial.

Confrontation Clause of the Sixth Amendment gives defendants the right to confront witnesses against them. The right is applicable, if: (1) the statement was testimonial, (2) the declarant is unavailable to testify at trial, and (3) the defendant has not had an opportunity to cross−examine the witness before trial. When witnesses make statements with the primary purpose to assist police to meet an ongoing emergency, these are not testimonial.

Here, the defendant had no opportunity to cross−examine the caller, since the caller did not appear at trial. Additionally, the statement is nontestimonial. The caller telephoned the police for assistance during the boyfriend's assaulting. The sister was bleeding and the boyfriend was out of control. It is likely for the court to conclude that the caller's statement is to make the police to meet an ongoing emergency.

In sum, the caller's statement is admissible, since it is nontestimonial.

3. The sister's statement is admissible, since it falls within the excited utterance exception.

The sister's statement is hearsay, if it was used to prove whether the boyfriend threw a bottle at her. However, excited utterance is a statement relating to a startling event or condition, made while the declarant was under the stress or excitement that it causes.

Here, sister was in a highly agitated and emotional state, which means that the statement was made under the stress.

In sum, the sister's statement is admissible.

4. Admission of the officer's testimony violates the boyfriend's constitutional rights, since it is testimonial.

Confrontation Clause of the Sixth Amendment gives defendants the right to confront witnesses against them. The right is applicable, if: (1) the statement was testimonial, (2) the declarant is unavailable to testify at trial, and (3) the defendant has not had an opportunity to cross−examine the witness before trial. When witnesses make statements with the primary purpose to assist police to meet an ongoing emergency, these are not testimonial.

First of all, the declarant, sister was unavailable to testify at trial and the defendant had no opportunity to cross−examine her before trial. Additionally, the police officer found the boyfriend and let him seat in the patrol car and locked the door from the outside so that the boyfriend would stay in the car while the officer spoke to the sister. There were no emergency circumstances, and the sister's statement was merely describing past accident. It is testimonial. Thus, the officer's testimony violated the Confrontation Clause.

However, if statements were used for a non−truth purpose (to prove the caller's or sister's state of mind), it would not be barred by the Confrontation Clause.

해설

난이도: 하

핵심 단어 및 논점

- hearsay exception
  - present sense impression
  - excited utterance exception
- Confrontation Clause
- testimonial

1번, 3번 문제

답안요령

> 1. Relevance★
>   + analysis
> 2. Hearsay 기본 rule: 정의 + inadmissible
>   + analysis (hearsay에 해당한다)
> 3. However, [business record] exception + rule
>   + analysis

2번, 4번 문제

답안요령

> 1. Confrontation Clause
> 2. Requirements
> 3. "Testimonial"
> 4. "Primary purpose"
> 5. Analysis

1. Alice and Carla do not have any legal basis to object to Bob's co−ownership, because of the opt−out provision.

An LLC is a business association that combines corporations and partnerships features. Like general partnerships, LLCs provide members flexibility for decision making and each member has fiduciary duties, duty to care and duty to loyalty, to each other. However, the members can agree to restrict or limit the duty of loyalty, with the opt−out provision in the operating agreement. In most states that permit opt−outs of the duty of loyalty. If it is not manifestly unreasonable, the operating agreement may restrict or eliminate the duty to refrain from competing with the company before the dissolution of the company.

Here, Alice, Bob and Carla have a duty of care and duty of loyalty each other. ABC is building, owning, and running a 100−room luxury hotel in the hometown. Metro Inn, co−owned by Bob is very similar with the ABC hotel project and Metro Inn is competitive with ABC. Bob's co−ownership of the Metro Inn is a breach of loyalty, since it is competing with the company. However, the ABC's Operating Agreement contains opt−out provision. The provision identifies activities (managing, owning, having interest competitive with ABC) and it is not unreasonable. Thus, the opt−out provision is valid provision.

In sum, Alice and Carla do not have any legal basis to object to Bob's co−ownership, because of the opt−out provision.

2(a). Alice, Bob, and Carla are personally liable to the designer, since the winding up process was improper.

Like corporations, LLC's investors (members) have limited liability for company's debts. This rule is not applicable, when: (1) the proper procedure for dissolution and winding up has not been followed or (2) a court decides to pierce the LLC veil. After dissolution, as the winding process, the LLC must provide notice of the dissolution to creditors.

Here, Alice and Carla sold all ABC's property and assets without responding to the designer. There was no notice of the dissolution to creditors. Thus, the winding process did not follow the proper procedure.

When the procedures were not followed and the LLC's asserts were distributed to the members, then a creditor's claim against the LLC may be executed against each member to the extent of the member's proportionate share of the claim or to the extent of the assets of the LLC distributed to the member in liquidation, whichever is less.

In sum, the designer can recover proportionately from Alice, Bob, and Carla personally to the extent of the amount that each member received during the winding up process.

2(b). Alice, Bob, and Carla are jointly and severally liable for the designer under the piercing the LLC veil theory.

Piercing the veil is used to prevent members from hiding behind the veil of limited liability when members improperly used the LLC form. To pierce the veil, it needs to analyze whether members have treated the LLC as a separate entity or whether it has become the alter ego of the members.

Courts usually consider whether the dominant shareholder siphoned corporate funds under the alter ego doctrine.

In this case, the designer would suggest that three members improperly distributed to themselves the proceeds of the asset sale and member disregard the economic separateness of firm. Additionally, court would find that entity finance and members' finance were not separate, since Alice paid the concrete suppliers bill from her own personal funds and then obtain reimbursement from ABC. The designer would argue that altering the financial statements is fraud and it is justifiable to pierce the LLC veil.

However, three members could argue that the failure of an LLC to observe any formalities relating to management of its activities is not a proper basis for personal liability on members for company's liability. Additionally, using Acme's personal funds had no harm to the designer and it actually had a positive effect. However, it does not make the improper distribution process during the winding up.

In sum, Alice, Bob, and Carla are jointly and severally liable for the designer.

해설

난이도: 하

핵심 단어 및 논점

- limited liability company (LLC)
- opt-out provision
- dissolution
- piercing the veil rule (LLC)
- alter ego doctrine

1. The manufacturer and the chef entered into an agreement for ten carving knives.

A contract for the sale of goods is governed by UCC2. Under UCC2, a contract can be formed in any manner sufficient to show agreement.

Here, the carving knife is "good" and the agreement is governed by UCC2. The chef stated he will send a check and the manufacturer stated that he will ship the 10 knives to chef's restaurant in a few weeks. These statements are sufficient to show agreement.

In sum, the manufacturer and the chef entered into an agreement for ten carving knives.

2. The contract for six knives satisfies SOF requirements under the document on May 15.

Under the Statute of Frauds (SOF), a contract for the sale of goods for $500 or more is enforceable against a party only when it is written and signed by the party against whom enforcement is sought.

Here, the contract is for 10 knives and each knife is for $100 each. The contract price is $1,000 and it should be written and signed. On May 15, the manufacturer sent six knives and a document on his letterhead. The document is writing. It states "our agreement" and it clearly shows that a contract for sale has been made. The term "signed" is a broad than normal term of "signature." In some cases, a billhead or letter head constitutes a signed writing when there is intent to accept the writing. Here, the letter on May 15 was on the manufacturer's letterhead and it would constitute a signed document, depending on whether it was with intent to accept the writing.

The contract is not enforceable beyond the quantity of goods shown in such writing. Here, the writing shows only 6 knives. Thus, under the writing, the quantity of the contract is 6 knives, rather than 10 knives as their oral agreement.

In sum, the contract for six knives satisfy SOF requirements under the document on May 15.

3. Only 6 knives are enforceable against the manufacturer, since there are no exceptions for SOF that can be applied in this case.

There are some SOF exceptions, including: (1) when the goods are accepted and payment has been made for it, (2) when the goods are specially manufactured, (3) when a document constitutes confirmation memo, or (4) when the party against whom enforcement admits in pleating or testimony.

Regarding the first exception, the chef sent the manufacturer a check for $600, which is the amount for six knives, and accepted them. Thus, the remaining four is not enforceable.

Regarding the second exception, there is no fact showing that the knives are especially manufactured.

Regarding the confirmation memo, when a contract is between merchants and the party seeking enforcement of the contract has sent the other party a signed confirmation of the contract. Merchants are who have knowledge or skills to the goods of the transaction. The confirmation memo should be signed by the party seeking enforcement of the contract.

Here, both the chef and the manufacturer are merchants. The chef sent the manufacturer an unsigned note to the manufacturer, stating "requesting the remaining four knives." It confirms that the contract was for 10 knives. However, the note was unsigned by the chef and handwritten note is not sufficient to satisfy signature requirement. Thus, it does not constitute a confirmation memo.

Regarding the last exception for SOF, there is no pleading and testimony of the manufacturer that admits contract for 10 knives.

In sum, only 6 knives are enforceable against the manufacturer, since there are no exceptions for SOF that can be applied in this case.

해설

난이도: 중

핵심 단어 및 논점

- formation of contract (UCC2)
- Statute of Frauds (SOF)
- confirmation memo (merchant's firm offer)

1. The man is likely to prevail against the builder to recover the $80,000, because of the implied warranty against latent defects.

In modern, a home builder makes implied warranties against the latent defects. There are various terms of the warranty, such as an implied warranty against latent defects, an implied warranty of merchantability, an implied warranty of habitability. This rule is similar with the UCC2 implied warranty of merchantability. In most states, the buyer is not required to prove that the house would have been uninhabitable. It is enough that the defect is major.

Here, water seeped into the basement of the house during a major storm, causing substantial damage. Thus, the buyer can raise an action against the woman for losses caused by the defective concrete.

Regarding warranty, there are different approaches. In some jurisdictions, the implied warranty against the latent defects extends to remote grantee, when the grantee is in private with the original owner. In some other jurisdictions, courts do not require the privity in contracts.

Here, the man purchased the house from the woman, and he had no privity in contracts with the builder, the original seller.

In sum, the man is likely to prevail against the builder to recover the $80,000, because of the implied warranty against latent defects.

2. The man is not personally liable for the outstanding balance on the mortgage note in most jurisdictions.

Because the seller's mortgage obligation was recorded, the buyer took the house subject to the mortgage, and the bank's interest had priority over the buyer's. Because the bank has priority, it can foreclose when the mortgage is in default. However, the recording of a mortgage does not automatically make the man personally liable for the mortgagor's obligations.

In majority jurisdictions, if a remote grantee takes subject to a mortgage but the grantee did not assume the mortgage, the remote grantee is not personally liable on the debt. The remote grantee is personally liable only when he expressly assumes a mortgage. In the minority of jurisdictions, a remote grantee is deemed as he impliedly assumed when a remote grantee did not expressly assume a mortgage, but the remote grantee paid the seller only the difference between the fair value of the house and the outstanding balance on the mortgage obligation.

Under the majority approach, the man did not expressly assume the mortgage. Thus, the man is not personally liable on the mortgage. Under the minority approach, the mortgage was recorded and the man paid only $160,000, which is the amount less than the worth of the house, $360,000. Additionally, the man immediately began to make the woman's monthly mortgage payments to the bank after the closing. Thus, the man would be deemed as he impliedly assumed the mortgage and is personally liable to it.

In sum, the man is not personally liable for the outstanding balance on the mortgage note in most jurisdictions.

3. The man will not be able to recover damages from the woman, because she gave him a quitclaim deed.

The buyer can raise an action against the seller for the breach of covenants against encumbrances, only when the seller warranted it. However, a quitclaim deed contains no warranties of title.

Here, the woman sold the house to the man with a quitclaim deed. Although there was woman's mortgage obligation that she made no reference to him, a quitclaim deed contains no warranties of damages from encumbrance, the mortgage here. Additionally, the bank has priority over the man, because it recorded the mortgage before the man purchased the house. Thus, the man has no cause of action against the woman.

In sum, the man will not be able to recover damages from the woman, because she gave him a quitclaim deed.

해설

난이도: 하

핵심 단어 및 논점

- implied warranty of merchantability
- remote grantee
- mortgage
- priority
- recording
- covenants against encumbrances (covenants of title)
- quitclaim deed

1(a). Mary is a beneficiary of John's will, since the premarital agreement does not have effect on the John's bequest to his spouse.

Even if a premarital agreement waives rights to a share of each other's assets upon death or divorce, either spouse can make a subsequent gifts or bequests to the other spouse. Such a premarital agreement can be applied only to involuntary bequests or gifts.

Here, John executed a valid will after making a premarital agreement, stating that he leaves his entire estate to his wife, Mary. It was made voluntarily, and it is a valid bequest.

In sum, Mary is a beneficiary of John's will, since the premarital agreement does not have effect on the John's bequest to his spouse.

1(b). Mary is entitled to her share under John's will, since the divorce proceeding is pending.

A bequest may be revoked by operation of law when there is a change in circumstance that makes it unlikely the testator would have wanted a beneficiary to take under the will. If the decedent is divorced after the execution of the will, a bequest to the decedent's former spouse is revoked by operation of law. However, revocation by operation of law does not occur when a divorce proceeding is pending.

Here, Jon and Mary's divorce decree was entered one month ago. When John was killed in a car accident, the divorce proceeding was pending. Thus, revocation by operation of law is not occurred.

In sum, Mary is entitled to her share under John's will, since the divorce proceeding is pending.

1(c). Whether Son is entitled to the share of John's estate depends on the state's adopting rule.

Under UPC, an adoption typically severs the parent—child relationship between the child and his biological parents. In the majority of jurisdictions, nonmarital child is entitled to a share of biological parent only if the biological parent intended to include an adopted—out child. In a few states, the parent—child relationship does not severe when the child is adopted by a relative of a biological parent.

Here, it is the issue how to interpret the term "my children" in John's will. Under UPC, John's nonmarital child was adopted by his Aunt and the adoption severs the parent—child relationship. Thus, Son is not included in the John's children and is not entitled to the share. In a few states, Son is entitled to the share. The evidence regarding John's intent is not conclusive. John gave Son up for adoption to Aunt, and after the death of Aunt he brought Son to his home. John admitted to Mary that Son is his son. However, there is no evidence that John is attempting to formalize his relationship with Son. If the court finds that John intended to include Son, Son is entitled to the share. If the court finds that John does not intend to Son, Son is not entitled to the share.

In sum, whether Son is entitled to the share of John's estate depends on the state's adopting rule.

2. Mary should be appointed as the personal representative.

Personal representative has priority to receive letters testamentary from the court overseeing the administration of the estate. Commonly, personal representative is appointed in a testator's will.

Where the will is silent regarding the appointment of the personal representative, typically, the decedent's surviving spouse is the individual with the first priority. If testator did not appoint the personal representative in the will, the court will appoint a qualified person following the governing statute. A surviving spouse has first priority only if the spouse is a devisee of the decedent. Even if the spouse is not a devisee, she would still be entitled to be appointed because decedent's devisees are minor.

Here, John did not specify the personal representative in his will. Mary is a surviving spouse and she has a share in the will. Thus, Mary is qualified as a personal representative. Even if she would not be a devisee, she would still be personal representative because Son is a minor.

In sum, Mary should be appointed as the personal representative.

해설

난이도: 하

핵심 단어 및 논점

- premarital agreement
- divorce (revocation)
- adoption
- personal representative

1. The city ordinance is not an unconstitutional taking, since it is a regulatory taking satisfying the balancing test.

There are two types of taking: physical and regulatory taking. Regulatory taking (non−physical taking) is recognized when: (1) the government denies all economic value of the private property (total regulatory taking), (2) several factors are considered and regulatory taking is recognized (Penn Central taking), (3) when an exaction was imposed by a government in exchange for a discretionary benefit conferred by the government (land−use exaction), or (4) a permanent physical occupation of property is authorized by the government, (Loretto taking).

Here, total regulatory taking is not recognized since there is minimum economic impact and not all economic value is denied. Land−use exaction is also not recognized since there is no fact indicating that the government imposes an exaction.

For Penn Central taking, balancing test must be satisfied: (1) there is the economic impact of the regulation on the claimant, (2) the owner's primary expectation for use of the property is interfered by the ordinance, and (3) the regulation is for public use.

In this case, first, there is minimum economic impact, since the study estimated cost $1,000 and the study estimated that owner can get increased earnings. Additionally, the ordinance is not interfering with the operation of the business, the owner can earn a reasonable return. Second, the ordinance does not interfere the operation of the restaurant and it does not prevent the restaurant from expanding. Third, the ordinance is to enhance public safety. The ordinance is clearly a valid exercise of the police power, and therefore it satisfies public use requirement.

In sum, the city ordinance is not an unconstitutional taking.

2. The city's requirement is an unconstitutional taking, since the city did not make efforts to quantify its findings.

The exaction is not a taking if: (1) there is an essential nexus between the public need that the proposed development contributes and the permit condition and (2) the government makes some individualized determination that the required dedication is roughly proportional both in nature and extent to the impact of the proposed development.

First, the city requested easement and it has essential nexus between the city's interest in crime prevention and public safety. Increased business traffic at the restaurant may attract additional crimes to the area and installing of surveillance equipment would be essential for the additional crimes. Second, the government must make some effort to quantify its findings in support of the dedication beyond the conclusive statement. Here, the city simply estimated that the increased patronage "would result" from the increased capacity of the restaurant and it "might attract" additional crime, and the installing "might alleviate" this increased crime. There was no state's effort to quantify the findings. Thus, the exaction is an uncompensated taking.

In sum, the city's requirement is an unconstitutional taking, since the city did not make efforts to quantify its findings.

해설

난이도: 하

핵심 단어 및 논점

- Taking Clause (Fifth Amendment)
- regulatory taking
- total regulatory taking
- Penn Central taking
- land-use exaction
- exaction

1번 문제

본 답안은 NCBE 해설과 다소 차이가 있다. NCBE 해설은 taking을 크게 physical taking과 regulatory taking으로 구분하고, regulatory taking 판단의 기준으로 Penn Central taking의 세 요건을 서술하였다. 그러나 본 답안은 taking을 physical taking과 regulatory taking으로 우선 구분하고, regulatory taking의 네 유형(total regulatory taking, Penn Central taking, land-use exaction, Loretto taking)을 모두 서술하였다. NCBE 해설은 total regulatory taking은 법원에서 잘 인정하지 않는 유형이고 본 사안에서 exaction이 존재하지 않으므로, Penn Central taking 유형을 기준으로 판단한 것으로 보인다. 그러나 최근 기출문제(2020Sep)는 regulatory taking의 각 유형을 구체적으로 구분하도록 요구하고 있어, 주어진 사안이 regulatory taking의 네 유형 중 어떤 유형에 해당하는지 명확히 서술해주는 것이 중요하다 생각된다.

> **답안요령**
>
> 1. Taking Clause
> 2. Regulatory taking 유형(×4)
> 3. Analysis + 결론

TIP1 Regulatory taking에 대해 논하기 전, Taking Clause에 대한 기본적인 설명하는 것이 고득점 포인트다.

TIP2 2번: 세 유형 중 "Penn Central" taking의 경우, 세 개의 고려사항을 구분하여 각각 analysis하는 것이 고득점 포인트다. Land-use exaction의 경우, exaction이 taking으로 인정되지 않는 예외 rules를 고려하는 것 또한 고득점 포인트다. "Loretto" taking의 경우, 정부의 목적(public interest)과는 무관하다는 점을 명시하는 것이 고득점 포인트다.

2번 문제

본 문제는 easement, 즉 exaction이 taking인지 그 여부를 판단하는 문제로서, regulatory taking 중 land-use exaction에 초점을 둔 문제이다. 앞서 1번 문제에서 regulatory taking에 대한 전반적인 내용을 서술하였으므로, 2번에서는 exaction이 taking으로 인정되지 않는 예외 rules에 대해 서술한다.

__1. Cash dividends and rents are allocable to income. Sales proceeds and stock dividends are allocable to principal. These are distributed to the son prior to the receipt of the son's letter.__

Receipts during the administration of a trust are allocable either to income or to principal. Under UPAIA, rents and cash dividends received are allocable to income and are distributable to the income beneficiary of the trust. Sales proceeds and dividends are allocable to principal.

In this case, Son is the sole beneficiary until the trustee received the son's letter stating renouncement. Thus, rents and cash dividends would be distributed to Son. Sales proceeds and dividends would be allocated to principal and hold by trustee. Thus, trustee would distribute it to the ultimate remaindermen of the trust.

In sum, cash dividends and rents are allocable to income. Sales proceeds and stock dividends are allocable to principal. These are distributed to the son prior to the receipt of the son's letter.

__2(a) Under the common law, the distribution to the grandchildren should be delayed until Son dies regardless of the Son's disclaimant, since there is a survivorship contingency. If there are grandchildren survives Son they will be entitled to the trust principal, while testator's heirs living at the son's death will be entitled to the trust principal if there are no grandchildren survives Son.__

Under the rule of convenience, the class closes when at least one member of the class is entitled to possession of his or her share of the remainder. When a beneficiary timely disclaims an interest in a trust, it is deemed that he predeceased the testator.

In this case, if Son disclaimed adequately following the state statute, he would be treated as he predeceased the testator. It would close the class of the remaindermen, testator's grandchildren, and the daughter's child would be entitled to the trust principal. However, Son disclaimed after nine months of the testator's death and it is not consistent with the state statute.

When the statutory requirement is not applicable, the common law rule is presumably applicable. Under the common law, disclaimers can renounce anytime. Under the common law, if a life estate disclaimed, the remainder interest accelerates and becomes immediately distributable to the remaindermen of the trust only when the remainder is not contingent.

In this case, the will shows survivorship contingency, stating "grandchildren who shall survive the son." Thus, the remaindermen, the distribution to the testator's grandchildren cannot be accelerated and the distribution would occur at the time of the Son's death.

In sum, under the common law, the distribution to the grandchildren should be delayed until Son dies regardless of the Son's disclaimant, since there is a survivorship contingency. If there are grandchildren survives Son they will be entitled to the trust principal, while testator's heirs living at the son's death will be entitled to the trust principal if there are no grandchildren survives Son.

3. Trust principal should be hold by trustee and trustee has three approach to distribute trust income during this period. Each approach has different methods of distribution.

When the trust principal is not immediately distributable, the trustee must hold trust assets until the ultimate remaindermen are ascertained. During this period, trust income could be distributed in three approaches.

In this case, Son failed to make an appropriate disclaimant and remaindermen (grandchildren) have survivorship contingency. Thus, trustee should hold trust principal until the Son dies. During this period, trustee would distribute trust income in three approaches.

First approach is to distribute trust income to testator's heirs. This is because the trust income during this period is intestate. Second approach is for trustee to accumulate and distribute trust income to ultimate remaindermen. This is because the person who is ultimately entitled to trust principal is entitled to the trust income. Third approach is to distribute trust income to would—be remaindermen, daughter's minor child until there is another testator's grandchild is born.

In sum, trust principal should be hold by trustee and trustee has three approach to distribute trust income during this period. Each approach has different methods of distribution.

해설

난이도: 상

핵심 단어 및 논점

- principal and income allocation
- UPAIA
- rule of convenience
- class gift
- disclaimant
  - acceleration (life tenant)
  - survivorship contingency
- trustee hold the trust assets

2014Feb Secured Transactions

1. The bank has a superior claim to the business's equipment.

The security interest is effective and attaches, when: (1) debtor signed a security agreement. (2) debtor has rights in the collateral, and (3) secured party gave money to secured party.

Under the agreement between the owner and Bank, Bank has security interest in the owner's business's present and future equipment. This interest is effective and attaches, because the owner authorized the agreement by signing on it, owner has right in the equipment, and Bank loaned money to the owner.

A security interest is perfected when the security interest attaches and any required additional steps have occurred. Generally, the required additional steps are filing a financial statement or possession of the collateral by the secured party. A financing statement is effective when it contain: (1) the name of the debtor, (2) the name of the secured party, and (3) an indication of the collateral. Here, the bank properly filed a financing statement. The statement indicated the name of the business as the debtor and equipment as the collateral. The fact that the financing statement was filed before the security interest was created does not have impact on the perfection. Even though the business owner had not yet signed the agreement, he authorized the filing of the financing statement. Thus, the bank properly perfected its security interest.

Finance company also has enforceable and attached security interest in the owner's equipment, because it loaned money to the business, the business has rights in the collateral, and the business signed the agreement. The finance company filed a financing statement, and therefore the finance company perfected its security interest in the owner's equipment.

Under the first to file or perfect rule, between two perfected security interests, the security interest that was the earlier to be either perfected or the subject of a filed financing statement has priority. Here, the finance company's security interest was perfected on March 15 before the bank's on March 22. However, the bank's finance statement was filed on March 2 and therefore the bank's security interest has priority.

In conclusion, the bank has a superior claim to the business's equipment.

2. The claims of the bank and the finance company to the business's equipment continue in the item of equipment sold to the competitor.

Generally, a security interest continues after sale of the collateral. However, a buyer in ordinary course of business (BIOCOB), the buyer takes free of perfected security interest which was created by the buyer's seller. BIOCOB is a buyer who (1) buys goods in good faith, (2) without knowledge that the sale violates the rights of another, (3) from a person in the business of selling goods of the kind in the ordinary course of the seller's business.

Here, the competitor bought the business's equipment when both Bank and the finance company perfected their security interest in the equipment. The competitor was not a BIOCOB. Although the competitor purchased the equipment in good faith without knowledge on the security interest, it was the first time the business had ever sold any of its equipment and therefore the business was not in the business of selling goods of the kind. In short, BIOCOB exception is inapplicable here.

In sum, the claims of the bank and the finance company to the business's equipment continue in the item of equipment sold to the competitor.

해설

난이도: 하

핵심 단어 및 논점

- effectiveness of security interest
- perfection
- priority
- first to file or perfect rule
- buyer in ordinary course of business (BIOCOB)

1번 문제

본 기출은 매우 basic한 문제로서, priority를 판단하는 흐름을 연습하기에 좋다.

Priority를 판단하는 로직은 다음과 같다.

Priority 판단 ← Perfection 여부 판단 ← Attach 여부 판단(security interest의 유효성 판단)

2번 문제

> **답안요령**

---

1. Security interest 기본 rule(collateral에 지속된다)★
2. 그러나 [BIOCOB]인 경우 예외 rule 적용
    + analysis
3. Shelter rule★
    + analysis

---

1. The court should order the customer to turn over the engineer's report, since it is not a work product.

A party may obtain discovery about any nonprivileged matter that is relevant to any party's claim or defense. Under the work product rule, a party can refuse to turn over documents that are prepared in anticipation of litigation. The work product needs to be disclosed to an adverse party, only when the adverse party can demonstrate a substantial need for the documents and an inability to obtain substantially equivalent information without undue hardship.

Here, the engineer's report is not a work product. The customer hired a structural engineer to examine the foundation of the house. The hiring was not in preparation of the anticipation of litigation, since it was before the builder filed suit. The customer merely hired engineer for the builder's cooperative attitude.

In sum, the court should order the customer to turn over the engineer's report, since it is not a work product.

2(a). The court should sanction the builder for the destruction, since he anticipated the litigation.

In general, destruction of evidence is improper if the party spoliated evidence when the party knew or should have known that the evidence is relevant to future litigation. It is improper for a party to destroy electronic information relevant to pending litigation, even if the destruction occurs before there is any request or order seeking the information. When a party anticipates litigation, it must suspend its routine document destruction policy and put in place a litigation hold to ensure the preservation of relevant documents.

Here, the customer may obtain discovery and it includes emails or other electrically stored information. The customer requested the engineer to provide copies of all emails concerning construction of the foundation of the house. Even though the builder informed the customer that he destroyed them according to the builder's standard practice of permanently deleting, he is subject to the sanction. This is because he had notice on the future litigation when he destroyed information. He destroyed the emails on August 2, and he directed its attorney to prepare a draft complaint against the customer for nonpayment before August 2. Thus, he anticipated the litigation.

In sum, the court should sanction the builder for the spoliation, since he anticipated the litigation.

2(b). The court may not impose severe sanction to the builder, since his spoliation does not have severe impact on the customer's allegation.

There are wide range of sanctions: the payment of expenses incurred by the other party as a result of the spoliation, an instruction to the jury authorizing it to draw an adverse inference from the spoliation of the evidence, a shifting the burden of proof, or even judgment against the responsible party.

In determining appropriate sanctions for spoliation, courts consider both: (1) the level of fault of the spoliating party and (2) the degree of prejudice the loss of evidence has caused the other party. Many courts impose severe sanctions only when there is evidence of bad faith with an intentional effort to hide information. In other courts, negligence is enough to impose severe sanctions.

First, the evidence was destroyed according to the builder's standard document destruction plan, and there is no fact to show that the builder spoliated emails with bad faith. Second, the loss of the evidence would not substantially obstruct to the customer's allegation. There are other ways to prove that the foundation was not properly constructed. Thus, a court is unlikely to impose severe sanction to the builder and the court requires the builder to reimburse expenses or shifts the burden of proof to the builder. Thus, the court may not impose severe sanction to the builder.

In sum, the court may not impose severe sanction to the builder, since his spoliation does not have severe impact on the customer's allegation.

해설

난이도: 하

핵심 단어 및 논점

- discovery
- work-product doctrine
- destruction of evidence (spoilation)
- anticipated the litigation
- sanctions

1번 문제

답안요령

> 1. General rule
> 2. Work-product doctrine
> 3. 예외
>   + analysis

2번 문제

답안요령

> 1. Range of sanctions
> 2. 고려사항
> 3. Severe sanction 판단기준
> 4. Analysis

TIP 본 답안요령은 sanction에 대한 개괄적인 내용을 작성하는 경우를 기준으로 작성되었으나, 최근 기출문제는 주어진 상황에 맞는 sanctions에 구체적으로 논하도록 요구하고 있어 위 4번 analysis를 자세히 작성하는 것이 중요하다.

2014Feb Criminal Law and Procedure

1. The trial court did not err when it denied the motion to dismiss on double jeopardy grounds, since theft and burglary are not same offenses.

Under the Double Jeopardy Clause of the Fifth Amendment, a defendant should not be prosecuted twice for the same offense. When the elements of the lesser charge are wholly contained in the greater charge, the double jeopardy occurs.

Here, the defendant was charged for both felony theft and burglary. The crime of burglary requires the entry into the building or dwelling with such intent. The crime of theft requires the taking and carrying away of an item of personal property of another with the intent to steal or permanently deprive the owner of possession. "Taking and carrying away" is not required in burglary crime. In short, the theft is not wholly contained in burglary and burglary is also not wholly contained in the theft. Thus, there is no double jeopardy issue here.

In sum, the trial court did not err when it denied the motion to dismiss on double jeopardy grounds, since theft and burglary are not same offenses.

2. The trial court erred in its instruction to the jury on the burglary charge, since it violated the Due Process Clause.

Under the Due Process Clause, prosecutor should prove all elements of the crime beyond a reasonable doubt. The burden of proof cannot be shifted to the defendant by a presumption of element with other elements of the offense. The shifting burden of persuasion with respect to any element of a criminal offense is contrary to the Due Process Clause.

Here, for the burglary charge, the prosecutor should prove entry into a building or dwelling with the specific intent to commit a felony beyond a reasonable doubt. The jury instruction state that jury may presume the intent if the fact that the defendant entered the dwelling without the owners' consent is proved beyond a reasonable doubt.

This instruction creates either a rebuttable presumption or an irrebutable presumption. A reasonable jury could believe that the instruction creates a rebuttable presumption by interpreting the statement as: the jury must find the defendant's intent, unless the defendant provides some evidence to rebut the presumption. Jury instructions that shifting the burden of proof to the defendant are unconstitutional. A reasonable jury could believe that the instruction creates an irrebutable presumption by interpreting the statement as: once the facts trigger the presumption, it is irrebutable. It relieves the prosecution the burden of proof for the intent element, and it violates due process.

In sum, the instruction creating either a rebuttable presumption or an irrebutable presumption violates due process.

3. The trial court erred when it sentenced the defendant to an additional year of incarceration, because the defendant's right to a jury trial was violated.

Under the Sixth Amendment, a defendant has right to a jury trial. When there is any fact, that was not provided in prior conviction and increases the penalty that increases the penalty for a crime beyond prescribed maximum, it must be submitted to a jury, and proved beyond a reasonable doubt. Statutory maximum is the maximum sentence a judge may impose solely on the basis of the facts that were the grounds for the jury verdict or that were provided by defendant. Any fact exceeding the maximum authorized by the facts established by a plea of guilty or a jury verdict must be admitted by the defendant or proved to a jury beyond a reasonable doubt.

Here, theft is a Class D felony if the value of the item taken is between $2,500 and $10,000. The jury found that the diamond value was at least $2,500 and the statutory maximum is three years' incarceration according to the verdict. However, at sentencing hearing, an expert witness testified that the diamond ring was worth between $7,000 and $8,000 which increases the maximum sentence for the theft. The judge imposed one year longer incarceration than the maximum sentence that would otherwise have been allowed without providing the statement of the expert witness to the jury. In short, the judge's finding was by preponderance of the evidence rather than beyond a reasonable doubt. In sum, the defendant's right to a jury trial was violated.

In sum, the trial court erred when it sentenced the defendant to an additional year of incarceration, because the defendant's right to a jury trial was violated.

해설

난이도: 하

핵심 단어 및 논점

- Double Jeopardy Clause
  (Fifth Amendment)
- Due Process Clause
- rebuttable presumption

- irrebutable presumption
- right to a jury trial
  (Sixth Amendment)
- penalty beyond prescribed maximum

1번 문제

답안요령

> 1. Double jeopardy
> 2. Analysis (elements of the charge) + 결론

TIP1 두 범죄의 서로 다른 요소만을 서술해도 충분하며, charged된 죄책의 모든 element를 모두 서술할 필요는 없다.

TIP2 2번: 각 주마다 범죄 구성요건을 다르게 규정하므로, "대부분은 이렇게 정의한다"는 표현을 사용한다.

활용하기 좋은 표현: Most states define [larceny] as ….

2번 문제

답안요령

> 1. DP clause (beyond reasonable doubt)
>   + analysis (charged crime + DP)
> 2. Analysis (jury instructions)★

TIP1 별도의 문제가 출제되지 않는다 하더라도 charged crime의 intent가 specific intent와 general intent 중 어느 것에 해당하는지 서술하는 것이 고득점 포인트다.

TIP2 문제에서 주어진 jury instruction에 대해 analysis하는 경우, rebuttable presumption 및 irrebuttable presumption과 연관지어 서술하는 것이 고득점 포인트다.

1(a). Adam was personally liable on the claim.

There is an apparent authority, when the partner acted in the ordinary course of the partnership business and a third party has no actual knowledge that the member lacks authority. Acts of the partner with an apparent authority create the partnership obligations. Partners of a general partnership are jointly and severally liable for all obligations of the partnership.

Here, Ben made a false representation that a famous movie star had once owned the car. The statement was made in the ordinary course of the partnership, buying and selling antique automobiles. Thus, Ben's wrongful action created partnership obligation and therefore Adam is jointly and severally liable for the collector's claim.

In sum, Adam was personally liable on the claim.

1(b). Diane is not personally liable on the claim, since he was admitted as a partner after the claim.

A partner is not personally liable for any partnership obligation which was created before his admission to the partnership.

Here, Diane was admitted to Empire as a general partner after the collector sued Adam, Ben, and Empire. Even though a general partner is jointly and severally liable for all obligations of partnership, Diane is not liable for the claim. Although Diane is not personally liable, his investment is at risk for the satisfaction of existing partnership debt.

However, the facts that Diane learned of the collector's claim and stated her concern that she might become liable if the claim were reduced to a judgment do not make change on the result. This is because partner can assume liability to third parties by private contractual guarantees or modification of the partnership agreement. Here, there are no facts regarding it.

In sum, Diane is not personally liable on the claim.

2(a). Adam and Ben are jointly and severally liable on the collector's claim.

A general partnership can become a limited liability partnership (LLP) when: (1) the partners approve unanimously by vote and (2) the partnership files a statement of qualification.

Here, a general partnership, Empire was sought to change into LLP. All partners agreed to the change and the partnership filed a statement of qualification. Thus, Empire became an LLP.

Under an entity theory, an LLP is a same entity that existed prior to becoming an LLP. Thus, the obligation on the collector's claim created before the partnership becomes the obligation of the LLP, and limited liability protection is inapplicable in this case. Thus, Adam and Ben are jointly and severally liable on it as partners of a general partnership.

In sum, Adam and Ben are jointly and severally liable.

2(b). No one is personally liable on the driver's estate's claim.

Under the limited liability protection, any obligation which is incurred when a partnership is LLP is obligation of LLP. A partner in a limited liability partnership is not liable for partnership's debts.

Here, the driver's estate's claim was created after the partnership becomes LLP. Thus, the obligation is the obligation of LLP and therefore Adam, Ben, and Diane is not jointly and severally liable for it. Thus, they are under the limited liability protection. If there is evidence that a partner was negligent or acted wrongfully by not telling the driver about the bad front suspension, the partner would be personally liable for the obligation.

In sum, no one is personally liable on the driver's estate's claim.

해설

난이도: 하

핵심 단어 및 논점

- apparent authority (ordinary course of business)
- entity theory
- limited liability protection

1(b)번 문제

논점: New partner and partnership

답안요령

1. Partner가 된 시기에 관해 analysis
2. General rule(prior debt에 대해 책임이 없다.)
   + analysis
3. New partner's contribution★

TIP 　3번: 새로운 partner의 contribution(investment)은 회사채무를 위해 사용될 수 있다는 점을 명시하는 것이 고득점 포인트다.

2(a)번 문제

논점: LLP로 변경되기 '전' 발생한 partnership debt에 대한 partner's 책임

답안요령

1. 이전 회사에서의 partner's liability(무한책임/유한책임)
2. Limited liability protection
3. Analysis(결론)

TIP1 　GP에서 LLP로 변경된 case에서 analysis의 logic은 다음과 같다.
GP에서 partner는 jointly and severally liable하다(personally liable하다). →
Entity theory에 의거하여 partnership debt의 성격은 GP에서 발생한

partnership debt의 성격을 띤다. → 따라서 limited liability protection 적용되지 않는다. → Partner는 해당 partnership debt에 대해 personally liable하다.

TIP2 · 본 문제에서는 LLP로 변경되기 '전' 발생한 partnership debt에 대한 partnership의 책임에 대한 질문 없이 partner의 책임에 대해서만 논하는 바, entity theory에 대한 자세한 설명이 필요하다.

3번 문제

논점: LLP로 변경된 '후' 발생한 partnership debt에 대한 partner's 책임

LLP로 변경된 후 발생한 partnership debt에 대해 partner의 책임유무를 논하라는 문제는 'LLP partnership debt에 대한 partner의 책임유무'를 논하라는 문제이다. 이러한 문제는 두 유형이 있는데, ① LLP로 변경되기 전과 후 발생한 partnership debt의 성격을 비교하는 문제와 ② LLP partnership debt에 대한 partner 책임, 즉 limited liability에 대해 논하는 문제가 그것이다. 따라서 문제의 질문의도를 파악하여 답안을 서술하는 것이 고득점 포인트다. 본 문제는 ①유형에 해당한다.

1. The defective did not violate the suspect's Sixth Amendment right to counsel, since there was no formal judicial proceedings for five burglary commenced.

Under the Sixth Amendment, which applies to the states through the Fourteenth Amendment, the accused have the right to counsel when formal judicial proceedings commenced. Once Sixth Amendment is attached, any attempts to deliberately elicit statement from the accused are barred. The right to counsel under the Sixth Amendment is offense specific, and therefore the right did not guarantee counsel for the unrelated crime.

Here, the suspect's lawyer represents the suspect for aggravated assault charge pending against him. Thus, the suspect's right to counsel is limited only to the assault charge, not to five burglaries. There is no formal judicial proceeding commenced for five burglaries, and therefore the suspect had no Sixth Amendment right to counsel. The fact that the detective did not inform the suspect of the lawyer's presence does not make a different result, since formal judicial proceeding did not commence.

In sum, the defective did not violate the suspect's Sixth Amendment right to counsel.

2. The suspect did not effectively invoke his right to counsel, since his statement was not unambiguous.

A suspect who is subject to in custody interrogation has a right to consult with counsel and to have counsel present during questioning. When a suspect invokes his right to counsel, law enforcement officer must stop all questioning. A suspect must unambiguously invoke his right to counsel which means that a reasonable officer would understand the statement to be a request for counsel.

Here, the suspect said, "I think I want my lawyer here before I talk to you." Hearing this statement, a reasonable officer would understand that the suspect might be invoking the right to counsel. In short, the statement was not unambiguous to invoke the right to counsel. Thus, the detective was not required to stop questioning of the suspect.

In sum, the suspect did not effectively invoke his right to counsel.

3. The suspect's waiver of his Miranda rights was valid, since it was knowing, intelligent, and voluntary.

A valid waiver of Miranda rights must be voluntary, knowing, and intelligent. In other words, the waiver must make a waiver with a full awareness of both the nature of the right being abandoned and the consequences of the decision. When the fact which occurs outside of the presence of a suspect was completely unknown to the suspect, it does not impair the suspect's capacity to understand the consequence of the waiver and to relinquish the constitutional right.

Here, the suspect signed a Miranda waiver from after he received Miranda warnings. Police did not use physical or psychological pressure, because the interview lasted only 45 minutes. Thus, the waiver was voluntary. Additionally, the detective did not inform the suspect of the lawyer's presence, but he informed the suspect his right. The suspect's reply on the Miranda warnings indicates that he understood his right to counsel. The suspect's statement, "I probably should keep my mouth shut, but I'm willing to talk to you for a while," indicates that he understood the result of the waiver. Thus, the waiver of the right to counsel was made knowingly and intelligently.

In sum, the waiver was valid.

해설

난이도: 하

핵심 단어 및 논점

- right to counsel (Sixth Amendment)
- offense specific
- invoke the right

- unambiguously
- waive the right
- knowing, intelligent, voluntary

1. The business's obligation to perform is preexisting duty and the conservatory is not required to pay additional $60,000.

Generally, a promise is enforceable when it is supported by consideration, and there is consideration if it is bargained for in exchange for a return promise or performance. However, under the preexisting duty rule, promise of performance already owed to a promisor is not consideration. Here, the business has a duty to repair the organ under the contract that he already owed to the music conservatory. Thus, the business cannot require additional amounts for the repair under the preexisting duty rule.

There is an exception to the preexisting duty rule: (1) when there is an unanticipated changed circumstance, (2) the change was not anticipated by the parties when the contract is made, and (3) the modification is fair and equitable. Usually, the exception is applicable when there is impracticability.

Here, the conservatory would argue that the business did not encounter such difficulties. The business can perform its obligation without impracticability, since the cash crunch has no effect on performance. Even if the business succeed to demonstrate impracticability, there were no unanticipated changed in circumstances. When the business made the contract, it expected that the contract price is enough to perform its obligation.

In sum, the business's obligation to perform is preexisting duty and the conservatory is not required to pay additional $60,000.

2. The promise to pay extra amounts is enforceable and the conservatory must pay additional $40,000.

A contract for the sale of goods is governed by UCC2. The term "goods" means movable things at the time of making a contract. Here, the contract to buy a new organ if governed by UCC2.

Under UCC 2, an agreement of modifying a contract needs no consideration, but the modification must satisfy the good faith requirement. Good faith means honesty and the following of reasonable commercial standards of fair dealing.

Here, the conservatory agreed to pay the extra amounts based on cash crunch. The cash crunch was unanticipated and the business requires additional money to enable its perform. Thus, the agreement of modification was made in good faith.

In sum, the promise to pay extra amounts is enforceable and the conservatory must pay additional $40,000.

3. The conservatory's agreement to modify the contract may not be wrongful. Thus, the defense of duress is not applicable and the conservatory is required to pay additional price.

Under the both common law and UCC2, parties may raise the defense of duress. A contract is voidable when there was economic duress by threat. The defense is established when (1) there was a threat to the conservatory, (2) the threat was wrongful, (3) the threat induced the manifestation of agreement to the modification, and (4) the threat was sufficiently serious to justify the assent.

Here, the business said "If you don't agree to pay us the extra money, I doubt that we will ever be able to perform either contract." It was a threat to conservatory and it induced the conservatory's agreement to the modification. If the conservatory did not agree with the business's modification, it would lose its prior payment, $325,000. There were no alternatives. However, the business would argue that the threat was not wrongful and it is nothing more than stating its financial difficulties to the conservatory. A mere threat to breach the contract with economic duress is not itself improper.

In sum, the conservatory's agreement to modify the contract may not be wrongful. Thus, the defense of duress is not applicable and the conservatory is required to pay additional price.

해설

난이도: 1번 문제: 상
2번 문제: 상
3번 문제: 하

핵심 단어 및 논점

- consideration
- preexisting duty rule
- modification (UCC2)
- duress (defense of formation of contract)

1번 문제

답안요령

> 1. General rule (modification is enforceable with consideration.)
>   + analysis
> 2. Preexisting rule
> 3. Preexisting rule 예외
>   + analysis

1(a). State A court does not have jurisdiction to modify the child support order.

Regarding a jurisdiction to modify child support award, the personal jurisdiction is not enough. This is because UIFSA governs child support order. Under UIFSA, an issuing state has continuing and exclusive jurisdiction to modify a support order when: (1) the child or any party continues to live in the state and (2) there is any party who does not consent to the jurisdiction of another forum.

Here, the State A has personal jurisdiction over the wife, since she was personally served in State A. However, it is not enough. Under UIFSA, the wife and daughter continue to live in State B, and the wife did not consent to the jurisdiction of another forum.

In sum, State A court does not have jurisdiction to modify the child support order.

1(b). The State A has jurisdiction to modify the marital-residence-sale-proceeds provision.

UIFSA is not applicable to divorce property division issues.

Here, the husband brought the action to adjudicate all domestic relations issues in State A. The petition to modify the property settlement is a domestic relations issue. State A has personal jurisdiction over the wife, since she was personally served in State A.

In sum, State A has jurisdiction to modify the marital-residence-sale-proceeds provision.

2(a). The husband cannot obtain retroactive modification of his child support obligation.

Retroactive modification of child support obligations is completely forbidden.
Thus, the husband cannot obtain retroactive modification of his child support obligation.

2(b). The husband would obtain prospective modification of his child support obligation, unless the state bars modification whenever petitioner voluntarily shifted income.

Modification of future child support order is typically available only when the petitioner can show a substantial change in circumstances. A significant decrease in income is typically treated as a substantial change. However, when a parent wants to modify a child support obligation because he has voluntarily reduced his income, the parent is required to prove many things. Some courts considers petitioner's intentions and permit downward modification if he has acted in good faith. Some courts refuse to modify whenever the income shift was voluntary. Many courts balance the interests of both parent and child under a multi−factor approach.

Here, husband was offered a job and he voluntarily accepted the job. He voluntarily reduced his salary. In the states that refuse to modify whenever the income shift was voluntary, husband's petition would be denied. Under the good faith approach, the husband changed his job because the job has much better promotion opportunities. The husband acted in good faith and therefore he could obtain downward modification. Under a multi−factor approach, the court would consider the impact on the child because of the income loss, the possible duration of the husband's income loss, and the possibility of a promotion.

In sum, husband would obtain prospective modification of his child support obligation.

2(c). The husband could not obtain modification of the marital−residence−sale−proceeds provision.

A property division cannot be modified after a divorce decree has been entered, because a property division award divides assets based on the equities at the time of divorce and it reflects the past. By contrast, support obligation reflects future and it could be modified if there is substantial change in circumstances. Here, the husband is seeking a modification of a property division award which was obtained at the time of divorce.

In sum, the husband could not obtain modification of the marital−residence−sale−proceeds provision

해설

난이도: 하

핵심 단어 및 논점

- child support order
- jurisdiction of child support order
- personal jurisdiction
- modification of child support order
- substantial change in circumstances
- property division order
- modification of property division order

1번 문제

논점: Child support order 중 modification order

State A 법원에서 내린 child support order에 대해 State B 법원이 modify할 수 있는 재판권이 있는가?

```
답안요령

1. UIFSA 적용
   + analysis(결과)
3. PJ와 무관함
   + analysis
```

TIP 생각 route ①

Child support order에 대해 UIFSA가 적용된다. → 두 요건을 모두 충족하므로 original court, 즉 State A 법원이 재판권을 가진다. → State B 법원은 재판권이 없다. → State B 법원이 피고에 대해 personal jurisdiction을 가지나 이것으로는 not enough하다.

생각 route ②

State B 법원은 피고에 대해 personal jurisdiction을 가지나 이것으로는 not enough하다. → Child support order에 대해 UIFSA가 적용된다. → 두 요건이 모두 충족되지 못하였으므로 original court, 즉 State A 법원은 재판권을 가지지 못한다. → State B 법원이 재판권을 가진다.

2(b)번 문제

답안요령

---

1. UIFSA 적용
2. Burden on proof
3. 고려사항
   + analysis
4. Modification of custody order와의 연관성★
   + analysis

TIP1 3번: 배우자의 수입이 감소되어 modification을 신청한 경우 수입감소가 배우자의 '자발적인' 행위였는지 그 여부를 구체적으로 논해야 한다.

TIP2 4번: 본 문제는 modification of child support order를 신청하는 자가 동시에 modification of custody order를 신청하는 경우이므로 양자간 관계를 서술하는 것이 고득점 포인트다.

1. The federal district court must allow the logging party to join the litigation as a party, since it met all three conditions.

Intervention is the process that a nonparty joins the litigation. A person must be permitted to intervene when: (1) the movant claims an interest that is related to the transaction that is the subject of the action, (2) the movant is so situated that outcome of the action may obstruct the movant's protection of its interest as a practical matter, and (3) existing parties do not adequately represent the movant's interest.

First, the USFS accepted the logging company's bid and the logging company is awaiting a logging permit. Thus, the logging company has an interest in subject matter of the litigation, since the nonprofit alleges the USFS cannot issue the logging permit. Second, the outcome of the claim may have impact the logging company's interest. If the USFS loses the lawsuit, the logging company should wait for the preparation of an environmental impact statement, and it delays the company's exercise of its rights. Third, although both the logging company and the USFS wish to avoid the preparation of the statement, their interests are distinct. The logging company's interest is making a profit from logging, while the USFS's interest is management of the forest system. Thus, the federal district court must allow the logging party to intervene in the action.

In sum, the federal district court must allow the logging party to join the litigation as a party, since it met all three conditions.

2. The federal district court is likely to grant TRO and a preliminary injunction to the nonprofit organization.

There are two types of relives that the nonprofit could seek to stop the USFS from issuing a logging permit: TRO and a preliminary injunction.

A temporary restraining order (TRO) can be issued without notice to the adverse party, but only in limited circumstances and only for no longer than 14 days. To secure a TRO without notice, the moving party would need to submit an affidavit that demonstrates a risk of immediate and irreparable injury. In deciding whether to grant a TRO, courts will also consider the same factors that are used in deciding a preliminary injunction.

Here, the nonprofit organization could argue that clearing of 5,000 acres of old−growth forest is home to a higher concentration of wildlife than can be found anywhere else in the western U.S and there would be an immediate and irreparable injury for the nonprofit organization to protect natural resources. Thus, the nonprofit could seek to obtain a temporary restraining order.

Preliminary injunction is an injunction that seeks to protect the plaintiff from irreparable injury and to make the court grant a meaningful decision after a trial on the merits. Preliminary injunctions can be granted only with notice to the adverse party, and only if the movant gives security in an amount that the court considers proper to pay the costs and damages suffered by any party found to have been wrongfully enjoined or restrained. The courts typically considers: (1) the significance of the irreparable harm to the plaintiff if the injunction is not granted, (2) the balance between the irreparable harm and the injury on the defendant because of the injunction, (3) the probability that the plaintiff will succeed on the merits, and (4) the public interest.

First, environmental damage creates a significantly irreparable. Second, the USFS will have to wait and the logging company will lose money if the delay is continued. However, these risks could be compensated by money and therefore the injunction could be granted. Third, the nonprofit organization alleges that NEPA requires an environmental impact statement for the logging project, and the USFS did not. It seems the nonprofit organization is able to show its possibility of succeed in the action. Fourth, the courts must consider the policy considerations. The public interest could be served (protecting the natural resources) when an environmental impact statement is prepared. Thus, the court is likely to preliminary injunction with the notice to the USFS.

In sum, the federal district court is likely to grant TRO and a preliminary injunction to the nonprofit organization.

해설

난이도: 하

핵심 단어 및 논점

- intervention of right
- temporary restraining order (TRO)
- preliminary injunction (PI)

1(a). The felony distribution of marijuana is admissible to impeach the inmate.

When convictions are used to impeach, (1) the nature of the crime, (2) the amount of time that has passed, and (3) (only in criminal cases) whether the witness is the defendant are considered. In civil cases, the admission of evidence of a felony conviction is subject to Rule 403, which says that a court may exclude relevant evidence if its probative value is substantially outweighed by the risk of misleading the jury, waste of time, injustice prejudice, and confusion of the issues.

There are two types of convictions that can be admitted for impeachment: felonies and the crime relating to a dishonest act or false statement. The crime that has been passed more than 10 years should not be admitted. 10-year time limit runs from the date of either the witness's conviction or release from confinement for it, whichever is later.

Here, the witness convicted of felony and he was released from prison nine years ago, satisfying the 10 years time limit. The felony has probative value to prove the witness's credibility. Its probative value is not substantially outweighed, and it is admissible.

In sum, the felony distribution of marijuana is admissible to impeach the inmate.

1(b). The perjury misdemeanor is admissible, since it is regarding dishonest.

The inmate's perjury misdemeanor is a crime regarding dishonest, and it must be admissible regardless of the time limit.

Thus, the perjury misdemeanor is admissible, since it is regarding dishonest.

1(c). The felony sexual assault is not admissible, since its probative value is substantially outweighed by the danger of unfair prejudice.

The felony was conducted seven years ago, satisfying the time limit. However, the felony has a low probative value, but has high risk of the danger of unfair prejudice.

Here, sexual assault is a type of sex crimes and it is not considered relevant to credibility. Additionally, the fact that the victim was the inmate's daughter makes danger of unfair prejudice. Thus, the court should not admit the evidence regarding the felony.

In sum, the felony sexual assault is not admissible, since its probative value is substantially outweighed by the danger of unfair prejudice.

2(a). The guard's resume must be admitted, since it is regarding truthfulness.

The witness could be subject to cross−examination regarding prior dishonest behavior, if the probative value is not substantially outweighed by the other dangers.

Here, the guard submitted a resume to the state and it is a prior dishonest behavior. It has probative value based on the fact that it shows untruthfulness and it was made recently. Since the probative value is very strong and there are no other dangers of prejudice, the court should permit inmate's counsel to cross−examine.

In sum, the guard's resume must be admitted, since it is regarding truthfulness.

2(b) The official copy should not be admitted, since it is an extrinsic evidence.

Although a counsel is permitted to cross−examine the witness regarding prior bad act, extrinsic evidence is not admissible.

Here, as mentioned above, the inmate's counsel may cross−examine the guard about false statement on his resume. However, the inmates' counsel cannot introduce the guard's resume or transcript which was extrinsic evidence.

In sum, the official copy should not be admitted, since it is an extrinsic evidence.

해설

난이도: 하

핵심 단어 및 논점

- impeachment
  - conviction
  - bad act
- extrinsic evidence (bad act, impeachment)

2(a)번 문제

Bad acts는 substantive evidence 또는 impeachment 목적으로 제출될 수 있는 증거로서, 각 경우의 admissibility 판단 기준이 다르다. 따라서 '제출목적'이 명시되어 있지 않은 문제의 경우, 해당 증거가 substantive evidence(character evidence)로 사용된 경우와 impeachment 목적으로 사용된 경우로 구분하여 서술하는 것이 고득점 포인트다. 그러나 본 문제에서는 impeachment 목적으로 제출되었음을 명시하고 있는 바, substantive evidence에 대한 내용은 불필요하다.

2014July Corporations

1. The investor's proposed bylaw provision is consistent with the state law.

Internal affairs of the corporation are governed by the state's corporate statute. Shareholder may amend the corporations' bylaws. In this case, state statute follows the MBCA and the shareholder's amendment is consistent with the law.

The bylaws may contain any provision that is consistent with law or the articles of incorporation. In addition, proxy access must be addressed and the bylaws may contain a requirement that the corporation must include in its proxy materials one or more individuals nominated by a shareholder. Typically, the director nomination procedures are found in the bylaws.

In this case, the provision regarding director nomination procedures in the bylaw is consistent with the law.

In sum, the bylaw provision is consistent with the state law.

2. The bylaw amendment would not take precedence over the investor's, since shareholders expressly limited the board's amendment.

Shareholders have the power to amend the bylaws. Existing bylaw provisions can be amended by the bylaw provisions that shareholder approved. This rule is applicable even when the original provisions are approved by the board. The board does not have this power, if: (1) the corporation's articles grant that power exclusively to the shareholders or (2) the amending shareholders expressly stated that the board of directors may not amend or repeal that bylaw.

However, even if shareholders does not allow board's changes the board still has the power to tinker with the bylaw to safeguard the voting process, but could not repeal the shareholder—approved bylaw.

Here, the amended provisions expressly indicate no board repeal clause, stating that Board of Directors may not be amended. Thus, the board does not have the amendment power. The board's amendment repealed the shareholders' amendment regarding nomination procedures.

In sum, the bylaw amendment would not take precedence over the investor.

3. The investor is not needed to make a demand before bringing suit, since it is a direct suit.

There are two types of suits that shareholders could bring against the company: derivative and direct suit. In determining whether the suit is derivative or direct suit, it depends on how the shareholders frame it.

A derivative claim is one regarding fiduciary breach by directors or challenging allegedly illegal action by management. If a claim is to vindicate shareholder's rights, it is a direct suit. If a transaction could be challenged either by derivative or direct suit, court permits a direct suit. While derivative proceeding requires prior demand to company, direct suit does not requires it.

In this case, the investor is bringing a suit regarding management's refusal to include the investor's proposed bylaw provision and the board's amendment.

In sum, the investor is not needed to make a demand before bringing suit, since it is a direct suit.

해설

난이도: 하

핵심 단어 및 논점

- corporation
- bylaws: bylaws에 포함되는 내용들
- power to amend the bylaws
- power to tinker
- derivative suit v. direct suit

2번 문제

논점: Bylaw를 수정할 수 있는 권리(BOD v. shareholders)

BOD에 의해 수정된 bylaw는 이후 shareholder가 제안한 bylaw에 우선하는가?

답안요령

> 1. Shareholder's right to amend
> 2. No board repeal clause (No board repeal clause에 의해 BOD가 bylaw를 amend할 수 없다)
> 3. Power to tinker
>   + analysis

1(a). The driver would be an employee, rather than an independent contractor.

Principal is liable for torts committed by the agent if the Principal employed him as an employee who acts within the scope of his employment, rather than an independent contractor. A person is an employee when the person's physical conduct in the performance is under the employer's control. There are several factors to be considered: level of skills required, whether the work is part or whole of Principal's business, whether the work was under the principal's control, whether the person is paid for regular work, and the length of the relationship.

First of all, delivering furniture to its customers does not require high level of skills. Secondly, the delivering work is ongoing, not the job required only for specific project. Third, the driver received a flat hourly payment based upon 40 work hours per week, not based on projects of business. Fourth, while "Independent Contractor Agreement" stated that each driver would provide a van for making deliveries, the store is responsible for the van, since it offered each driver the opportunity to lease a delivery van from the store at a below−market rate. Thus, the store is responsible for the expense of the van. Fifth, delivery is a regular business of the store. Finally, "Independent Contractor Agreement" stated that the driver is an independent contractor but it is not determinable.

In sum, the driver would be an employee, rather than an independent contractor.

1(b). The delivery was acting within the scope of his employment.

An employee was acting within the scope of his employment if: (1) the act is of kind that the employee is employed to perform, (2) it occurs substantially within the authorized time and space limits, and (3) it is motivated to serve the employer.

First of all, the driver's conduct that caused the accident was parking and it is the kind of the acts that the driver is employed to perform, driving. Second, the time and space changes from authorized activities were not substantial. Driver drove six blocks from the driver's next delivery, and the delivery added no more than half an hour to his workday. Finally, the driver was motivated to help the customer and he believed that the deliver would create good reputation of the store.

In sum, the delivery was within the scope of the driver's employment.

1(c). The driver would be liable for the passenger's injuries, since he was negligent per se.

An actor is negligent per se, if (1) the actor violates a statute that is designed to protect against the type of accident that the actor caused and (2) the victim is within the class of persons that the statute is designed to protect.

Here, the local traffic ordinance restricts double parking. The ordinance may be to prevent traffic jam and any damage from the traffic accidents. The driver's double—parking of the delivery van was the type of accident that the ordinance is designed to protect and the passenger is within the class of persons that the statute is designed to protect. The fact that 80% of deliveries are made while the delivery van is double—parked does not make any change.

In sum, the driver would be liable for his negligence.

2. The store is entitled to identification from the driver.

The paying defendant can be entitled to Indemnification from nonpaying defendant, when the paying defendant was not at fault in causing the plaintiff's injuries. By contrast, a joint tortfeasor is entitled only to contribution.

Here, the store was not at fault in causing the passenger's injuries. The store is liable to the passenger only because of the vicarious liability.

In sum, the store is entitled to identification from the driver.

해설

난이도: 하

핵심 단어 및 논점

- vicarious liability
- employee v. independent contractor rule
- doctrine of respondeat superior
- negligence per se
- indemnification

1. The Act does not violate the Equal Protection Clause, since it satisfies the rational basis test.

Under the Fourteenth Amendment, no state shall deny to any person within its jurisdiction the equal protection of the laws. There are three levels of scrutiny for equal protection claims: strict, intermediate, and rational basis scrutiny. The Court applies rational basis scrutiny to age based discrimination. Under the rational basis scrutiny, the discrimination must reasonably related to the state legitimate interest.

Here, State A enacted the Act that discriminates firefighters based on the age. The Act would be valid, if it satisfies the rational basis scrutiny. State A has its legitimate interest, because the act will improve workforce quality, enhance social safety, and save money. Additionally, mandatory retiring age is reasonable to improve the workforce fitness, in general. The fact that the firefighter is in excellent physical condition does not make a different result, since the issue is whether State A has a reasonable reason to believe that one's physical conditioning and ability to be a firefighter declines with age, in general. The Act is also reasonably related to the purpose to reduce expenses. Thus, the Act satisfies the rational basis test.

In sum, the Act does not violate the Equal Protection Clause, since it satisfies the rational basis test.

2. Congress has no authority under Section Five of the Fourteenth Amendment, since there is no constitutional injury.

Congress's powers are limited by the Constitution and therefore Congress must have legislative authority in the Constitution to enact a law. Congress has enforcement power and it may enact legislations that remedies constitutional violation.

Congress's power is remedial. When legislation lacks a connection between the constitutional injuries to be prevented or remedied and the means adopted, Congress can rely on its enforcement power. Congress cannot rely on its Fourteenth Amendment enforcement power to prohibit a kind of behavior that is unlikely to involve a constitutional violation at all.

Here, under the Act, the classification is based on age and it reasonably related to a legitimate state interest. There is no constitutional violation. Thus, Congress's primary goal would be to outlaw a kind of discrimination that does not violate the Fourteenth Amendment.

In sum, Congress has no authority under Section Five of the Fourteenth Amendment, since there is no constitutional injury.

해설

난이도: 하

핵심 단어 및 논점

- Equal Protection Clause
- RR test (age)
- enforcement power (Congress)
- remedial

2번 문제

논점: Enforcement power

| 답안요령 |

1. Congress's power is limited.★
2. Enforcement power
3. "Remedial"
4. Analysis(State가 제정한 법이 합헌인지)
5. Analysis(Congress의 remedy 방법이 적합한지)

TIP 1번: "Congress에게 해당 행위를 할 수 있는 권한이 있는가?"라는 질문에는 답안 첫 문장에는 "Congress's power is limited"임을 명시해야 한다.

1. Bank has an enforceable security interest in Acme's property properly described in the loan agreement.

The security interest is effective and attaches, when: (1) debtor signed a security agreement containing a description of the collateral, (2) debtor has rights in the collateral, and (3) secured party gave money to secured party.

First, Acme signed the loan agreement which described the collateral as inventory and accounts, Acme has rights in its inventory and accounts, and Bank loaned money to Acme. Thus, Bank's security interest in Acme's inventory and accounts was effective and had attached.

In sum, Bank's security interest in Acme's property which are inventory and accounts that are properly described in the loan agreement is effective and had attached.

2(a). Bank has an enforceable security interest in these rights, because these are accounts.

Accounts are defined as rights to payment for services rendered or to be rendered.

Here, Acme's rights to payment for repair services provided on credit are accounts. Thus, these rights to payment are subject to Bank's security interest.

In sum, Bank has an enforceable security interest in these rights, because these are accounts.

2(b). Bank has an enforceable security interest in used violins, because these are inventories.

Inventory is defined as raw materials, work in process, or materials used or consumed in debtor's business.

Here, the used violins are used for sale and therefore it is inventory. Thus, the used violins are subject to Bank's security interest.

In sum, Bank has an enforceable security interest in used violins, because these are inventories.

2(c). Bank has no enforceable security interest in violins in Acem's possession, because these are not owned by Acme.

First, those violins are not inventory, because they are not held by Acme for sale or lease. Second, the violins are owned by customers who brought them to Acme for repairing. Thus, Acme has no rights in those violins and no power to transfer rights in them to a secured party.

In sum, Bank has no enforceable security interest in violins in Acme's possession.

2(d). Bank has no enforceable security interest in wood, because these are inventory.

Woods are used by Acme in repairing violins and it is raw materials that are consumed in the business of Acme. Thus, those woods are subject to Bank's security interest.

In sum, Bank has no enforceable security interest in wood, because these are inventory.

2(e). Bank has no enforceable security interest in the Gambretti plane, since it is equipment.

The Gambretti plane is not inventory, because it is not held for sale or lease by Acme. It is equipment which is not covered by Bank's security interest.

Thus, Bank has no enforceable security interest in the Gambretti plane, since it is equipment.

2(f). Bank has no enforceable security interest in the Red Rosa violin, since the violinist is a buyer in ordinary course of business.

Generally, a security interest continues after sale of the collateral. However, a buyer in ordinary course of business (BIOCOB), the buyer is free from the security interest which was created by the buyer's seller. BIOCOB is a buyer who (1) buys goods in good faith, (2) without knowledge that the sale violates the rights of another, (3) from a person in the business of selling goods of the kind in the ordinary course of the seller's business.

Here, the violinist purchased the Red Rosa in the ordinary course of Acme's business. There is no fact to show the violinist's bad faith or knowledge on the rights of Bank. Thus, the violinist took the Red Rosa free of Bank's security interest in it.

In sum, Bank has no enforceable security interest in the Red Rosa violin, since the violinist is a buyer in ordinary course of business.

2(g). Bank's claim is superior to that of the judicial lien creditor, because Bank perfected its security interest before the lien creditor obtains lien.

A judgment lien creditor takes priority over a security interest only when the creditor became a lien creditor before the conflicting security interest is perfected. As mentioned above, Bank's security interest in Acme's inventory and accounts was effective and had attached. Bank filed a financing statement before the creditor, a judgment lien creditor, became a lien creditor.

In sum, Bank's claim is superior to that of the judicial lien creditor, because Bank perfected its security interest before the lien creditor obtains lien.

해설

난이도: 하

핵심 단어 및 논점

- effectiveness of security interest
- accounts
- inventory
- equipment
- buyer in ordinary course of business (BIOCOB)
- judgment lien creditor

2(f)번 문제

답안요령

1. Security interest 기본 rule(collateral에 지속된다)★
2. 그러나 BIOCOB인 경우 예외 rule 적용
   + analysis
3. Shelter rule★
   + analysis

1. The buyer acquired title to the two and one−half acres of the three−acre tract by adverse possession.

To acquire title by adverse possession, the possession must be: (1) actual, (2) open and notorious, (3) exclusive, (4) continuous, and (5) hostile.

To be actual, possession must be same with the possession of a reasonable owner if in possession. Here, the possession of the man and his sister was to build a cabin and to plant a vegetable garden. These acts were same with how reasonable owner possess the land. Thus, the possession was actual.

To be open and notorious, the owner can notice the adverse possession if the owner inspected the land. Here, the garden and the cabin that occupied the half an acre of the three−acre tract were visible.

Regarding hostility, in most states, hostility exists when a possessor is on the land without the owner's permission. In some states, the possessor must have a good−faith belief that she has a good title to the land. In some other states, the possessor must believe that she does not have a good title to the land. In most states, the possession of the man, his sister, and the buyer satisfies the hostility requirement.

Regarding continuous, the period that creates title by adverse possession is determined by state statute. Here, a state statute provides that the period is 10 years. The period starts to run when a wrongful possession occurs. Here, man's wrongful possession occurred fifteen years ago. When a multiple possessors are in privity with each other, the period of each possessor can be aggregated for the purpose of the statutory period. The possessors are in privity when there was a voluntary transfer, descent, or testamentary succession.

Here, a man possessed the land for seven years and he bequeathed the land to his sister. The man and the sister ware in privity with each other, since there was a testamentary succession. The sister and the buyer were also in privity, since the sister voluntarily transferred the land to buyer. Thus, the 10 year statutory period is satisfied and the buyer acquired title by adverse possession to the one−half−acre portion of the three−acre tract.

The buyer acquired title by adverse possession only to the one−half−acre portion of the three−acre tract. This is because the man, his sister, the buyer did not possess the other portion of the three−acre tract.

Under the constructive adverse possession doctrine, the possessor constructively extend its possession when a possessor enters under color of title and the possessor takes possession of only a portion of the land described in the instrument. Here, neither the man nor his sister entered under color of title. Thus, the constructive adverse possession doctrine is inapplicable here.

In sum, the buyer acquired title to the two and one−half acres of the three−acre tract by adverse possession.

2. The buyer can recover damages from the sister because the sister breached the covenant of seisin and the right to convey.

A general warranty deed that contains all six title covenants includes the covenant of seisin, right to convey, the covenant against encumbrances, covenant for quiet enjoyment, covenant of warranty, and covenant for further assurances.. Here, when the sister sold the land to the buyer by a general warranty deed, she did not own the three−acre tract.

In sum, the buyer can recover damages from the sister because the sister breached the covenant of seisin and the right to convey.

3. The buyer cannot compel the sewer company to remove the sewer line under the garden as the title of the owner.

When an adverse possessor acquires title by adverse possession, the title is not greater than the title of the holder of the cause of action.

Here, the holder of the cause of action is a property owner and he granted a sewer−line easement to a private sewer company. Thus, the buyer's title is also subject to the easement as the holder's title.

The man, his sister, and the buyer could argue that their possession interfered the right of easement. However, there is no fact showing that planting and maintaining garden interfered the use of an underground sewer line. Thus, there was no interference by the easement and the company has no cause of action against the possessors.

In sum, the buyer cannot compel the sewer company to remove the sewer line under the garden as the title of the owner.

해설

난이도: 하

핵심 단어 및 논점

- adverse possession
- constructive adverse possession doctrine
- coventna of title
  - covenant of seisin
  - covenant of the right to convey
- easement

1번 문제

> **답안요령**

---
1. Adverse possession 성립요건(×5)
2. Analysis
3. 결론(acquire title only to the portion of the tract)

TIP 2번: 5개의 요소 중 'continuance'와 'in privity'에 대한 analysis가 가장 중요하다.

3번 문제

> **답안요령**

---
1. General rule(정's right ≤ 갑's right)
2. Analysis
3. Termination of easement
4. Analysis + 결론
---

1. The service of process of MedForms was sufficient, since it serves documents to CEO.

Service upon a corporation is effective (1) when it followed state law where the district court sits or where service is made, or (2) by delivering a copy of the summons and of the complaint to an officer.

Here, the district court sits in State A and the service was made in State B. According to the State A and State B, each authorizes service of process on corporations only by personal delivery of a summons and complaint to the corporation's secretary. MedForms did not serve the secretary of the company. However, the company's chief executive officer was served with process. Typically, the term "officer" includes the CEO, who is sufficiently integrated with the corporation so that he will realize his responsibilities and know what he should do with the served paper. The service was reasonably sufficient to provide the company actual notice of the case, and therefore it satisfies constitutional requirements.

In sum, the service of process of MedForms was sufficient, since it serves documents to CEO.

2. The district court has subject matter jurisdiction, since MedForms and the company have diverse citizenship and the amount in controversy exceeds $75,000.

MedForms's third-party complaint is alleging the breach of contract which is governed by the state law. Thus, there is no federal question jurisdiction.

Regarding diversity jurisdiction, the citizenship of the corporation can be dual. A corporation is a citizen of the state where the corporation has been incorporated and it has principal place of business. The principal place of business is the corporation's nerve center where the corporation maintains its headquarters. Here, MedForms is incorporated and has its principal place of business in State A, and therefore its citizenship is in State A. The company is incorporated and has its principal place of business in State B. Thus, there are diverse citizenship between MedForms and the company. The amount in controversy ($500,000) exceeds $75,000. Thus, the district court has diversity jurisdiction.

In sum, the district court has subject matter jurisdiction, since MedForms and the company have diverse citizenship and the amount in controversy exceeds $75,000.

3. The company as a third－party defendant is improper joinder and MedForms cannot bring the company as the third party defendant.

A defendant can join a nonparty as a third party defendant into an action, only when the defendant claims that the third party is or may be liable to the defendant for the claim against it.

Here, MedForms attempts to bring the company into the action, alleging the company breached its contract. MedForms does not allege that the company is or may be liable to the company for the woman's claim against MedForms. Additionally, there is no fact showing that the company needs to indemnify MedForms as a MedForm's supervisor for the woman's claim. MedForms alleged claim against the company is an independent claim with the woman's claim.

In sum, the company as a third－party defendant is improper joinder and MedForms cannot bring the company as the third party defendant.

해설

난이도: 하

핵심 단어 및 논점

- service of process (upon corporation)
- jurisdiction
- diversity of citizenship jurisdiction (DCJ)
- corporation citizenship
- joinder
- third party defendant (impleader)

1. The husband's will was not revoked because there is no evidence of the intent.

A will may be revoked by physical act or by the execution of a new will, if the testator revokes with the intent to revoke the will. The burden of proof to establish that a validly executed will has been revoked is upon the party who seeks to revoke the will.

Here, the husband extended over the words in the will. It could be a physical act to revoke a will, but there is no evidence that shows testator's intent to revoke the will. Husband wrote that estate plan should be changed. It is showing that there is a need to change the will, but it does not mean it is revoked. "Call lawyer to fix" statement shows intent to do something in the future after consultation with his attorney, not right now. The fact that the will was found on his desk and the voice massage was on the phone shows that the testator recognized problem on the will very recently, not that he revoked it.

In sum, the husband's will was not revoked because there is no evidence of the intent.

2. The husband's daughter is not entitled to a pretermitted child's share, since daughter's other parent, the testator's wife, were bequeathed substantially all of his estate.

Pretermitted child statutes ensure the intestate share of children who were born after the execution of the will. A child born to a testator after the execution of the will is entitled intestate share of decedent's estate, unless the will evidences testator's intent not to do so. However, in some states, an afterborn child is denied a share of the decedent parent's estate if decedent parent bequeathed all or substantially all of his estate to the child's other parent.

Here, testator specified that he did not want to grand the share of his estate to his children with the statement "regardless of whether we have children." Thus, either in some states, the husband's daughter is not entitled to a pretermitted child's share.

In sum, the husband's daughter is not entitled to a pretermitted child's share, since daughter's other parent, the testator's wife, were bequeathed substantially all of his estate.

3. Wife could be entitled to one−half of the trust or the whole of the trust, depending on the meaning of the term "illusory."

Under the law of the state, a revocable trust created by a husband during the marriage is deemed illusory. However, the statue is ambiguous regarding the remaining one−half of the trust's assets after the distribution to wife. If the statute means it is illusory to the extent of wife's share, wife receives one−half of the trust and University gets one−half of the trust. If the statute means it is illusory at all, the trust is void. Wife would be entitled to the trust as residuary legatee.

In sum, wife could be entitled to one−half of the trust or the whole of the trust, depending on the meaning of the term "illusory."

해설

난이도: 1번 문제: 하
　　　2번 문제: 하
　　　3번 문제: 중

핵심 단어 및 논점

- revocation by physical act
- testator's intent
- pretermitted child
- illusory

1. A jury could find the friend liable to the boy for his injuries, since they engaged in an adult activity.

In a negligence action, child's action is compared with the standard of other child who has similar age, intelligence, and experience. However, when a child engaged in a hazardous activity which is normally undertaken by adults, they will be held to the standard of adult.

Here, friend was only 10 years old, but he was an experienced snowmobiler. Snowmobiling is an adult activity and the friend should be held to the standard of adult in negligence action. A reasonable adult snowmobiler would perceive that turning off a designated snowmobiling trail onto a logged trail that is not maintained for snowmobiling has a foreseeable risk of injury. The logging trail was not marked or maintained for snowmobiling.

In sum, a jury would find that the friend was negligent.

2. A jury could find the landowner liable to the boy for his injuries, if the boy is a licensee. If the boy is classified as a trespasser, the landowner is not liable for his injuries because he involved in adult activity.

The landowner has a duty to a trespasser or a licensee. A trespasser is one who enters upon the landowner's land without a privilege to do so. Here, the boy had no privilege to enter the landowner's property, and the boy may be a trespasser.

However, the entrant can be classified as a licensee, when a reasonable person would interpret that the landowner is in fact willing for another to enter upon his land. Here, the landowner blocked the logging trail by a chain with "No Trespassing" sign. However, the landowner's land was in a northern state where three to four feet of snow typically blankets the ground throughout the winter.

The landowner should have foreseen that the sign would be covered by snow. Thus, the boy and the friend would be classified as licensees.

The landowner owes licensee a duty to show hidden dangers that the landowner knows or should have known and the licensee was not likely to discover. Here, the landowner should have known that the dangers by a chain and therefore, if the boy is classified as licensees, the landowner would be liable to them.

If the boy is classified as trespasser, the landowner owes him duty only when attractive nuisance doctrine is applicable. Under the attractive nuisance doctrine, the landowner is liable for the physical harm to a trespassing child if all factors are satisfied: (1) landowner knows or should have known that there is an dangerous artificial condition on the land, (2) landowner knows or should have known that children are likely to trespass, (3) those children cannot recognize the risk of dander, and (4) burden of maintaining the condition is slight compared to the risk of the danger.

Here, the land should have known that a logging trail would be dangerous. The boy and his friend could not recognize the risk of the danger, since it was hidden by snow. The landowner's burden was very slight, since he can avoid the danger by posting a sign warning sufficiently high not to be covered by snow. However, the attractive nuisance doctrine is applicable only for children. Here, the boy and his friend engaged in an adult activity and the attractive nuisance doctrine is inapplicable.

In sum, if the boy is classified as a licensee, the landowner violated his duty of care. If the boy is classified as a trespasser, the landowner is not liable for his injuries.

3. A jury could not find the woman liable to the boy for his injuries.

Generally, there is no duty to come to the aid of another. However, once an actor renders services to reduce the risk of harm to another, the actor owes a duty of reasonable care to the other person if: (1) an actor increases the risk of harm compared to the risk without the undertaking or (2) the person who received the services relies on the actor's exercising reasonable care in the undertaking.

Here, a woman saw the boy and his friend as she was snowmobiling on the snowmobile trail. She called 911 and reported the accident. It was to render service to reduce the risk of harm. The calling did not increase the risk of harm compared to the risk without calling 911. Although the boy and the friend suffered injuries from frostbite, it was not because of woman's delay. There are no facts showing that the boy and the friend relied on the woman.

In sum, a jury could not find the woman liable to the boy for his injuries

4. The boy could not raise the negligence claim under the contributory negligence doctrine, while his damage award would be reduced by his negligence under the comparative negligence approach.

Under the common law contributory negligence doctrine, the plaintiff cannot recover damages from the defendant when the plaintiff's negligence was a cause in fact and proximate cause of his injuries. This doctrine is applicable in a few states. Under the modern comparative negligence approach, the court apportion fault among them when two or more parties are negligent. In some comparative negligence jurisdictions, the apportionment is available only when the jury concludes that the plaintiff is less than 50 percent at fault.

Here, the boy was an experienced snowmobiler and he should have foreseen the risk of harm. Thus, the boy was negligent in allowing the friend to drive the snowmobile. Under the contributory negligence doctrine, the boy cannot recover damages from the defendant. Under the comparative negligence approach, the boy can recover damages which are reduced by his negligence.

In sum, the boy could not raise the negligence claim under the contributory negligence doctrine, while his damage award would be reduced by his negligence under the comparative negligence approach.

해설

난이도: 1번 문제: 하
2번 문제: 중
3번 문제: 하
4번 문제: 상

핵심 단어 및 논점

- negligence
- child's adult activity (duty of care)
- licensee
- trespasser

- attractive nuisance doctrine
- duty to aid
- contributory negligence doctrine
- comparative negligence approach

2번 문제

답안요령

1. Landowner's duty → trespasser? licensee?
2. Trespasser/Licensee 정의
3. Rule (landowner's duty + 기타)
4. Analysis (If the π is a licensee, …)
5. Analysis (If the π is a trespasser, …)
6. Even if trespasser, attractive nuisance doctrine★
   + analysis
7. 결론

TIP1 Landowner는 상대방의 신분(trespasser/licensee)에 따라 그들에 대한 다른 의무를 지지만, 그 상대방의 신분을 명확하게 구별할 수 없을 경우 trespasser일 경우와 licensee일 경우로 나누어 각각 analysis하는 것이 고득점 포인트다.

TIP2 상대방의 신분이 trespasser인 경우, landowner는 상대방에게 자신의 땅에 존재하는 위험요소에 대해 고지할 의무가 없다. 다만 상대방이 trespasser이더라도 attractive nuisance doctrine이 적용될 수 있는 사안이라면, landowner는 trespasser인 상대방이 landowner's 땅에 존재하는 인공적 위험요소에 의해 입은 신체적 피해에 대해 책임을 진다.

TIP3 Child의 행위가 adult activity에 해당하는지 그 여부를 판단하는 것은 jury의 몫이므로, 문제에서 주어진 사안만으로는 단정할 수 없다. 따라서 attractive nuisance doctrine에 관련한 답안을 서술할 경우, "if" 표현을 사용하여 아이의 행동을 adult activity인 경우와 아닌 경우를 가정하고 각각 analysis하는 것이 고득점 포인트다.

3번 문제

답안요령

1. No duty to aid
2. 예외(duty가 인정되는 경우)
3. Analysis (i 요건)
4. Analysis (ii 요건)

1(a). The State A federal district court has personal jurisdiction over the corporation, since the corporation established minimum contacts in State A.

Federal district courts exercise personal jurisdiction to the same extent as the courts of general jurisdiction of the state where the district court sits. Here, State A's long−arm statute has been interpreted to extend personal jurisdiction as far as the U.S. Constitution allow.

Under the Due Process Clause of the Fourteenth Amendment, a state court can have personal jurisdiction over a nonresident defendant who established minimum contacts with the state. Even if the contacts in State B is not continuous and systematic required to establish general jurisdiction, a nonresident defendant is subject to specific jurisdiction when his contacts with the forum state demonstrate purposeful availment of the benefits of the forum state, and it was foreseeable that the defendant may be hauled into the forum state's courts.

Here, the corporation's salespeople hold sales presentation in State A and they spoke to prospective buyers about purchasing super solar panels. The corporation shipped the panels to the woman in State A. By these actions, the corporation purposefully availed itself of the privilege of doing business in State A and received the benefits from State A. The corporation could foresee that it might be hauled into a State A court if its contacts in State A are wrongful. The woman's claim was directly related to the corporation's actions. Thus, the corporation has sufficient contacts with State A.

Even though there are defendant's minimum contacts with the state, the exercise of personal jurisdiction over the nonresident may offend due process if it is unfair. The defendant has the burden of proof to show that the fairness considerations outweigh the existence of minimum contacts.

Here, the woman lives in State A and the panels were installed in State A. There is no fact showing that the litigation in State A would impose serious burden on the corporation. In sum, there is no better State compared to State A Thus, the

State A federal district court has personal jurisdiction over the corporation.

In sum, the State A federal district court has personal jurisdiction over the corporation, since the corporation established minimum contacts in State A.

1(b). The State A federal district court has no personal jurisdiction over the engineer, since he merely put the brochures in the stream of commerce.

Stream of commerce theory is rejected. This is because it is insufficient basis for jurisdiction that the defendant has predicted that its goods will reach the forum state. Transmission of the goods to the forum can be a basis for jurisdiction only when the defendant has targeted the forum.

Here, the engineer has never been physically present in State A and there is no fact showing the engineer was trying to do business in State A. Even though he prepared the brochures and he reasonably foresee that the brochures would be distributed to a prospective buyer in another state, he was not targeting State A. He was merely put the brochures in the stream of commerce. Thus, the State A court has no personal jurisdiction over the engineer.

In sum, the State A federal district court has no personal jurisdiction over the engineer, since he merely put the brochures in the stream of commerce.

2(a). The State A federal district court has subject matter jurisdiction over the woman's claim, since it arises under a federal law.

Federal courts have original jurisdiction over all civil actions arising under the federal laws or Constitution. Under the well-pleaded rule, plaintiff's complaint must state that his own cause of action is based upon federal laws or the Constitution. Merely mentioning of the federal statute to rebut an anticipated defense or to deny the applicability of the law does not establish federal-question jurisdiction.

Here, the woman's claim is based on the allegations that the defendants made false representation under the federal statute. The woman's claim is central to the federal statute.

In sum, the State A federal district court has subject matter jurisdiction over the woman's claim, since it arises under a federal law.

2(b). The State A federal district court has supplemental jurisdiction over the engineer's cross-claim, since it forms part of the same case or controversy.

The engineer's cross-claim is based on the state statute, so there is no federal question jurisdiction. The engineer resides in State B and the corporation is incorporated and has its principal place of business in State B, so there is no diversity jurisdiction.

However, under the supplemental jurisdiction statute, district courts may hear claims that could not be heard, if those claims that are part of the same or controversy under Article III, if they derive from common nucleus of operative fact.

When courts determines whether the claims arises out of the same transaction or occurrence, they considers many factors, such as: (1) whether the issues of fact and law in the claims are same, (2) whether the same evidence would support or refute the claims, (3) whether there is a logical relationship between those claims, and (4) whether res judicata would bar a subsequent suit on the cross-claim.

Here, there are many overlapping facts between the engineer's cross-claim and the woman's claim. The engineer alleges that the corporation must indemnify the engineer based on a consulting contract, and the woman's claim is regarding misrepresentation on the brochures engineer prepared. The material the engineer prepared is related to both woman's claim and engineer's claim. Additionally, the corporation would be liable to the engineer under the contract, only when the engineer first became liable to the plaintiff. The two claims have logical relationship.

The district court has discretion to decline to exercise supplemental jurisdiction in three situations: (1) there are complex issue on state claim, (2) state claim predominates federal claim, (3) federal court dismissed all claims that it had original jurisdiction, or (4) there are other compelling reasons.

Here, there are no facts showing any reasons for refusing jurisdiction.

In sum, the State A federal district court has supplemental jurisdiction over the engineer's cross-claim, since it forms part of the same case or controversy.

해설

난이도: 하

핵심 단어 및 논점

- personal jurisdiction (PJ)
- long-arm statutes
- stream of commerce theory
- federal question jurisdiction (FQJ)

- well-pleaded rule
- cross-claim
- supplemental jurisdiction (SPJ)

1번 문제

답안요령

> 1. (Federal PJ = state)
> 2. △ = nonresident (long-arm & due process)
> 3. DP (minimum contact & notice)
> 4. "Minimum contact"
> 5. Analysis (stream of commerce theory)
> 6. Fairness

2(a)번 문제

답안요령

> 1. FQJ
> 2. Well-pleaded doctrine★
> 3. Analysis + 결론

TIP　법원의 FQJ 유무여부를 판단하는 경우, well-pleaded doctrine에 대해 논하는 것이 고득점 포인트다.

2(b)번 문제

논점: Cross-claim 중 jurisdiction (SPJ)

답안요령

1. SPJ에 대한 기본 rule
2. Considering factors (×4)
   + analysis
3. Court's discretion (×3)
   + analysis
4. 결론

TIP1   본 답안요령은 법원이 SPJ를 가지는지 그 여부를 논하는 모든 경우에 사용될 수 있는 바, joinder 또는 intervention이 jurisdiction 측면에서 허용가능한지 판단할 때에도 본 답안요령이 적용된다.

TIP2   SPJ에 대한 답안은 analysis를 최대한 자세히 논하는 것이 고득점 포인트다.

2015July Contracts

1. The contract is enforceable against the buyer.

A contract for the sale of goods is governed by UCC2. The term "goods" means movable things at the time of making a contract. Under UCC2, a contract can be formed in any manner sufficient to show agreement. Under the Statute of Frauds (SOF), a contract for the sale of goods for $500 or more is enforceable against a party only when it is written and signed by the party.

Here, a seller and a buyer made an agreement on antique doll. Antique doll is a "good" and it is governed by UCC2. The buyer telephoned the seller to discuss buying the doll. It is sufficient to show agreement. Although the contract was oral, the buyer signed and mailed a letter to the seller on May 2 satisfies SOF. The letter stated "we agreed" and it clearly shows the contract for sale. Additionally, the letter stated "the 1820 doll" and it shows that the contract was for only one doll. Thus, the letter from the buyer is sufficient to satisfy the requirements under UCC2 and SOF.

In sum, the contract is enforceable against the buyer.

2. The buyer breached that contract, since his attempt to retract was unsuccessful.

When either party repudiates the contract before the due date of the performance, the damaged party may wait performance by the repudiating party for a reasonable time or find any remedy for breach. The repudiation occurs when there is (1) a clear communication of intention, (2) an action that makes performance impossible, or (3) a clear demonstration of determination not to continue with performance.

Here, the buyer's letter said "I have decided not to buy the 1820 doll." It is clear statement of buyer's determination not to buy. The buyer's failure to buy substantially impairs the value of the contract to the seller. Thus, the buyer's letter is a repudiation of the contract.

In sum, the buyer breached that contract, since his attempt to retract was unsuccessful.

A repudiating party may retract its repudiation. However, the power to retract a repudiation terminates when the nonbreaching party has done following: (1) cancelled, (2) materially changed his position, or (3) otherwise indicated that he considers the repudiation final.

Here, on May 5, the buyer indicated that he will buy the doll from the seller on the terms they agreed to. However, On May 3, the seller immediately telephoned the buyer and said he considers the letter to be the final end to their deal. Additionally, the seller agreed to resell the doll to the other collector, and the seller materially changed his position. Hence, the buyer's attempted retraction is ineffective.

In sum, the buyer breached the contract, since his attempt of retraction was unsuccessful.

3. The seller can recover in damages for $1,000 plus incidental damage of $150.

The purpose of the remedies is to put the aggrieved party in as good a position as if the other party had fully performed. Under UCC2, when a buyer breaches or repudiates, the seller has several remedies, including reselling the goods. The seller can recover the difference between the contract price and the resale price plus incidental and consequential damages only when the resale is made in good faith and in a commercially reasonable manner. Incidental damages include any expenses incurred in return or resale of the goods. If the resale is by private sale, this remedy is available only if the seller gives the buyer a reasonable notification of the resale.

Here, when the seller resale the doll to the collector, the seller acted in good faith and in a commercially reasonable manner. On May 2, the seller told the buyer that he will sell the doll to someone else. Thus, the seller is entitled to recover $1,000, which is the difference between $12,000 and $11,000. Additionally, the seller spent $150 for the express delivery service and the seller can recover $150 as incidental damages. There is no fact regarding consequential damages.

In sum, the seller can recover in damages for $1,000 plus incidental damage of $150.

해설

난이도: 1번 문제: 중
　　　　2번 문제: 하
　　　　3번 문제: 하

핵심 단어 및 논점

- formation of contract (UCC2)
- Statute of Frauds (SOF)
- breach of contract
- repudiation
- retraction of repudication
- remedy
- cover damages

1. The business judgment rule does not apply to the board's decision, since the transaction was director's conflicting interest transaction and it was not approved by qualified directors.

Conflicting interest transaction is a transaction that the director had knowledge and material financial interest. It is called as self−dealing in common law.

Here, each director has one fourth ownership of LLC and it made them difficult to consider the transaction objectively. Thus, the director's financial interest in the transaction was material. Directors had knowledge, because all the directors were aware that the transaction was with their LLC. Additionally, the transaction was with the corporation and LLC that the directors had indirect interests. Thus, the sale of the tower was a director's conflicting interest transaction.

Under the safe harbor rule, a director's conflicting interest transaction is protected when: (1) there is an approval by disinterested directors or shareholders, (2) a director fully disclosed all relevant information, and (3) a director played no part in the disinterested directors' vote directly or indirectly. When the safe harbor rule is inapplicable, the business judgment rule is not applicable and the directors must show the fairness of the transaction.

Here, the sale of the tower was not approved by qualified directors, because it was approved by the directors who had interest in the transaction. Thus, the presumption of the business judgment rule that the directors were fully informed and acted in good faith is not available in this case.

In conclusion, the business judgment rule does not apply to the director's decision.

2. The directors breached their duty of loyalty and duty of care.

Even if the directors' decision is not protected by the business judgment rule, the directors can satisfy their duty of loyalty, when the transaction was fair to the corporation. Directors have burden to show that the transaction was fair price and fair dealing. The courts would consider (1) whether the transaction price was comparable to what might have been obtained and (2) whether the director's process in reaching their decision was appropriate.

Here, the directors could argue that the $12 million price was substantively fair because the price was within the range of received offers and the corporation will have time to relocate to a new headquarters. Additionally, the procedure was fair because the directors had known all information about the transaction and no reason for additional inquiries. However, the transaction was not either substantively or procedurally fair. Regarding substantive fairness, the CEO rejected the received offers ranging from $8 million to $13 million because the CEO thought it was insufficient. Regarding procedural fairness, the board's meeting was only for 10 minutes and the decision was based on the past appraisal of fair market value.

Thus, the directors breached their duty of loyalty.

A director has duty of care, which requires a director to exercise the care that a reasonable person in a like position would exercise and to be fully informed.

Here, the business judgment rule is inapplicable since the directors were engaged in a conflicting interest transaction. The directors were grossly negligent regarding the sale of the tower, because they hold the meeting only for 10 minutes and they used two year appraisal.

In sum, the directors breached their duty of care.

해설

난이도: 하

핵심 단어 및 논점

- corporation
- limited liability company (LLC)
- business judgment rule (BJR)
- safe harbors rule
- fairness
- fiduciary duty

2번 문제

논점: Director's duty of loyalty & Safe harbor rule

답안요령

1. Duty of loyalty (conflicting interest transaction)
   + analysis
2. Safe harbor rule
   + analysis
3. Fairness
   + analysis

TIP1 본 기출문제는 conflicting interest transaction에 관한 case로서, safe harbor rule을 우선 적용하고 safe harbor rule의 요건을 만족하지 못한 경우 추가적으로 fairness에 대해 analysis한다.

TIP2 1번: Conflicting interest transaction 용어가 modern과 CL에서 차이가 있다는 점을 서술하는 것이 고득점 포인트다.

TIP3 3번: Fairness 여부를 판단해야 할 행위가 어떤 유형의 행위인지 그 여부에 따라 entire fairness review(fair price와 fair dealing)의 적용여부가 다르다.

1. The woman cannot establish an NGRI defense, because her schizophrenia did not prevent her recognizing whether her conduct was wrong or wrong.

State A statute limits the defense to a defendant who can show that, she suffered from a severe mental disease of defect at the time of the charged crime, she suffered from a severe mental disease of defect, and that, as a result of the disease, she did not know whether her conduct was wrong or wrong. It is the M'Naghten test of the insanity defense.

First, schizophrenia satisfies the severe mental disease when it impairs a defendant's capacity to recognize reality. The expert's written reports suggest that the woman suffered schizophrenia at the time of the crime.

Second, the defendant must prove that his mental disease made him unable to distinguish right from wrong. In some states, courts permit the defense if the defendant's severe mental disease prevented her from knowing that her acts were legally wrong. In some other states, courts permit the defense when a defendant did not know that her actions were morally wrong, even if the defendant knew that her actions were legally wrong.

Here, the woman stated "Forget the speed limit" and it supports that she recognized her action was legally wrong. The fact that the woman took a knife and she was motivated by the following photographers from another planet also suggests that she knew that her action was criminal. Additionally, there is no evidence that the woman committed the alleged crime, because the schizophrenia prevented her from knowing that her actions were morally wrong. Even if she believed that she is followed by photographers from another planet, it does not prevent her from recognizing whether her action is morally wrong or not. She could sufficiently recognize that kidnapping and forcing the other person with knife are morally wrong.

In short, the woman's schizophrenia did not prevent her from recognizing whether her actions were right or wrong.

2. The man can be charged with manslaughter.

A person can be charged with depraved—heart murder when the person recklessly causes the death of another with extreme indifference to the value of human life. However, depraved heart murder is appropriate when reckless diving is combined with other factors, such as intoxication.

Here, there was no fact to show aggravating factors, and therefore the man cannot be charged for depraved heart murder.

In most jurisdictions, defendant can be guilty of manslaughter when defendant's conduct causes the death of another human being and he acted with criminal negligence.

Here, the man sped up to 85 miles per hour, violating the traffic laws and it created substantial risk of an accident and serious injury to others. His driving also was both the actual and proximate causation. The motorcyclist would not have died but for his high speed driving, and there was no unforeseeable intervening causation of the death.

Regarding mens rea, some states require the defendant's criminal or gross negligence. If the defendant's action was gross deviation from the standard of reasonable person under the defendant's circumstance, the defendant can be convicted. Other states require the defendant's recklessness. If the defendant was aware that his conduct can create a risk of death, the defendant can be convicted. In some states, the defendant can be convicted when a death occurs as a result of defendant's unlawful act.

Here, the man sped up to 85 miles per hour and it was unlawful act. The ordinary person would have been recognized that doing so creates a substantial risk of death. Additionally, the man must have been aware that such driving can create an accident and a death. Thus, the man satisfies mens rea element under any jurisdictions.

In conclusion, the man can be convicted for manslaughter.

3. The defense of duress will be available to the man.

Generally, the defense of duress can be hold, if their conduct was committed under the pressure of an unlawful threat from another person to harm the defendant. Under the MPC, the defense of duress is defined as a threat that a reasonable person would be unable to resist it. Under the common law, duress is not available as a defense to any kind of intentional homicide.

Here, driving with high speed was because of the woman's threat of death or serious bodily harm. He was reasonable to feel fear, because the woman took a knife and held it against the man's throat. Additionally, he was already driving before the woman took a knife, and he was unable to flee from the threatening situation. The man had no intention to kill the motorcyclist, and therefore he could also raise the defense of duress.

In sum, the defense of duress will be available to the man.

해설

난이도: 하

핵심 단어 및 논점

- insanity (defense)
- M'Naghten test
- depraved—heart murder
- manslaughter
- duress (defense)

1번 문제

사안에 명시된 statute가 M'Naghten test를 의미하는 바, M'Naghten test와 MPC를 비교분석할 필요는 없다.

1. The son's interest in the trust would not terminate upon the son's marriage, since it violates public policy.

Trust provisions that restrain a first marriage violate public policy. The provisions of trusts that violate public policy are void.

In this case, the wife's testamentary trust states that trust income will be distributable to the wife's son for so long as he shall live or until such time as he shall marry. This provision restricts son's marriage and it is void.

However, if the wife's motive was to support son only during the beneficiary is single, a restrain on marriage might be upheld. Here, there are no facts to support it. Thus, the son's interest in the trust should be distributed to son.

In sum, the son's interest in the trust would not terminate upon the son's marriage, since it violates public policy.

2. The trustee breached the duty of loyalty, self-dealing, and there are two remedies for the breach: rescission or seeking damages award.

Trustees have a duty of loyalty to beneficiaries, such as the duty not to do self-dealing. Self-dealing includes the purchase of trust assets by the trustee in his individual capacity. Under the no further inquiry rule, there is no need to inquire into the motivation for the self-dealing transaction.

In this case, trustee purchased the stock himself for $1.2 million. It is self-dealing and breached the duty of loyalty. Thus, trust beneficiary can rescind the self-dealing transaction or get a damage award against the trustee.

First, to rescind, the trust property purchased by the trustee would be returned to the trust and the amount the trustee paid for the property would be refunded by the trust. Here, because of the declined in value to $450,000, the trust property returned to the trust would be valued only $450,000. Additionally, current trust assets in portfolio value $1 million. Because trustee would be returned $1.2 million which is larger amount than current trust assets, rescission is not a good method.

Secondly, damages are based on the difference in the fair market value of the trust assets at the time of the self−dealing transaction and the amount paid by the trustee. Here, the fair market value of the trust assets at the time of the self−dealing transaction is $1.5 million and the amount paid by the trustee is $1.2 million. Thus, the trust would get damages award for $300,000.

Additionally, the trustee also breached his duty of care, because he sold the stock without the testing of the market.

In sum, the trustee breached the duty of loyalty, self−dealing, and there are two remedies for the breach: rescission or seeking damages award.

3. The trustee did not breach any duties in acquiring and retaining the portfolio of mutual funds.

A trustee has a duty of care, which requires a trustee to administer the trust as a prudent person with reasonable care. A trustee is under a duty to invest and manage trust assets as an ordinary invest would. The obligation to invest prudently normally requires the trustee to diversify trust investment. The obligation to manage the trust requires trustee to monitor investments prudently made to assure that retention of those investments remains prudent.

In this case, trustee chose to invest in a balanced portfolio and it satisfies the diversification requirement. Trustee is not liable for declines in value because it is result of a downturn resulting from general economic conditions. Thus, there is no breach of duty to care, including duty to invest diversify and duty to manage the trust.

In sum, the trustee did not breach any duties in acquiring and retaining the portfolio of mutual funds.

해설

난이도: 하

핵심 단어 및 논점

- violating public policy (restraint of marriage)
- duty of loyalty (self-dealing)
- remedy for duty of loyalty
- duty of care
- duty to invest prudently
- duty to diversify

2번 문제

논점: Self-dealing

답안요령

---

1. Self-dealing
   + analysis
2. No further inquiry rule★
   + analysis
3. Beneficiary's remedy
   + analysis

TIP Self-dealing에 관한 경우, no further inquiry rule과 이에 대한 analysis가 고득점 포인트다.

1. The finance company has no an interest in the home entertainment system, since the buyer is a buyer in the ordinary course of business, and the shelter rule is applicable here.

The security interest is effective and attaches, when: (1) debtor signed a security agreement containing a description of the collateral, (2) debtor has rights in the collateral, and (3) secured party gave money to secured party.

Here, the finance company's security interest attached, because the retailer signed the loan agreement which has a description that the collateral is the retailer's present and future inventory, the retailor had rights in its inventory, and the finance company loaned money to the retailor. Moreover, the finance company perfected its security interest by filing the finance statement in the appropriate state filing office.

Generally, a security interest continues after sale of the collateral. However, a buyer in ordinary course of business (BIOCOB), the buyer takes free of security interest which was created by the buyer's seller. BIOCOB is a buyer who (1) buys goods in good faith, (2) without knowledge that the sale violates the rights of another, (3) from a person in the business of selling goods of the kind in the ordinary course of the seller's business.

Here, the buyer is a BIOCOB. First, she purchased the home entertainment system in good faith and had no knowledge of the retailer's agreement with the finance company. Second, the retailer was the person in the business of selling home electronic equipment in the ordinary course of its business. Thus, the buyer took the home entertainment system free of the finance company's security interest.

Under the shelter rule, once a buyer acquired goods free of security interest which was created by the buyer's seller, any subsequent buyer is free from the security interest. Here, the friend purchased from the buyer, who took the home entertainment system free of the finance company's security interest. In short, the friend is also free of the finance company's security interest.

In conclusion, te finance company has no an interest in the home entertainment system, since the buyer is a buyer in the ordinary course of business, and the shelter rule is applicable here.

2. The retailer has no security interest in the home entertainment system, following the consumer to consumer exception.

Reservation of title by a seller of goods notwithstanding delivery to the buyer is limited to a reservation of security interest in effect.

Even though the agreement specified that the retailer retain title until the buyer pays for it, the retailer's interest in the home entertainment system purchased by the buyer is limited as a security interest. This security interest was effective and had attached, because the buyer signed a credit purchase agreement, the buyer purchased the home entertainment system, and the retailer gave it to the buyer on credit.

When the collateral is a consumer goods and it secures a purchase money obligation on that collateral, the security interest is a purchase money security interest (PMSI) in consumer goods. A purchase money security interest is automatically perfected upon attachment. Consumer goods are goods that are used primarily for personal, family, or household purposes.

Here, the security interest in the home entertainment system was created to secure buyer's remainder of the purchase price. Additionally, the buyer got home entertainment system constitutes consumer goods Thus, the retailer's security interest in the home entertainment system is a PMSI and therefore it was perfected when the system took it.

Generally, a security interest continues after sale of the collateral. However, under the consumer to consumer exception, a subsequent buyer is free of security interest created by the original seller when: (1) the collateral is used primarily for personal, family, or household purposes, (2) the subsequent buyer acquired the collateral for value, (3) the subsequent buyer had no actual knowledge of the security interest, and (4) before a filing of a finance statement with the respect to that security interest.

Here, the friend purchased the home entertainment system which was collateral of the retailor. First, the home entertainment system was used for primarily for household purposes. Second, the friend acquired it for $4,000. Third, the friend had no knowledge of the buyer's agreement with the retailer. Fourth, the friend acquired the home entertainment system when none of finance statement about the security interest in it. Thus, the exception is applicable in this case and therefore the retailer's security interest in the home entertainment system does not continue.

In conclusion, the retailer has no security interest in the home entertainment system, following the consumer to consumer exception.

3. The retailer has an interest in the $4,000 check, since it is cash proceeds.

Here, the friend gave the buyer a check for $3,000 and the check is proceeds of the home entertainment system.

A perfected security interest will automatically attach to any identifiable proceeds from the disposition of collateral. This automatic perfection for proceeds continues for only 20 days after attachment.

Here, the retailer had a perfected security interest in the home entertainment system when the friend bought it. Thus, the retailer has interest in the check and security interest in the check was automatically perfected.

However, that perfection ceases after 20 days, unless (1) the security interest is perfected when the security interest attaches to the proceeds or within 20 days thereafter, (2) the proceeds are identifiable cash proceeds, or (3) the security interest in the original collateral was perfected by a filing in the same office in which a security interest in the proceeds could be perfected by filing.

Here, the proceeds is identifiable cash proceeds and, therefore, the perfection is continuously perfected.

In sum, the retailer has an interest in the $4,000 check, since it is cash proceeds.

해설

난이도: 상

핵심 단어 및 논점

- enforceability of security interest
- buyer in ordinary course of business (BIOCOB)
- shelter rule
- perfection
- consumer to consumer exception
- PMSI in consumer goods
- cash proceeds

본 사안을 간단히 정리하면 다음과 같다.

Retailer와 finance company 간 home entertainment system(이하 system)을 담보로 하는 security interest 생성. 이후 retailer가 buyer에게 system을 판매함. 이후 buyer가 friend에게 $4,000 check을 받고 system을 판매함.

1번 문제는 system에 대한 finance company의 interest를 묻고 있으므로, 우선 buyer와 finance company 간 priority를 판단해야 한다. Finance company는 perfection을 한 상태였으므로 담보물에 대한 security interest는 지속되는 것이 원칙이나, buyer가 BIOCOB이므로 예외 rule이 적용되어 finance company의 security interest는 더 이상 지속되지 않는다. 즉, buyer는 security interest로부터 free하다. 본 문제에서는 friend에게 shelter rule이 적용되므로, finance company와 friend 간 priority를 별도로 판단하지 않아도 된다. 만약 finance company가 buyer를 상대로 priority를 가지고 있었다면, finance company와 friend 간 priority를 판단해야 했을 것이다.

2번 문제는 system에 대한 retailer의 interest를 묻고 있으므로, 우선 retailer와 buyer 간 관계를 파악해야 한다. 이들이 체결한 계약은 본질적으로 security interest를 생성하는 바, retailer와 buyer 간 priority를 파악해야 하는데, 해당 security interest는 PMSI in consumer goods이므로 자동적으로 perfection된다. 따라서 retailer가 priority를 가진다(retailer>buyer). Retailer의 perfection이 인정되므로 담보물에 대한 security interest는 지속되는 것이 원칙이나, buyer와 friend 간 계약에 consumer to consumer exception이 적용되는 바, retailer의 security interest는 더 이상 지속되지 않는다. 즉, friend는 security interest로부터 free하다.

본 기출문제의 핵심은 BIOCOB에 대한 rule과 PMSI in consumer goods에 대한 rule을 구별하는데 있다.

1번 문제

답안요령

1. Security interest 기본 rule(collateral에 지속된다)★
2. 그러나 [BIOCOB]인 경우 예외 rule 적용
   + analysis
3. Shelter rule★
   + analysis

1. The police officer's testimony recounting the witness's statement is admissible, since it is hearsay exception and it did not violate the Confrontation Clause.

Hearsay is an out−of−court statement offered in evidence to prove the truth of the matter asserted. Witness's statement is not made at trial and it is used to prove the person described by witness is matched. However, it fits hearsay exception for present sense impression and excited utterance.

Present sense impressions exception exists when there is a statement describing an event or condition made while or immediately after the declaration after the declarant perceived it. Excited utterance is a statement relating to a startling event or condition, made while the declarant was under the stress or excitement that it causes.

In this case, a police officer arrived five minutes later and it is enough time to fits present sense impressions exception. The witness was wringing her hands and pacing when he made the statements and it shows that he was under the stress.

Thus, the police officer's testimony recounting the witness's statement is admissible under the hearsay exceptions.

Confrontation Clause of the Sixth Amendment gives defendants the right to confront witnesses against them. The right is applicable, if: (1) the statement was testimonial, (2) the declarant is unavailable to testify at trial, and (3) the defendant has not had an opportunity to cross−examine the witness before trial. When witnesses make statements with the primary purpose to assist police to meet an ongoing emergency, these are not testimonial.

The statement could be considered nontestimonial. The witness made the statement when the police arrived at the scene of the robbery under emergency circumstance. A robbery had recently occurred, and the suspect was armed, having the potential damage to public. If the court decides the statement is testimonial, the Confrontation Clause is not violated.

The statement could be considered testimonial. The witness made the statement when there is no suspect. The judge could conclude that the witness statement was describing past crime. The witness did not stand at trial and the defendant did not have an opportunity to cross−examination. Thus, its admission would violate the Confrontation Clause.

In sum, the police officer's testimony recounting the witness's statement is admissible, since it is hearsay exception and it did not violate the Confrontation Clause.

2. The police officer's testimony recounting the victim's statement is admissible, since it is identification statement.

The statement is deemed nonhearsay, if (1) the declarant prior statement identifies a person who declarant perceived before and (2) the declarant is subject to cross−examination at trial.

In this case, victim's statement was out−of−court statement to prove the truth of the matter asserted, and it is hearsay. However, the victim identified the defendant through voice based on the experience of it and the victim is subject to cross−examination at trial.

In sum, the police officer's testimony recounting the victim's statement is admissible, since it is identification statement.

3. The police officer's testimony that the defendant is a known drug dealer is inadmissible, since it is character evidence.

Character evidence is not admissible to prove that a person acted in conformity with the particular character trait. Evidence of crimes or other acts may be admissible for another purpose, such as motive, opportunity, intent, plan, identity, or absence of mistake.

In this case, the purpose of the police officer's testimony is to suggest that defendant is the sort of person who would commit a robbery. It is character evidence. It is hard to conclude that the defendant's hanging around is to prove his motive, opportunity, or something. Thus, police officer's statement is character evidence and it is inadmissible.

In sum, the police officer's testimony that the defendant is a known drug dealer is inadmissible, since it is character evidence.

해설

난이도: 중

핵심 단어 및 논점

- Confrontation Clause
- hearsay
- prior identification statement (officially non−hearsay)
- character evidence

1번 문제

> 답안요령

1. Hearsay 여부 판단★
   ① Hearsay 기본 rule
   ② 그러나 hearsay exception에 해당하여 admissible 가능
   ③ Exception rule
   ④ Analysis
2. Confrontation Clause
   ① Requirements
   ② "Testimonial"
   ③ "Primary purpose"
   ④ Analysis

TIP 본 답안요령은 문제가 세분화되어 있지 않고 '특정 statement의 admissibility를 판단하라'와 같이 해당 statement에 관한 '모든' 논점을 고려해야 하는 문제를 기준으로 작성되었다. 이 경우, Confrontation Clause뿐만 아니라 hearsay에 대한 내용을 서술하는 것이 고득점 포인트다. 한편, 동일한 statement에 대해 hearsay를 판단하는 문제와 Confrontation Clause 위반여부를 판단하는 문제가 구분되어 출제되었다면, 각 논점에 대해 서술한다.

1. LLP is liable to the bank on the loan, because the man had apparent authority.

When a partner has either actual or apparent authority, a limited liability partnership is bound by the partner's acts. There is an apparent authority, when the partner was carrying on in the ordinary course of the partnership business and a third party has no actual knowledge that the member lacks authority.

Here, the man loaned $25,000 from the bank without actual authority, since he had no consent of woman. However, the man regularly borrowed amounts from the bank. From the bank's perspective, the man was acting as a partner and had apparent authority to borrow money, because borrowing was for the ordinary course of the partnership business as LLP anticipated regular borrowings of up to $25,000 to cover maintenance expenses. Additionally, the loan officer had no actual knowledge that the man lacks authority. He asked the man if he had authority and checked a copy of the partnership agreement. He did not know the statement of partnership authority which was never filed. Thus, man had apparent authority.

In sum, LLP is liable to the bank on the loan, because the man had apparent authority.

2. The woman is not personally liable to the bank on the loan, since she is limited liable for the partnership's debts.

A partner in a limited liability partnership is not liable for partnership obligations just because he is the partner. Partners can become liable for partnership liability based on the doctrine of piercing the corporation's veil or member's direct liability.

Here, the loan is partnership's debts and the woman is not personally liable to the bank just because she is a partner of the partnership. There is no fact showing woman's personal liability or reason for piercing the corporation's veil.

There could be an argument that the woman was negligent to supervise or control the man. However, each partner is co—equal each other and no partner is under the other's supervision or control.

In sum, the woman is not personally liable to the bank on the loan.

3. The man is liable for breaching his fiduciary duties both to partnership and to woman.

A partner has the duty of loyalty and duty of care both to the partnership and to the other partners. Thus, partners are liable for damages to partnership and co—partners when they breach their duties. Duty of loyalty includes duty not to appropriate partnership assets for personal use. Duty of care includes a duty not to do intentional misconduct and violations of law knowingly.

Here, the man breached the duty of loyalty, since he used the $25,000 to pay his personal gambling debts. The money was what he loaned from the bank in the conduct of the partnership. He also breached his duty of care, since he did not give the loan officer a copy of the statement of partnership authority and tell him its existence.

In sum, he breached the duty of loyalty and duty of care.

When a partner breached his duties, the partnership can bring an action against the partner for the violation of the fiduciary duties. Additionally, the other partner can bring an action against another partner to enforce the partner's rights with or without accounting.

Here, the woman can bring a direct action to let the man make whole for any losses caused by the breach of duties. The woman can also bring an accounting action to let the man account to the partnership for the money that he used for his personal use. The partnership can bring a suit to seek damages for the man's breach of duties.

In conclusion, the man is liable for both partnership and the woman.

해설

난이도: 하

핵심 단어 및 논점

- LLP 특징
- apparent authority (ordinary course of business)
- fiduciary duty

1번 문제

답안요령

> 1. Agency rule
> 2. Partner's actual authority
>   + analysis
> 3. Apparent authority
>   + analysis: Ordinary course of business에 관한 계약 → apparent authority 인정
> 4. 결론(LLP's liability)

TIP 본 기출문제는 agent가 apparent authority를 가지고 있는 사안이다.

3번 문제

논점: Fiduciary duty

답안요령

> 1. Fiduciary duty to (partnership + partners)
> 2. Duty of loyalty
> 3. Duty of care
> 4. 피해본 partner가 소송할 경우★

1. Section 1 is constitutional, because it does not discriminate either on its face or in practical effect and there is no unduly burden on interstate commerce.

State laws that discriminate against out of state commerce in favor of in state commerce are subject to strict scrutiny.

Here, Section 1 is not facially discriminatory. It has an objective standard, requiring 50% of the electricity come from environmentally friendly energy sources. However, Section 1 is discriminatory in practical effect, since it favors State A's energy over an out of state industry. The discriminatory impact test applies, when a discriminatory impact was in a market that is regulated by the state. Here, Section 1 has discriminatory impact on natural gas market, but State A is regulating generation of electricity. In short, Section 1 is not practically discriminatory.

Even if it is not discriminatory, the state laws that affect interstate commerce can be invalidated if there is unduly burden on interstate commerce. It is so-called Pike balancing test. Here, there is no fact to show excessive burden on interstate commerce.

In short, Section 1 is constitutional.

2. Section 2 is unconstitutional, since it is discriminatory on its face and there are less discriminatory alternatives.

Section 2 is discriminatory on its face, when the Public Service Commission of State A denied the public utility in State B. This is because the law creates an exception for urgent energy needs in State A only, only favoring State A's consumer of electricity from state coal burning power plants. Additionally, the utility would have been permitted if it provided evidence of urgent energy needs in State A, rather than energy shortages in State B. The permit denial discriminates against out of state consumers. Any legitimate environmental purpose could not be used to discrimination.

Even if the state laws are discriminatory, they could be valid when the laws are narrowly tailored to meet a legitimate purpose. A law is not narrowly tailored, if there are less discriminatory alternative means to accomplish the state's purpose.

Here, Section 2 would not be narrowly tailored to meet environmental protection. There could be alternative ways that are less discriminatory, such as strict environmental regulations of all in state coal burning power plants or exception for urgent energy needs that does not discriminate against out of state consumers. In conclusion, Section 2 is unconstitutional.

3. Section 3 is constitutional, since State A's role is a market participant.

The state may discriminate in favor of in−state residents, when the state is acting as a market participant.

Under the Section 3, State A is required to buy goods and services only from environmentally friendly vendors located within the state. The law is discriminative in favor of in state vendors, but State A is acting as a market participant.

Thus, Section 3 is constitutional.

해설

난이도: 하

핵심 단어 및 논점

- dormant commerce clause (state)
- discriminatory impact
- unduly burden
- Pike balancing test
- market participant exception

논점: Dormant commerce clause

답안요령

1. General rule
2. Analysis(요건 ⅰ: discrimination)
3. Analysis(요건 ⅱ: unduly burdensome)★
   + analysis

그러나 본 기출에서는 dormant commerce clause 논점이 세 문제로 나누어 출제되었다. 따라서 각 문제가 초점을 두고 있는 내용에 대해서만 서술해야 한다. MEE에서는 출제의 도를 파악하고 해당되는 내용을 간단명료하게 작성하는 것이 중요하기 때문이다. 따라서 1번 답안에는 discrimination 요건(답안요령 2번)을, 2번 답안에는 discrimination과 unduly burdensome 요건(답안요령 2번과 3번)을, 3번 답안에는 exception rules(답안요령 4번)를 서술한다.

한편, 2번 답안 중 unduly burdensome 요건 서술 시, Pike balancing test를 근거로 판단하는 것이 고득점 포인트다.

1. An agent under a durable health−care POA has the power to make health care decision, whenever the principal lacks capacity to make such decisions.

All states authorize advance directives (living will) and durable health−care powers. An advance directive specifies whether the patient prefer treatment or non−treatment when he becomes incapacitated. Unless a durable POA specifies otherwise, a designated agent is empowered to make health−care decisions for the principal whenever the principal lacks capacity to make such decisions. The power is not limited to particular illness or for a particular time period.

Here, the patient singed a durable health care POA shortly after receiving the cancer diagnosis. A designated agent is empowered to make not only for cancer related decisions, but also for decisions related to other health care. Thus, the attorney's decisions following the automobile accident were empowered.

Under the advance directive, a designated agent shall make decisions for the principal for the principal's best interest. Here, the patient's son was confident that his mother would not want to be kept on life support if she were permanently unconscious. Additionally, the doctor noted that prior large risk or a stroke would substantially increase the risk, causing unconsciousness. Thus, the son's decision not to resuscitate seems consistent with the best interest of the patient. The fact that the sisters disagreed with their brother's decision does not make a difference on the result, because the designated agent may act on behalf of the principal without consulting family members. Thus, the decision of the designated agent, son, was proper.

In sum, an agent under a durable health−care POA has the power to make health care decision, whenever the principal lacks capacity to make such decisions.

2. The sons is not liable in a wrongful death action, since he acts in good faith.

An agent who made health care decisions in good faith is protected from civil and criminal liability. A health care decision is to provide, or withhold all forms of health care. Health care means any care, treatment or procedure that affect an individual's physical condition.

Here, There were many facts that supports son's good faith: the son was confident that the patient, his mother would not want to be maintained in a permanently unconscious condition, there was a more than 50% risk that the patient would not regain consciousness, patient was over age 80, and cardiac arrest and stoke enhance the risk of unconsciousness. The fact that the patient designated his son as an agent also supports that the patient trusts his decision. There are no facts supporting son's bad faith. Thus, the son acted in good faith.

In sum, the sons is not liable in a wrongful death action, since he acts in good faith.

3. The son is entitled to a share of the patient's estate, since he did not intentionally cause the patient's death.

Under the slayer statute, a beneficiary is not entitled to the share when he intentionally caused the decedent's death. Slayer statute does not apply to an agent under durable health−care POA.

Here, the son did not "intentionally" cause the patient's death and his decision was based on many circumstantial considering. Additionally, Son did not cause the death, but cardiac arrest is the direct arrest since there is no evidence that a resuscitation attempt would have been successful. Penalizing the agent based on a decision caused death of principal would undermine the important purpose of empowering a durable power of attorney. Thus, the son should not be barred from taking a share of his mother's estate.

In sum, the son is entitled to a share of the patient's estate, since he did not intentionally cause the patient's death.

해설

난이도: 하

핵심 단어 및 논점

- advance directives (living will)
- durable health−care power of attorney (POA)
- health care decision
- in good faith
- slayer statute

본 기출문제는 POA에 대한 세 개의 논점이 구분되어 있다. 1번 답안에는 'power가 not specific하다'는 점, 2번 답안에는 POA가 good−faith를 가지고 판단했는지 그 여부, 3번 답안에는 slayer statute와의 관계성에 대해 서술한다.

한편, 2번 답안 서술 시, POA에서 지정된 agent는 작성자의 특정 질병에 한해 권한을 가지는 것이 아니라는 점과 agent의 good−faith가 있었음에 대해 analysis한다.

2016Feb Family Law

1. The premarital agreement is enforceable.

The state follows UPAA, and therefore an agreement is unenforceable if the party against whom enforcement is sought shows: (1) involuntariness or (2) unfairness and lack of adequate disclosure.

Regarding involuntariness, it could be established by fraud, duress, or coercion, and there are many factors to be considered, such as lack of opportunity to talk with independent counsel, reasons for proceeding with the marriage (pregnancy), financial losses and embarrassment arising from cancellation of the wedding, maturity of parties, and prior experience of marriage.

Here, the woman presented the man with a proposed premarital agreement one week before the wedding. The man could argue that he had no enough time to concerning about it and it was involuntarily made. However, he had time to contact a lawyer friend and get advice. Even though the lawyer urged him not to sign it, he voluntarily signed the agreement. Additionally, they married at City hall, and there are no facts showing any hardship from cancellation of the wedding. Thus, there was no involuntariness in making the agreement.

Woman presented the man with the agreement and an asset list. Thus, there was adequate disclosure and therefore the premarital agreement is enforceable.

In sum, the premarital agreement is enforceable.

2. Condominium is separate property, and the portions of brokerage account and royalties are marital. The characteristic of the lottery depends on approach. Marital property would be divided in the court's discretion.

Marital property is divisible at divorce. By contrast, separate property is not divisible at divorce. The property is marital if it was granted during the marriage by any methods, except for gift, descent, or devise. A separate asset can be transformed into marital property, if marital funds or significant efforts by the owner's spouse enhance its value or build equity during the marriage. When courts decide property division order, only marital property is considered.

Here, woman purchased the condominium before she married the man, and therefore it is separate property. It worths $400,000 as a result of market appreciation. It was by the nature of the economy, rather than by man's contribution during the marriage or by the marital property.

Regarding woman's brokerage account, its portion is marital property. This is because its value was increased by additional investments that the woman made with employment bonuses she received during the marriage, which is marital property. The portion of brokerage account that was made before marriage is separate property.

Regarding the royalties, it is not clear how long he wrote the novel before the marriage. If the man wrote significant portion of the novel during the marriage, significant portion of the royalties is marital property. It depends on the portion of the novel completed during the marriage.

In the majority of jurisdictions, marital property continues to accrue until a final divorce decree is entered. In the minority of jurisdictions, marital property stops accruing after the date of permanent separation or the date of filing for a divorce.

Here, the woman won, but has not yet received, a $5 million lottery jackpot. In the majority of jurisdictions, the lottery will accrue until a final divorce decree is entered and therefore it is marital property. In the minority of jurisdictions, the lottery is separate property, since they separated before awarding the lottery.

In sum, condominium is separate property, and the portions of brokerage account and royalties are marital. The characteristic of the lottery depends on approach.

When courts divide property, they divide marital property equitably, not equally. They consider many factors, such as the duration of the marriage, each spouse's future needs, and the parties' contribution to the marriage and to the acquisition of assets.

Here, the woman worked as an investment banker, while the man worked part−time as a bartender. It seems that the woman has better social position compared to the man. Additionally, the woman won lottery. The woman and man had no child and the man had no contribution during the marriage as a parent. There are no facts showing man made contribution during the marriage as a homemaker. By contrast, the woman made contribution to man's novel.

In sum, it is hard to predict how the court divides the marital property.

해설

난이도: 하

핵심 단어 및 논점

- premarital agreement
- property division order
- marital property
- separate property
- accrue

1번 문제

논점: Enforceability of premarital agreement

- Enforceability와 관련하여 적용되는 두 개의 rule이 있으며, 하나는 요건 중 하나 (or)만 만족하면 되는 한편, 다른 하나는 모든 요건을 모두(and) 만족해야 한다는 점을 명시하는 것이 고득점 포인트다. 다만, 일부 기출문제에서는 UPAA를 적용하는 법원임을 명시하는 경우도 있는데, 그런 경우에는 UPAA의 rules에 대해서만 논하면 충분하다. 본 문제가 그러하다.

- UPAA가 적용되고 부부간 full disclosure가 존재하는 경우, unconscionability에 대한 analysis를 생략하고 바로 involuntariness에 대한 analysis를 하는 것이 좋다. Full disclosure가 존재한다면 unconscionability 존재여부와 무관하게 UPAA의 premarital agreement's enforceability 두 번째 요건을 만족하지 못하기 때문이다.

- 각 state마다 unconscionability를 판단하는 '기준시점'이 다르므로, 다양한 기준에 입각하여 analysis하는 것이 고득점 포인트다.

1. A member−managed LLC was created, since the certificate of organization fails to specify the type of LLC.

Here, the certificate of organization fails to specify whether the LLC is member−managed or manager−managed. The LLC is presumed to be member−managed.
Here, two siblings filed a certificate of organization to form a limited liability. The certification did not specify the type of the LLC. Thus, the LLC is a member−managed LLC.
In sum, a member−managed LLC was created, since the certificate of organization fails to specify the type of LLC.

2. The LLC is bound under the tire contract, since the brother had both actual and apparent authority.

Each member in a member−managed LLC has equal rights in the management and conduct of the company's activities. Thus, general agency law principles are applicable. If a member made a contract with both actual and apparent authority, member's acts can bind the company to the contract. A member has actual authority if the member carried out the company's ordinary business. A member has apparent authority when the opposing party of the transaction could rely on the appearance of the member.
Here, the brother had actual authority to make the tire contract, since his purchasing 100 bike tires is the company's ordinary business, a bike shop. He also had apparent authority, because he had purchased tires for the LLC twice in the past, and the manufacturer could rely on the appearance that the brother was properly acting for the LLC.
In sum, the LLC is bound under the tire contract, since the brother had both actual and apparent authority.

3. The LLC is not bound by the farmland sales contract, since the cousin lacked actual and apparent authority.

When a member made a nonordinary transaction, the actual authority depends on the operating agreement of the LLC, which governs relationship between members and the LLC and the activities of the company. When a member made a nonordinary transaction, the apparent authority cannot exist, because it is hard for the third party of the transaction to reasonably believe that the member properly acted for the company.

In this case, the operating agreement provides that the LLC's farmland may not be sold without the approval of all three members. However, cousin sold the LLC's farmland to a third-party buyer without consents of brother and sister. Cousin's transaction was made in violation of the agreement. Thus, cousin lacks actual authority. The LLC did not manifest that cousin was authorized and sale of the farmland is not in the ordinary course of bike shop business. Thus, cousin lacks apparent authority.

However, acts of members not in the ordinary course of the company's business bind the company only if the members were authorized by the other members.

In this case, cousin acted not in the ordinary course of the company's business without authorization of the other members. Thus, cousin lacks apparent authority.

In sum, The LLC is not bound by the farmland sales contract.

4. The brother's email is a dissociation from the LLC.

When a member expresses will to withdraw, it constitutes dissociation. Dissociation is different from dissolution, which requires all consents from members. Dissociation results in: (1) loss of his rights to participate in the LLC, (2) rights to distributions only if made by the continuing members, and (3) loss of the right to payment for his LLC interest, unless the operating agreement specifies otherwise.

In this case, the brother's email states "I want out of our business," and it constitutes dissociation, not dissolution. As a result of dissociation, the brother has no right to payment for his LLC, a check for his share here.

In modern, when a member of an at-will LLC withdraws, it is treated same as when a partner in an at-will general partnership withdraws. Dissociated member's interest in at-will LLC must be purchased by LLC.

In sum, the brother's email is a dissociation from the LLC.

해설

난이도: 하

핵심 단어 및 논점

- limited liability company (LLC)
- default rule (member-managed LLC v. manager-managed LLC)
- actual authority
- apparent authority
- dissolution v. dissociation

1, 2, 3번 문제

논점: Member의 법률행위는 LLC에 귀속되는가

답안요령

1. LLC 유형 & Member's authority
    + analysis
2. Actual/Apparent authority
3. Analysis (actual authority)
4. Analysis (apparent authority)

TIP1 1번: Manage할 권한을 가진 member 행위에는 'agency rule'이 적용됨을 서술한다.

TIP2 2번: 대부분의 기출문제는 member's 행위가 '회사 경영을 위한 통상적인 행위(ordinary course of business)'인 사안으로 출제된다.

2016July Evidence / Criminal Procedure

1. The officer's testimony is admissible, since the defendant was not in custody.

Law enforcement officers are required to read Miranda warnings to a suspect when the suspect is subject to an in−custody interrogation. There is custody when reasonable person under similar circumstances would believe she was not free to leave. There is interrogation when police either expresses questioning or elicit an incriminating response from the suspect.

In this case, the defendant was under interrogation because the officer asked him. However, the defendant was not in custody, since he voluntarily invited the officer. Additionally, Miranda protects only protect testimonial or communicative evidence. Crying is not the type of communication protected by the privilege against self−incrimination. Thus, defendant's Miranda right has not been violated.

There is no hearsay issue here, since crying is just an action and it is not a statement.

In sum, the officer's testimony should be admissible, since the defendant was not in custody.

2. Permitting the officer to read her handwritten notes is proper, since it falls within a recorded recollection exception.

Hearsay is an out−of−court statement offered in evidence to prove the truth of the matter asserted.

The notes is double hearsay: first level is the notes itself and the second level is the defendant's statement to the officer.

The first level is admissible under the hearsay exception for recorded recollection. A recorded recollection is a record regarding a matter that the witness knew but now cannot recall enough to testify, and it was made when to refresh the witness's memory.

Here, the handwritten notes is recorded recollection, since the officer recorded it with personal knowledge but now cannot remember exactly what he said.

The handwritten notes can be read to jury if the witness cannot remember even after refreshing. According to the facts, the officer states that he cannot remember the events after reviewing her notes, and she identified the document as notes she had made on December 2. Thus, the first level fits hearsay exception.

The second level hearsay is admissible under an admission exception. Defendant's statement to officer is used against defendant. Thus, the second level hearsay is admissible. Thus, the notes are properly read to jury.

In sum, permitting the officer to read her handwritten notes is proper, since it falls within a recorded recollection exception.

3. Admitting the officer's handwritten notes as an exhibit is not proper, since it was not requested by opposing party.

Although there is a hearsay exception for recorded recollections, the record may be received as an exhibit only if it is offered by an adverse party.

Here, the notes were recorded recollection hearsay exception as mentioned above, and it is provided as an exhibit by the prosecutor, not by opposing party, defendant.

Therefore, the notes cannot be admitted as an exhibit.

In sum, admitting the officer's handwritten notes as an exhibit is not proper, since it was not requested by opposing party.

4. Admitting the officer's testimony recounting the defendant's statement is proper, since the defendant voluntarily initiated communication.

If a custodial suspect who has invoked his right to counsel initiates post–invocation communication with the police, the suspect's subsequent statements may be admissible.

In this case, the defendant was read Miranda warnings and he invoked the right to counsel. After his invocation of right, the officer stopped questioning. However, defendant voluntarily initiates communication, stating "I want to make a deal." Thus, defendant's subsequent statement "I have some information that can really help you with this case" is admissible.

Additionally, the statement is an opposing party statement and not considered as hearsay.

In sum, admitting the officer's testimony recounting the defendant's statement is proper, since the defendant voluntarily initiated communication.

5. Admitting the officer's testimony recounting the defendant's statement is proper.

If a suspect has been released from in-custody interrogation, the police obligation to honor an invocation of the Miranda right to counsel terminates after 14 days.

In this case, on December 1, the defendant re-invoked the right to counsel. However, he was arrested on December 20, which is the date after 20 days and the police obligation to honor the right to counsel is terminated. On December 20, the officer properly read Miranda warnings and the defendant voluntarily waived his rights. Thus, admitting the defendant's statement does not violate Miranda right.

The statement is not hearsay because it falls within an admission exception.

In sum, admitting the officer's testimony recounting the defendant's statement is proper.

해설

난이도: 2번 문제: 중
　　　　그 외 문제: 하

핵심 단어 및 논점

- Miranda rights (Fifth Amendment)
- in-custody interrogation
- hearsay
- double hearsay
- recorded recollection
  (hearsay exception)
- admission exception
  (hearsay exception)
- exhibit (recorded recollection)
- waive the right to counsel
- 14-day honor

2번 문제

답안요령

1. Analysis(해당 증거의 relevance에 대한)
2. Hearsay 정의
   + analysis
3. Double hearsay exception rule
   + analysis
4. 1st level이 해당하는 exception rule
   + analysis
5. 2nd level이 해당하는 exception rule
   + analysis
6. 결론

TIP Double hearsay인 경우, 바깥에 있는 hearsay(first level)부터 analysis한다.

3번 문제

논점: Past recorded recollection as an exhibits

답안요령

1. Recorded recollection 정의
   + analysis
2. Exhibit 제출 요건
   + analysis

4번 문제

답안요령

1. 상황설명
2. Post-invocation communication
3. "Willingness"
   + analysis
4. Hearsay issue★
   + analysis

5번 문제

답안요령

1. 상황설명
2. Rule (honor invocation only for 14 days)
   + analysis
3. Hearsay issue★

1. The physician is not liable to the man under tort law.

Negligence action can be raised when the defendant failed to exercise reasonable care. The doctor's actions should be complied with the standard of other typical doctor.

Here, the man could argue that the physician was negligent in suggesting that drinking the herbal tea might lower his cholesterol. However, there is no fact showing that the physician suggested the herbal tea, knowing that the herbal tea would be contaminated with toxic pesticides. Additionally, the physician offered to prescribe a drug first as the ordinary physician does, but the man stated that he did not want to start taking drugs and want to take natural remedies first. The physician told the man that natural remedies are not as reliable and urged the man to come back in three months for another blood test. Thus, the physician was not negligent in suggesting the herbal tea.

The man could also argue that the physician was negligent to correctly find that his symptoms were because of the herbal tea. However, the physician underwent another blood test and he responded to the test that showing an elevated white blood cell count by taking more tests. The physician properly referred the man to a medical specialist who had expertise in liver diseases. Even the liver expertise recognized the symptoms with the several patients with inflamed livers and elevated white blood cell counts like the man. Thus, the physcian took prompt and proper care for the patient.

In sum, the physician was not negligent to the patient.

2. The five U.S. companies are liable for the breach of warranty of merchantability, while they are not liable under the product liability.

A commercial seller is subject to strict product liability for physical harm thereby caused, when he sells any defective product that is unreasonably dangerous to the consumer. The commercial seller is defined as one who engaged in the business of selling products.

Here, the five U.S. companies that processed packaged, and sold the herbal tea to the health—food store are commercial sellers. The fact that man is not a direct purchaser of the herbal tea from those companies does not make a different result. This is because the privity of contract is not required in raising strict product liability.

A product is defective when it is unreasonably dangerous. A product could have a manufacturing defect, a design defects, or inadequate warnings. A product has a manufacturing defect, when the consumer would not expect the unreasonable danger. Here, the product was herbal tea, and the existence of the harmful ingredient is a manufacturing defect. The man could not expect that the herbal tea was contaminated with a highly toxic pesticide. The man is not required to show the companies' negligence for the strict product liability.

In a products liability action, the plaintiff must show that the defendant caused the injury. When the plaintiff cannot directly link the exact defendant's product and the plaintiff's injury (symptoms), there are several doctrines to be used: market share liability doctrine, alternative liability doctrine, and joint venture doctrine.

Under the market share liability doctrine, jury could apportion the damages based on the market shares of manufacturers of a defective product. However, this doctrine is applicable only when the defective products are fungible in relation to their capacity to cause harm. Here, the investigation has established that the levels of contamination and toxicity were not consistent. Thus, the defective products are not fungible and therefore the market share liability doctrine is not applicable.

Under the alternative liability doctrine, jury can find two defendants liable when each was negligent and either individual could have caused the plaintiff's injuries. Here, there are five companies and there are no facts showing each are negligent. Thus, the alternative liability doctrine is inapplicable.

Under the joint venture doctrine, the jury imputes one defendant's negligence to other defendants who are engaged in a common project. Here, there is no fact showing that the five companies are in common project, such as sharing common warehouse with exporters. Thus, the joint venture doctrine is inapplicable.

Under the UCC2, the contract of sale includes an implied warranty of merchantability when the products were sold by merchants. To be merchantable, the goods must fit for the ordinary purpose for which the goods are used. Here, the herbal teas are "goods" and it is governed by UCC2. The contaminated herbal tea does not fit for the ordinary purpose and the five companies breached the implied warranty of merchantability.

In conclusion, the five U.S. companies are liable for the breach of warranty of merchantability, while they are not liable under the product liability.

3. The health—food store is liable to the man under the strict product liability and the implied warranty of merchantability.

A commercial seller is subject to strict product liability for physical harm thereby caused, when he sells any defective product that is unreasonably dangerous to the consumer. The commercial seller is defined as one who engaged in the business of selling products. "Commercial sellers" include a retailer even if it has no control over the design and manufacture of a product.

Here, the health—food store is the retailer, and therefore it is liable under the strict product liability because it sold contaminated herbal tea.

Regarding the causation, the man purchased all the herbal tea from the same health—food store. Therefore, the man is not required to identify exact the product that caused his injury.

Under the implied warranty theory, the retailer is a merchant. Therefore, the man can recover damages for the breach of the warranty.

In sum, the health—food store is liable to the man.

해설

난이도: 중

핵심 단어 및 논점

- negligence
- strict product liability
- product defect
- market share liability doctrine
- alternative liability doctrine
- joint venture doctrine
- strict product liability
- implied warranty theory

2번, 3번 문제

논점: Products liability based on strict liability

답안요령

> 1. strict products liability 정의
> 2. NG proof 필요 없음★
> 3. Commercial seller"
>   + analysis
> 4. "Defective" product(manufacturing/design defect)
> 5. Causation
> 6. Analysis

> **TIP** Strict liability를 입증하는데 있어, '피고의 negligence 유무는 무관하다'는 점을 명시하는 것이 고득점 포인트다. 이는 products liability뿐만 아니라 일반적인 strict liability에 관해 논하는 경우에도 그러하다.
>
> "In a strict products liability action, the plaintiff can recover against a producer without proof of negligence if the plaintiff could show that a producer sold the product that caused his injury."
>
> "Whether there was negligence does not change the result."

1. Ion's disablement does not incur any liability to PTT, since Ion can sent its technician to the PTT facility without breach of the peace.

The security interest is effective and attaches, when: (1) debtor signed a security agreement containing a description of the collateral, (2) debtor has rights in the collateral, and (3) secured party gave money to secured party.

Here, Ion has effective security interest in the proton-therapy equipment. PTT authenticated a security interest that described the proton therapy equipment, PTT purchased the equipment, and Ion gave the equipment to PTT on credit.

When a debtor defaulted and the collateral is equipment, a secured party may leave the equipment in place and make it unusable. A secured party may pursue this option without judicial process without breach of the peace. Equipment is defined as goods other than inventory, farm products, or consumer goods.

Here, PTT defaulted, so Ion will be sending a technician to the PTT facility to disable the equipment so that it cannot be used by PTT until PTT pays what it owes to Ion. This option will no breach the peace, because the technician was to perform regular maintenance on the equipment. There is nothing indication of the technician's violent, disruptive, or illegal behavior.

In conclusion, Ion's disablement does not incur any liability to PTT, since Ion can sent its technician to the PTT facility without breach of the peace.

2. Bank has a superior claim to the proton-therapy equipment, since Ion did not made fixture filing.

Bank has security in PTT's land and all structures erected on the land. Under State A law, the proton therapy equipment attached to PTT's building is considered a fixture. Thus, Bank extends its security interest to the equipment.

Ion's security interest in the proton therapy equipment was effective and had attached, since PTT signed the agreement, PTT had rights in the equipment by purchasing it, and Ion sold it on credit.

Whether a filing of a financing statement is proper to perfect the security interest is governed by the state law in which a debtor is located. Here, PTT is located in State A and therefore the State A law governs the filing. Ion filed a properly completed financing statement with the office of the Secretary of State of State A, and therefore Ion perfected its security interest.

Even if a security interest in fixtures is perfected, it is generally subordinate to a conflicting interest of an encumbrancer of the related real property. However, the security interest in fixtures would have priority over conflicting interest of an encumbrancer of the related real property when: (1) the fixture is subject to a purchase money security interest (PMSI) and (2) the secured party made fixture filing before the collateral became a fixture or within 20 days thereafter. Fixture filing should provide a description of the real property that the collateral is related and must be filed in the office in which a mortgage on the related real estate would be filed, not in the state's central filing office.

Here, the equipment constitutes fixture which is subject to Ion's PMSI. The equipment secures PTT's obligation to pay the remaining purchase price. However, the financing statement that Ion filed does not constitute fixture filing, because it did not includes the description of the building and it was filed in the office of the Secretary of State of State A. In short, Ion is subordinate to Bank's interest.

In conclusion, Bank has superior claim to the equipment.

3. Ion has an enforceable and perfected security interest PTT's rights in the lease contract.

Proceeds is defined as whatever is obtained on the sale or lease of the collateral. A secured party that has a security interest in collateral also has security interest in any same proceeds of the collateral.

Here, PTT's rights under the lease with Oncology are proceeds of the proton therapy equipment and therefore Ion has a security interest in PTT's rights.

As security interest in proceeds of collateral is perfected for at least 20 days if the security interest in the original collateral was perfected. The security in the equipment's proceeds will remain after the 20−day period, if the security interest in the original collateral was perfected by a filing in the same office in which a security interest in the proceeds could be perfected by filing.

Here, Ion's security in the equipment is perfected by the filing and its security in the equipment's proceeds is perfected for at least 20 days. A security interest in the chattel paper, created between Oncology and PTT, may be perfected by filing a financing statement in the Secretary of State's office in State A, which is the same office in which PTT filed the financing statement with respect to the equipment. In short, the security interest in the chattel paper is perfected as well. In conclusion, Ion has an enforceable and perfected security interest PTT's rights in the lease contract.

해설

난이도: 상

핵심 단어 및 논점

- effectiveness of security interest
- equipment
- conflict of laws
- fixture
- real property
- priority
- purchase money security interest (PMSI)
- fixture filing
- proceeds
- 20−day rule

2번 문제

논점: fixture와 real property의 priority

두 collateral에 대한 security interest가 모두 perfection되어 있는 것을 전제로 할 때, 대부분 경우 "fixture < real property"이다. 그러나 fixture에 대한 security interest가 PSMI이면서 그것이 생성되기 전 또는 생성된 후 20일 이내로 fixture filing을 한 경우에는 "fixture > real property"이다.

답안요령

1. 상황설명, Fixture 개념
2. 병's security right의 attachment, perfection
   + analysis
3. 원칙 (perfected fixture < real property)
4. 예외 rule (요건×3)
   + analysis
5. 결론

TIP1 답안작성 로직은 다음과 같다.

　① 'Fixture'에 대한 attachment 및 perfection을 설명

　② Fixture에 대한 담보물권은 perfection 유무와 상관없이 real property에 대한 담보물권에 subordinate한 것이 원칙이다. (fixture < real property)

　③ 그러나 예외의 rule이 있다. 요건들을 충족하면 (fixture > real property) 인정 O.

　④ 결론

TIP2 'Fixture'에 대한 담보물권을 먼저 설명한다.

TIP3 위 1번: Collateral 유형에 대해 주 법 조항이 문제에 명시되어 있는 경우, 해당 조항을 기준으로 collateral 유형을 판단한다.

TIP4 위 2번: Fixture에 대한 담보물권의 perfection 성립요건은 collateral이 위치한 주 법에 의해 규율된다는 점과 fixture filing이 file되어야 하는 office에 대해 서술하는 것이 고득점 포인트다.

1. The neighbor would succeed in a breach of contract action against the painter.

Generally, contracts are assignable. However, a contract is not assignable if the assignment: (1) would materially change the duty of the obligor, (2) would materially increase the burden imposed on the obligor, (3) would impair the obligor's chance of obtaining return performance, (4) is forbidden by statute or by public policy, or (5) is validly precluded by contract. To be an effective assignment, it needs: (1) that the assignor manifests his/her intent to transfer the right to the assignee, without reserving any right to confirm or nullify the transfer and (2) that the assignee manifests assent to the assignment.

Here, a homeowner assigned the contract with the painter to neighbor. The obligation of the painter under the contract was to paint the homeowner's house within 14 days. First of all, the two houses of the homeowner and the neighborhood have identical exteriors. Thus, the assignment would not materially change the duty of the painter. Secondly, those two houses are next to each other and therefore the assignment would not increase the painter's burden to travel. Thirdly, there is no fact showing that the painter's chance of obtaining $6,000 and the assignment is forbidden by statute, public policy, or the contract. Thus, the contract is assignable.

Regarding the effectiveness of the assignment, the homeowner and the neighbor agreed to the assignment though clear communication. The assent from the obligor is not required. Thus, the assignment is effective.

In sum, the neighbor would succeed in a breach of contract action against the painter.

2. The retiree would not succeed in a breach of contract action, since he is not an intended third beneficiary.

Here, the homeowner's assignment was to the neighbor, not to the retiree. Thus, the retiree has no cause of action against the painter.

There are two types of third party beneficiary: incidental beneficiaries and intended beneficiaries. If the parties knew that the contract benefits third party when the contract is made, the beneficiary is intended beneficiary. Only the intended beneficiaries can enforce a promise.

Here, the retiree is not an intended beneficiary. When the painter and the homeowner made the contract, they did not intended that the contract will benefit the retiree.

In sum, the retiree would not succeed in a breach of contract action, since he is not an intended third beneficiary.

3. The painter could succeed in a contract claim against either the neighbor or the homeowner, since the assignment includes a delegation of the homeowner's duty.

Generally, assignment includes a delegation of the assignor's unperformed duties under the contract.

Here, the contract between the neighbor and the homeowner is not only an assignment but also a delegation to the neighbor to make a payment to the painter. When the contract is made, the homeowner let the neighbor pay the painter $6,000 and the neighbor agreed it. Thus, the painter has a cause of action against him for his already done performance, even if the neighbor was not a party to the original contract between the homeowner and the neighbor.

If an obligor does not agree to discharge an assignor, the assignor's delegation to the assignee does not relieve assignor's obligation to the obligor. Here, there is no fact showing the painter agreed to discharge the homeowner. Thus, if the neighbor does not make a payment to the painter, the painter can also raise a cause of action against the homeowner.

In sum, the painter could succeed in a contract claim against either the neighbor or the homeowner, since the assignment includes a delegation of the homeowner's duty.

해설

난이도: 1번 문제: 하
2번 문제: 하
3번 문제: 중

핵심 단어 및 논점

- assignment
- intended third beneficiary
- delegation

2016July Civil Procedure

1. The court has personal jurisdiction cover the man, since he was served when he was voluntarily present in State C.

Federal district courts exercise personal jurisdiction to the same extent as the courts of general jurisdiction of the state where the district court sits. Under the Due Process Clause of the Fourteenth Amendment, a state court can have personal jurisdiction over a nonresident defendant who was served with process when he voluntarily present in the forum state.

Here, State C's courts may exercise personal jurisdiction to the limits allowed by the U.S. Constitution. The man was personally served when he visit the woman in the hospital. Additionally, his traveling was purposefully availed himself of benefits in the State C, such as benefits of police, fire, and emergency medical protection. The man has the burden of proof that holding the case in State C is unfair, but the modern transportation would not be helpful for alleging unfairness. Thus, the court has personal jurisdiction cover the man.

In sum, the court has personal jurisdiction cover the man, since he was served when he was voluntarily present in State C.

2. The federal court may exercise federal question jurisdiction over the woman's Safety Act claim and supplemental jurisdiction over the woman's negligence claim.

Federal courts have federal question jurisdiction over all civil actions arising under the federal laws or Constitution. Under the well—pleaded rule, plaintiff's complaint must state that his own cause of action is based upon federal laws or the Constitution. Merely mentioning of the federal statute to rebut an anticipated defense or to deny the applicability of the law does not establish federal question jurisdiction.

Here, the woman's complaint was based on a Safety Act which is the federal law. Thus, the federal question jurisdiction exists. Regarding the woman's state-law negligence claim, The U.S. District Court for the District of State C does not have federal question jurisdiction. Additionally, both the woman and the man are living in State A, and there is no citizenship diversity. State citizenship for individual U.S. citizens is determined by their domicile, the home where the individual intends to return. Even though the woman stayed in State C while she was in the hospital, she had no intent to change domicile. Thus, the woman is domiciled in State A.

Under the supplemental jurisdiction statute, district courts may hear claims that could not be heard, if those claims that are part of the same or controversy under Article III, if they derive from common nucleus of operative fact.

Here, the woman's Safety Act and negligence claims arise from common nucleus of operative facts: the man's disabling of his gun's safety features and the resulting accidental shooting of the woman. Thus, the federal court may exercise supplemental jurisdiction over the negligence claim.

The district court has discretion to decline to exercise supplemental jurisdiction in three situations: (1) there are complex issue on state claim, (2) state claim predominates federal claim, (3) federal court dismissed all claims that it had original jurisdiction, or (4) there are other compelling reasons.

Here, the woman could argue that the negligence claim substantially predominates over the federal question claim, because the damages on the negligence claim are larger than the damages on the federal claim. However, there are many overlapping evidences between the claims, and the court is unlikely to dismiss the negligence claim.

In sum, the federal court may exercise federal question jurisdiction over the woman's Safety Act claim and supplemental jurisdiction over the woman's negligence claim.

3. The U.S. District Court for the District of State C is not appropriate venue, since the man resides in State A, and the substantial part of the accidental shooting occurred in State A.

Venue is appropriate in a judicial district where: (1) any defendant resides if all defendants are residents of the forum state, (2) a substantial part of the events which is the basis of the claim occurred, or (3) (if none of the above apply,) any defendant is subject to the court's personal jurisdiction.

First, the man resides in State A, and State C is a not proper venue. Second, the woman's claim is based on the accident of shooting and it was occurred in State A. Typically, in the personal injury torts claim, the district where the defendant's torts actions occurred, rather than the district where the plaintiff received medical treatment. Third, State A is a proper venue under the prior two provisions, and the third provision is inapplicable in this case. Thus, the man's motion to dismiss for improper venue should be granted.

In sum, the U.S. District Court for the District of State C is not appropriate venue, since the man resides in State A, and the substantial part of the accidental shooting occurred in State A.

해설

난이도 : 하

핵심 단어 및 논점

- personal jurisdiction (PJ)
- federal question jurisdiction (FQJ)
- well-pleaded rule
- supplemental jurisdiction (SPJ)
- venue

2번 문제

FQJ와 SPJ 모두에 대해 논해야 한다.

> **답안요령1**

> 1. FQJ
> 2. Well-pleaded doctrine★
> 3. Analysis + 결론

> **답안요령2**

> 1. SPJ에 대한 기본 rule
> 2. Considering factors (×4)
>   + analysis
> 3. Court's discretion (×3)
>   + analysis
> 4. 결론

> **TIP** SPJ에 대한 답안은 analysis를 최대한 자세히 논하는 것이 고득점 포인트다.

1. The contract between the cook and the neighbor is governed under UCC2.

A contract for the sale of goods is governed by UCC2. The term "goods" means movable things at the time of making a contract. Common law is applicable regarding aspects that are not displayed by UCC.

Here, a contract is for sale of tomatoes, which are movable.

In sum, the contract between the cook and the neighbor is governed under UCC2.

2. The gardener is not binding by the promise to open the offer open and he could revoke the offer anytime before acceptance.

There is an offer when the person communicates to another a statement of willingness to enter into a bargain and to justify for the other person to understand that his assent is invited and the assent will conclude it. Here, the cook handed a document to the gardener and it constitutes gardener's willingness to enter into a bargain of tomatoes.

An offer can be revoked by the offeror at any time before acceptance. However, offer cannot be revoked when option contract exists. An option contract is enforceable when there is a consideration. Here, the document stated that the gardener will hold open this offer for 14 days. However, there is no consideration for holding the offer open. Thus, the promise to hold the offer open is not enforceable.

Under a firm offer rule, a promise hold open the offer without consideration is enforceable. This rule applies only to an offer by merchant. Merchants are who have knowledge or skills to the goods of the transaction. Here, the offer was made by the gardener who is an amateur gardener with no business experience.

The gardener is not a merchant and a firm offer rule is inapplicable.

In some cases, an offer is as an option contract when: (1) the offerer should reasonably expect to induce action or forbearance the offeree before acceptance and (2) the offer actually induced action or forbearance. There is no fact to apply this rule in this case.

In sum, the gardener is not binding by the promise to open the offer open and he could revoke the offer anytime before acceptance.

3. The gardener revoked his offer with clear notice to the cook and is not bound by the contract.

A revocation occurs when the offeror manifests an intention not to enter into the proposed contract. Notice of the revocation must be communicated to the offeree to terminate the offeree's power to accept the offer.

Here, as soon as the cook identified herself, the gardener told the cook that "I can't sell them to you because I have sold them to someone else." It is a manifestation that shows the gardener's intention not to enter into the contract for sale of tomatoes with the cook. Thus, it terminates the cook's power to accept the offer.

In sum, the gardener revoked his offer with clear notice to the cook and is not bound by the contract.

해설

난이도: 하

핵심 단어 및 논점

- offer
- revocation of offer
  - firm offer rule
  - option contract

2, 3번 문제

아래 답안요령은 revocation 전체에 대한 것이며, 본 기출의 3번 문제는 답안요령 5번이 별도로 출제된 것이다.

답안요령

1. Governed by CL/UCC2★
2. Offer 정의
3. General rule (offer is revocable, unless~)
4. Exceptions + 해당 rule
   + analysis
5. Communication requirement
   + analysis

2017Feb Trusts & Future Interests

1. It is proper for the trustee to accumulate trust income, because the testator has the right to amend.

A power to revoke includes the power to amend.

In this case, Settlor revoked the trust instrument which stated to distribute trust income to Settlor for life. Trust instrument stated that Settlor's power of revocation was exercisable only during Settlor's lifetime and by a written instrument. Settlor followed all requirements to revoke and it is valid.

In sum, it is proper for the trustee to accumulate trust income, because the testator has the right to amend.

2. Charity would be entitled to the share for children of Settlor's son, since children of Settlor's son is not permissible appointees. Charity would take the share in the trust assets as a taker in default of appointment.

The donee of a special power can appoint the property only to permissible appointees or objects of the power. Permissible appointees are the persons to whom an appointment is authorized. Objects of a power include only those who receive a beneficial interest.

In this case, Settlor's "children" is permissible objects. There might be an argument in interpreting "children" term in the trust instrument. However, in the Settlor's valid will, Settlor used "to my descendants, other than my children" and it could be an evidence that Settlor distinguish descendants and children. Settlor may be used the "children" to include only his son and daughter, not including grandchildren. Thus, the distribution of the trust assets to the children of Settlor's son is ineffective appointment.

If the special power is ineffectively appointed, the property passes to taker in default of appointment designated by the donor of the power. Here, the portion of the trust assets which was directed to children of Settlor's son would be passed to Charity. The portion of the trust assets for Settlor's son is effective and Charity does not have right on it.

In sum, Charity would be entitled to the share for children of Settlor's son, since children of Settlor's son is not permissible appointees. Charity would take the share in the trust assets as a taker in default of appointment.

3. Under the statue in this jurisdiction, husband will be entitled to $50,000. However, husband could raise the claim of an elective share including both probate and trust assets based on the illusory−transfer doctrine and the fraudulent−transfer doctrine. Then the husband can get $150,000.

Under the statute in this jurisdiction, a descendant's elective share is applicable only to probate estate. Probate assets do not include trust assets which are determined by the trust instrument. However, there are the illusory−transfer doctrine and the fraudulent−transfer doctrine, permitting the surviving spouse to claim an elective share of trust assets.

In this case, the statute allows husband claim an elective share. However, husband is entitled to $50,000 under the will and the elective share is $33,333. Thus, husband would not raise an elective share claim. However, the husband could claim an elective share on both probate assets and trust assets based on the illusory−transfer doctrine and the fraudulent−transfer doctrine.

Under those doctrines, husband will be entitled to receive $200,000 (1/3 of $600,000). However, $200,000 should be reduced by $50,000 which is entitled to husband under the will. Thus, husband would be entitled to $150,000.

In sum, under the statue in this jurisdiction, husband will be entitled to $50,000. However, husband could raise the claim of an elective share including both probate and trust assets based on the illusory−transfer doctrine and the fraudulent−transfer doctrine. Then the husband can get $150,000.

해설

난이도: 중

핵심 단어 및 논점

- power to revoke
- power to amend
- donee of a special power
- permissible appointees
- default of appointment

- children 해석
- elective share
- illusory-transfer doctrine
- fraudulent-transfer doctrine

1. Andrew have a claim to a share of the lottery winnings and the portion Andrew could get depends on how the court consider Andrew's contribution.

To establish a valid common law marriage, it requires that the spouses: (1) cohabitated, (2) made a present agreement to be married, and (3) held themselves out to others as a married couple. Under the conflict of laws principles, a valid marriage is valid anywhere, unless it violates public policy of another state. Thus, once one state permitted a common law marriage, other states that do not permit common law marriage should hold the marriage valid.

Here, Andrew and Brenda lived together and they agreed to marry "in the eyes of God," even though they did not obtain a marriage license or have a formal wedding. They held themselves out to others by using Andrew's last name, listing Brenda as his spouse, and filing joint income tax returns. Thus, there was common law marriage between Andrew and Brenda. In sum, State B court should recognize Brenda's common law marriage to Andrew as State A court.

Marital property is divisible at divorce regardless of the title. By contrast, separate property is not divisible at divorce. The property is marital if it was granted during the marriage by any methods, except for gift, descent, or devise. In the majority of jurisdictions, marital property continues to accrue until a final divorce decree is entered. In the minority of jurisdictions, marital property stops accruing after the date of permanent separation or the date of filing for a divorce. When courts decide property division order, only marital property is considered.

Under the majority approach, the lottery winning is marital property, since Andrew and Brenda remain married. Under the majority approach, the lottery winning is separate property, since Brenda purchased it after they separated. If it is marital property, Andrew has a claim to a share of it.

Marital property is divided equitably, not equally. Courts consider many factors, such as the duration of the marriage, each spouse's future needs, and the parties' contribution to the marriage and to the acquisition of assets.

In sum, Andrew has a claim to a share of the lottery winnings and the portion Andrew could get depends on how the court considers Andrew's contribution.

2. Daniel would have a claim based on a share of the lottery winnings based on putative−spouse doctrine or unmarried cohabitants doctrine.

Bigamy is illegal. Individual cannot have more than one legal spouse at a time. If first marriage was not legally terminated, a second marriage has no legal effect. It is presumed that the latest marriage is valid, but it can be rebutted only by evidence that the prior marriage still exists or by clear and conclusive evidence.

Here, Brenda and Daniel obtained a State B marriage license. The presumption arises that the marriage with Daniel is valid. If Brenda can show that she had valid common law marriage with Andrew and there is no evidence of the termination of it, Daniel could not obtain equitable share of Brenda's lottery winnings as her spouse.

However, even if Brenda rebutted the presumption, Daniel could have a claim on the lottery winnings. Under the putative−spouse doctrine, a would−be spouse who participated in a marriage ceremony with a good−faith but with mistaken belief in its validity can be treated like a spouse in equitable distribution of the marital property. Under unmarried cohabitants doctrine, property between cohabitants arises with an express or implied contract to share assets. Attempted marriage implies an agreement to share their property.

In sum, Daniel would have a claim based on a share of the lottery winnings based on putative−spouse doctrine or unmarried cohabitants doctrine.

3. Daniel can obtain court−ordered visitation with Chloe, since it would be in the best interest of Chloe.

Parents have a fundamental constitutional right to control to upbringing of their children, including decisions about visitation right. When a parent objected third party's visitation, parent's reasons should be specially weighted before the court overrules the parent's objection.

Here, Chloe lived with Daniel for significant period and regarded him as her father and called him "Dad." Thus, Daniel would be regarded as de facto parent. Additionally, rejecting visitation of Daniel would be not in the best interest of

Chloe, since when Chloe learned about the divorce, she became very upset because she continues to regard Daniel as her father. Unlike Troxel case, Brenda planned to cut off all contact with Daniel.

In sum, Daniel can obtain court—ordered visitation with Chloe, since it would be in the best interest of Chloe.

해설

난이도: 하

핵심 단어 및 논점

- common law marriage
- property division order
- bigamy
- putative—spouse doctrine

- unmarried cohabitants doctrine
- child custody order
- Troxel case

3번 문제

논점: Custody order

> **답안요령**

> 1. General rule (best interest test)
> 2. Parents' constitutional right
> 3. Analysis(Troxel case와 비교)★

TIP Custody order에 대한 합헌성은 Troxel case와 비교분석하는 것이 고득점 포인트다. 비교분석 시, ① 제3자에게 주어진 권리(visitation/custody)와 ② 친부모로서 가지는 헌법적 권리에 중점을 둔다.

2017Feb Corporations

1. The shareholder is entitled to inspect the documents, since it has a proper purpose to protect corporation's interest.

A shareholder has a right to inspect corporate books and records for a proper purpose. A proper purpose is a purpose reasonably related to a person's interest as a shareholder.

Here, the shareholder has an interest in determining whether MEGA's directors did illegal conduct, since it could make the corporation pay civil or criminal penalties. The news story in a leading financial newspaper and the board's fail to deny the illegal conduct could be the basis of the investigation. In sum, the shareholder's purpose is proper.

Under the MBCA, a shareholder is allowable to inspect only relevant part of board minutes directly connected with the shareholder's purpose. Shareholder can demand only for financial documents. The corporation may refuse inspection of nonfinancial documents even if those are related to shareholder's interest.

Here, the shareholder made a demand for accounting records which is financial records, and there would be many information regarding illegal conducts, foreign bribes in this case. Accounting records are directly connected with shareholder's purpose.

In sum, the shareholder has a right to inspect board's minutes and accounting records.

2. The board may not obtain dismissal of the derivative claim, since there was no reasonable investigation.

Under the MBCA, the board may dismiss the shareholder's derivative action, if a majority of the boards' qualified directors determines in good faith based on a reasonable inquiry which shows that continuance would be contrary to the corporation's best interests. Even though a complete investigation is not necessary, the board's request for dismissal must have some reason in the findings of the inquiry.

Here, the letter of June 1 to the shareholder shows that there is no investigation or inquiry, and the court should not grant the motion to dismiss the derivative action.

In sum, the board may not obtain dismissal.

3. The board's decision not to investigate or take further action is not consistent with the duty to act in good faith, and is not protected by the business judgment rule (BJR).

A director owes a duty to act in good faith. When a board knew that a transaction is to violate law, there is a lack of good faith. The duty to act in a good faith requires directors to ensure the corporation's compliance with legal norms. Even if an illegal activity is resulted in a financial benefit to the corporation, directors are required to comply with the law.

Here, the MEGA's directors failed to investigate alleged illegal foreign bribes and it made the corporation under the penalties. Thus, it is not in good faith.

Under BJR, there is a presumption that a board makes a decision (1) in a good faith, (2) in an informed manner, (3) based on a rational basis, and (4) for the best interest of the corporation. In sum, BJR is not applicable when there is fraud, illegality, or conflict of interest.

Here, the alleged illegal foreign bribe is illegal, and the directors are not protected by BJR.

In sum, the board's decision not to investigate or take further action is not consistent with the duty to act in good faith, and is not protected by the business judgment rule (BJR).

해설

난이도: 1번 문제: 하
2번 문제: 하
3번 문제: 중

핵심 단어 및 논점

- corporation
- right to inspect
- board's dismissal of derivative action
- business judgment rule (BJR)

1번 문제

<blockquote>답안요령</blockquote>

1. Right to inspect
2. "For proper purpose"
   + analysis
3. "Corporate books and records"
4. Procedural requirements
   + analysis

> TIP　주주의 right to inspect에 관한 문제는 크게 ① 주주가 해당 요청에 대해 권한을 가지는지 그 여부를 판단하는 문제와 ② 해당 요청 과정의 적합성을 판단하는 문제(위 4번)로 구분되는 바, 문제의 출제의도를 파악하여 서술하는 것이 중요하다. 본 기출문제의 1번 답안은 유형①에 해당한다.
>
> 유형①의 경우, 주주가 열람을 요청한 서류의 유형에 따라 서술하는 방향이 다르다.
>
> (a) Board minutes: 주주의 purpose가 "proper purpose"에 해당하는가. 해당한다면 minutes 전체가 아닌 주주의 목적에 해당하는 부분에 한해 열람이 가능하다.
>
> (b) Accounting records: 주주의 purpose가 "proper purpose"에 해당하는가. accounting records가 "corporate books and records"에 해당하는가.

3번 문제

논점: Director's duty of care & BJR

답안요령

> 1. BJR
>   + analysis (본 사안과 BJR간의 관계 및 관련 rule)
> 2. S/H's rebutting
>   + analysis
> 3. 결론

TIP1 본 답안요령은 directors가 행한 특정 행위에 대해 책임을 져야 하는지 그 여부를 판단하는 문제에 적용되는 답안요령으로써, 다음과 같은 logic을 가진다.

BJR에 따르면 director의 행위는 보호되는 바, 책임을 지지 않는다.

→ Director가 한 특정 행위는 BJR과 연관이 있다.

→ 다만, 주주(director에게 책임을 묻고자 하는 자)는 director의 행위가 not good faith임을 증명할 것이다.

→ 주주의 증명으로서 BJR이 적용될 수 없는 바, director는 그 행위에 대해 책임이 있다.

TIP2 본 기출의 3번 문제는 ① board의 특정 행위에 대한 act in good-faith 여부를 판단하고 ② 이에 근거하여 BJR의 적용여부를 판단하는 문제로서, 문제 자체가 good faith에 초점이 맞추어져 있다. 따라서 상기 답안요령을 적용하기보다는 good faith의 의미에 비중을 두어 analysis하는 것이 더 나을 것이다.

<u>**1. The investor is not liable on the contract, since the woman lacks authority. The woman is liable to the manufacturer because of the breach of implied warranty.**</u>

A principal is liable on a contract made by an agent when the agent has either actual or apparent authority. Actual authority exists when a principal makes an agent to believe that the principal wants the agent to act on behalf of principal. Apparent authority arises when (1) a third party reasonably believes that the actor is authorized, (2) that belief is from the principal's manifestation, and (3) the third party has no notice.

Here, the woman had no actual authority. This is because the inventor told woman to purchase only Series A computer chips. However, she purchased Series B chips and she exceeded her actual authority. The woman had no apparent authority, since the inventor did not mention to the chip manufacturer that the woman had authority to acquire Series B chips. Additionally, there is no fact showing the manufacturer reasonably believed the woman has authorization. In sum, a principal is not liable on the contract with the manufacturer.

However, when a person claimed that he makes a contract as an agency without authority, there is an implied warranty of authority to the third party. A person is liable for damages of breach of contract when the person breaches the warranty. Thus, the woman is liable to the manufacturer for the breach of implied warranty. In sum, even though a principal is not liable on the contract, the woman is liable to the manufacturer.

<u>**2. Both investor and woman are liable to the blue−lens manufacturer.**</u>

A principal is liable on a contract made by an agent when the agent has either actual or apparent authority. This rule is also applicable when the principal is undisclosed principal.

Here, when she made the contract, she did not tell the manufacturer that she is acting as anyone's agent. The inventor was undisclosed principal on the contract. The woman had actual authority, since she purchased 25 blue lenses that cost no more than $300 each. Thus, the inventor is liable on the contract even though the woman had no apparent authority.

The woman is also liable on the contract, since she claimed that she makes the contract on her behalf. The principal was an undisclosed principal. Thus, the woman is liable.

In sum, both investor and woman are liable to the blue—lens manufacturer.

3. Both investor and woman are liable to the shutoff—switch manufacturer under the Second Restatement. However, under the Third Restatement, only the woman is liable.

The principal is a partially disclosed principal, when a third party knows that the opposing party is an agency but a third party does not know the identity of the principal. A partially disclosed principal is liable when an agency has actual or apparent authority.

Here, the woman told the manufacturer that she was acting as someone's agent but did not disclose the identity of her principal, and therefore the investor is a partially disclosed principal. The woman had neither actual nor apparent authority, since she purchased shutoff switches that are not in less than one second and there is no basis for the manufacturer to reasonably believe woman is authorized.

However, when the principal ratifies the agent's act, the principal is liable on the contract regardless of agent's authority.

Here, inventor used switches to build lawn mowers. It means ratification and when the principal ratifies the agent's act, the agent is deemed to have acted with actual authority. Thus, inventor is liable for the contract. Additionally, an agent who acted on behalf of partially disclosed principal is liable on the contract. Thus, the woman is deemed to have acted with actual authority and therefore she is liable.

In sum, both investor and woman are liable to the shutoff—switch manufacturer under the Second Restatement. However, under the Third Restatement, only the woman is liable.

해설

난이도: 하

핵심 단어 및 논점

- actual authority
- apparent authority
- partially disclosed principal
- ratification

1, 2번 문제

답안요령

1. General agency rule
2. Principal's liability
   i. Actual authority
      + analysis
   ii. Apparent authority
      + analysis
3. Agent's liability
   i. Principal status(해당하는 status)★
   ii. Reasoning
4. Analysis + 결론

3번 문제

논점: Principal's ratification

Ratification에 관한 문제가 undisclosed principal의 경우로 출제된 경우, Second Restatement와 Third Restatement를 구분하여 논하는 것이 고득점 포인트다. 즉 agent 의 행위가 act인지 또는 purport인지 그 여부를 판단하는 것이 가장 중요한 논점이다. 그러나 본 사안은 Second Restatement와 Third Restatement의 구별실익이 없는 partially disclosed principal의 경우로, 두 법을 비교분석할 필요가 없다.

1. The landlord would argue that his reason of withholding the consent is valid under either majority or minority jurisdictions.

A restriction on assignment is a valid restraint on alienation. Here, the lease contained the provision that "Tenant shall not assign this lease without the Landlord's written consent." This restriction is valid.

The silent consent clause is a clause that does not include a standard or condition when the giving or withholding the consent. Under the majority jurisdictions, the landlord can give or withhold consent for any reason, even for no reason under a silent consent clause. Under the minority jurisdictions, the landlord's refusal must be reasonable.

Here, the landlord withholds the consent on the assignment, based on his personal experiences. Under the majority of jurisdictions, the landlord's withholding is valid. The landlord could argue that his reason based on his personal experiences is reasonable and is also valid under the minority of jurisdictions.

In sum, the landlord would argue that his reason of withholding the consent is valid under either majority or minority jurisdictions.

2. The landlord would argue that there was no acceptance of the abandonment.

Abandonment occurs when: (1) tenant vacates premises, (2) before the end of the term, (3) with no intent to return, and (4) has unpaid rent. Under the common law, a landlord has three options when a tenant abandons the premises: (1) accept the surrender, and extinguish the tenant's duty to pay rent due after the acceptance of surrender, (2) re-let or attempt to re-let the premises on the tenant's behalf, and recover damages from the tenant based on the difference original tenant rent fee and re−letting rent fee, or (3) leave the premises vacant, and recover for unpaid rent as it accrues.

Here, on July 25, 2015, the tenant vacated the apartment and left the keys in an envelope in the landlord's mail slot, stating that she was moving overseas and would not be back before her lease ends, and would not pay any rent from August 1 on. The landlord emailed the tenant the next day and Stated that "Although this is a problem you created, I want to be a nice guy and help you out. I feel pretty confident that I can find a suitable tenant who is not a lawyer to rent your apartment."

The landlord would argue that he did not voluntarily accept the keys, but it was merely placed in the mail slot. He would also argue that he merely stated to attempt to re−let the premises on the tenant's behalf. His email exactly stated that it was a problem the tenant created. Additionally, the fact shows that there was a recent precipitous decline in the local residential rental property market, and therefore the landlord would not voluntarily suffer financial loss by re−letting the premises.

In sum, the landlord would argue that there was no acceptance of the abandonment.

3. Landlord would argue that he has no mitigation duty. Even if he owes it, he could argue that he satisfied it.

Under the common law no mitigation rule, the nonbreaching party has no duty to mitigate.

Here, the landlord would argue that he had no duty to mitigate under the common law. This is because he did not accept the tenant's surrender and therefore he is entitled to the unpaid rent for 17 months. Even in a jurisdiction that requires mitigation duty, the landlord would argue that he satisfied it. This is because he placed advertisements in the newspaper and on a website listing all of apartment for rent. The landlord showed all four vacant apartments, including the tenant's apartment, to each prospective tenant. They would determine that his actions are sufficient to satisfy the mitigation duty.

The mitigation duty does not require that the mitigation must be successful. Thus, the fact that the landlord was unable to rent apartments does not make a different result.

If the landlord has the mitigation duty, he is entitled to the damage based on the difference between the original rent and the apartment's fair rental value. The landlord would argue that he was unable to rent the apartments at any price, and the fair rental value is $0. Thus, the landlord would be entitled to $34,000.

In sum, if the landlord did not accept the surrender, he is entitled to $34,000 for the rent of 17 months and the result would be same with the amount when the landlord has the duty to mitigate.

4. The tenant would argue that the landlord's objection was not reasonable and it is invalid.

The tenant would argue that the landlord must act reasonably in rejecting the assignment. Regarding reasonableness, many factors should be considered, such as the suitability of the premises for the proposed assignee's use, the proposed assignee's financial ability to pay, and the need for alterations to accommodate the proposed assignee's use. It should be commercially reasonable and the personal reasons are not reasonable.

Here, the attempted assignee was a lawyer and a lawyer had financial ability to pay. There was no fact that the landlord was going to use the premises for residence use. The landowner objected the assignment because of his personal experiences and it was not commercially reasonable.

In sum, the tenant would argue that the landlord's objection was not reasonable and it is invalid.

5. The tenant would argue that the landlord accepted the surrender, and he had no duty to pay rent.

The landlord stated that "Although this is a problem you created, I want to be a nice guy and help you out. I feel pretty confident that I can find a suitable tenant who is not a lawyer to rent your apartment." These words express landlord's willingness to help the tenant by reletting himself.

In sum, if the surrender was accepted by landlord, it extinguishes the tenant's duty to pay rent due after July 26, 2015.

<u>**6. The tenant would argue that the landlord had a duty to mitigate, even if he did not accept the surrender.**</u>

Regarding the mitigation duty, the duty is satisfied when there are reasonable efforts. In some jurisdictions, the reasonable efforts are defined as steps that are following local rental practice for similar properties.

Here, the landlord showed all four vacant apartments, including the tenant's apartment. The tenant will argue that the landlord should have shown the tenant's apartment, except for other three vacant apartments. The tenant will further argue that the fact the landlord was unable to rent apartments at any price is irrelevant, since he failed to mitigate. Alternatively, fair rental value is $1,000 based on the rent of the landlord rented two apartments. Thus, the tenant will argue that the landlord's damage would be $17,000.

In some jurisdictions, because the landlord failed to satisfy the duty to mitigate, tenant has no liability for rent or damages after the abandonment. Thus, landlord is entitled to nothing.

해설

난이도: 하

핵심 단어 및 논점

- restriction on assignment
  (landlord and tenant)
- silent consent clause
- surrender/abandonment (tenant)
- duty to mitigate
- reasonable objection (landlord)
- duty to pay rent

2017July
2017July Torts

__1. Under the First and Third Restatement, fireworks displays would be an abnormally dangerous activity which are subject to strict liability and the judge was incorrect. However, under the Second Restatement, fireworks displays would not be an abnormally dangerous activity which are not subject to strict liability and the judge was correct.__

To establish a strict liability case, the following elements must be shown: (1) the nature of the defendant's activity imposes an absolute duty to make safe, (2) the dangerous aspect of the activity is the actual and proximate cause of the plaintiff's injury, and (3) the plaintiff suffered damage to person or property. Under the First Restatement, the strict liability is applied to ultra-hazardous activities. However, under the Second and Third Restatement, the strict liability is applied to abnormally dangerous activities. Meanwhile, Second Restatement uses different factors in determining whether an activity is unduly dangerous and the result under the First and Third Restatement would be different from one under Second Restatement.

Under the First and Third Restatement, an activity is abnormally dangerous, if: (1) the activity creates a foreseeable and highly significant risk of physical harm even when with reasonable care and (2) the activity is not common usage. The term "common usage" has broader definition and activities can be in common use even if they are engaged in by only a limited number of actors.

In this case, the parties show that there are accidents involving fireworks cause about 9,000 injuries and 5 deaths each year, even with careful use by experts, fireworks mortars. Thus, the first element is satisfied. However, the fireworks are activities that are common in community. Second element is not satisfied and, therefore, defendants are not liable for strict liability.

Under the Second Restatement, multi-factor approach is used and six factors are totally considered. Unlike the First and Third Restatements, the Second

Restatement considers the value of the activity to the community. Additionally, the Second Restatement defines "common usage" as by many people in the community (or by great mass of mankind).

Under the Second Restatement, the result would be different from one under the First and Third Restatement. Many people enjoys fireworks and the value of it to the community is relatively high. Even if the court does not recognize fireworks are in common usage, multi−factor approach is used. Thus, there is a likelihood that the defendants is not liable for strict liability.

In sum, under the First and Third Restatement, fireworks displays would be an abnormally dangerous activity which are subject to strict liability and the judge was incorrect. However, under the Second Restatement, fireworks displays would not be an abnormally dangerous activity which are not subject to strict liability and the judge was correct.

2. The judge incorrectly granted the motion for the fireworks company on the negligent claim. This is because there was a foreseeable risk of harm that would be reduced without unduly burden.

An actor who does not complied with all statutory standards is negligent per se.

Here, state statute does not refer to fireworks launched on water regarding a safety zone. Thus, the fact that neither the homeowners association nor the fireworks company established such a zone does not make them liable for negligence per se.

However, an actor who is not liable for negligence per se can be negligent if his conduct is not reasonable under the circumstances. In determining whether the actions are reasonable, jury would consider appropriate precautions to avoid foreseeable risks. Jury may consider the likelihood that the risk will eventuate and the burden of taking precautions against such foreseeable risk.

Here, all the fireworks company's employees were state−certified fireworks technicians and the company followed all governmental fireworks regulations. However, there are plaintiff's evidences that 15% of the accidents involving fireworks are caused by mortars misfiring in the course of professional fireworks displays, and some of these accidents occur despite compliance with governmental fireworks regulations. It is clear that the probability that foreseeable risk of a misfiring mortar will occur even with due care is very high. Additionally, a state statute requires a "safety zone" of 500 feet from the fireworks site on land. It is arguable, but the statute provides a reasonable standard for determining a safety zone for a fireworks display on water. A reasonable jury could have concluded that both the risk of injury and the utility of a 500-foot safety zone were known to the fireworks company. Additionally, with very little cost or inconvenience, the fireworks company or the homeowners association could have identified the four viewing spots within 500-foot safety zone and warned potential spectators of the hazard of watching from those locations.

In sum, the court erred in directing a verdict for the fireworks company on the negligence issue.

3. The judge erred in granting the motion, since danger invites rescue.

Typically, liability extends only to individuals within the zone of risk, or to foreseeable hazards.

Here, husband was inside the house and he was outside of the area in which risks from a fireworks display were to be anticipated. Additionally, he suffered fracture which is a different injury that which one would usually anticipate from fireworks exposure, such as burns.

However, injuries caused when running from danger are foreseeable. Moreover, because danger invites rescue, the wrong that imperils life is a wrong to his rescuer.

Here, the husband was a rescuer and his injuries, fracture, is a typical injury caused rushing from a dangerous situation. Thus, the misfiring mortar was the proximate cause of the husband's injuries.

In sum, the judge erred in granting the motion, since danger invites rescue.

4. The trial judge incorrectly found that the homeowners association cannot be held liable for the fireworks company's acts or omissions, because the homeowners association is an independent contractor.

An independent contractor is one who possesses independence in the manner in performing the work through a contract. Independent contractors are usually paid by the job, not salaries, and they are not supervised by individuals who hired them. One who employs independent contractor is not vicariously liable for the contractor's acts or omissions. However, when one employed an independent contractor to do work involving a special danger to others which the employer knows or has reason to know to be inherent in the normal work, he is subject to liability for physical harm by the contractor's failure to take reasonable precautions against such danger.

Here, a fireworks company is an independent contractor, since they was hired by the homeowners association for a specific job, to plan and manage the fireworks display. The homeowner association had reason to know that the fireworks are inherently risky even when fireworks are used by experts.

In sum, the trial judge incorrectly found that the homeowners association cannot be held liable for the fireworks company's acts or omissions, because the homeowners association is an independent contractor.

해설

난이도: 하

핵심 단어 및 논점

- strict liability for abnormally dangerous activities
- abnormally dangerous
- negligence per se (statute)
- negligence
- duty of care (precaution)
- zone of danger (foreseeable plaintiff)
- proximate causation (rescuer)
- vicarious liability
- independent contractor

1번 문제

답안요령

1. Strict liability for abnormally dangerous activities 기본 rule
   (First, Second, Third Restatement마다 다른 용어로 표현함★)
2. First, Second, Third Restatement마다 다른 기준을 가지고 있음★
3. First 및 Third Restatement의 요건(×2)
   + analysis
4. Second Restatement의 요건(multi-factor approach, 요건×6)
   + analysis

TIP1 First and Third Restatement와 Second Restatement로 구분하여 각각의 판단 기준으로 결론을 내는 것이 핵심이자 고득점 포인트다. Blasting은 strict liability이다, 아니다 식의 명확한 결론을 내야 할 필요가 없으며, 모든 사안은 다양하게 해석될 수 있다는 점에 유념한다.

TIP2 위 2번: "Second Restatement uses different factors in determining whether an activity is unduly dangerous and the result under the First and Third Restatement would be different from one under Second Restatement."

TIP3 위 4번: 여섯 개의 요건을 모두 암기하여 서술할 필요는 없다. Value to the community 요건을 중점적으로 analysis하며, 이 요건은 First 및 Third Restatement에서 고려되지 않음을 명시한다.

2번 문제

답안요령

---

1. statute 위반 → NG per se
   analysis(actor가 statute 준수하였으므로 NG per se 인정×)
2. statute 준수하더라도, NG 가능
   + analysis(actor의 행동이 unreasonable함)★

TIP 2번: Actor 행동의 reasonability를 판단하는 경우, ① 주의(precaution)를 기울임에 있어 actor의 부담과 그 ② 행동의 위험(probability)을 비교하는 것이 고득점 포인트다.

1. The bank cannot maintain a suit in federal court against State A for damages, since states are immune from suits for damages in federal court under the Eleventh Amendment.

Under the Eleventh Amendment, states are immune from any suit against one of the United States by citizens of another State for damages in federal court.

Here, the bank, a resident of State B is suing State A for damages in federal court. The immunity under the Eleventh Amendment can be waived by the state, but there is no evidence that State A has done so in this case.

In sum, the bank cannot maintain a suit in federal court against State A for damages.

2. The bank can maintain a suit in federal court against the state Superintendent of Banking.

Official capacity actions against state officials for prospective relief are not treated as actions against the State. Even though the Eleventh Amendment bars damages claims against the state, a suit against public officials in their official capacity seeking an injunction can be maintained.

Here, the bank could maintain the action in federal court.

3. The State A statute would constitutional, if the benefits of the security measures required by State A are substantial enough to justify the burdens.

Congress has the power to regulate interstate commerce. When a state law discriminates against interstate commerce, it is unconstitutional. A nondiscriminatory state law that imposes an incidental burden on interstate commerce will nonetheless be unconstitutional, if the burden is clearly excessive to the local benefits. The benefits of the law must be weighed against the burden it imposes. Here, the State A law is facially nondiscriminatory, since it applies equally to local banks and to banks from other states. Additionally, the law imposes a heavier burden on out−of−state banks compared to the burden on in−state banks (banks in State A).

State A has interest in protecting local businesses from the significant losses that can result from electronic funds transfer fraud. The fact that State A adopted its law in response to lobbying by a local business does not affect the fact that the law serves a legitimate state interest. However, it is unclear whether the security measures required by State A produce real and substantial benefits.

Compliance with the law requires the bank to make substantial changes to its banking system at a cost of $50 million. This cost is substantial enough to deter the bank from offering certain services in State A at all. Thus, there are real and substantial benefits.

In sum, if the benefits of the security measures required by State A are substantial enough to justify the burdens, the statute is constitutional.

해설

난이도: 하

핵심 단어 및 논점

- Eleventh Amendment
- Commerce Clause
- Dormant Commerce Clause (state)
- interstate commerce

1. The bank has a superior right to the claims against the retail stores, since the bank perfected its security interest.

The UCC9 governs a sale of accounts, even though the transaction is not one in which property secures an obligation. Here, the sale by the manufacturer to the finance company of the right to be paid by the retail stores is a sale of accounts. Thus, the agreement of sale between the manufacture is a security agreement.

The security interest is effective and attaches, when: (1) debtor signed a security agreement containing a description of the collateral, (2) debtor has rights in the collateral, and (3) secured party gave money to secured party. Thus, the security interest is enforceable and has attached and finance company, but it is not perfected, since the company did not filed a financing statement.

The bank also has an enforceable and attached security interest in the right to be paid by the retail stores. First, the bank loaned money to the manufacturer. Second, the manufacturer still had rights in the collateral (the sold accounts). Even though the manufacturer sold the accounts to the finance company, the finance company's interest was unperfected. Third, the manufacturer signed the security agreement. Moreover, the bank perfected its security interest by filing a financing statement.

An unperfected security interest is subordinate to a perfected security interest in the same property.

In sum, the bank has a superior right to the claims against the retail stores.

2. The retail stores are incorrect, since they received authenticated notifications of the assignment of their accounts to the bank.

Under UCC9, an account debtor of assigned accounts is entitled to discharge its obligation by paying the assignor. However, once the account debtor receives notice of the assignment that directs the account debtor to make payment to the assignee, the account debtor is entitled to discharge only paying the assignee. The notice of the assignment would be authenticated by either the assignor or the assignee.

Here, the retail stores are "account debtors" on the accounts. The retail stores have received a notice of the assignment authenticated by the bank directing them to pay the assignee.

In sum, the retail stores can discharge their obligations on the accounts only by paying the bank, the assignee.

해설

난이도: 하

핵심 단어 및 논점

- accounts
- effectiveness of security interest
- perfection
- priority
- account debtor

1. Testator's will was validly executed, but it could be invalid under the common law.

There are requirements for a will to be validly executed: a writing, a signature of the testator, and at least two witnesses.

Here, in 2012, Testator wrote a document and signed it at the end in witnesses' presence. There were two witnesses: Bob and his neighbor. Bob has interest in a will and he is an interested witness. While a will that is witnessed by an interested witness would be invalid under the common law, most of jurisdictions do not adopt such a strict requirement.

In sum, Testator's will was validly executed, but it could be void under the common law.

2. The share to Bob would be valid either under the republication−by−codicil doctrine or under UPC.

Under the republication−by−codicil doctrine, defects in a previously validly executed will can be cured if the will is republished in the properly executed codicil. Under the doctrine, the provisions of the original will that have no conflicts with the codicil are deemed as it was recited in the codicil and witnessed by the witnesses to the codicil. Curing an interested witness problem by codicil is a typical example of the republication−by−codicil doctrine.

In some statutes, the will is required to be witnessed by disinterested witnesses. If not, the will is defective even though it is validly executed. However, under UPC, interested witnesses are allowed.

Here, the first will has defects but it is validly executed if the state statute requires disinterested witness. In 2015, the will was replicated by codicil in 2015 with two disinterested witnesses. Thus, the share to Bob in the first will would be cured by the codicil and the bequest to Bob is valid. Moreover, the share to Bob is also valid under UPC.

In sum, the share to Bob would be valid either under the republication−by−codicil doctrine or under UPC.

3. Testator's memorandum is not incorporated in a will under the incorporation by reference doctrine, while it is incorporated under UPC.

Under the incorporation by reference doctrine, only a document can be incorporated into a will if: (1) it exists when or before the will was signed and (2) it is sufficiently identified in a will.

Here, a memorandum was dated three days after Testator's codicil was duly executed. It could not be incorporated in Testator's codicil, and aunt has no interest on Testator's furniture.

However, under UPC, documents that exist when, before, or even after the will was signed can be incorporated by reference, if the will evidences an disposal intent.

Here, the first will clearly specified that it incorporates the memorandum and it shows testator's intent to incorporate. Thus, the aunt is entitled to the furniture.

In sum, Testator's memorandum is not incorporated in a will under the incorporation by reference doctrine, while it is incorporated under UPC.

4. Testator's bequest to Sam's children who attain age 25 is valid under the common law Rule Against Perpetuities.

Under the Rule Against Perpetuities (RAP), no interest is no interest is valid, unless it must vest, if at all, within 21 years of one or more lives in being at the time of its creation.

Here, Testator's codicil is ambulatory and the time limit for RAP purpose starts to run when testator dies.

A class gift will vest for purpose of the RAP when the class is closed and all member of the class have met any conditions precedent. Because Sam predeceased Testator, Sam's children who attain age 25 would be entitled to the trust principal. However, When Sam dies, no Sam's children reached age 25 and trust principal should be hold by trustee until they satisfy the age contingency.

Here, the class of Sam's children closed when Sam died. As a result, the two children became members of the class and these members need to reach age 25 to be vest. Thus, measuring life is children themselves. If either satisfy the contingency and take the gift or they will die before reaching age 25 and the gift will fail. If all children, Amy and Dan, reached 25, they share the trust principal in equal shares. If only one child reached 25, the child will be entitled to whole trust principal. If no child reached 25, the trust principal will be distributed to testator's heirs.

In sum, Testator's bequest to Sam's children who attain age 25 is valid under the common law Rule Against Perpetuities.

해설

난이도: 4번 문제: 상
　　　　그 외 문제: 하

핵심 단어 및 논점

- validity of will
- interested witness
- republication−by−codicil doctrine (curing defects)
- incorporation by reference doctrine
- Rule Against Perpetuities (RAP) − wills

1. The testimony from the woman should be admissible, since it is relevant and it is hot hearsay.

Evidence is relevant if it has tendency to make a fact more or less probable than it would be without the evidence. Here, the testimony from the woman is relevant to suggest self-defense of woman. This testimony can suggest woman's fear of man and the possibility of woman's reasonable belief that her use of force was immediately necessary to protect herself.

Hearsay is an out-of-court statement offered in evidence to prove the truth of the matter asserted. The woman's statement is not made at court, but it is not required for jury to think whether the man made woman happy or unhappy to prove woman's fear of man.

In sum, the testimony from the woman is relevant and it is not hearsay. It is admissible.

2. Testimony from the police officer is admissible, since it is admission exception and there is no violation of Miranda right.

Hearsay is an out-of-court statement offered in evidence to prove the truth of the matter asserted. However, there is an admission exception, if an out of court statement is made by an opposing party and used against the party.

In this case, the testimony from the police officer is relevant, since it can be used against woman's self-defense. It could help prosecution that woman used improper force, since it is no use of force in immediate protecting herself. However, the testimony from the police officer is the statement made by woman, and it is used against the woman. It falls within an admission exception. Thus, the testimony from the police officer is not hearsay and is admissible.

Law enforcement officers are required to read Miranda warnings to a suspect when the suspect is subject to an in−custody interrogation. There is custody when reasonable person under similar circumstances would believe she was not free to leave. There is interrogation when police either expresses questioning or elicit an incriminating response from the suspect. However, Miranda warnings are not always required in in−custody interrogation. Under the Miranda public safety exception, when police intended to protect public safety, there could be a limited interrogation without Miranda warnings.

In this case, the woman is in−custody, since a police officer blocked the doorway so that the woman could not leave and no one could enter. There was an interrogation, since the officer asked her. However, there are a number of people gathered outside the doorway of the woman's office. Police's questioning whether there are any other weapons is to protect public safety and it falls within the Miranda public safety exception.

In sum, the officer did not violate Miranda right of the woman, and the testimony from the police officer is admissible.

3. Testimony from the police officer is admissible, since it falls within the present sense exception and excited utterance exception.

The testimony from the police officer made by a custodian is out−of−court statement and it is used to prove whether woman committed the crime. However, there are hearsay exception for present sense impressions and excited utterance exception. Present sense impressions exception exists when there is a statement describing an event or condition made while or immediately after the declaration after the declarant perceived it. Excited utterance is a statement relating to a startling event or condition, made while the declarant was under the stress or excitement that it causes.

In this case, the testimony by a custodian is made 20 minutes after of the accident. It would be an enough time to fit present sense impressions exception. Additionally, the court would find under the facts in this case that the custodian is startling and he was ender the stress under the accident. Thus, the statement would fit excited utterance exception. The fact that the custodian is unavailable to testify at trial does not make a different result.

In sum, the testimony from the police officer made by the custodian falls within the hearsay exception, and it is admissible.

해설

난이도: 하

핵심 단어 및 논점

- hearsay
- Miranda rights (Fifth Amendment)
- hearsay exception
  - present sense impressions
  - excited utterance exception

1. The court should consider the woman's motion to dismiss for insufficient service of process, since she properly amended her motion.

When a party initially makes motion to dismiss under the Rule 12(b), the party must join all other motions permitted by Rule 12 with the motion which are available to the party. If a party fails to join available motions, the defense is waived. However, a party may amend the motion to dismiss before the motion is heard, so long as the adverse party is not prejudiced by the amendment and no delay results in the prosecution and determination of the case.

Here, the woman initially made a motion to dismiss the action for failure to state a claim upon which relief can be granted. Two days after filing the motion to dismiss, she amended the motion. The amendment was effective, since she amendment the motion before Taxes had responded to the motion. Additionally, there is no fact to show that amendment could make Taxes prejudiced or the amendment would cause the proceedings to be delayed.

In sum, the court should consider the woman's amended motion to dismiss for insufficient service of process, since she properly amended her motion.

2. The court must grant the motion, since she moved out of her parent's home in State A.

Regarding service of process upon individual personally, leaving a copy of each at the individual's current dwelling or usual place of abode with someone of suitable age and discretion who resides there is permitted.

Here, the service was made at the woman's parents' home in State A. Even though she had lived in parents' home before, but moved out of the home and moved into an apartment now. Thus, the parents' home is not a current dwelling.

In sum, the court must grant the motion to dismiss for insufficient service of process, since she moved out of her parent's home in State A.

3. The court must follow State A's choice of law approach, under the Erie doctrine.

Under the Erie doctrine, a federal court applies the substantive law of the forum state when it has diversity jurisdiction. Choice of law rule is substantive.
Here, the federal court sits in State A.
In sum, the federal court should follow State A's approach, the Second Restatement of Conflict of Laws.

4. The court should enforce the noncompete covenant, because State A has substantial relationship to the parties, and authorizing the noncompete covenants does not violate State B's fundamental policy.

Generally, the Second Restatement of Conflict of Laws permits the enforcement of choice of law clauses, unless (1) the chosen state has no substantial relationship to the parties or the transaction or (2) application of the law of the chosen state would be contrary to a fundamental policy of a state.
Here, the written employment contract between the woman and Taxes includes the provision stating the contract was governed by State A law. First, State A has substantial relationship to the parties. The parties entered into the contract in State A, and the woman was hired and trained to work in State A. Second, application of State A's law would not violate State B's fundamental policy. State B considers the noncompete covenants in the contract unreasonable, simply because it exceeds 18 months duration. There is no fact showing the authorizing the noncompete covenants violates State B's fundamental policy. Thus, the court should enforce the noncompete covenant.
In sum, the court should enforce the noncompete covenant, because State A has substantial relationship to the parties, and authorizing the noncompete covenants does not violate State B's fundamental policy.

해설

난이도: 하

핵심 단어 및 논점

- motion to dismiss (Rule 12(b))
- service of process (upon individual)
- Erie doctrine
- choice of law clauses

1. Either spouse may successfully enforce the premarital agreement, except for the provision regarding child custody.

The enforceability of the premarital agreement depends on three factors: voluntariness, fairness, and disclosure. Under UPAA, an agreement is unenforceable if the party against whom enforcement is sought shows: (1) involuntariness or (2) unfairness and lack of adequate disclosure.

Here, David provided an accurate list of his net assets, a list of his liabilities, and his tax returns for the past three years. Thus, Meg cannot establish inadequate disclosure. Regarding involuntariness, it could be established by fraud, duress, or coercion, and there are many factors to be considered, such as lack of opportunity to talk with independent counsel, other reasons for proceeding with the marriage (pregnancy), financial losses and embarrassment arising from cancellation of the wedding, maturity of parties, and prior experience of marriage. Here, David presented the proposed agreement one week before their wedding. There is no fact to show that Meg did not have time to confer with counsel. They were married in a small wedding held at the grandmother's house and therefore Meg had no financial loss arising from cancellation of the wedding. Meg cannot establish involuntariness. Thus, the premarital agreement is valid.

However, the premarital agreement includes a provision regarding child custody. Because the child custody should be in the best interest of child, provisions regarding child custody in the premarital agreement are ineffective.

In conclusion, a premarital agreement is effective except for the provision regarding child custody.

2. A part of David's repair business and the home are divisible at divorce, because they are marital property.

Marital property is divisible at divorce. By contrast, separate property is not divisible at divorce. The property is marital if it was granted during the marriage by any methods, except for gift, descent, or devise. A separate asset can be transformed into marital property, if marital funds or significant efforts by the owner's spouse enhance its value or build equity during the marriage. In the minority jurisdictions, all assets whenever or however acquired are separate property. When courts decide property division order, only marital property is considered.

Here, Meg inherited stocks, so stocks are separate property. David's auto repair business was initially separate property, because David initiated his business before the marriage. However, he had worked full−time in the business during the marriage and therefore the business is at least partially marital property. The home is marital property because employment income was used for the down payment and all mortgage payments.

In sum, a part of David's repair business and the home are divisible at divorce, because they are marital property.

3(a). David may not obtain sole physical custody of Anna based on Meg's adultery, since there is no evidence that Meg's adultery would cause Anna harm.

Child custody should be in the child's best interest. Custody is deprived when a parent endangers child's health or safety.

Here, David discovered that Meg had been having an affair with a coworker for the past year. However, it is hard to say that Meg's adultery endanger Anna's health or safety. Thus, it is insufficient evidence to allow David's sole physical custody of Anna.

In sum, David may not obtain sole physical custody of Anna based on Meg's adultery, since there is no evidence that Meg's adultery would cause Anna harm.

<u>3(b). David may obtain sole physical custody of Anna, but the court may need more evidences.</u>

In determining child custody, courts consider many factors, such as (1) the wishes of the child's parent or parents, (2) the wishes of the child, (3) the interaction and interrelationship of the child with other person, such as his parents who significantly affect the child's best interest, (4) the child's adjustment to his home, school, and community, and (5) the mental and physical health.

Here, Meg lived with Anna only for short time. David lived with Anna throughout this period and provided care for her when he was not working. The grandmother acted as a primary caregiver to Anna and she has continued to provide care. These factors support David's sole physical custody of Anna.

However, evidence is lacking regarding Anna's wishes, Anna's current relationships, and each parent's mental and physical health. Thus, without such evidences, it is hard to predict the outcome.

In conclusion, David may obtain sole physical custody of Anna.

해설

난이도: 하

핵심 단어 및 논점

- premarital agreement
- enforceability of the premarital agreement
- property division order
- marital property
- separate property
- child custody order
- best interest of child

1번 문제

논점: Enforceability of premarital agreement

지문에서 "adoped a statute modeled after the UPAA"임을 명시하였으므로, UPAA (and 요건)를 기준으로 작성해야 한다.

1. The prosecution should be suspended because of the defendant's incompetence.

Competence to stand trial is required that means a defendant's ability to participate in criminal proceedings. The defendant must have (1) sufficient present ability to consult with his lawyer with a reasonable degree of rational understanding and (2) a rational and factual understanding of the proceedings against him. Whenever a defendant can establish a bona fide doubt about the defendant's decision making abilities, the court must hold a hearing to determine competence to stand trial. The burden of evaluating competency is placed on the courts and court—appointed experts.

First, the defendant said "My mother told me I did something bad, but I can't remember what." It shows that the defendant cannot provide information about the armed robbery. Additionally, the defendant said "She's nice" and "She comes to see me and helps me." It means he cannot understand the role of his appointed counsel. Second, the defendant responded "I don't know what they are talking about" and described the judge as "the guy in charge." These facts show the lack of rational and factual understanding of the trial proceedings.

In short, the defendant is incompetent and his competence in the future can be reassessed in the future.

2. The jury would not find that he is NGRI under the M'Naghten test, because he did not satisfy the second prong.

Under the M'Naghten test of the insanity defense, a defendant needs to show that (1) she suffered from a severe mental disease of defect, at the time of the charged crime and (2) the mental disease left her either unable to know the nature and quality of the act or unable to know that the act was right or wrong.

Here, the evidence provided by two psychiatrists showed that the defendant was having some mental health difficulties because of the struggling business. The defendant stated to his best friend, "I cannot attract customers because the United Nations has organized a secret boycott of my new business." These evidences support defendant's mental disease. However, the court should consider that: the defendant's mental health difficulties apparently did not impair his relationships with his family and friends, he had not sought mental health treatment, and he maintained his ability to manage his everyday life and operate his business.

In sum, even if the defendant was suffering some mental disease at the time of armed robbery, it is insufficient to satisfy the first prong.

Regarding insanity defense, states have different definition of "wrong." Some states permit the defense only if the defendant did not know that his acts were legally wrong as the result of his mental disease. Some states permit the defense only if the defendant did not know that his acts were morally wrong as the result of his mental disease.

Here, the defendant texted his best friend the day before the armed robbery: "I've been a victim for too long. I've decided to start making up for my losses," which indicates that the defendant understood the robbery as a solution to his financial loss. The defendant planned to flee and he instructed his friend to destroy evidence and to lie to the police. With these facts, the defendant knew the nature and quality of robbing the store. Moreover, regardless how the state defines the wrongfulness, the defendant's actions show that he knew his acts were morally and legally wrong.

In sum, the defendant's actions satisfy the first prong but do not satisfy the second prong. Thus, the jury would not find that he is NGRI under the M'Naghten test.

해설

난이도: 하

핵심 단어 및 논점

- incompetence to stand trial
- insanity (defense)
- M'Naghten test

2번 문제

본 문제는 "State A uses the M'Naghten"임을 명시하였으므로, MPC와 비교분석할 필요가 없다.

2018Feb Contracts

1. Whether those disputes are governed by common law or UCC2 depends on the predominant purpose test.

Contract for the sale of goods are governed by UCC2. Most contracts are governed by the common law of contracts. When the contract contains both sale of goods aspects and nongoods aspects, it is a hybrid contract. Generally, courts use predominant purpose test to determine which body of law applies to the whole contract.

Here, the sale of goods aspects is for $5,000, regarding the equipment and tools. It is larger than the amount for the services portion ($4,000), and UCC2 would govern the contract. However, it is arguable because woman's main interest of the contract is improving her pottery skills and being enable her to create some pottery items that she could sell. Considering her main interest, the disputes would be governed by the common law of contract.

In conclusion, there are persuasive arguments on whether UCC2 or common law governs the disputes.

2. Under the parol evidence rule, whether the lodging agreement binds on the parties depends on how the writing is integrated.

Under the parol evidence rule, the terms of oral agreement that predates a written agreement can become part of the resulting contract when a contract has been reduced to a writing that is integrated and the writing constitutes final expression of an agreement. If the writing is completely integrated, the writing discharges prior agreements. If the writing is partially integrated, it discharges prior agreements only to the extent that the written agreement is inconsistent with the prior agreement. In determining whether the writing is completely or partially integrated, the court consider various factors.

Here, the contract between the woman and the professional potter signed the document which includes the provision "This is our complete agreement." The statement shows their intent to regard the document as a final expression of an agreement. However, the statement is not enough to prove complete integration, and the court needs additional inquiry. If the court concludes that the writing is completely integrated, the oral agreement does not bind on the parties. By contract, if the court concludes that the writing is not completely integrated, the oral agreement binds on the parties, because there the lodging agreement is not inconsistent with the written agreement.

In conclusion, whether the lodging agreement binds on the parties depends on how the writing is integrated.

3. The oral agreement lowering the price for the apprenticeship is not binding on the parties, because there was no consideration.

Under the common law, modification of the contract must be generally supported by consideration. Performance for preexisting duties is not consideration.

Here, under the modified agreement, the woman had the same duties to the potter. Nothing was exchanged in return for the potter's agreement to lower the amount of money to which he was entitled. Thus, there is no consideration for the lower price.

In sum, the oral agreement lowering the price for the apprenticeship is not binding on the parties, because there was no consideration.

해설

난이도: 하

핵심 단어 및 논점

- predominant purpose test
- parol evidence rule
- modification
- consideration
- preexisting duty

3번 문제

답안요령

1. General rule (Modification is enforceable with consideration.)
   + analysis
2. Preexisting rule
3. Preexisting rule exception
   + analysis

1. The developer breached the covenant against encumbrances under the merger doctrine. However, the court would conclude that there is no breach of the covenant against encumbrances.

A warranty deed contains six title covenants, including three present covenants and three future covenants. The three present covenants are: covenant of seisin, covenant of right to convey, and covenant against encumbrances. Under the merger doctrine, contractual promises are merged into the deed at the time of closing and delivering the deed.

Here, the contract provided a conveyance by a warranty deed excepting all easements and covenants of record. However, at the closing, the deed contained no exceptions to the six covenants.

An encumbrance is some outstanding right or interest in a third party which does not totally negate the title which the deed purports to convey. Here, the land conveyed to the man was subject to an easement, and the covenant against encumbrances was breached.

The merger doctrine applies only when the use of the doctrine may result in the parties' probable intent. Here, the developer could argue that the omission of the exception is mere a clerical mistake. If the court accepts this argument and does not apply the doctrine, there is no breach of the covenant against encumbrances.

In sum, the developer breached the covenant against encumbrances under the merger doctrine. However, the court would conclude that there is no breach of the covenant against encumbrances.

2. Assuming that there was a breach of the present title covenants, the man cannot recover damages from the developer for the breach since he had constructive notice of the easement. Additionally, the easement did not reduce the value of the land.

If the covenant against encumbrances was breached, the buyer is entitled to damages when the easement is not plain, obvious, or is not known to the buyer. Here, the man had notice of the easements. Although the sewer and utility lines were installed underground and not visible, the man had constructive notice of the easement, because the easement was recorded. Additionally, the easement is beneficial to the man, and the breach of the covenant against encumbrances would not be recognized. Thus, the man cannot recover damages.

However, the man could argue that the developer intended to give him the warranty and he is entitled to damages for the breach of the covenant. If the court accepts this argument, the man is entitled to damages only when he proves that the easement reduced the value of the land. The damages is measured as the difference between the value of the land not subject to the easement and the value of the land as restricted by the easements.

Here, the easement was to install underground sewer and utility lines. It is hard to say that sewer and utility lines reduce the value of the land. Thus, the man is not entitled to damages even if his argument is accepted.

In sum, assuming that there was a breach of the present title covenants, the man cannot recover damages from the developer for the breach since he had constructive notice of the easement. Additionally, the easement did not reduce the value of the land.

3. The man cannot force the utility company that installed the underground sewer lines to remove them from the land, since he had constructive notice of the easement.

Whether the man can force the utility company to remove is depending on the man's knowledge on the easement when he purchased the land.

Here, the man had constructive notice of the easement, because the easement was recorded. The man recorded the deed after the recording of the easement. Thus, he is subject to the easement regardless of the recording statute (notice, race−notice, or race).

In sum, the man cannot force the utility company that installed the underground sewer lines to remove them from the land, since he had constructive notice of the easement.

4. The man may recover the $5,000 in damages from the developer, since the developer breached implied warranty.

In the past, a home builder makes no implied warranties regarding the condition of the premises. However, in modern courts, a home builder makes implied warranties regarding the condition of the premises, because a buyer relies upon the builder's skill and integrity, and ordinary buyers are not in a position to discover latent defects.

Here, an expert determined that the cause of the rainwater influx was a defect in the construction of the home's foundation. Thus, the developer breached implied warranty and the man is entitled to recover damages for losses resulting from defective construction, $5,000.

In sum, the man may recover the $5,000 in damages from the developer, since the developer breached implied warranty.

해설

난이도: 하

핵심 단어 및 논점

- present covenants of title
- covenant against encumbrances
- merger doctrine
- damages for breach of covenant
- easement
- constructive notice
- implied warranty of merchantability

1번 문제

- 문제에서 "present title covenants"라 명시하였으므로, present covenants만 나열해도 충분하다.
- Merger doctrine이 적용되는 경우와 그렇지 않은 경우를 구분하여 analysis하는 것이 고득점 포인트다. Merger doctrine이 적용되지 않을 경우의 argument point를 서술하는 것이 핵심이다.

3번 문제

지문에서 recording statute를 명시하지 않았으므로, 모든 유형의 recording statutes를 고려하여 답안을 작성해야 한다. 본 사안에서는 모든 유형에 있어 동일한 결과가 도출되는 바, "recording statute 유형과 상관없이 ~하다"고 서술하였다.

2018Feb Civil Procedure

1(a). The court may properly grant the plaintiff's motion for sanctions for improper denials of factual and legal contentions.

All pleadings must be signed by an attorney or by a party if the party is not represented. An attorney's signature on a pleading certifies that to the best of the person's knowledge, information, and belief after a reasonable inquiry. Here, the defendant driver and the moving company filed an answer to the complaint and the answer is a pleading. It was signed by the attorney. However, the defendant's attorney made a general denial.

General denial is allowed only if the party intends in good faith to deny all the allegations of a complaint with the jurisdictional reasons. A defendant's answer must respond to both legal conclusions and factual allegation stated in the complaint. Generally, a general denial is improper in most cases.

Here, the complaint filed by the passenger includes factual allegation, such as state of citizenship and the driver's employment at the time of the accident. Because the defendant's attorney made a general denial, these factual allegations were denied at all. These denials were proper only if they were warranted on the evidence. Defendant's denial of the propriety of venue was also unwarranted by the facts or by existing law. The attorney is required to investigate the statutory provision regarding the venue before filing the answer.

Even if a lawyer filed an inaccurate pleading, he is not subject to sanctions when he acted in good faith with a pre—filing inquiry that was reasonable under the circumstances. Reasonableness should exist at the time the pleading was submitted and reasonableness is determined with some factors: investigation time that was available to the signer, whether he had to rely on a client for information, and whether the pleading and motion were based on a plausible view of the law.

Here, the defendant's attorney had relatively short time to investigate. However, the attorney or another member of the firm should have known simple facts.

Even a brief conversation with the clients would have permitted verification of those facts.

In conclusion, the court may properly grant the plaintiff's motion for sanctions for improper denials of factual and legal contentions.

1(b). The court may properly gave the defendants' attorney an opportunity to correct the pleading before granting the sanction.

Before a party seeks sanctions, the party must serve on the opposing party a motion that describes the specific conduct that allegedly violated Rule 11. The opposing party has 21-day period to withdraw or correct the challenged pleading. If the safe harbor period passes without corrected pleading, the motion for sanctions may be filed with the court.

Here, the plaintiff's lawyer requested that the defendants withdraw their original answer and file an amended answer admitting the allegations that the defendants had admitted in their response to the Requests for Admission. The defendants failed to withdraw or amend their answer within the safe harbor period. Thus, the court may impose sanctions on defendants.

In sum, the court may properly gave the defendants' attorney an opportunity to correct the pleading before granting the sanction.

2(a). A sanctions award that fully compensates the plaintiff for the costs may be proper to promote deterrence.

The court has discretion in imposing sanctions. The purpose of any sanctions award should be to deter similar future conduct by this lawyer or others. Sanctions can be monetary or nonmonetary. The monetary sanctions include an order to pay a penalty into court or an order to pay to the movant of part or all of the reasonable attorney's fees and other expenses directly resulting from the violation. The nonmonetary sanctions include striking the offending paper or requiring participation in educational programs. In determining among the range of sanctions, court may consider many factors, such as whether the improper conduct was willful or negligent and whether it was intended to injure.

Here, the defendants denied the allegations which were same denials in the original answer. It suggests that the defendants were not willfully seeking to impose any burden on the plaintiff. The court should also consider whether seven hours are directly resulted from the violation. Seven hours and the billing rate ($300) do not seem unreasonable.

In sum, a sanctions award that fully compensates the plaintiff for the costs may be proper to promote deterrence.

2(b). Sanctions may be ordered against defendants' attorney, his law firm, and the defendants, but monetary sanctions for asserting an unwarranted legal contention may not be imposed upon the driver and the moving company.

The court may impose sanctions on any attorney, law firm, or party that violated the rule or is responsible for the violation. Generally, the attorney's law firm is jointly responsible, unless there are no exceptional circumstances. A party should be sanctioned, when the party authorizes its attorney to pursue a claim that it knew was legally and factually baseless.

Here, the court may impose sanctions on attorney of driver and moving company, and the attorney's law firm, because there are no applicable exceptional circumstances. There are no facts indicating that the driver and the moving party knew the content of the answer, thus they were not responsible for the attorney's decision to make an unwarranted general denial. Additionally, the sanction for general denial based on an unwarranted legal contention should not be imposed upon the driver and the moving company.

In conclusion, sanctions may be ordered against defendants' attorney, his law firm, and the defendants, but monetary sanctions for asserting an unwarranted legal contention may not be imposed upon the driver and the moving company.

해설

난이도: 하

핵심 단어 및 논점

- pleadings
- general denial
- sanction (Rule 11)
- safe harbor period
- sanction on law firm

1. The man properly withdrew from the partnership, because the partnership is at−will partnership.

A partner may withdraw from a partnership by giving notice at any time. A partner has power to withdraw by express will, even if the withdrawal is wrongful or violates partnership agreement. When a partner withdraws from an at−will partnership, dissolution occurs.

Here, the man's email to the woman constituted a withdrawal from the partnership and it did not violate the partnership agreement. There is no indication that the partnership is for a definite term or for particular undertaking and therefore the partnership is at−will partnership.

In sum, the man's withdrawal from their at−will partnership was proper.

2. The man's withdrawal from the partnership caused dissolution, but it did not terminate the man's duties during the winding−up process.

Dissolution of a partnership results in a change in the legal relation of the partners, but it does not immediately terminate the partnership or the rights of the partners. The partner's legal relationship and the partnership terminate when all of the partnership affairs are completely wound up. A partnership at will is properly dissolved by the express will of any partner, and any partner of the dissolved partnership has the right to participate in the winding up process.

Here, the man's withdrawal caused the dissolution of their at−will partnership, but the man still has duties to the woman and the partnership during the winding up process. Because his withdrawal was not wrongful, he had right to participate in the winding up process and his actions bound the partnership.

In conclusion, the man's withdrawal from the partnership caused dissolution, but it did not terminate the man's duties during the winding−up process.

3. The man breached the duty to account and duty of good faith and fair dealing by not performing the opportunity to purchase the building, because the fiduciary duty continues during the winding−up process.

During the winding−up process, partners who participate in the winding up process continue to have a fiduciary relationship both to the partnership and the other partners. The partner has a duty to account to the partnership for any benefit derived by the partner from the appropriation of any partnership opportunities. A partner who learns of a business opportunity during the term of a partnership may not appropriate that opportunity during the winding−up process or after the partnership term ends. Moreover, the partner has a duty to perform in good faith and for fair dealing.

Here, the man knew that landlord's intent to sell the building before he withdrew from the partnership. The opportunity to purchase the building constituted a partnership opportunity. Partnership had expectancy to purchase the building and there is no fact to show partnership's lack of monetary capacity for the purchase. In sum, by not informing the woman of the opportunity to purchase the building, the man breached the fiduciary duty to account and duty of good faith and fair dealing.

In conclusion, the man breached the duty to account and duty of good faith and fair dealing by not performing the opportunity to purchase the building, because the fiduciary duty continues during the winding−up process.

해설

난이도: 하

핵심 단어 및 논점

- at−will partnership
- dissolution & winding−up
- fiduciary duty to account & good−faith

1. Section 11 of the Federal Drug Abuse Prevention Act is unconstitutional, since the law violates federalism principle under the Tenth Amendment.

Under the Tenth Amendment dual sovereignty system, states have sovereign authority and Congress cannot require states to govern according to Congress' instructions.

Under the federalism principle, Congress may not command the states to regulate private conduct. When legislating to force the state law enforcement officials to take certain actions as agents of the State is federal government's acting to control their actions with an effort to direct the functioning of the state executive, the law is unconstitutional.

Here, Section 11 of the Federal Drug Abuse Prevention Act (FDAPA) requires a State A law enforcement officer or agency to undertake investigations and it is to detect violations of federal drug laws. The law also requires reporting to federal authorities on suspected violations. It seeks to compel state officers to participate in the enforcement of the federal laws against the use of marijuana.

In sum, the law violates federalism principle and is unconstitutional under the Tenth Amendment.

2. Section 15 of FDAPA is a constitutional exercise of federal power, since it is a correct exercise of Congress's power to spend.

Congress may use a threat to withhold federal money to induce a state to exercise its sovereign authority to achieve congressional goals. Congress may condition the states' receipt or use of federal funds on state compliance with federal statutory and administrative directives.

To be constitutional, (1) the spending must be for the general welfare, (2) the condition must be unambiguous, (3) the condition must be related to the federal interest, (4) the condition must not be used to induce the states to engage in unconstitutional activities, and (5) a condition should not be so coercive.

Here, Section 15 is probably constitutional. First, both the federal spending program and the imposed condition are for the general welfare. Second, the condition imposed on states is unambiguous. Third, the condition relates to the purpose of the federal funding. Fourth, the requirement that the states criminalize the use of certain drugs does not induce any state to engage in unconstitutional activity. Fifth, the threat of a loss of Justice Assistance Grant funds is not so coercive. This is because the amount of money involved in this case, $10 million, is only a small fraction of State A's law enforcement budget. This is not a substantial economic loss.

In sum, although the funding condition acts as an incentive for State A to adhere to federal policy, it is a proper exercise of Congress's spending power.

해설

난이도: 하

핵심 단어 및 논점

- federalism principle
- dual sovereignty (Tenth Amendment)
- spending power (Congress)
- general welfare

<u>The transaction between the homeowner and the neighbor is governed by UCC2, since it is goods. They are not merchants.</u>

UCC2 governs transactions in goods. The term "goods" means movable things at the time of making a contract.

Here, the lawn mowers are goods, and the transaction is governed by UCC2.

Merchant is a person who deals in goods of the kind at issue.

Here, the homeowner and the neighbor are not merchants.

In sum, the transaction between the homeowner and the neighbor is governed by UCC2, since it is goods. They are not merchants.

<u>1. The homeowner was not bound by his promise to keep his offer open for a week, since there is no consideration, no merchant, and no detrimental reliance.</u>

To create an option contract, the contract should be supported by consideration and the offer should be made in a signed writing.

Here, the homeowner renewed the offer and promised to hold it open for a week. However, there was no consideration and a signed writing for the offer. Thus, the offer is not bound to be open.

Under a firm offer rule, a promise hold open the offer without consideration is enforceable. This rule applies when (1) an offer is made by a merchant and (2) an offer is made in a signed writing.

Here, homeowner is not a merchant, and the offer by her was oral. Thus, a firm offer rule does not apply here and the homeowner's promise to hold the offer open was not binding.

When the offeror should reasonably expect to induce action on the part of the offeree before acceptance and the offer induces in fact such action or forbearance, the offer is enforceable as an option contract.

Here, there are no facts supporting this rule.

In sum, the homeowner was not bound by his promise to keep his offer open for a week, since there is no consideration, no merchant, and no detrimental reliance.

2. The neighbor's statement did not create a contract with the homeowner, since the homeowner revoked her offer.

The power of acceptance may be terminated by revocation by the offeror. Revocation of an offer occurs when the offeror made a manifestation of intention not to enter into the proposed contract. It can be communicated to the offeree indirectly, when the offeror takes definite action inconsistent with an intention to enter into the proposed contract and the offeree got reliable information.

Here, the homeowner took definite action inconsistent with an intention to sell the lawn mower to the neighbor. Moreover, the neighbor acquired reliable information that the homeowner did not intent to enter into the proposed contract with the neighbor. The acquaintance told the neighbor about the homeowner's contract and he showed her their written agreement. Thus, there was an indirect revocation of the homeowner's offer.

In sum, the neighbor's statement did not create a contract with the homeowner, since the homeowner revoked her offer.

해설

난이도: 하

핵심 단어 및 논점

- UCC2
- "goods"
- offer
- revocation of offer
- consideration
- firm offer rule
- merchant
- detrimental reliance
- rely on/induce
- power of acceptance
- definite action
- indirectly

예상질문

Q. 본 사안의 계약은 "goods"에 대한 것이므로 UCC2가 적용된다. 그러나 NCBE 해설(point sheet)에는 'CL 룰'들을 적용하여 결론을 도출하였다. UCC2가 적용되는데, 왜 CL을 적용해야 하는가?

하나의 계약에, CL과 UCC2 중 딱 하나만 적용되는 것이 아니다. UCC2가 적용되는 "goods"에 대한 계약의 경우, UCC2가 '우선 적용'되는 것일 뿐, CL이 일체 배제되는 것이 아니다. CL과 UCC2 중 어떤 룰을 적용해야 하는지에 대한 정확한 룰은 다음과 같다: Common law principles remain applicable to the extent not displaced by the UCC(UCC에서 규정되어 있지 않은 부분에 대해서는 CL을 적용한다).

1. The expansion can be arguably interpreted. It would not be a nonconforming use, since a change could be inconsistent with the zoning law when any doubts are resolved against the change.

Under the nonconforming−use doctrine, zoning ordinance can allow uses that existed prior to the enactment of the ordinance. A nonconforming use cannot be extended in ways that constitute a substantial change, while insubstantial changes are permitted. Owners are entitled to make reasonable alterations to repair their facilities and render them practicable for their purposes. A change could be inconsistent with the zoning law when any doubts are resolved against the change.

Here, the expansion is not a nonconforming use. The goal of the protection of nonconforming use under the zoning ordinance is to protect prior investment, not a change of the existing use. The man hopes to increase the intensity of the use in the newly zoned residential neighborhood, and it would impose more traffic and externalities in the residential community.

However, the expansion could arguably be treated as a permissible nonconforming use. This is because the expansion is necessary for the man's store to compete effectively with the three other stores in the area. Other local convenience stores sell gas and have small dining areas within them. Thus, the expansion could be viewed as merely a normal expansion of a prior nonconforming use. Additionally, the goal of the protection of nonconforming use is to protect the persons who purchased the property in reliance on the law in place when the property was acquired. The man had expected that in the future he would expand the store when he purchased the store.

In sum, it is more likely that the expansion is not a nonconforming use.

2. The bank is not obligated to disburse further funds, since its obligation is optional with the condition of the bank's determination.

A future advance mortgage is a loan that the lender will advance funds to the borrower over a fixed period. The lender secures a mortgage on the property for the entire amount of the money, including future advances. There are two types of future advances mortgage: obligatory advances and optional advances.

If a future advances mortgage is obligatory, the lender has a duty to advance the funds, while the lender has no duty to advance funds but has discretion whether to make future advances under an optional future advances mortgage. When a lender has no definite obligation to advance any funds, it is an optional future advance mortgage.

Here, the agreement between the bank and the man is a future advance mortgage. It requires a satisfactory-progress condition. The bank would disburse at such times and in such amounts when the bank determined to be appropriate. Thus, the future advance mortgage is optional. Thus, the bank officer's concerns could justify withholding funding.

In sum, the bank is not obligated to disburse further funds, since its obligation is optional with the condition of the bank's determination.

3. With respect to the $50,000 payment, the bank's mortgage has priority, since it preceded the filing of the mechanic's lien. With respect to the $40,000 payment, the results are different under the majority and minority rules.

With respect to the $50,000 payment, the bank properly filed its security interest in the local land records office. It preceded the filing of the mechanic's lien, and therefore the bank has priority over the mechanic.

With respect to the $40,000 payment, if payments under a future-advances mortgage are obligatory, then the junior lender's lien is junior regardless of the time when the junior lien was recorded.

Here, if the loan is obligatory and the bank must make the future payments, those payments are deemed to have been made when the mortgage was created. Thus, bank has priority over the mechanic with respect to the $40,000 payment.

If a future-advances mortgage are optional, the junior lender has a priority as to the amounts that junior lender transferred to the mortgagee and recorded it. This is applicable only when the mortgagee has notice of the subsequent lien when it makes the advance.

Under the majority jurisdictions, mortgagee has notice only when he has actual notice based on the reason that the mortgagee has no burden of a title search each time it makes an advance.

Here, the bank had no notice of the mechanic's lien when the third advance was sought. Thus, the bank would have priority over the subcontractor with respect to $50,000 and $40,000. With respect to the additional future advances (the third advance), the bank has no priority.

Under the minority jurisdictions, mortgagee is charged with constructive notice when junior lender's lien is properly recorded. Here, mechanic's lien is properly recorded, and therefore, with respect to $50,000, the bank has no priority over the mechanic.

In sum, with respect to the $50,000 payment, the bank's mortgage has priority, since it preceded the filing of the mechanic's lien. With respect to the $40,000 payment, the results are different under the majority and minority rules.

해설

난이도: 하

핵심 단어 및 논점

- nonconforming use
- zoning ordinance
- future advance mortgage

3번 문제

답안요령

1. Future-advances mortgage 정의
2. Optional v. Obligatory
3. Analysis + 결론

2018July Trusts & Future Interests

<u>1(a). The trustee breached his duty of loyalty when he rented a trust-owned apartment to himself.</u>

A trustee owes trust beneficiaries the duty of loyalty. A trustee is prohibited from making transactions that place the interest of the trustee or another above the interest of trust beneficiaries. The duty of loyalty prohibits two types of transactions: self-dealing and conflict of interest. Self-dealing is a transaction that the trustee deals with trust property for the trustee's personal benefit.

Here, the trustee's lease of a trust owned apartment to himself was self-dealing. Under the no further inquiry rule, there is no need to inquire into the motivation for the self-dealing transaction or even its fairness.

Here, the fact that the trustee paid a market rate is irrelevant to the conclusion that the trustee engaged in self-dealing.

In sum, the trustee breached his duty of loyalty when he rented a trust-owned apartment to himself.

<u>1(b). The trustee breached his duty of care when he failed to purchase fire insurance on the real property.</u>

A trustee has the duty of care, which requires a trustee to administer the trust as a prudent person with reasonable care. A trustee shall take reasonable steps to take control of and protect the trust property.

Here, the trustee failed to purchase a fire policy on the trust's rental property and it results in a loss to the trust. Such insurance is customarily taken by a prudent person.

In sum, the trustee breached his duty of care when he failed to purchase fire insurance on the real property.

<u>1(c). The trustee breached his duty to administer the trust in accordance with applicable law when he allocated the repair expense to trust income.</u>

A trustee has the duty to administer the trust diligently and in good faith in accordance with the terms of the trust and applicable law.

Under the UPAIA, all ordinary expenses incurred in connection with the preservation of trust property, including ordinary repairs are allocated to income. Extraordinary repairs are allocated to principal. Ordinary repairs are repairs required by day to day wear and tear. Extraordinary repairs are repairs required by an unusual or unforeseen occurrence.

Here, the roof repair was extraordinary because it was required by an unforeseen occurrence, a fire. Thus, it should be allocated to principal, not income. However, the trustee charged this expense to trust income, instead to liquid assets. The trustee did not act in accordance with the UPAIA.

In sum, the trustee breached his duty to administer the trust in accordance with applicable law when he allocated the repair expense to trust income.

<u>2. Upon Albert's death, the trust principal should be distributed to Betty's husband, since she devised her vested remainder in the trust to him.</u>

Under the terms of the trust, the testator created a life estate in Albert and a remainder interest in Betty. Betty's interest was vested because there is no contingency on Betty's interest. Thus, if the remainderman is not living when the remainder becomes possessory, it passes to the devisee of the interest under the deceased remainderman's will.

Here, the trust principal became possessory at Albert's death, and Betty was not living at that time. Betty's will left Betty's entire estate to her husband. Thus, the principal should be distributed to Betty's husband upon Albert's death.

In sum, upon Albert's death, the trust principal should be distributed to Betty's husband, since she devised her vested remainder in the trust to him.

해설

난이도: 하

핵심 단어 및 논점

- fiduciary duty
- duty of loyalty (self-dealing)
- no further inquiry rule
- duty of care
- duty to administer the trust diligently and in good faith
- allocation of principal and income
- UPAIA
- life estate and remaindermen
- predecease

1(a)번 문제

논점: Self-dealing

답안요령

1. Self-dealing
   + analysis
2. No further inquiry rule★
   + analysis
3. Beneficiary's remedy
   + analysis

TIP　Self-dealing에 관한 답안 작성 시, no further inquiry rule과 이에 대한 analysis가 고득점 포인트다.

1. The mechanic's testimony is admissible either as lay witness testimony or as expert witness testimony.

Evidence is relevant if it has any tendency to make a fact more probable or less probable than it would be without the evidence.

Here, the mechanic's testimony is relevant because it tends to make it more probable that a brake malfunction may have caused the accident.

Lay witness opinion is admissible if: (1) the opinion is rationally based on the witness's perception, (2) the opinion held to determine a fact in issue, and (3) the opinion is not based on scientific, technical, or other specialized knowledge

Here, the mechanic's opinion is rationally based on his personal perception and would be helpful to the jury's determination of whether the woman or the man caused the accident. A court could also find that because the mechanic's opinion is based on his personal perception, it is not an expert opinion.

In the alternative, the mechanic may be qualified as an expert based on his technical skill or specialized knowledge. Expert opinion is admitted when (1) the expert's scientific, technical, or other specialized knowledge will help the trier of fact to understand the evidence or to determine a fact in issue, (2) the testimony is based on sufficient facts or data, (3) the testimony is the product of reliable principles and methods, and (4) the expert has reliably applied the principles and methods to the facts of the case.

Here, the mechanic used his technical skills to reliably form the opinion that the woman's truck brakes required repair, making the opinion testimony admissible.

In sum, the mechanic's testimony is admissible either as lay witness testimony or as expert witness testimony.

2. The invoice will be admissible under the business records hearsay exception.

The invoice for the new parts for the woman's truck brakes is relevant, because it has some tendency to make it more probable that the woman's truck brakes were, in fact, in need of repair and may have malfunctioned, causing the accident.

The hearsay is an out of court statement that is offered in evidence to prove the truth of the matter asserted in the statement.

Here, the invoice is hearsay. First, it is mechanic's written assertion and is a statement. Second, the mechanic made the statement out of court. Third, the statement will be offered to prove the cause of the accident.

However, the invoice fits business records exception. A business record may be a record of an event or condition made by someone with knowledge, if kept in the course of a regularly conducted activity of a business, and if making the record was a regular practice of that activity. The fact must be shown by the testimony of the custodian of the record or another qualified witness.

Here, the mechanic was a person with knowledge because he ordered the truck brake parts. The facts that receipt was signed by the mechanic and he kept it in his cabinet among similar receipts for other customers support mechanic kept the receipt in the ordinary course of his repair business.

In sum, the invoice will be admissible under the business records hearsay exception.

3(a). The doctor's testimony is not protected by the physician—patient privilege, because the woman placed her medical condition in issue.

The doctor's proposed testimony is relevant because it has some tendency to make it less probable that the accident caused the onset of the woman's neck pain.

The physician—patient privilege has been adopted by statute in most jurisdictions, while the common law does not recognize the privilege. In determining whether to honor the assertion of a privilege, courts must balance the public interest in nondisclosure against the need of the particular litigant for access to the privileged information, keeping in mind that the burden of persuasion rests on the party seeking to prevent disclosure.

In most jurisdictions, patient communications or disclosures made for the purpose of medical diagnosis or treatment are privileged. However, there are some exceptions to prevent the privilege from being used as a shield for fraud. When the patient places a physical condition in issue in a personal injury lawsuit, the privilege is inapplicable.

Here, the woman used her medical condition, putting the cause of the pain into the issue of the lawsuit.

In sum, the doctor's proposed testimony is not protected by the physician—patient privilege.

3(b). The doctor's testimony is admissible, because (1) it is officially non—hearsay and (2) it is the hearsay exception for statements made for medical diagnosis or treatment.

The doctor's statement repeats an out—of—court statement by the woman for the truth of the matter asserted. However, it is not hearsay and admissible. This is because it is an opposing party's statement of which the declarant is the plaintiff, the woman here.

In the alternative, hearsay exception for statements made for medical diagnosis or treatment is applicable when (1) the statement describes medical history and provides information about patient's past or present symptoms or sensations, or their general cause and (2) it is made for medical diagnosis or treatment.

Here, the woman's statement describes the onset and nature of her neck pain. It is medical history and made for medical treatment to her doctor.

In sum, the doctor's testimony is admissible, because (1) it is officially non—hearsay and (2) it is the hearsay exception for statements made for medical diagnosis or treatment.

4. The roommate's testimony is admissible, since it is admissible habit evidence.

Evidence of a person's habit may be admitted to prove that on a particular occasion the person acted in accordance with the habit. A person's habit is defined as his or her consistent response to a specific situation. Testimony involving habit evidence may be given by the person who has personal knowledge.

Usually character evidence is inadmissible when it is used to prove that on a particular occasion the person acted in accordance with the character, and habit evidence can be inadmissible when the habit evidence is described similarly to evidence of a person's character. Thus, courts limit habit evidence to proof of relevant behaviors that are not just consistent but semi−automatic.

Here, the roommate would testify that texting is the man's constant and consistent practice. The texting is volitional and it would be considered a semi−automatic habit as admissible habit evidence.

In sum, the roommate's testimony is admissible, since it is admissible habit evidence.

해설

난이도: 하

핵심 단어 및 논점

- lay witness opinion
- expert witness opinion
- hearsay
- business records exception (hearsay exception)
- physician−patient privilege

- admission exception (hearsay exception)
- medical treatment (hearsay exception)
- habit
- semi−automatic

2번 문제
논점: Hearsay exception

답안요령

> 1. Relevance★
>   + analysis
> 2. Hearsay 기본 rule: 정의 + inadmissible
>   + analysis (hearsay에 해당한다)
> 3. However, business record exception + rule
>   + analysis

3(a)번 문제

논점: Physician-patient privilege

답안요령

1. Analysis(해당 증거의 relevance에 대한)
2. General rule
3. Balancing test
   + analysis
4. Exceptions
   + analysis

4번 문제

논점: Habit

답안요령

1. Relevance
   + analysis
2. Habit rule + 정의
3. Character evidence와 비교★
4. Analysis(증거가 habit이라는 점에 대해)

TIP1 증거력을 판단하는 문제에 대한 답안은 '증거의 relevant 유무'에 대한 내용으로 시작되어야 한다.

TIP2 특정 증거가 character가 아닌 habit인 경우, character evidence와 비교분석하는 것이 고득점 포인트다.

1. The Solar Inc. came into existence on December 10, when its articles of incorporation were filed by the Secretary of State's office.

A corporation is formed when the articles of incorporation is filed with the Secretary of State.

Here, the articles were not filed on November 10 when they were received by the Secretary of State. This is because the woman filed to include in the document the number of authorized shares, as required by the business corporation ac of State X. The woman revised articles and it were filed on December 10.

In sum, the Solar Inc. came into existence on December 10.

2(a). The woman is not personally liable to the installer, because she did not know that the business had not been properly incorporated when she made the contract under the MBCA.

Persons purporting to act on behalf of a corporation and knowing there was no incorporation are jointly and severally liable for all liabilities created while so acting. An erroneous but in good faith belief that incorporation has happened does not constitute knowledge.

Here, the woman did not actually know that the original articles had not been filed by the Secretary of State when she entered into the employment contract with the installer in the corporate name.

In sum, the woman is not personally liable to the installer.

2(b). The woman is not personally liable to the installer under common law doctrines, de facto corporation doctrine and incorporation by estoppel doctrine.

Co-owners of a business for profit that has not been properly incorporated are treated as partners in a partnership and are jointly and severally liable for all business obligations.

However, de facto corporation doctrine and incorporation by estoppel doctrine show corporate limited liability.

Under the de facto corporation doctrine, courts recognize corporate limited liability when: (1) there was good faith attempt to incorporate and (2) there was actual use of the corporate form, such as by carrying on the business as a corporation or contracting in the corporate name.

Here, the woman mailed to the Secretary of State of State X a document with good faith attempt to incorporate. This would have led to a validly formed corporation but for omitted the number of authorized shares. Moreover, the woman used the corporate form by entering into the employment contract in the corporation's name. Thus, the woman is not personally liable under the de facto corporation doctrine.

Under the incorporation by estoppel doctrine, most jurisdictions recognize corporate limited liability when (1) a third party deals solely with the corporation and (2) third party has not relied on the personal assets of the promoter.

Here, the woman signed as president of Solar Inc. With the phrase "President, Solar Inc." in the contract, the installer was dealing with the corporation, not with the woman and he was not relying on the personal assets of the woman.

In sum, the woman is not personally liable to the installer under common law doctrines, de facto corporation doctrine and incorporation by estoppel doctrine.

3. The man is not personally liable to the installer, because he was an inactive investor in the business.

Under the defective incorporation principles, an inactive investor, who did not purport to act on behalf of the non-existent corporation, is not personally liable. Here, the man did not sign the contract with the installer and therefore he is not an inactive investor in the business. Thus, the man is not personally liable to the installer.

Moreover, even though a co-owner in a business for profit may have been a partner in the unincorporated business, a corporate would have limited liability for the co-owner under the de facto corporation and corporation by estoppel doctrines. Those doctrines are applicable to all participants of the business, including those who are inactive.

Here, the man would not have personal liability for the same reasons that are available to the woman.

In sum, the man is not personally liable to the installer.

해설

난이도: 하

핵심 단어 및 논점

- corporation
- articles of incorporation (AOI)
- de facto corporation doctrine
- incorporation by estoppel doctrine
- defective incorporation principles

1. A court could find that the woman was negligent even though she was driving below the posted speed limit. This is because the actor can still be liable for negligence even if he/she did not violate the statute.

An actor who does not complied with all statutory standards is negligent per se. However, an actor who is not liable for negligence per se can be negligent if his conduct is not reasonable under the circumstances. In determining whether the actions are reasonable, jury would consider appropriate precautions to avoid foreseeable risks. Jury may consider the likelihood that the risk will eventuate and the burden of taking precautions against such foreseeable risk.

In this case, the woman did not violate the state statute, driving 40 mph at the time of the accident. However, the accident was occurred on an icy highway during a winter storm. The speed limit is for normal weather and the jury could consider the woman is negligent for driving 40 mph.

In sum, a court could find that the woman was negligent even though she was driving below the posted speed limit. This is because the actor can still be liable for negligence even if he/she did not violate the statute.

2. A court properly find that the woman is liable for the man's damages resulting from the infection. This is because the woman's negligence proximately cause the infection.

An actor is liable for harms that are a foreseeable consequence of his negligence. Usually, subsequent medical treatment is foreseeable risk.

In this case, man was rushed to a local hospital after the accident. Hospitalization and surgery are foreseeable consequences of the woman's negligence. Thus, woman is liable for man's damages resulting from the infection that are caused in the hospital, since woman's negligence proximately caused the injury.

In sum, a court properly find that the woman is liable for the man's damages resulting from the infection. This is because the woman's negligence proximately cause the infection.

3. A court properly find that the hospital is liable for the man's damages resulting from the infection based on res ipsa loquitur doctrine.

In negligence cases, the plaintiff must show that defendant was negligent and it caused his/her damages. However, under the res ipsa loquitur doctrine, jury can infer duty and breach, even if the plaintiff fails to find a specific action that is negligent, when: (1) the event is of a kind which ordinarily does not occur in the absence of negligence, (2) the negligence is within the scope of the defendant's duty to the plaintiff, and (3) the defendant was exclusive to the control.

In this case, the tests revealed that the serious infection would be caused by the exposure to contaminated blood products or improperly sterilized medical instruments, or failure of staff to follow proper handwashing techniques, staff failure to properly identify and discard certain used medical instruments. These reasons are usually not occurred in the absence of negligence and the first element is satisfied. Secondly, it is clear that the hospital has duty to protect the patient from infections. Lastly, medical instruments are not substances that is under the control of hospital, rather than the man (patient). Handwashing techniques are also controlled by hospital. Thus, the res ipsa loquitur is applicable in this case.

In sum, a court properly find that the hospital is liable for the man's damages resulting from the infection based on res ipsa loquitur doctrine.

4. The woman's liability could not be limited to $100,000 for injuries the man suffered in the accident, since the woman and the hospital are jointly and severally liable for the man's damages.

If more than one defendant were negligent, those defendants would be jointly and severally liable for the damages. Any one of the defendants is liable for the full amount of the plaintiff's damages.

In this case, the woman and the hospital are jointly and severally liable for the man's infection.

In sum, the woman's liability could not be limited to $100,000 for injuries the man suffered in the accident, since the woman and the hospital are jointly and severally liable for the man's injuries.

해설

난이도: 하

핵심 단어 및 논점

- negligence per se (statute)
- negligence
- proximate causation
- res ipsa loquitur
- joint and several liability

1번 문제

'Woman이 statute를 준수했음에도 불구하고 court가 woman의 과실을 인정할수 있는지' 그 여부를 판단하는 문제이다. Woman에게 과실이 '있는지/없는지' 판단하는 것이 아닌, court가 과실을 인정할 '수' 있다/없다를 판단하는 문제이다. 본래 negligence 유무를 판단할 때 행위자의 행동이 reasonable한지 판단하기 위해 precaution과 probability, 이 두 요소를 비교형량하여야 하나, 주어진 사안에서는 두 요소에 대한 구체적인 내용을 명시하고 있지 않는 바, statute를 준수했음에도 불구하고 court가 woman의 과실을 인정할 수 있다는 로직을 보여주면 충분하다.

> **답안요령**

> 1. statute 위반 → NG per se
>   + analysis(actor가 statute 준수하였으므로 NG per se 인정×)
> 2. statute 준수하더라도, NG 가능
>   + analysis(actor의 행동이 unreasonable함)★

> **TIP** 2번: Actor 행동의 reasonability를 판단하는 경우, ① 주의(precaution)를 기울임에 있어 actor의 부담과 그 ② 행동의 위험(probability)을 비교하는 것이 고득점 포인트다.

2019Feb Secured Transactions

1. The company has claim against the bank with respect to the sale of the gramophone, since the bank did not notice the company before the sale.

After default, a secured party may dispose the collateral. A secured party must send an authenticated notification of the disposition to the debtor. The only exception to this notification requirement is if the collateral is perishable or sold on a recognized market.

Here, the bank, secured party, did not sent authenticated notification to the company. Additionally, there are no fact indicating that exception rules are applicable in this case.

In sum, the company has claim against the bank with respect to the sale of the gramophone, since the bank did not notice the company before the sale.

2. The bank had a superior claim to the gramophone, since the bank's security interest is perfected before the judgment lien is created.

A judgment lien creditor takes priority over a security interest only when the creditor became a lien creditor before the conflicting security interest is perfected. Here, the security interest of the bank is effective and is perfected. A security interest attaches to collateral when: secured party gave value to debtor, debtor has rights in the collateral, and the collateral is not a certificated security and the collateral is in the possession of the secured party pursuant to the debtor's security agreement. The company borrowed money from the bank and it owned the gramophone. The bank took possession of gramophone under the oral agreement with the company's owner. Thus, the bank's security interest is attached and effective. Moreover, there are many ways to perfect the security interest. The collateral can be perfected by taking possession of it. Thus, the security interest of the bank is perfected.

The security interest of the bank was perfected several months ago and the judgment creditor obtained a judicial lien last month. Thus, the bank takes priority.

In sum, the bank had a superior claim to the gramophone, since the bank's security interest is perfected before the judgment lien is created.

3. The bank does not have an enforceable security interest in any personal property of the company other than the gramophone. This is because the loan agreement does not describe the security interest in those assets.

The security agreement must describes the collateral. Although the description is not required to be detailed, but it must reasonably identifies what is described.

Unlike the gramophone, the bank does not take possession of other personal property of the company. Then, the attachment of the bank's security interest is recognized only if the company authenticated (signed) the security agreement. Here, the company signed the loan agreement, but the description "all personal property" is insufficient. The provision does not reasonably identify the collateral. Thus, the security interest in any personal property of the company other than the gramophone is ineffective.

In sum, the bank does not have an enforceable security interest in any personal property of the company other than the gramophone. This is because the loan agreement does not describe the security interest in those assets.

해설

난이도: 하

핵심 단어 및 논점

- notice (disposal)
- effectiveness of security interest
- perfection
- lien creditor
- description of the collateral

2번 문제

Judgment lien creditor와 perfection한 creditor(bank) 간 priority를 판단하는 문제이나, 답안을 서술할 때에는 bank의 attachment와 perfection에 대해 자세히 논해야 한다. 로직은 다음과 같다.

Judgment lien creditor와 perfection한 creditor(bank) 간 priority ← Bank의 채권은 perfection이 되었는가? ← Bank의 채권은 attached되었는가?

3번 문제

본 사안은 attachment는 ineffective하고 filing, 즉 perfection은 effective한 경우이다. 그러나 attach되지 않은 security interest는 perfected될 수 없는 바, 채권자는 채무자의 personal property에 대해 권리가 없다.

1. Radiology Services is a general partnership at will, since LLC has not been created and Carol, Jean, and Pat are recognized as co−owners.

An LLC is formed when an articles of organization is filed with the Secretary of State. A general partnership is formed when two or more persons do a business for profit as co−owners. No formalities and no intent are required.

Here, even though Carol, Jean, and Pat wanted to create an LLC, they forgot to sign the documents and they have never done so. Thus, LLC has not been created. Instead, they agreed to split the profits equally and to run the practice together in a manner that would be competitive. The intent to from GP is not required to create a GP. Thus, Radiology Services is a general partnership. Moreover, there is not fact indicating that the partners agreed to the GP's fixed period or specific undertaking, and the GP at−will is established.

In sum, Radiology Services is a general partnership at will, since LLC has not been created and Carol, Jean, and Pat are recognized as co−owners.

2. Carol had the actual authority to purchase the imaging machine, since the purchase of the machine was the acts for ordinary course of business.

Each partner has equal rights in the management and control of the partnership's business. Thus, the scope of a partner's authority is governed by agency law principle. If the partnership agreement is silent on the scope of the agent (partner)'s authority, a partner has actual authority to usual and customary matters, unless that partner has reason to know that: (1) other partners might disagree or (2) consultation with other partners is appropriate for some other reason.

Here, Carol purchased for the practice a state−of−the−art imaging machine and it is in the ordinary course of business. Although Jean, other member, was worried about overspending on imaging equipment, she did not express her concern to Carol. Thus, Carol has actual authority to make the purchase.

In sum, Carol had the actual authority to purchase the imaging machine, since the purchase of the machine was the acts for ordinary course of business.

3. Jean's statements to Carol constituted a withdrawal from Radiology services, since the oral statement shows her intent to withdraw.

A partner can dissociate from the partnership at any time when the partner expressed his will to withdraw as a partner. The notice of the partner's dissociation need not be in writing.

Here, Jean told Carol, "I'm out of here and never coming back." This statement shows her intent of withdrawal and it constitutes a dissociation. As mentioned above, the general partnership is an at−will partnership and Jean's dissociation is rightful dissociation.

In sum, Jean's statements to Carol constituted a withdrawal from Radiology services, since the oral statement shows her intent to withdraw.

4. Jean's statements were sufficient to entitle her to receive a buyout payment, since she made a rightful dissociation. However, there is no time limit for the partnership to make the payment since she did not made an written demand.

A partner's dissociation in an at−will partnership results in its dissolution and the business must be wound up. However, remaining partners can waive the dissolution by the affirmative vote or consent of all remaining partners. When a dissociating partner made a rightful dissociation, the partner is entitled to the value of his interest. If the dissociating partner makes a written demand for payment and no agreement is reached within 120 days after the demand, the partnership must pay in cash the amount it estimates to be the buyout price.

Here, Jean dissociated but Carol and Pat agreed to continue their participation in Radiology Services without Jean. As mentioned above, Jean made a rightful dissociation, and she is entitled to receive payment of a buyout price. However, Jean did not made a written demand for the payment, and there is no time limit for the partnership to make the payment.

In sum, Jean's statements were sufficient to entitle her to receive a buyout payment, since she made a rightful dissociation. However, there is no time limit for the partnership to make the payment since she did not made an written demand.

해설

난이도: 하

핵심 단어 및 논점

- LLC formalities
- general partnership (GP)
- actual authority
- dissociation (GP)
- rightful dissociation
- right to receive payment

1번, 3번 문제

Jean의 dissociation이 rightful하며 유효하다. Rightful한지 그 여부는 GP의 유형에 따라 달리 판단되는 바, 3번 문제에서 GP at-will임을 근거로 rightful하다고 작성하는 것이 중요하다. 그런데 GP의 유형(GP at-will)을 판단하는 것은 1번 문제에 해당하는 바, 1번 답안에 GP의 구체적 유형, 즉 GP at-will임을 작성하는 것이 고득점 포인트다.

1(a). The state citizenship of the woman is State C and the state citizenship of the airline is State A. The parties are diverse.

A federal court has jurisdiction of a complaint based on state law if the amount in controversy exceeds $75,000 and there is complete diversity between the parties.

State citizenship for individual U.S. citizen is determined by their domicile. When the plaintiff changes his/her domicile, residence in a state and an intent to remain in that state at the time the complaint was filed should be considered.

Here, the woman lived in State C. Even though she was planning to start working at a new job in State A and found apartment in State A, she continues to live in State C after the accident. In other words, the woman did not physically take up residence in State A. Thus, the state citizenship of the woman is State C.

A corporation is a citizen of any state where it has been incorporated and of state where it has its principal place of business. Principal place of business is the corporation's nerve center, where the corporation maintains its headquarters.

Here, the airline is incorporated in State A and its corporate headquarters are located in there. Thus, its nerve center is in State A and the state citizenship of the airline is State A.

In sum, the state citizenship of the woman is State C and the state citizenship of the airline is State A. The parties are diverse.

1(b). The amount in controversy exceeds $75,000 and the court has diversity jurisdiction.

In determining whether the amount in controversy exceeds $75,000, courts rely on the plaintiff's good-faith allegations unless it appears to a legal certainty that plaintiff cannot recover the amount alleged.

Here, the woman is seeking for damages in excess of $1 million and it is for the woman's personal injury. The fact indicated that she suffered serious and permanent injuries during the emergency landing and has been unable to work.

In sum, the amount in controversy exceeds $75,000 and the court has diversity jurisdiction.

2. There is no personal jurisdiction for the airline and, therefore, the court should grand the motion to dismiss.

Federal district courts may exercise personal jurisdiction to the same extent as the courts of general jurisdiction of the state in which the district court sits.

Here, the federal court is in State B and State's long-arm statute allows its courts to exercise personal jurisdiction to the maximum extent allowed by the Fourteenth Amendment of the U.S. Constitution.

The Due Process Clause of the Fourteenth Amendment permits a state court to exercise jurisdiction over a defendant if he have established minimum contacts with the state such that the exercise of personal jurisdiction would not offend traditional notions of fair play and substantial justice. In determining whether there is minimum contact, the relatedness between the cause of action and the defendant's contacts with the forum is considered.

When the contacts between the business and the State is so continuous and systematic to render the corporation is essentially at home in the State, general jurisdiction can be established.

Here, in State B, the facility in which the airline receives and processes online and telephone reservation requests is located. Moreover, there are only 150 employees in State B while more than 12,000 of its 15,000 employees are located in other state (State C). Thus, it is hard to conclude that the airline is essentially at home in State B.

Specific jurisdiction can be established when the contacts demonstrate purposeful availment of the benefits of the forum state and render it foreseeable that the defendant may be hauled into the forum state's courts.

Here, there was a contact between the woman and the airline in State B when the woman called the reservation center there. However, the case is not for the reservation, but the emergency landing accident which occurred in State A. It is hard to conclude that the airline can foresee that it may be hauled into State B's courts because of once reservation for the accident.

In sum, there is no personal jurisdiction for the airline and, therefore, the court should grand the motion to dismiss.

해설

난이도: 1번 문제: 하
　　　　 2번 문제: 상

핵심 단어 및 논점

- diversity of citizenship jurisdiction (DCJ)
- citizenship of corporation
- citizenship of individual
- personal jurisdiction (PJ)
- general jurisdiction
- specific jurisdiction

1번 문제

- 사안에서 'woman이 state-law tort claim을 근거로 federal court에 소송을 제기했음'을 명시하였는 바, 이는 woman이 FQJ가 아닌 DCJ를 근거로 소송을 제기했음을 의미한다. 따라서 FQJ에 대해서는 논할 필요가 없다.
- NCBE 해설은 AIC, domicile 순서로 논하였으나 본 답안은 domicile, AIC 순서로 작성되었다. 순서는 중요하지 않으므로 수험자 편의대로 서술하면 되겠다.

2번 문제

본 기출문제는 PJ를 판단하는 요소 중 minimum contact에 관한 것, 특히 피고(airline)와 State B와의 관계(relatedness)유무에 중점을 두고 있는 바, general jurisdiction과 specific jurisdiction을 구분하여 작성하는 것이 고득점 포인트다.

1(a). The trustee could have properly distributed trust assets to the son to enable him to pay his hospital bill.

The power of distribution given to trustee is limited under the trust. In this case, the trust is a discretionary trust with a spendthrift clause and it is a support trust. In discretionary trusts, a trustee has uncontrolled discretion and a trustee controls the distribution unless there is an abuse of the discretion by the trustee. A spendthrift clause prevents a beneficiary's creditors from reaching trust assets. However, it is allowed for the beneficiary to reach trust assets himself when a trustee abused his discretion. A support trust permits distributions from the trust to enable the beneficiary to maintain his or her accustomed standard of living.

Here, trust assets were distributed to son to enable him to pay his hospital bill. Hospital bill is treated as support.

In sum, the trustee could have properly distributed trust assets to the son to enable him to pay his hospital bill.

1(b). The trustee could not have properly distributed trust assets to the son to enable him to pay the loan to purchase the computer−gaming system without additional proving.

The "support" term includes more than necessities or bare essentials and it is interpreted in various ways depending on the fact patterns. In determining whether the distribution is to support a beneficiary or not, a beneficiary's accustomed lifestyle is considered which is determined at the time the beneficiary's trust interest is created.

Here, the son has earned, on average, less than $35,000 per year during the past and it is hard to say that computer−gaming system is necessary to maintain son's life style. Thus, the distribution to enable son to pay the loan to purchase the computer—gaming system could not be recognized as a distribution for son's support. However, if the son shows that the purchasing the system is necessary to allow him to live in accordance with his accustomed lifestyle, the distribution could be allowed.

In sum, the trustee could not have properly distributed trust assets to the son to enable him to pay the loan to purchase the computer—gaming system without additional proving without additional proving.

1(c). The trustee could have properly distributed trust assets to the son to enable him to pay child support.

The term support includes the reasonable amounts to support minority children.

Here, the son has three living children, now 9, 11, 14 years of age and he has been judicially ordered to pay child support. The fact that these children currently live with their mother, not the son does not change the result.

In sum, the trustee could have properly distributed trust assets to the son to enable him to pay child support.

2. The trustee abused his discretion in refusing to make any distributions to the son during the past seven years.

As mentioned above, a trustee has uncontrolled discretion and a trustee controls the distribution unless there is an abuse of the discretion by the trustee, under a discretionary trusts. The trustee must have reasonable reasons when he withholds payments from a beneficiary. Additionally, all beneficiaries have same priority on the distributions and there should be no impartiality when there are more than one beneficiary.

Here, although the son's and daughter's financial needs were similar, the trustee has distributed $80,000 from trust income and principal to the settlor's daughter. However, trustee has no specific reasons not to make distributions to son. The trustee frequently told others, behind the son's back and without any direct basis, that the son was an "adulterer" and a "terrible father." Moreover, the trustee often referred to the son as a "bum," and he told the settlor's daughter without any explanation, "Your brother is rude to me."

In sum, the trustee abused his discretion in refusing to make any distributions to the son during the past seven years.

3.(a) The son's former wife may obtain orders requiring the trustee to pay her claim against the son from trust assets, since the claim is for child support.

A spendthrift clause prevents creditors of a trust beneficiary from reaching trust assets until trust assets are distributed to the beneficiary. However, even with a spendthrift clause, claims against a beneficiary for unpaid child support can be enforced against the trust when there is a trustee's abuse of discretion under UPC.

Here, the claim raised by son's wife is for child support.

In sum, the son's former wife may obtain orders requiring the trustee to pay her claim against the son from trust assets, since the claim is for child support.

3(b). The hospital may obtain orders requiring the trustee to pay their claims against the son from trust assets with the trustee's abuse of discretion in some jurisdictions adopting the necessaries exception. However, the hospital may not obtain orders in other jurisdictions where do not adopt the necessaries exception.

In some jurisdictions, creditors who provided the beneficiary with necessaries may reach the beneficiary's interest in satisfaction of any unpaid debt even when there is a spendthrift clause. However, this rule applies only when there is abuse of discretion.

Here, the hospital is a creditor who provided the son with medical treatment, which is surely recognized as necessary. Moreover, as mentioned above, the trustee abused his discretion in distributing the distribution to the son. Thus, the hospital may obtain orders requiring the trustee.

In other jurisdictions, the necessaries exception is not recognized. In these jurisdictions, the hospital cannot reach the son's interest in the trust in satisfaction of its claim.

In sum, the hospital may obtain orders requiring the trustee to pay their claims against the son from trust assets with the trustee's abuse of discretion in some jurisdictions adopting the necessaries exception. However, the hospital may not obtain orders in other jurisdictions where do not adopt the necessaries exception.

<u>3(c). The friend may not obtain orders requiring the trustee to pay their claims against the son from trust assets, since the friend did not provide necessaries to son.</u>

As mentioned above, computer–gaming system is not recognized as necessary. Thus, the exception rule is inapplicable to the friend.

In sum, the friend may not obtain orders requiring the trustee to pay their claims against the son from trust assets, since the friend did not provide necessaries to son.

해설

난이도: 중

핵심 단어 및 논점

- discretionary trust
- spendthrift clause
- support trust
- "support" 해석
- child support
- abuse of discretion
- necessaries exception

1번과 3번 문제의 경우, 필자는 세 명의 creditors를 각각 title화하여 작성하였다. 1번 문제에서 각 creditor들을 (a), (b), (c)로 구분하고 있고, 세 명의 creditors에게 적용되는 rules가 많아 각 creditor에 적용되는 rule을 구분하여 작성하기 불편했기 때문에, 1번 문제뿐만 아니라 3번 문제에 대해서도 문제를 세분화하여 작성하였다. 수험자는 본인에게 편한 방식으로 답안을 작성하면 되나, 각 creditor를 구분하지 않고 작성할 때에는 모든 rules를 빠짐없이 작성하도록 유의하여야 하고, 어떤 rule이 어떤 creditor에게 적용되는지 명확히 서술해야 할 것이다.

1. Ben should not be charged with burglary because he had no intent to commit burglary.

At common law, burglary is defined as the breaking and entering of the dwelling house of another in the night with the intent to commit a felony.

In this case, Ben pushed the window fully open and climbed into the house without the consent from neighborhood. The house was neighbor's dwelling structure and Ben acted in night. However, Ben intended to retrieve his own painting, rather than to commit burglary. Thus, Ben has no intent necessary to be charged with burglary.

In sum, Ben should not be charged with burglary because he had no intent to commit burglary.

2. Ben should not be charged with larceny because he had no intent to steal and he did not act without consent.

At common law, larceny is defined as: (1) the misappropriation of another's personal property, (2) by means of taking it from his possession, (3) without his consent. Larceny requires an intent to steal.

In this case, the neighbor suggested Ben to hang the unsigned print. Thus, Ben's taking of the print was not without consent. Additionally, Ben did not acted with the intent to steal the print, but acted following the neighbor's permission. Thus, Ben had no intent necessary to be charged with larceny.

In sum, Ben should not be charged with larceny because he had no intent to steal and he did not act without consent.

3. Ben should be charged with embezzlement because he sold the dealer neighbor's print with the requisite intent.

Embezzlement is generally defined as: (1) a lawful possession, (2) of another person's property, and (3) wrongfully misappropriates such property. Embezzlement requires an intent to permanently deprive the lawful owner of the property is required.

In this case, the neighborhood permitted Ben to hang the print in his house just temporarily. However, Ben had been so angry with the neighbor about his arrest and he had sold the dealer the print. It was a wrongful misappropriation of neighbor's property (print). Additionally, Ben's actions strongly suggest that he intended to permanently deprive the neighbor of the print.

In sum, Ben should be charged with embezzlement because he sold the dealer neighbor's print with the requisite intent.

4. The art dealer should be charged with receiving stolen property, since all surrounding circumstances shows her knowledge that the property was stolen.

Receiving stolen property is defined as the receipt of stolen property. In most jurisdictions, receiving stolen property requires: (1) knowledge that the property was stolen and (2) intent to deprive the owner of her property. Stolen property includes properties that are obtained through larceny, embezzlement, or false pretenses.

In this case, the dealer received the print from Ben and the print was obtained through Ben's embezzlement.

Knowledge is recognized if an actor knew the property was stolen at the moment of receiving it. In some jurisdictions, defendant's actual subjective knowledge is required. In other jurisdictions, knowledge is recognized from all surrounding circumstances.

In this case, Ben offered to sell the print at a very low price and he told the art dealer, "I can sell this print to you at such a good price only because I shouldn't have it at all." The art dealer failed to investigate the ownership history of her purchases. Moreover, an hour after the sale, she contacted a foreign art collector and sold him the print for 10 times what she had paid for it. These facts strongly shows that the art dealer had knowledge that the property was stolen.

In sum, the art dealer should be charged with receiving stolen property, since all surrounding circumstances shows her knowledge that the property was stolen.

해설

난이도: 하

핵심 단어 및 논점

- burglary
- larceny
- embezzlement
- receiving stolen property
- knowledge (intent)

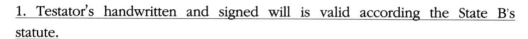

1. Testator's handwritten and signed will is valid according the State B's statute.

At common law, the validity of a testator's will was determined under the law of the state where the testator was domiciled at the time of his death. Here, Testator died while domiciled in State B. State B recognizes "wills in a testator's handwriting so long as the will is dated and subscribed by the testator." Testator's handwritten will includes the Testator's name at the end of the will and it was dated.

In sum, Testator's handwritten and signed will is valid according the State B's statute.

2. A court is likely to determine that the Testator's death in City is merely motive, rather than a condition of execution of his will, considering various factors.

In determining whether the testator's death in City is a condition of execution of his will, a court must first determine whether the happening of the testator's death in City is a condition, or whether it was merely a motive. For this issue, lots of facts are considered.

First, the handwritten will of January 4, 2010, was found in Testator's bedside table. The fact that Testator had kept his will after he came back from City shows that the death in City was a motive. Second, there were no other testamentary documents. Third, if the testator's death in City is recognized as a condition, it would result in intestacy and Testator's son, Robert would be one of beneficiaries. It would be a result that is inconsistent with Testator's intent, since Testator did mention only John. With these facts, a court is likely to determine that the Testator's death in City is merely motive, rather than a condition of execution of his will.

In sum, a court is likely to determine that the Testator's death in City is merely motive, rather than a condition of execution of his will, considering various factors.

3. Regarding the ambiguous phrase "delightful wife of many years," a court may rule that Martha is a beneficiary of the will considering the facts and circumstances surrounding the execution of the will.

When there is ambiguities in a will, the facts and circumstances surrounding the execution of the will are considered.

Here, the will contains phrase stating "to my son John and his delightful wife of many years." John's wife name is not clearly stated and it is ambiguous, since Martha died and John later married Nancy. When Testator died, Nancy had been married only for two months. However, Martha had been married for seven years when the will was executed in 2010. Moreover, Testator had known Martha and her parents for many years, and Testator had introduced Martha to John. For these reasons, the phrase "delightful wife of many years" is strongly construed in favor to Martha, rather than Nancy.

In sum, regarding the ambiguous phrase "delightful wife of many years," a court may rule that Martha is a beneficiary of the will, considering the facts and circumstances surrounding the execution of the will.

4. Martha's two children should take the share to which Martha would have been entitled under the State B's statute.

State B provide that "if a beneficiary under a will predeceases the testator, the deceased beneficiary's surviving issue take the share the deceased beneficiary would have taken unless the will expressly provides otherwise." This statute is a type of anti−lapse statute.

Here, Martha is a beneficiary who predeceased Testator two years ago. Thus, Martha's two children who are surviving issues should take the share to which Martha would have been entitled.

In sum, Martha's two children should take the share to which Martha would have been entitled under the State B's statute.

5. Robert is not entitled to intestate share since there is no fact indicating that he born after 2020.

A child born to a testator after the execution of the will is entitled to intestate share of decedent's estate, unless the will shows testator's intent not to do so.

Here, Robert would be entitled to intestate share if he is a permitted child even when Testator did not mention him in his will. However, there is no fact indicating he born after 2020. Thus, Robert is not entitled to intestate share.

In sum, Robert is not entitled to intestate share since there is no fact indicating that he born after 2020.

해설

난이도: 2번 문제: 중
　　　　그 외 문제: 하

핵심 단어 및 논점

- validity of will
- conflict of laws
- condition v. motive
- ambiguous term
- anti-lapse statute
- permitted child

- 본 답안의 1번은 NCBE 해설의 Point One과 Point Two에 해당한다.
- 본 답안의 5번은 본 기출문제에 할당된 전체점수 중 적은 비중(10%)을 차지하나, 문제에서 명시하지 않은 논점을 수험자가 스스로 찾아내야만 작성할 수 있다는 점에서 고득점 포인트다.

1. The court did not err in denying the motion to suppress based on the interrogating the woman on March 15 after she had invoked her Miranda right to counsel on February 4. This is because more than 14 days had been passed after the invocation of the Miranda right to counsel.

Law enforcement officers are required to read Miranda warnings to a suspect when the suspect is subject to an in-custody interrogation. After invocation, counsel must be provided before a suspect can be questioned unless the suspect: (1) initiates contact with law enforcement, (2) is given a fresh set of Miranda warnings, and (3) executes a knowing and voluntary waiver. However, If a suspect has been released from interrogative custody, the police obligation to honor an invocation of the Miranda right to counsel terminates after 14 days.

In this case, on February 1, the woman returned to her cell after the interrogation. The interrogation on March 15 was raised after more than five weeks and the detective had read her Miranda warning. Thus, the woman's right to counsel had terminated by March 15.

Meanwhile, the fact that the woman remained in her cell for about five weeks is regardless of this issue. Custodial interrogation ends only when a person is released from interrogation and back into his normal life.

In sum, the court did not err in denying the motion to suppress based on the interrogating the woman on March 15 after she had invoked her Miranda right to counsel on February 4. This is because more than 14 days had been passed after the invocation of the Miranda right to counsel.

2. The court did not err in denying the motion to suppress based on the conveying to the woman her Miranda right to counsel by the statements he made on March 15. This is because the warning reasonably conveys woman's right to counsel.

The lawful enforcement must inform that a suspect has a right to the presence of an counsel after being informed of her Miranda rights. Miranda warnings must reasonably convey to a suspect his rights as required by Miranda. It is not required to be the clearest possible formulation.

Here, Both warnings on February 4 and March 15 reasonably convey suspect's rights. Even considered with the warnings on February 4 which is the state's standard, the warning on March 15 reasonably conveys woman's right to counsel.

In sum, the court did not err in denying the motion to suppress based on the conveying to the woman her Miranda right to counsel by the statements he made on March 15. This is because the warning reasonably conveys woman's right to counsel.

3. The court did not err in denying the motion to suppress based on the interrogating the woman on March 15 after she had invoked her Miranda right to counsel on March 15. This is because she did not unambiguously invoke her right.

To invoke the right to counsel, a suspect's request must be unambiguous, which means that the suspect must articulate the desire for counsel sufficiently clearly that a reasonable officer would understand the statement to be a request for counsel.

Here, the woman said, "I might need a lawyer." This statement is not an unambiguous invocation of the right to counsel. Moreover, the detective responded to her statement, "That's your call, ma'am," and it shows that the detective did not understand the woman's statement to be a request for counsel. Thus, the woman did not invoke her right to counsel.

In sum, the court did not err in denying the motion to suppress based on the interrogating the woman on March 15 after she had invoked her Miranda right to counsel on March 15. This is because she did not unambiguously invoke her right.

해설

난이도: 하

핵심 단어 및 논점

- Miranda rights
- right to counsel (Fifth Amendment)
- reasonably convey (no formulation)
- unambiguously (invocation)
- 14-day honor

1. Parent did not breach any duties to HomeSolar with respect to HomeSolar's no−dividend policy, since it is rational under the business judgment rule.

A parent corporation that is a controlling shareholders of a subsidiary owes fiduciary duties to subsidiary. When the transactions do not involve self−dealing, business judgment rule (BJR) is used. According to the BJR, there should be a rational business justification for the activity. The rule bars judicial inquiry into actions of corporate directors taken in good faith and in the exercise of honest judgment in the lawful and legitimate furtherance of corporate purposes.

In this case, the no−dividend policy does not involve Parent's interests, since it does not have any effect on shareholders both of Parent and HomeSolar. Thus, fairness test is not used. Here, HomeSolar has explained that the policy is for its research and development budget, and a rational business justification is recognized. Thus, the policy does not breach any duty of care.

In sum, Parent did not breach any duties to HomeSolar with respect to HomeSolar's no−dividend policy, since it is rational under the business judgment rule.

2. Parent breached duty of loyalty to HomeSolar with respect to HomeSolar's contract with SolarMaterials for the purchase of rare earth minerals, since the contract is an unfair dealing. There is no breach of duty of care.

Under the safe harbor rule, parent's self−dealing is allowed if, after disclosure of all relevant facts, qualified directors or shareholders authorized the transaction. "Qualified directors or shareholders" are defined as whom did not have an interest in the transaction.

Here, the contract with SolarMaterials is a self−dealing and it breaches duty of loyalty since it is a transaction that Parent has interest. However, there was no fact showing that disinterested directors or HomeSolar shareholders approved the contract. Thus, under the safe harbor rule, it is not allowed.

When the transactions involve self−dealing, fairness test is used. Generally, the directors have the burden to show that the transaction as a whole was fair in terms of "fair price" and "fair dealing." However, in intra−group corporate dealings, the entire fairness review (showing both fair price and fair dealing) is not required and showing that it was reasonably to yield favorable results for the corporation is enough.

Here, the contracts sets prices significantly higher than the current market prices under similar long−term contracts for such minerals, and it could not be a favorable result for HomeSolar. Thus, Parent breached its duty of loyalty.

Additionally, there is no fact indicating that Parent breached is duty of care.

In sum, Parent breached duty of loyalty to HomeSolar with respect to HomeSolar's contract with SolarMaterials for the purchase of rare earth minerals, since the contract is an unfair dealing. There is no breach of duty of care.

3. Parent did not breach any duties to HomeSolar by denying HomeSolar the opportunity to apply for the government grant, since it is more possible that the grant is given to Industrial Solar compared to SolarMaterials.

A parent corporation has discretion in allocating business opportunities within the group considering the best interest of subsidiaries. Business opportunity is defined as an opportunity that would be of interest of the corporation or that is closely related to a business in which the corporation is engaged or expects to engage.

Here, the government grant was to develop industrial−scale solar projects. SolarMaterials is exclusively for the residential solar power market and it is clear that it is not capable of using the government grant. Moreover, Industrial Solar is exclusively for the industrial solar power market and it is more possible that the grant is given to Industrial Solar compared to SolarMaterials.

In sum, Parent did not breach any duties to HomeSolar by denying HomeSolar the opportunity to apply for the government grant, since it is more possible that the grant is given to Industrial Solar compared to SolarMaterials.

해설

난이도: 하

핵심 단어 및 논점

- fiduciary duty
- parent and subsidiary
- business judgment rule (BJR)
- fairness test

- entire fairness test
- safe harbor rule
- corporate opportunity

1. The damages recoverable by the owner include $50,000, since the owner is entitled to recover expectation damages.

Nonbreaching party is entitled to expectation damages for breach of contract. The party has a right to damages based on the party's expectation interest. The purpose of the remedies is to put the nonbreaching party in as good as a position as if the other party had fully performed.

Here, the contractor did not perform his contractual obligation and the owner found a substitute contractor that agreed to install the seats for $150,000 by September 15. The owner spent more $50,000 than the original contractor had performed under the contract. Thus, $50,000 is adequate as expectation damages.

In sum, the damages recoverable by the owner include $50,000, since the owner is entitled to recover expectation damages.

2. Whether the owner may recover for lost profits resulting from the cancellation of the film festival depends on whether the loss was foreseeable.

Usually, consequential damages are lost profits resulting from the breach. Consequential damages may be recovered only if it is: (1) reasonably foreseeable, (2) sufficiently certain, and (3) unavoidable (plaintiff's duty to mitigate).

Here, the original contractor may argue that lost profits were not reasonably foreseeable with the following reasons: the festival was canceled because the seats were not installed. It is hard to say that cancellation of the festival is ordinary course of events from breach of installation of the seats. Additionally, the judge has made the fact that the contractor was unaware that the owner was planning to hold a film festival when it entered into the contract. If the original contractor's argument is right, the owner may not recover for lost profits. Meanwhile, the owner may argue that lost profits were reasonably foreseeable since installation of the seats was for the owner's new movie theater and it is reasonable to think that a festival would be held after the installation. If the owner's argument is right, the owner may recover for lost profits.

In sum, whether the owner may recover for lost profits resulting from the cancellation of the film festival depends on whether the loss was foreseeable.

3. The amount the owner would recover is depending on whether the owner's actions satisfy duty to mitigate.

Nonbreaching party has duty to mitigate. Duty to mitigate requires the injured party to take reasonable steps to reduce the damages. However, the alternative may not be substantially different from or inferior to the originally planned business. It should not involve undue risk or burden.

Here, the judge has made the fact that the owner would have made a profit of $35,000 if the seats had been installed as scheduled on September 1−10. The lost profits would be measured as $35,000 if the owner's actions satisfy duty to mitigate. However, the fact indicates that the owner could have relocated the film festival to a nearby college auditorium that was available September 1−10 and, if this had occurred, the owner would have made a profit of $25,000. The original contractor would argue that the owner had an alternative plan to hold the festival in a nearby college auditorium but he did not. The owner breached his duty to mitigate and he is entitled only to $10,000. Meanwhile, the owner would argue that holding the festival in another place is substantially different from the original plan. Thus, the fact that the owner canceled the festival does not mean that the owner breached his duty to mitigate, and he is entitled to $35,000 as consequential damages.

In sum, the amount the owner would recover is depending on whether the owner's actions satisfy duty to mitigate.

해설

난이도: 하

핵심 단어 및 논점

- expectation damages
- consequential damages
- foreseeability
- duty to mitigate

2번, 3번 문제

- 2번, 3번 문제 모두 consequential damages에 대한 것으로, 2번은 consequential damages의 성립요건 중 "foreseeability"에 초점을 두고 있고 3번은 "unavoidability (duty to mitigate)"에 초점을 두고 있다.

- Original contractor와 owner의 arguable points를 짚어내는 것이 고득점 포인트다. Yes/No로 답을 내야 한다는 생각을 버리자.

1. Frank may not obtain spousal support from Wendy, since there is no marriage separation.

Spousal support award is allowed only when a couple is separated.

Here, Frank filed one month ago and it is when they live together.

In sum, Frank may not obtain spousal support from Wendy, since there is no marriage separation.

2. Frank's constitutional challenge will not prevail, since his parental right is limited.

A parent has constitutional right to care, custody, and control their child. However, this fundamental right is limited when a parent imperils child's health and safety or increase social burdens.

In our case, Frank, based on his personal, nonreligious beliefs, has consistently refused to allow Danielle to receive any vaccinations. Danielle was not permitted to enroll in school. Vaccination is directly connected to the child's health and safety and contagious disease is social burden. Additionally, disallowing unvaccinated student is within the state's police power.

In sum, Frank's constitutional challenge will not prevail, since his parental right is limited.

3. The aunt must file a custody petition in State A, since it was the home state and Danielle's parents continue to live in the state.

Under UCCJEA or PKPA, home sate has jurisdiction over child custody. A state where the child lived with a parent for six consecutive months immediately before the commencement of a child–custody proceeding or a state where was the home state within six months and the child is absent from the State but a parent continues to live in the state.

In this case, Danielle was born in State A and had continued to live in State A. Two weeks ago, Danielle went to visit her aunt in State B. State A was the home state and her parents continue to live in State A. Thus, State A was the home state and has jurisdiction over the child custody.

In sum, the aunt must file a custody petition in State A, since it was the home state and Danielle's parents continue to live in the state.

4. The court is unlikely to grant legal custody of Danielle to her aunt, since Danielle's opinion is not determinative.

Any person could petition for visitation rights. However, as mentioned above, every parent has constitutional right. In Troxel case, grandparent petitioned for visitation but the court concluded that it violated parent's constitutional right.

Here, the aunt petitioned for 'custody,' which is greater right than visitation in Troxel case. It is unlikely that the court grant legal custody to the aunt.

The child's preference should be considered in determining child custody. However, it is not determinative.

Here, Danielle told her aunt that she did not want to return to her parents' home. Danielle is 11 years old and she is mature enough to express her opinion. However, it was because "Mom is always traveling, Dad is really depressed." Depression does not mean his care is inadequate. Thus, it may be interpreted in favor to Danielle's parents rather than nonparent aunt.

In sum, the court is unlikely to grant legal custody of Danielle to her aunt, since Danielle's opinion is not determinative.

해설

난이도: 하

핵심 단어 및 논점

- spousal support
- right to care, custody, and control
- fundamental/constitutional right
- child custody order
- jurisdiction of child custody order (UCCJEA or PKPA)
- home state
- best interest of child
- visitation order
- child's opinion (not determinative)
- Troxel case

4번 문제

논점: Custody order

- NCBE 해설에서는 'aunt의 child custody가 인정되지 않을 것이다'는 결론을 도출하였다. 이에 대한 근거로는, child's opinion이 반드시 반영되는 것은 아니라는 점과 Danielle이 주장한 근거 중 father's depression은 inadequate child care를 의미하지는 않는다는 점을 들었다. 그러나 반드시 NCBE 해설과 동일한 결론이 도출되어야 하는 것은 아니고, 충분한 논거로 로직한 답안을 작성하면 된다. 예컨대, child's opinion은 반영되어야 하고 11세는 충분히 본인의 의사를 표명할 수 있는 나이라는 점, Mom의 부재는 child care에 상당한 영향력을 미친다는 점, Frank의 personal beliefs로 인해 입학이 거부되었다는 점 등을 근거로 'aunt의 child custody를 인정할 것이다'는 결론을 도출할 수 있다.

- Troxel case와 주어진 사안을 비교분석하는 것이 고득점포인트다. ① 제3자에게 주어진 권리(visitation/custody)와 ② 친부모로서의 헌법적 권리에 중점을 둔다.

- 기출문제 2012July Family Law와 함께 공부하면 좋다.

> **답안요령**
>
> 1. General rule (best interest test)
> 2. Parents' constitutional right
> 3. Analysis(Troxel case와 비교)★

1. The court has subject—matter jurisdiction over the state—law claim raised by the class action, pursuant to 28 U.S.C. §1332.

Following 28 U.S.C. §1332, a federal district court exercises diversity jurisdiction over a class action if: (1) any class member is diverse citizenship from any defendant ("minimum diversity"), (2) the AIC in the aggregate exceeds $5 million, and (3) at least 100 members in the proposed class or classes.

Here, the court has diversity jurisdiction over the class action raised by the man. First, state citizenship for individual U.S. citizen is determined by their domicile and a corporation is a citizen of any state where it has been incorporated and of state where it has its principal place of business. Trident Healthcare Inc., is incorporated in State X and its headquarters in State X. Thus, the citizenship of Trident is State X. As to the plaintiffs' citizenship, the fact indicated that there are 10,000 patients living in State Y and 15,000 patients living in State Z. Moreover, most of patients are U.S. citizens who are domiciled in the states where they receive their health care. Thus, at least one of 30,000 patients is a citizen of State Y or State Z, and the diversity requirement is satisfied. Third, there are at least 30,000 patients whose information was taken during the hacking. Thus, all three requirements are satisfied.

In sum, the court has subject—matter jurisdiction over the state—law claim raised by the class action, pursuant to 28 U.S.C. §1332.

2. The action should not be dismissed because of the state law, since the federal procedure governs procedural issues under the Erie doctrine.

When the federal court has jurisdiction based on the diversity, the federal court must apply forum state law for the substantive rules. Federal procedural law would continue to govern, even if the federal procedure affected the outcome of the litigation.

Here, as mentioned above, the federal court of State X has diversity jurisdiction. Thus, federal procedural rules govern the class action despite the state law barring class actions to recover statutory damages, if the class action is authorized by FRCP.

In sum, the action should not be dismissed because of the state law, since the federal procedure governs procedural issues under the Erie doctrine.

3. The man has standing to bring a statutory damages claim, since concrete and particularized injury is traceable to Trident's conduct and it would be redressed.

Federal court jurisdiction is limited by Article III of the Constitution to subject matter, parties, and cases or controversies. To establish standing, a plaintiff must show: (1) an injury in fact, (2) fairly traceable to the challenged conduct of the defendant, and (3) likely to be redressed by a favorable judicial decision.

As to the injury requirement, a concrete injury is required. An injury cannot be concrete just because the injury is recognized under the statutes. In other words, the plaintiff must show particularized injury. However, actual monetary harm is not required but intangible injury also satisfies the requirement.

Here, the action is based on the invasion of privacy. Even though patients suffered no actual damages because information has not been used, they would suffer emotional distress knowing the hacking incident. Additionally, it is traceable to Trident's failure to keep patient medical information private under the absolute duty required by the State X Privacy Protection Act. Moreover, statutory damages would be redressed under the State X statute.

In sum, the man has standing to bring a statutory damages claim, since concrete and particularized injury is traceable to Trident's conduct and it would be redressed.

해설

난이도: 하

- diversity of citizenship jurisdiction (DCJ)
- CAFA
- class action
- Erie doctrine
- standing

1(a). Common law governs the kitchen contract, since it is mainly to provide service.

A contract for the sale of goods is governed by UCC2. The term "goods" means movable things at the time of making a contract. Here, a contract between the homeowner and the contractor is for the renovation of the kitchen, and it is governed by common law.

Additionally, even though the contract contains the purchase of materials and fixtures, courts typically use a predominant purpose test to determine which body of law applies to the whole contract. Here, the fact indicates that the price was based mostly on labor costs because the cost of materials and fixtures was relatively small.

In sum, common law governs the kitchen contract, since it is mainly to provide service.

1(b). The homeowner is not required to pay the contractor under the kitchen contract, since the contractor did not provide substantial performance.

Under the common law, nonbreaching party can recover when there is a material breach. A material breach occurs when a party does not provide substantial performance. When courts determine whether there is a material breach, they consider various factors: (1) the extent to which nonbreaching party will lose the reasonably expected benefit, (2) the extent to which nonbreaching party will be compensated for the part of benefit that the party will lose, (3) the extent to which breaching party will suffer forfeiture, (4) the possibility that the breaching party will cure his failure, and (5) the extent to which the breaching party acted in good faith and fair dealing.

Here, the contractor did make a material breach. First, what the homeowner reasonably expected was vinyl flooring because he wanted to be reminded of his youth. It is non-economic reason and it is impossible for the homeowner to be compensated for it. Second, the contractor intentionally breached the contract and he did not act in good faith.

In sum, the homeowner is not required to pay the contractor under the kitchen contract, since the contractor did not provide substantial performance.

2(a). Common law governs the bathroom contract, since it is mainly to provide service.

Here, a contract between the homeowner and the contractor is for the renovation of the bathroom, and it is governed by common law.

Additionally, even though the contract contains the purchase of materials and fixtures, courts typically use a predominant purpose test to determine which body of law applies to the whole contract. Here, the fact indicates that the price was based mostly on labor costs because the cost of materials and fixtures was relatively small.

In sum, common law governs the bathroom contract, since it is mainly to provide service.

2(b). The homeowner is required to pay the contractor under the bathroom contract, since the contractor provided substantial performance.

Here, the contractor did not make a material breach. First, the contractor did not intentionally breached the contract and he acted in good faith. Second, even though the homeowner expected 30-inch space between the vanity and the bathtub, the benefit provided with 29-inch space is not substantially inferior than the benefit provided with 30-inch space. Third, the forfeiture the contractor would suffer is significant. The only way to make 1-inch space is to remove either the vanity or the bathtub and to obtain and install a smaller custom-made model.

In sum, the homeowner is required to pay the contractor under the bathroom contract, since the contractor provided substantial performance.

2(c). The contractor is entitled to $9,500 which is calculated by deducting $500 from the final payment($10,000). This is because the homeowner is entitled to recover $500 from the contractor under the waste doctrine.

Generally, damages for breach of construction contract is measured by the reasonable cost of replacement of cost of completion. However, when an award for the cost of completion is wasteful, a court may apply the waste doctrine. The waste doctrine will apply if: (1) the contract is for construction, (2) the contractor performs in good faith but defects nevertheless exist, and (3) the cost of completion greatly exceeds the difference in value.

Here, the contract is for remodeling bathroom and it is a construction contract. Second, as mentioned above, the contractor performs in good faith but 1-inch shortage occurred. Third, the cost of completion is $7,500 and it is much higher than the difference in value, $500. Thus, damages would be measured by the the difference in value, $500. The contractor is entitled to the amount which is calculated by deducting $500 from the final payment ($10,000),

In sum, the contractor is entitled to $9,500 which is calculated by deducting $500 from the final payment ($10,000). This is because the homeowner is entitled to recover $500 from the contractor under the waste doctrine.

해설

난이도: 2(c)번 문제: 상
　　　그 외 문제: 하

핵심 단어 및 논점

- predominant purpose test
- substantial performance (CL)
- waste doctrine
- damages ($산정)

1(a)번, 2(a)번 문제

사안에 부가적으로 설명된 내용을 활용하여 analysis하는 것이 고득점 포인트다. 지문 맨 마지막 문단에 "cost of materials and fixtures가 비교적 적었다"는 내용은, 본 사안에 CL과 UCC2 중 CL을 적용해야 한다는 결론을 뒷받침할 아주 좋은 근거이다.

1. The husband's execution of the mortgage severed the joint tenancy, since State A applies the title theory.

Under the title theory, the mortgagee takes title to the property for the duration of the mortgage. Thus, a mortgage severs the joint tenancy and therefore it would convert the joint tenancy into a tenancy in common.

Here, State A applies the title theory of mortgages. Thus, the husband's execution of the mortgage severed the joint tenancy since it severed both the unity of title and the unity of time.

In sum, the husband's execution of the mortgage severed the joint tenancy, since State A applies the title theory.

2(a). Whether the husband's execution of the lease severs the joint tenancy depends on the jurisdictions.

In most jurisdictions, a lease severs the joint tenancy. In some others jurisdictions, a lease does not sever. In some others jurisdictions, a lease severs only when the leasing joint tenant dies before the end of the lease term.

Here, the lease was for a 10-year period but husband died last year, and, therefore, the lease severs the joint tenancy.

In sum, whether the husband's execution of the lease severs the joint tenancy depends on the jurisdictions.

2(b). Assuming that the lease severed the joint tenancy, tenant's lease is valid and the tenant can occupy the building. However, the tenant cannot exclude the woman from possessing the building.

Assuming that the lease severed the joint tenancy, the woman and the husband owned the building as tenants in common. Thus, upon the husband's death, the tenant retains the interest and can occupy the building. However, the interest is no greater than the husband owned, and the tenant cannot exclude the woman from possessing the building.

In sum, tenant's lease is valid and the tenant can occupy the building. However, the tenant cannot exclude the woman from possessing the building.

3(a). During the spouses' lifetimes, the woman was entitled to half of the rental income payable to her husband under the lease.

When one joint tenant alone leases the property to a third party, each joint tenant is entitled to half of the rental income.

Here, the husband alone leases the building to the tenant, and the woman is entitled to half of the rental income.

In sum, during the spouses' lifetimes, the woman was entitled to half of the rental income payable to her husband under the lease.

3(b). At the husband's death, the woman owns the building free from the lease and the tenant's interest terminates.

If there is no severance of joint tenancy, the tenant who survives the another tenant owns the property alone. When the leasing tenant died, the lease made by the tenant terminates.

Here, the woman survived her husband, and she owns the building free from the lease.

In sum, at the husband's death, the woman owns the building free from the lease and the tenant's interest terminates.

해설

난이도: 하

핵심 단어 및 논점

- joint tenancy
- title theory (mortgage)
- lease (severance)
- rent (severance)

1번 문제

만일 문제에서 theory를 명시하지 않았다면, execution of the mortgage가 joint tenancy에 미치는 영향, title theory와 lien theory의 차이점, 등 전반적인 내용을 모두 서술해야 한다. 그러나 본 사안에서는 title theory가 적용된다는 것을 명시하였으므로, 간단히 서술하는 것으로도 충분하다.

1. The woman properly joined the man, AmCo, and CarCo as defendants, since the claims are arising out of the same transactions or occurrence and there are several common questions to all the parties.

Two or more plaintiffs or defendants may join their claims in a single lawsuit whenever: (1) the claims to be joined are arising out of the same transactions or occurrence and (2) there is a question of law or fact common to all the parties. In determining whether the claims are arising out of the same transactions or occurrence, courts often use the logical—relationship test. When the likelihood of overlapping proof and duplication in testimony indicates that separate trials would result in delay, inconvenience, and added expense to the parties and to the court, those claims were arising out of the same transactions or occurrence, or series of transactions or occurrences.

First, the claims are arising out of the same transactions or occurrence. Each fault of the defendants was caused by each defendant's negligence and there are two separate accidents, the accident in the state highway and the accident in an ambulance. However, two accidents are closely related because each accident is a part of a series of occurrence (woman's injury). Thus, the first requirement is satisfied. Second, there are several common questions to all the parties. Woman's claim is based on her injury and the nature and extent of it will be commonly raised in the case. Moreover, whether the woman is negligent in accidents are common question in negligence cases. Thus, the second requirement is satisfied.

In sum, the woman properly joined the man, AmCo, and CarCo as defendants, since the claims are arising out of the same transactions or occurrence and there are several common questions to all the parties.

2. CarCo properly joined LockCo as a party to the woman's action, since LockCo is an adequate third-party defendant in impleader.

If the defendant claims that the nonparty is or may be liable to the defendant for all or part of the claim against it, then the defendant may bring a third-party complaint against the nonparty and the nonparty may be joined as a third-party defendant. There are three requirements to bring impleader: (1) third-party is or may be liable to the defendant, (2) for all or part of a judgment against the defendant in the action, and (3) some derivative liability exists (indemnifications or contribution).

Here, LockCo is a nonparty in the action the woman raised and the defendant, CarCo, joined it. LockCo is the company that manufactured and supplied the seat belt locking mechanism that CarCo installed in the woman's car. The woman's claim is based on the seat belt malfunctioned and LockCo would be liable for the accident. Additionally, if LockCo is liable for the accident, CarCo would claim identification against LockCo. Thus, all three requirements are satisfied.

In sum, CarCo properly joined LockCo as a party to the woman's action, since LockCo is an adequate third-party defendant in impleader.

해설

난이도: 하

핵심 단어 및 논점

- permissive joinder
- logical-relationship test
- impleader (third-party claim)

1. Bank had a security interest in Construction Company's right to be paid $450,000 by the developer for the road−building project, since the security agreement between Bank and Construction Company is enforceable and its collateral is after−acquired collateral.

To be a valid security interest, (1) the debtor authenticated a security agreement, (2) the debtor has rights in the collateral, and (3) the creditor gave value,

In our case, (1) Construction Company's president on behalf of the company signed a security agreement. (2) The collateral is payments for any contracts for the construction or repair of bridges or roads. The company has right to them. (3) Construction Company borrowed $50,000 from Bank. Thus, the security agreement between Bank and Construction Company is valid and enforceable.

As mentioned above, the collateral is payments for any contracts for the construction or repair of bridges or roads. It is after−acquired collateral. After−acquired collateral is a collateral that a debtor acquires after the security agreement has been signed.

Here, the security agreement is signed on Feb 1 and the contract with the developer is made on March 1. Thus, Bank is entitled to be paid $450,000.

In sum, Bank had a security interest in Construction Company's right to be paid $450,000 by the developer for the road−building project, since the security agreement between Bank and Construction Company is enforceable and its collateral is after−acquired collateral.

2. The developer was not discharged from its payment obligation under the road−building contract by virtue of its having paid Construction Company, since Bank (assignee) notified the developer (account debtor) before the developer make a payment.

When a debtor defaulted, a creditor has right to notify account debtor to make payment directly to the creditor. Once account debtor received a notification, the account debtor may be discharged only by paying account to the creditor (assignee).

In our case, On September 1, Construction Company (debtor) defaulted on its obligations to Bank (creditor or assignee) under the agreement and Bank immediately sent a letter to the developer (account debtor). The letter said "... a security interest granted to us by Construction Company, all payments should be made to us." It clearly indicates an assignment. However, even after the letter was received by the developer on September 3, the developer's treasurer sent a check to Construction Company.

In sum, the developer was not discharged from its payment obligation under the road−building contract by virtue of its having paid Construction Company, since Bank (assignee) notified the developer (account debtor) before the developer make a payment.

해설

난이도: 중

핵심 단어 및 논점

- validity of security agreement
- after−acquired collateral
- account
- account debtor (developer)
- assignee (Bank)
- right to notify
- discharge

1번 문제
논점: Bank가 $450,000에 대해 권리를 가지는가(Bank가 $450,000에 대해 채권을 행사할 수 있는가)

- 이에 대한 답을 도출하기 위해서는, Bank와 Construction Company 간 체결한 security agreement의 '유효성'부터 판단해야 한다. 해당 security agreement가 유효하지 않다면, Bank의 채권은 존재하지 않는 바, 당연히 collateral에 대해서도 권리가 없다. 따라서 문제에 validity 논점이 언급되어 있지 않더라도 반드시 validity를 논해야 하며, 이것이 본 문제의 핵심 포인트다.
- 다시 말해, 본 문제는 다음과 같은 두 개의 논점을 함축하고 있다: ① Security agreement의 validity와 ② collateral 판단($450,000이 collateral이 맞는지).
- 채권자(Bank)의 collateral에 대한 채권행사는, security agreement의 validity가 있는 경우 가능하며, perfection이 필요한 것은 아니다. 즉 perfection은 대항요건으로서, perfection이 없어도 Bank의 채권행사가 가능한 바, perfection 내용은 불필요하다.

2번 문제

논점: account debtor의 채무이행 여부(discharge 여부)

- 본 문제는 1번 문제와 같이 developer의 채무이행 여부를 판단하기에 앞서, Bank가 letter에 담긴 내용을 developer에게 요구할 권리가 있는지 그 여부를 판단해야 한다. 다시 말해, 본 문제는 다음과 같은 두 개의 논점을 함축하고 있다: ① Bank의(assignee의) right to notify와 ② account debtor가 notification을 받은 이후 시점에서의 채무이행 여부 판단.
- ①논점에서 반드시 서술해야 하는 표현은 account, account debtor, assignee(assignment)다. Bank와 Construction Company 간 체결한 계약상 collateral은 after-acquired collateral이자 accounts다. Accounts란, 물건을 팔고 고객으로부터 받을 돈과 같이 '외상매입금'을 뜻하는 바, 제공한 서비스에 대한 Construction Company의 대금채권이 accounts다(그 서비스를 제공받았고 대금을 지불할 채무가 있는 developer가 account debtor다). 또한 본 권리는 Bank와 Construction Company 체결한 security agreement를 체결한 시점 '이후에' 발생된 바, after-acquired collateral이다. 한편, Construction Company의 대금채권(right)은, security agreement에 따라 default한 시점에 자동으로 Bank에게 이전(transfer)되었다. 즉 이는 right이 transfer된 경우(assignment)로서, Bank는 assignee다.
- ①논점에서 Bank의 notification은 구체적으로 (1) assignment가 이루어졌음(security agreement의 존재와 Bank의 default했다는 사실), (2) account debtor(developer)는 채무를 assignee(Bank)에게 이행해야 한다는 점, 이 두 가지를 포함한다.

1. Linda is liable to the sign shop for the purchase price of the signs, since the driver had apparent authority to purchase the signs.

An agent acting on behalf of a principal can bind the principal to contracts if the agent has either actual or apparent authority. Actual authority is recognized when agent reasonably believes that the principal wanted him to act through the principal's manifestation. Apparent authority is recognized when a third party reasonably believes that the person has authority to act as an agent, that belief is from the principal's manifestation, and the third party has no notice on the lack of authority.

Here, Linda clearly told the man not to spend more than $300, and the driver had no actual authority. As to apparent authority, there was an writing on the back of the card, "This is my agent to purchase signs for my store." It is reasonable for the store to believe the driver is an agent and this belief is traceable to Linda's writing. Moreover, the store had no knowledge that there was a price limitation allowed to the agent. Thus, apparent authority is recognized.

In sum, Linda is liable to the sign shop for the purchase price of the signs, since the driver had apparent authority to purchase the signs.

2. The driver is not liable to the sign shop for the purchase price of the signs, since the driver had apparent authority and Linda was a fully disclosed principal.

An agent is liable for the contract, unless he has authority and the principal is fully disclosed. The principal is a fully identified principal when the third party is aware of the existence and the identity of the principal.

Here, as mentioned above, the driver had apparent authority to make the purchase from the sign shop. And, the store got the card and the writing on the card's back helped the store to get aware of the identity of the principal. Even though the store did not realize that the driver made the purchase for Linda, it does not change the result.

In sum, the driver is not liable to the sign shop for the purchase price of the signs, since the driver had apparent authority and Linda was a fully disclosed principal.

3. Linda is vicariously liable to the customer for the injuries resulting from the driver's negligence, since the customer reasonably relied on apparent authority.

Principal will be liable for the agent's tortious conduct only if it occurred within the scope of his employment. However, this rule does not apply when the agent is an independent contractor, unless the third party relied upon apparent authority.

Here, the fact clearly indicated that the driver was an independent contractor, and Linda is not vicariously liable for the injuries. However, two facts indicate that the customer relied upon apparent authority: three weeks ago, Linda told her, "My driver is on his way" and when the accident occurred, the customer saw the signs on the van. It is reasonable for her to believe that the van is driven for Linda. Thus, Linda is vicariously liable for the injuries.

In sum, Linda is vicariously liable to the customer for the injuries resulting from the driver's negligence, since the customer reasonably relied on apparent authority.

4. Linda is directly liable to the customer for the driver's negligence, since Linda was negligent in hiring the driver as the agent.

Under the negligent selection rule, when a principal was negligent (or reckless) in selecting, training, retaining, supervising the agent, a principal is liable, regardless of vicarious liability.

Here, when Linda searched the driver on a website, the driver was listed on with the lowest hourly rate by a wide margin used his own delivery van for making deliveries. There were reviews of the driver citing his misbehavior, untrustworthiness, and bad driving. Additionally, the website reported that the driver had been sued three times for negligent driving and had been found liable in each case. The accident was foreseeable risk and it shows Linda's negligence in selecting her agent. Moreover, the accident caused the customer's injuries and Linda is liable for them.

In sum, Linda is directly liable to the customer for the driver's negligence, since Linda was negligent in hiring the driver as the agent.

해설

난이도: 하

핵심 단어 및 논점

- agency rule
- actual authority
- apparent authority
- fully identified principal
- vicarious liability
- independent contractor
- negligent
- foreseeable

1번 문제

본 문제와 Linda의 ratification은 무관하다. 본 사안에서 'sign이 deliver된 이후에 Linda가 approve했다'는 내용은, ratification이라 오해하기 쉬운 포인트다. Ratification은 agent(본 사안에서는 driver)에게 actual 또는 apparent authority가 없었던 경우에 고려되는 이슈로서, apparent authority가 인정되는 본 사안과는 무관하다. 그러나, 'agent에게 actual authority와 apparent authority가 모두 없었다'고 서술한 수험자의 경우에는, ratification도 반드시 서술해야 할 것이다.

3번, 4번 문제

3번은 vicarious liability에 대한 문제이고, 4번은 direct liability에 대한 것이다. 즉 3번은 driver의 행위에 대해 Linda가 책임이 있는지 그 여부를 판단하고, 4번은 Linda의 행위가 torts에 해당하는지 판단하는 문제이다.

4번 문제의 경우, driver를 selecting하는 과정은 Linda의 negligence를 의미한다는 것뿐만 아니라 그러한 negligence(driver를 잘못 select한 과실)가 해당 injuries를 야기했다는 점을 서술하는 것이 고득점 포인트다. 즉 negligence의 성립요건의 causation에 대해 서술하는 것이다.

2020Feb Evidence / Criminal Law

1. The woman could establish a common law affirmative defense of self-defense, depending on whether her force was proportionate to protect herself.

A defendant is not liable for harm to the plaintiff if he: (1) reasonably believed that the force was necessary to protect himself who is in danger of immediate bodily harm and (2) used reasonable force that was necessary to protect himself (or another). In some jurisdictions, a defendant is further required to prove: (1) the defendant was not an initial aggressor or (2) the defendant had tried to withdraw from or abandon the conflict before using the force if she were the initial aggressor.

Here, the woman punched the man in the nose when the man pocked her shoulder harder and harder with his finger. The man was using unlawful force and the poking involved increasing force. It causes the woman imminent bodily harm. Thus, the first element is satisfied. As to the second element, the woman used no weapon in respond to the man's force with no weapon. Whether the punching nose is proportionate to increasing forceful poking is a close call. Additionally, there is no fact indicating that the woman is an initial aggressor.

In sum, the woman could establish a common law affirmative defense of self-defense, depending on whether her force was proportionate to protect herself.

2(a). The eyewitness's testimony regarding the friend's statement is admissible, since it is nonhearsay.

Relevant evidence is any evidence that tends to make the fact more or less probable than it would be without the evidence.

Here, the eyewitness's testimony regarding the friend's statement is relevant. It could prove that the woman's act was not to defense herself from the man's poking, but it was because the man annoyed her with the intent to hurt him.

Hearsay is an out of court statement offered in evidence to prove the truth of the matter asserted.

Here, the testimony was offered to prove the purpose of the woman's action. It was not to prove that the friend and woman waited so long for those tickets. Thus, the testimony is nonhearsay.

In sum, the eyewitness's testimony regarding the friend's statement is admissible, since it is nonhearsay.

2(b). The eyewitness's testimony regarding the woman's nodding and thumbs–up signal is admissible, since it falls within the hearsay exceptions.

The eyewitness's testimony regarding the woman's nodding and thumbs–up signal is relevant. It could prove that the woman's act was not to defense herself from the man's poking, but it was because the man annoyed her with the intent to hurt him. Moreover, woman's nodding and thumbs–up signal are assertive conduct and it is hearsay. Thus, the statement would be inadmissible if there are no hearsay exceptions applicable.

Under the admission exception, a statement made by an opponent party and offered against that party is admissible as a non–hearsay.

Here, the person who offered the statement is the prosecution, the opposing party of the woman, and the statement is offered by the woman. Thus, the statement falls within the admission exception and is admissible.

Moreover, present state of mind exception is also applicable in this case. A present state of mind is a statement made by a declarant that conveys his then–existing state of mind, such as present intent, motive, or plan.

Here, the woman's nodding and thumb–up signal were made in reaction to the friend's statement. It shows that she intended to harm anyone who annoyed her and her friend.

In sum, the eyewitness's testimony regarding the woman's nodding and thumbs–up signal is admissible, since it falls within the hearsay exceptions.

2(c). The eyewitness's testimony regarding the woman's general attitude is inadmissible, since it is character evidence.

The eyewitness's testimony is relevant since it would prove that she has aggressive propensity. However, character evidence is usually inadmissible when it is used to prove that on a particular occasion the person acted in accordance with the character. It is admissible only in limited situations.

In criminal case, character evidence is admissible only when a defendant opens the door to offer relevant character evidence proving that the defendant did not committed charged offense. A defendant's character traits can be proven only: by testimony as to reputation or by testimony in the form of an opinion.

Here, there was no character evidence offered by the defendant before the witness (prosecutor) offered the testimony. Thus, the defendant did no open the door and the testimony is inadmissible as character evidence.

The evidence of crimes, wrongs, or other acts may be admissible for another non−propensity purpose, such as proving motive, opportunity, intent, preparation, plan, knowledge, identity, absence of mistake, or lack of accident.

Here, there is no fact indicating those non−propensity purposes.

In sum, the eyewitness's testimony regarding the woman's general attitude is inadmissible, since it is character evidence.

3(a). Defense counsel's cross−examination regarding conviction for shoplifting would be not permitted, since it is not a type of crimes admissible for impeachment purpose.

When convictions are used to impeach, the nature of the crime, the amount of that has passed, and (only in criminal cases) whether the witness is the defendant are considered. There are two types of convictions that may be admissible for impeachment: felonies and the crime relating to a dishonest act or false statement. Felony is a crime that is punishable by death or by imprisonment for more than one year.

Here, shoplifting is a crime punishable by a maximum sentence of six months in jail and it is not a felony. Then, the conviction could be offered for impeachment purpose only if it is classified as a crime relating to a dishonest act or false statement. Most courts recognize shoplifting as a crime relating to a dishonest act or false statement. This is because a person can commit shoplifting without dishonest act or false statement. However, the fact that dishonest act or false statement is used is proven by the woman's counsel, shoplifting would be admissible.

In sum, Defense counsel's cross−examination regarding conviction for shoplifting would be not permitted, since it is not a type of crimes admissible for impeachment purpose.

3(b). Defense counsel's cross−examination regarding a letter would not permitted, since it shows the eyewitness's bias.

Evidence showing that the witness has bias or motive to lie can be used for impeachment.

Here, a letter is offered by the prosecution that says "Thanks for 10 years of a great friendship." It shows long friendship between the eyewitness and the man and that the eyewitness is biased in favor of the man.

In sum, Defense counsel's cross−examination regarding a letter would not permitted, since it shows the eyewitness's bias.

해설

난이도: 하

핵심 단어 및 논점

- self−defense (battery에 대한 defense)
  - immediate bodily harm
  - reasonable force (proportionate)
- hearsay
  - to prove the truth the matter asserted
  - assertion
- character evidence
- conviction (impeachment)
- bias (impeachment)

2번 문제

− NCBE 해설에서는 eyewitness의 증언을 (a) friend's statement와 woman의 행동 (nodding, thumb−up), (b) 자신이 평소에 본 모습, 이렇게 두 부분으로 나뉘어져 있다. 그러나 hearsay여부를 판단하데 있어 각 증거의 성격이 다르기 때문에, 필자는 (a) friend's statement, (b) woman의 행동(nodding, thumb−up), (c) 자신이 평소에 본 모습, 이렇게 세 부분으로 나누어 서술하였다. 양자 중 본인에게 맞는

format으로 작성하면 되겠으나, 'woman의 행동이 assertion을 나타내므로 hearsay
에 해당한다'는 점을 반드시 언급해야 할 것이다.

- 본래 hearsay인 statement가 hearsay exception에 해당함과 동시에 Confrontation
Clause에 부합해야만 admissible하다. 그러나 본 기출문제는 헌법적 논점은 다루지
말 것("Do not discuss any constitutional issues.")을 명시하였으므로, Confrontation
Clause에 대한 답안작성은 불필요하다.

답안요령

1. "Statement"
2. Relevance 유무여부★
3. "To prove the truth asserted"
4. Hearsay exception

> **TIP1** 특정 증거가 hearsay인지 그 여부를 판단하는 경우, 해당 증거의 statement 여
> 부와 목적(to prove the truth asserted)을 상세히 analysis하는 것이 고득점 포인
> 트다.

> **TIP2** 4번: Statement가 hearsay인 경우 반드시 hearsay exception에 해당하는지 그
> 여부를 판단하고, 만약 해당한다면 statement 전체가 아닌 부분적 exception이
> 가능하다는 점에 유념한다.

2(c)번 문제

논점: Character evidence

Character evidence에 관한 문제는, ① 주어진 증거가 제출된 character evidence인지
아닌지 판단하는 문제와 ② character evidence가 admissible한지 그 여부를 판단하는
문제로 구분된다. 본 문제는 eyewitness's testimony의 admissibility를 판단토록 요구
하고 있는 바, ①과 ②의 내용을 모두 작성해야 한다. 답안 작성 로직은 다음과 같다.

Relevant한가?

→ Character evidence가 맞는가? (정의)

→ 맞다면, admissible한가? (위 ②번 유형)

→ MIMIC 목적은 아닌가? (위 ①번 유형)

②번 유형은 아래 답안요령1에 따라 작성한다.

답안요령1

> 1. Character evidence 기본 rule: not admissible
> 2. 그러나 in criminal case 가능
> 3. Limitation (R/O)
> 4. Analysis

①번 유형은 아래 답안요령2에 따라 작성한다.

답안요령2

> 1. Character evidence rule (usually not admissible)
>   + analysis
> 2. For "MIMIC" purposes
>   + analysis (character evidence가 사용된 목적)

3(a)번 문제

답안요령

> 1. Convictions to impeach 요건
> 2. Nature of the crime
> 3. Time

3(b)번 문제

본래 document의 '내용'을 증거로 제출할 경우, 해당 증거의 admissibility는 authentication과 best evidence rule(BER)을 기준으로 판단한다. 그러나 본 문제는 cross-examination에서 impeach하는 방법으로서 편지의 내용을 인용하는 것이 가능한지 묻고 있으며, 이는 bias를 이용한 'impeachment'에 중점을 두고 있다. 따라서 BER 내용은 서술하지 않아도 된다. 이는 document 자체의 admissibility에 대한 문제인 기출문제 2020July 2번과 차이가 있다.

1. In−court testimony from a trucking company representative should not be admitted, since the evidence is subsequent remedial measures and it violates public policy exception rules.

Subsequent remedial measures are inadmissible to prove negligence, culpable conduct, or a defect in a product or its design. The purpose of the rule is to encourage people to make such repairs. If subsequent remedial measures are used to prove other claim, they are admissible.

Here, the truck driver was fired the next day of the accident and it shows the driver's negligence. There are no facts indicating that other purposes of submitting this evidence. Thus, the evidence is inadmissible.

In sum, in−court testimony from a trucking company representative should not be admitted, since the evidence is subsequent remedial measures and it violates public policy exception rules.

2(a). A handwritten letter the woman received is admissible only if it can be authenticated.

Authentication of evidence is a prerequisite for its admissibility. To authenticate, the proponent must produce sufficient evidence to prove what the proponent claims it to be. Handwriting can be verified by: (1) a lay or expert witness with knowledge or (2) witness with knowledge.

Here, there is no fact clearly indicating that there are lay or expert witness who could authenticate the truck driver's handwriting. Additionally, the letter was signed with the name of the truck driver, but it does not mean the woman can authenticate it. Thus, it is a close call.

In sum, a handwritten letter the woman received is admissible only if it can be authenticated.

2(b). Assuming that the handwritten letter is authenticated, it should be admitted under the best evidence rule.

Assuming the letter is authenticated, it is admissible if it satisfies best evidence rule. According to the best evidence rule, in proving the contents of the writing, the original writing must be produced. A duplicate is defined as a counterpart produced by mechanical means. Duplicates are admissible to the same extent as the original unless: (1) a genuine question is raised as to the original's authenticity or (2) it would be unfair to admit the duplicate instead of original.

Here, the woman's cell phone has been examined by a neutral computer expert, and the expert reports that the photograph of the letter is clearly legible and that the image has not been altered in any manner. Thus, the photograph would be admissible as a duplicate.

The original is unavailable and secondary evidence is admissible if all of the originals are lost or destroyed without proponent's bad faith.

Here, the woman no longer has the original letter but there is no fact indicating that she lost it with bad faith. Thus, secondary evidence, duplicate, is admissible.

In sum, assuming that the handwritten letter is authenticated, it should be admitted under the best evidence rule.

2(c). Assuming that the handwritten letter is authenticated and satisfies the best evidence rule, it should be admitted since it falls within the hearsay exception as to statements against interest.

Hearsay is an out−of−court statement offered in evidence to prove the truth of the matter asserted.

Here, the letter is hearsay because it is made out of court while the woman was recuperating in the hospital. Additionally, the letter is submitted to prove that its content is true.

However, the testimony of a now unavailable declarant is admissible if the statement was against the declarant's pecuniary, or penal interest when it was made.

Here, the truck driver is unavailable to testify at trial because neither party has been able to procure his attendance and his whereabouts are unknown. Moreover, the letter (statement) says that "I am terribly sorry about the accident that I caused. It was all my fault. I was taking pain pills...." This statement was made by the driver and he clearly admits his fault in the accident. Thus, the exception rule is applicable in this case.

In sum, assuming that the handwritten letter is authenticated and satisfies the best evidence rule, it should be admitted since it falls within the hearsay exception as to statements against interest.

3. In-court testimony from the truck driver's doctor would not be admitted based on the physician-patient privilege, but it depends on the statute adopted by State A.

The physician-patient privilege belongs to the patient and patient communications or disclosures made for the purpose of medical diagnosis or treatment are privileged. Here, the truck driver (patient) is unavailable and the doctor is under the duty to assert the privilege and refuse to testify about her communications with the driver.

The woman could argue that the driver waived his privilege since he wrote the woman a letter stating about his pain pills. Some jurisdictions recognize such medical information to third party as implied waiver, while some other jurisdictions do not. Even if the court concludes that the letter is an implied waiver of the privilege, only the relevant testimony as to the pain pills is admissible.

In sum, in-court testimony from the truck driver's doctor would not be admitted based on the physician-patient privilege, but it depends on the statute adopted by State A.

해설

난이도: 하

핵심 단어 및 논점

- subsequent remedial measure
  (public policy exception)
- documentary evidence
- authentication
- BER

- HS
- HS exception
- statement against interest
- physician-patient privilege

2(c)번 문제

예상질문

Q1. Admission exception(officially non-hearsay)이 적용될 수는 없는가?

적용될 수 없다. Admission exception은 당사자가 해당 statement를 진술하였고, 그 당사자를 상대로(against) 제출되었을 때에만 적용되는 rule이다. 본 사안에서 statement는 truck driver가 진술한 내용인데, 그는 본 재판의 당사자(party)가 아니다.

예상질문

Q2. Admission exception이 'employer-employee 관계'에 확대 적용되었다고 볼 수는 없는가?

볼 수 없다. employer-employee 관계에 확대 적용되려면, employment 관계가 '유지 중'일 때 언급된 statement이어야 한다. 본 사안에서 truck driver는 사고 발생일 다음 날 해고되었고("the truck driver's being fired the next day"), letter는 사고 발생 일주일 후에 작성되었으므로("dated one week after the accident"), 해당 letter는 employment 관계가 '종료된 후에' 작성된 것이다. 따라서 admission exception이 적용될 수 없다.

Q₃. <u>Public policy exception 중 settlement에 해당하지 않는가?</u>

해당하지 않는다. settlement 과정 중 언급된 내용에 한해서만 public exception rule이 적용된다. 본 사안에서 letter는 settlement 과정 중 작성된 것이 아니다.

3번 문제

예상질문

Q. <u>Physician-privilege는 common law와 federal rule에서 인정하지 않는다. 그렇다면 본 사안에도 적용될 수 없는 것이 아닌가?</u>

Common law와 federal rule(FRE)에서 해당 privilege를 인정하지 않는 것은 맞다. 그러나 본 사안은 federal court에서 제기된 소송이면서 DCJ가 인정되는 바("diversity action"), Erie doctrine에 의거해 state law(state statute)가 적용되어야 한다. 모든 주에서는 physician-privilege를 적용하는 바, common law와 federal rule의 내용과 상관 없이 본 사안에 physician-privilege에 대한 룰을 적용할 수 있다.

[참고]

Federal rules(FRE)에서는 'psychotherapist와' patient 간 특권만을 인정하고 있어, 적용 범위가 매우 좁다.

1. The shareholder is entitled to inspect the requested board minutes, since the demand was for a proper purpose with reasonable particularity and was made in good faith.

A shareholder has right to inspect corporate books and records for a proper purpose. The document with reasonable particularity must be directly connected to the purpose. A shareholder must demand in good faith.

Here, (1) her purpose is to confirm those donations and seek to have the board desist from further waste of corporate assets. It is related to the demanding shareholder's interest, and proper. (2) The shareholder explained that her purpose is to confirm those donations and seek to have the board desist from further waste of corporate assets. All minutes of the meetings of Retailer's board of directors relating to donations made by Retailer to AFAW have reasonable particularity and are directly connected to the purpose. (3) She demanded only portion of the shareholder made the demand because of a respected national business magazine. It shows that her demand was made in good faith.

In sum, the shareholder is entitled to inspect the requested board minutes, since the demand was for a proper purpose with reasonable particularity and was made in good faith.

2. The shareholder's proposed resolution is not a proper subject for submission to Retailer's shareholders for their vote, since it is binding on BOD.

Shareholder resolutions are proper only when they are non-binding and precatory. When a resolution is recommendation or request to BOD, it is proper.

In our case, the resolution requires the BOD shall not approve any political expenditures by Retailer, unless such expenditures are specifically authorized by a majority vote of all outstanding shares of Retailer. It directly affects BOD's actions and binding on them. Thus, it is improper resolution.

In sum, the shareholder's proposed resolution is not a proper subject for submission to Retailer's shareholders for their vote, since it is binding on BOD.

3. The resolution would not infringe Retailer's First Amendment rights, since the it is not a governmental action.

Under the First Amendment, federal government should protect the citizen's right to freedom of speech. It applies to state and local governments through the Fourteenth Amendment.

In our case, even though the corporation's political donations constitute speech, the resolution is made by the shareholder. It is a private action, rather than governmental action. Thus, the First Amendment does not apply here.

In sum, the resolution would not infringe Retailer's First Amendment rights, since the it is not a governmental action.

해설

난이도: 중

핵심 단어 및 논점

- right to inspect
  - corporate books and records
  - for a proper purpose
  - directly connected to
  - with reasonable particularity
  - in good faith
- shareholder's resolution
- non-binding
- precatory
- right to speech (freedom of speech)
- First Amendment
- private action v. governmental action

1번 해설

- 단순히 right to inspect 유무만을 서술하면 full score가 나올 수 없다. Right to inspect가 구체적으로 무엇을 의미하는지 룰을 '세분화하여' analysis하는 것이 중요하다. Inspect하고자 하는 purpose가 proper해야 하는데, 이는 보호하고자 하는 interest가 있는 경우 인정된다. 한편, inspect를 하기 위해 요청하는 서류는 with reasonable particularity해야 하며, purpose와 서류 간 direct connection이 있어야 한다. Good-faith는 주주가 demand하게 된 근거가 credible한 경우(credible basis가 있는 경우) 인정된다.
- 본 답안은 룰을 세분화하여 analysis했음을 어필하기 위해 넘버링하였다.

2020July Decedents' Estates / Trusts & Future Interests

1. The trust endures for its stated duration since it is a charitable trust and not subject to RAP.

A charitable trust is a trust that is created for a charitable purpose. Improving communities is recognized as charitable purpose. In determining the nature of a benefit provided by a trust, only the trust instrument is considered, not a trust settlor's motivation.

Here, the trust instrument created by Ann requires the trustee to purchase and install seasonal plantings on all principal streets in the town where Ann grew up. It is beneficial for all communities in the town, not only for specific people. Thus, the trust is a charitable trust. Even though Ann created the trust in honor of the store owners, it is motivation and it does not change the result.

The rule against perpetuities (RAP) does not apply to charitable trust. A charitable trust can last in perpetuity. Thus, the trust endures for its stated duration.

In sum, the trust endures for its stated duration since it is a charitable trust and not subject to RAP.

2. A court could preserve the trust up to 21 years from the date of creation of the trust, but essential fact is missing.

To be a valid trust, the trust must have ascertainable beneficiaries. The rule does not apply for charitable trusts. Thus, a trust which has a noncharitable purpose and no ascertainable beneficiary is unenforceable. However, the transferee may apply the property to the designated purpose of a noncharitable trust providing mere beneficience to a group of indefinite beneficiaries, unless such application is made at a time beyond the period of RAP. The common law RAP 21-year period would be used.

Here, assuming that the trust is not a valid charitable trust, the trust is noncharitable but it provides beneficience to indefinite beneficiaries. Thus, the trustee would have power to apply the trust up to 21 years. However, there is no fact indicating when the trust is created in this case.

In sum, a court could preserve the trust up to 21 years from the date of creation of the trust, but essential fact is missing.

3. Ann's estate must be distributed equally to Ann's uncle and her niece under the consanguinity method, while Ann's estate must be distributed to her niece under the parentelic method.

In determining the identity of decedent's heirs, there are two methods: consanguinity method and parentelic method. Under the consanguinity method, kins equally share who are in the same degree of consanguinity to testator. Under the parentelic method, the issues of intestate's parent take to the exclusion of any issue of the intestate's grandparents.

Here, Ann's uncle and her niece are in same degree of consanguinity and both are recognized as Ann's heirs under the consanguinity method. Thus, Both are entitled to equal shares of Ann's estate. On the other hand, Ann's niece is a descendant of Ann's parents and Ann's uncle is a descendant of Ann's grandparents. Thus, the niece is a Ann's heir under the parentelic method and she is entitled to Ann's entire estate.

In sum, Ann's estate must be distributed equally to Ann's uncle and her niece under the consanguinity method, while Ann's estate must be distributed to her niece under the parentelic method.

해설

난이도: 1번 문제: 하
　　　　2번 문제: 상
　　　　3번 문제: 하

핵심 단어 및 논점

- charitable trust
- rule against perpetuities (RAP)
- ascertainable beneficiaries
- intestate succession
- consanguinity method
- parentelic method

1(a). A State A has jurisdiction to grant the wife a divorce, since she is domiciled in State A and satisfies State A statute's requirement.

The court has jurisdiction over a valid decree when one spouse was domiciled there. Domicile is based on residence with the intent to remain permanently or indefinitely.

Here, the wife took Sarah and moved to State A. She told the husband that she intended to remain in State A with Sarah. She found a job and moved into a nearby apartment in State A. Thus, she is domiciled in State A. Additionally, State A requires that either the divorce plaintiff or the defendant have been residing in State A for six months before the plaintiff may file a divorce petition. The wife satisfies this state statute's requirement.

In sum, a State A has jurisdiction to grant the wife a divorce, since she is domiciled in State A and satisfies State A statute's requirement.

1(b). A State A has jurisdiction to grant the wife a sole physical custody of the couple's daughter, Sarah, since it is Sarah's home state.

Under UCCJEA, home state has exclusive jurisdiction over child custody when. Home state is the state in which a child lived with a parent or a person acting as a parent for at least six consecutive months immediately before the commencement of a child— custody proceeding.

Here, one week ago, the wife commenced a divorce action against the husband in State A. Sarah moved to State A with her mom nine months ago. Thus, State A is Sarah's home state.

In sum, a State A has jurisdiction to grant the wife a sole physical custody of the couple's daughter, Sarah, since it is Sarah's home state.

1(c). A State A does not have jurisdiction to grant the wife a share of the couple's marital property, there is no minimum contract between State A and the husband.

When the court has jurisdiction over a divorce decree based on the plaintiff's domicile the court does not have jurisdiction over property and support rights. A state has personal jurisdiction over the defendant when there is minimum contacts between them.

Here, as mentioned above, the divorce decree was entered based on the woman's domicile. The husband was personally served with a summons and divorce complaint at his home in State B. Additionally, the husband has never been to State A except for the one-day stopover when he and the wife were married there. Thus, there is no minimum contract between State A and the husband.

In sum, a State A does not have jurisdiction to grant the wife a share of the couple's marital property, there is no minimum contract between State A and the husband.

2(a). The court could grant the wife a divorce based on the husband's fault, since the wife has suffered both physical and mental cruelty.

A divorce may be granted based on cruelty. Cruelty means bodily harm that endangers life or health and makes marital life unsafe. Both physical and mental cruelty are recognized.

Here, after the accident, the husband became physically and emotionally abusive toward his wife. It is unclear but the abusive acts have been more than a year. Additionally, the husband was convicted of assault after a physical attack led to the wife hospitalization. These facts show that the wife has suffered both physical and mental cruelty and it is sufficient basis for the divorce decree.

In sum, the court could grant the wife a divorce based on the husband's fault, since the wife has suffered both physical and mental cruelty.

2(b). The court could grant the wife sole physical custody of Sarah, since the best interest of Sarah would be given by it.

A child custody contest between parents is decided on the basis of the child's best interests.

Here, after having Sarah, the wife stayed at home to serve at her primary caregiver. The wife told the husband that she intended to remain in State A with Sarah. Additionally, the husband has drinking problem and he was convicted of assault after a physical attack led to the wife hospitalization. The husband has not worked since his injury, while the wife found a job in State A. All of these facts show that the sole physical custody provided by wife may be the best interest of Sarah.

In sum, the court could grant the wife sole physical custody of Sarah, since the best interest of Sarah would be given by it.

해설

난이도: 1번(c) 문제: 중
　　　　그 외 문제: 하

핵심 단어 및 논점

- jurisdiction
- divorce decree - domicile
- property division
- custody order - UCCJEA, home state

- marital property, PJ, ex parte
- fault divorce
- best interest of child

1(a). Bank has an enforceable interest in the power generator and it perfected the secured interest.

"Equipment" is goods other than inventory, farm products, or consumer goods. According to the security agreement, the company granted the bank a security interest in "all of the company's present and future inventory, accounts, and equipment." The power generator constitutes equipment.

A security interest attaches to collateral unless the parties have agreed to postpone the time of attachment, when: (1) secured party gave value to debtor, (2) debtor has rights in the collateral, and (3) debtor authenticated a security agreement.

Here, the bank loaned $100,000 to a company, the company owns (bought) the power generator, and the company signed the security agreement.

There are three methods to make a perfection: (1) filing a financing statement, (2) taking possession, or (3) control of the collateral. Bank filed, in the appropriate filing office, a properly completed financing statement. Thus, bank's security interest is effective and perfected.

In sum, Bank has an enforceable interest in the power generator and it perfected the secured interest.

1(b). The manufacturer has an enforceable interest in the power generator and the interest is perfected.

Here, the manufacturer sold the power generator to the company on credit, the company owns (bought) the power generator, and the company signed the security agreement. Moreover, the manufacturer filed, in the appropriate filing office, a properly completed financing statement. Thus, manufacturer's security interest is effective and perfected.

In sum, the manufacturer has an enforceable interest in the power generator and the interest is perfected.

1(c). The manufacturer's security interest has priority over the bank's security interest, since manufacturer's security interest is a purchase−money security interest (PMSI).

As mentioned above, security interests of both manufacturer and bank are perfected. Regarding a purchase−money security interest (PMSI) in non−consumer goods, the security interest takes priority over conflicting interests which arises between the time the security interest attaches and the time of filing, if a person files a financing statement with respect to a PMSI before or within 20 days after the debtor receives delivery of the collateral.

Here, security interest secures the company's obligation to pay the purchase price of the power generator, and the security interest is PMSI. The security interest was perfected at the time the power generator was delivered to the company. Thus, the manufacturer's security interest has priority over the bank's security interest.

In sum, the manufacturer's security interest has priority over the bank's security interest, since manufacturer's security interest is a purchase−money security interest (PMSI).

2(a). The bank has an enforceable interest in the retinal scanner and it perfected the secured interest.

According to the security agreement, a security interest is in "all of the company's present and future inventory, accounts, and equipment." Thus, the retinal scanner, equipment, is the accurate collateral.

The bank loaned the company, the company owns the retinal scanner (scanner was delivered to the company), and the company signed the security agreement. Moreover, the bank filed, in the appropriate filing office, a properly completed financing statement. Thus, bank's security interest is effective and perfected.

In sum, the bank has an enforceable interest in the retinal scanner and it perfected the secured interest.

2(b). The supplier has an enforceable interest in the retinal scanner, but the security interest is unperfected.

Under UCC9, the substance of a transaction controls, rather than its form.

Here, although the agreement was entitled "Lease Agreement," the supplier holds the title of the retinal scanner to ensure company's obligation to pay monthly lease payments. In other words, the supplier has security interest in the retinal scanner.

The supplier supplied the scanner on credit, the company owns the scanner, and the company signed the lease agreement. Thus, the security interest is enforceable. However, the supplier did no file a financing statement with respect to the transaction, and the security interest is unperfected.

In sum, the supplier has an enforceable interest in the retinal scanner, but the security interest is unperfected.

2(c). Bank's security interest is superior to the supplier's security interest, since Bank has perfected its interest while the supplier didn't.

Between an unperfected secured creditor and a perfected secured creditor, a perfected secured creditor has superior claim to the collateral.

Here, bank perfected its security interest while supplier didn't. Thus, Bank's security interest is superior to the supplier's security interest.

In sum, Bank's security interest is superior to the supplier's security interest, since Bank has perfected its interest while the supplier didn't.

해설

난이도: 하

핵심 단어 및 논점

- effectiveness of security interest
- equipment
- perfection
- priority
- purchase−money security interest (PMSI)

본 기출은 'security interest의 enforceability를 판단하는 문제'와 '담보물에 대한 priority를 판단하는 문제'로 구성되어 있다. 본래 enforceability와 perfection은 구별되는 개념이고 주어진 문제는 enforceability만을 묻고 있으나, perfection을 판단해야만 priority를 판단할 수 있으므로, 각 담보물권의 attachment와 perfection을 모두 판단한 내용을 서술하는 것이 고득점포인트다. 이와 비교하여 기출 2021Feb의 경우, 1번 문제는 enforceability, 2번 문제는 perfection, 3번 문제는 priority를 묻고 있는 바, 문제에서 enforceability와 perfection을 구별하고 있으므로 1번에는 attachment, 2번에는 perfection에 대해 각각 서술하면 되겠다.

1. The owner did not violate the Fair Housing Act of 1968 by refusing to rent to men and lawyers, since the Act does not apply in this case.

Under the Fair Housing Act of 1968, it is unlawful to refuse to sell or rent a dwelling to any person based on race, color, religion, sex, familial status, or national origin. However, the anti−discrimination rule does not apply if: (1) the owner occupies one of the units in a multiple−unit dwelling, (2) the dwelling contains no more than four units, and (3) the dwelling is occupied by persons living independently of each other.

Here, the owner refused to rent to lawyers and it is a discrimination based on the occupation and it is not subject to the Act. As to the refusal to rent to men, it is a discrimination based on the sex. However, the owner occupied the ground−floor apartment in three two−bedroom apartments and persons occupied all units independently. Thus, the Act does not apply to the refusal to rent to men.

In sum, the owner did not violate the Fair Housing Act of 1968 by refusing to rent to men and lawyers, since the Act does not apply in this case.

2. Both the owner and the newspaper publisher violated the Fair Housing Act of 1968 by publishing the owner's rental advertisement, since there is no exception applicable to publishing.

It is unlawful to make or publish any advertisement with respect to the sale or rental of a dwelling that indicates any discrimination based on race, color, religion, sex, familial status, or national origin. There is no exception rule.

Here, the owner made the statement which is discriminatory based on sex and the publisher published it. This rule is applicable both to a landlord and the publisher of the newspaper. Thus, both violated the Act.

In sum, both the owner and the newspaper publisher violated the Fair Housing Act of 1968 by publishing the owner's rental advertisement, since there is no exception applicable to publishing.

3(a). The television is not a fixture, since it is unreasonable to conclude that it was affixed or attached with the intent to make it a permanent part of the apartment.

Under the state's fixtures code, a fixture is an item of personal property affixed or attached to the real property by the seller unless a reasonable person would conclude that the item of personal property at the time was not affixed with the intent to make it a permanent part of the real property.

Here, the television on a wall mount was affixed to the wall over the fireplace. In contrast to past televisions, wall−mounted television is affixed and it could be recognized as a fixture. However, the television is one that is easily movable from the wall and is sometimes replaced by new ones. Additionally, the television is affixed by a person with a specific need or a desire to install it. These facts show that the owner had the intent to make the television a permanent part of the apartment.

In sum, the television is not a fixture, since it is unreasonable to conclude that it was affixed or attached with the intent to make it a permanent part of the apartment.

3(b). The chandelier is not a fixture, since it is unreasonable to conclude that it was affixed or attached with the intent to make it a permanent part of the apartment.

Here, the chandelier was of an ornate, old−fashioned styled and did not match the modern light fixtures in the apartment. Additionally, the owner commented to the buyer that it had come from her mother and meant a lot to her. These circumstances show that the owner had no intent to make the chandelier a permanent part of the apartment. Thus, the chandelier is not a fixture.

In sum, the chandelier is not a fixture, since it is unreasonable to conclude that it was affixed or attached with the intent to make it a permanent part of the apartment.

해설

난이도: 하

핵심 단어 및 논점

- Fair Housing Act (anti-discrimination rule)
  - based on sex
  - based on occupation
  - publishing
- fixture
- intent

3번 문제

핵심 논점: 설치자의 intent 유무

사안에 state code가 명시되어 있으므로, 그 내용을 바탕으로 analysis한다. 주어진 state code의 표현을 그대로 사용하면 좋다.

1. Whether the boyfriend has committed murder in the first degree is depending on how the statute defines deliberation and premeditation.

The statute provides that a person commits murder in the first degree when the person willfully, deliberately, and with premeditation kills another person.

In most jurisdictions, deliberation or premeditation is recognized when the person acts with a cool mind that is capable of reflection or there was a period of time for prior consideration.

Here, the boyfriend had no period of time for prior consideration. He immediately fired a single shot as he turned around just in time to see the pawnbroker push his girlfriend. Thus, the boyfriend cannot be committed murder in the first degree.

In other jurisdictions, circumstantial evidence is considered in determining deliberation and premeditation. In these jurisdictions, a specific intent to kill at the time of action shows deliberation and premeditation.

Here, the boyfriend had an intent to kill the pawnbroker since intent to kill can be referred by using gun. Thus, deliberation and premeditation could be inferred and jury could find him guilty.

In sum, whether the boyfriend has committed murder in the first degree is depending on how the statute defines deliberation and premeditation.

2. The boyfriend has committed voluntary manslaughter, since he acted without malice aforethought.

The main difference between murder and voluntary manslaughter is the presence of "malice aforethought" element. The defendant acted without malice aforethought if there was (1) adequate provocation and (2) heat of passion.

In this case, the boyfriend fired a shot as soon as he saw the pawnbroker push his girlfriend. Jury might conclude that the boyfriend did so because he was angry with the pawnbroker, and the heat of passion element is satisfied.

As to adequate provocation element, it is defined as a provocation that would cause a reasonable man to lose his normal self−control.

Here, the boyfriend had been standing in the rear of the shop and did not see the situation in which his girlfriend stole the necklace and it caused the pawnbroker to chase her. It is reasonable for the boyfriend to believe that the chase is unprovoked. Thus, adequate provocation could be recognized.

In sum, the boyfriend has committed voluntary manslaughter, since he acted without malice aforethought.

3. The facts do not present a valid legal defense (defense of others), since the boyfriend acted without a reasonable fear of imminent death or great bodily injury of girlfriend.

A defendant is not liable for harm to the pawnbroker if State A's self−defense doctrine is applicable. However, the boyfriend fired shot for his girlfriend and he should claim defense of others, rather than self−defense. In some jurisdictions, the defendant can claim defense of others only when the person being attacked could have acted in self−defense.

Here, it is unreasonable for the girlfriend to use the force to the pawnbroker, since she stole the necklace. The pawnbroker was lawfully trying to retrieve his stolen property from her. Additionally, the pawnbroker did not use force. Thus, it was not the case that the girlfriend could have acted in self−defense, and the boyfriend cannot raise a defense of others.

In other jurisdictions, the defendant can claim defense of others when he reasonably believed that the person being attacked had a right to act in self−defense.

Here, the fact that the boyfriend had been standing in the rear of the shop and had seen that the girlfriend stole the necklace supports that he was reasonable to believe that the chase is unprovoked. However, there was no reason to believe that immediate use of force against the pawnbroker is necessary. Thus, the boyfriend cannot claim defense of others.

In sum, the facts do not present a valid legal defense (defense of others), since the boyfriend acted without a reasonable fear of imminent death or great bodily injury of girlfriend.

4. The girlfriend has not committed murder in the first degree, since she did not commit a forcible felony.

Under the State A's statutes, murder in the first degree is defined as a murder caused by a person while he participates in a forcible felony. Forcible felony is generally defined as the crimes that involve the use or threat of physical force or violence against an individual.

Here, the girlfriend stole the necklace without any force and she did not commit any forcible felony.

In sum, the girlfriend has not committed murder in the first degree, since she did not commit a forcible felony.

해설

난이도: 하

핵심 단어 및 논점

- murder
- manslaughter
- deliberation and premeditation
- without malice aforethought
- self−defense and defense of others
- felony murder

1. The landlord owes the doctor the duty to repair the furnace and the doctor owes the landlord the duty to pay rent, since the privity of estate exists between them and duties run with the leasehold.

In every lease contract, a covenant of quiet enjoyment is implied. When there is a constructive eviction by the landlord, the covenant is breached. The constructive eviction occurs when the landlord breaches duty owed to the tenant that substantially deprives the tenant's use and enjoyment of the premises.

Here, the lease between the landlord and the tenant specified that the landlord would maintain the building, including the furnace, in "good working order and repair" during the term of the lease. However, the landlord failed to have the furnace repaired although it could have been repaired within three weeks. Thus, the landlord breached his duty.

When a tenant assigns his interest in a lease, the privity of estate arises between landlord and new tenant and the privity of contract remains between landlord and assignor. Duties of both landlord and tenant run with the leasehold.

Here, the tenant validly assigned the lease to a medical doctor, and the privity of estate arises between the landlord and the doctor. Thus, the landlord owes the doctor the duty to repair the furnace and the doctor owes the landlord the duty to pay rent.

In sum, the landlord owes the doctor the duty to repair the furnace and the doctor owes the landlord the duty to pay rent, since the privity of estate exists between them and duties run with the leasehold.

2. The doctor may raise a defense of constructive eviction and he has no duty to pay rent.

Under the doctrine of constructive eviction, a tenant has no duty to pay rent when he shows that: (1) the landlord breached his duty owed to the tenant, (2) the tenant gave the landlord notice of the breach, (3) the breach resulted in substantial interfering the tenant's enjoyment of the premises, (4) the tenant gave the landlord a reasonable opportunity to correct the breach, and (5) the tenant timely vacated the premises.

Here, the doctor has no duty to pay rent. First, as mentioned above, the landlord breached his duty to repair the furnace owed to the doctor. Second, the doctor promptly notified the landlord about the broken furnace. Third, because of the broken furnace, it was extremely cold in the building and he finally vacated the building. Fourth and fifth, the doctor waited the landlord for three weeks and it is enough time to repair it. Thus, doctor may raise a defense of constructive eviction.

In sum, the doctor may raise a defense of constructive eviction and he has no duty to pay rent.

3. The tenant may assert a defense that the landlord accepted his surrender, and he has no duty to pay rent.

Abandonment occurs when the tenant vacates premises before the end of the term with the intent not to return and defaults in the payment of rent. When the tenant abandoned the premises, the landlord has three options to: (1) accept the surrender, (2) re−let or attempt to re−let the premises on the tenant's behalf, or (3) leave the premises vacant.

Here, the doctor vacated the building and moved to an office in another location before the lease ends. The doctor tried to hand all the building keys to the landlord, but the landlord refused to accept them. The landlord could argue that refusing to accept the keys shows that he did not accept the doctor's abandonment, but he extensively remodeled the building immediately after the doctor vacated and leased it to an attorney. Remodeling strongly shows the landlord's acceptance of the abandonment and it could be interpreted as an attempt to mitigate damages. Thus, the doctor may assert as a defense that the landlord accepted his surrender, terminating the lease.

In sum, the tenant may assert a defense that the landlord accepted his surrender, and he has no duty to pay rent.

해설

난이도: 하

핵심 단어 및 논점

- covenant of quiet enjoyment
- constructive eviction
- assignment
- privity of estate
- doctrine of constructive eviction
- abandonment

1(a). The court should not refuse to give the codicil effect based on Testator's mental state, since there was no lack of mental capacity.

To be valid, a will must be executed by a testator who has mental capacity. Mental capacity is presumed and a contestant has burden of proving that the testator lacked mental capacity. A contestant must shows that a testator was unable to understand: (1) the nature and extent of his property, (2) the persons who are the natural objects of her bounty, (3) the nature of his act, and (4) the nature of the disposition he is making (relationship with an orderly disposition).

Here, Testator had minor cognitive decline with some memory loss when he executed the codicil in 2019. However, it is insufficient to prove Testator's mental capacity since it does not show that he was unable to understand four factors stated above. Thus, there was no lack of mental capacity.

In sum, the court should not refuse to give the codicil effect based on Testator's mental state, since there was no lack of mental capacity.

1(b). The court should refuse to give the codicil effect under the common law since it does not allow extrinsic evidence. Under UPC, the court should also refuse since there is no clear and convincing evidence of mistake. Additionally, DRR is inapplicable.

Generally, courts do not admit extrinsic evidence proving factual errors in order to correct them or to vary the literal meaning of the terms in the trusts, unless there are ambiguous terms or misdescriptions in the will. Thus, the court should refuse to give the codicil effect.

Under UPC, a donative instrument may be reformed to conform the donor's intention if it is established by clear and convincing evidence showing: (1) that a mistake of fact or law affected specific terms of the document or (2) what the donor's intention was.

Here, it is unclear whether Testator was motivated to revoke based on the belief of Son's illegal drug use or his friends' arrest for selling drugs. Thus, there is no clear and convincing evidence showing Testator's mistaken believes.

Under the dependent relative revocation doctrine (DRR), if a testator revokes a will or codicil based on a mistake of fact or law, the revocation is ineffective if it appears that the testator would not have revoked but for the mistake.

However, DRR usually applies when: (1) the bequests in a revoking document and in the revoked will are sufficiently similar, (2) there is an alternative plan of disposition in a revoking document, or (3) the mistake affecting the revocation is recited in the revoking document.

Here, the first and second prongs are inapplicable. Additionally, Testator's belief about Son's illegal drug use is not recited in Testator's 2019 codicil. Thus, DRR is inapplicable and the revocation is effective.

In sum, the court should refuse to give the codicil effect under the common law since it does not allow extrinsic evidence. Under UPC, the court should also refuse since there is no clear and convincing evidence of mistake. Additionally, DRR is inapplicable.

2. University is entitled to $5,000 from Testator's estate, since the 2014 document is validly incorporated by reference in the will.

Incorporation by reference is valid if: (1) testator intended to incorporate, (2) a writing existed at the time or before the will was executed, and (3) the writing is substantially identified in the will.

Here, the document on Testator's computer is not a holographic will since it is not in her handwriting and it is not a will since it is not witnessed. Moreover, incorporation by reference doctrine is inapplicable since the document did not exist when Testator executed her will in 2012. Incorporation by reference under UPC is also inapplicable since $5,000 is not tangible personal property. However, the 2019 codicil republished the 2012 will and it is deemed that 2019 is the execution date of the 2012 will. Thus, the 2014 document was in existence when the referring will is executed (2019). Testator intended to incorporate the document and the document is substantially identified in the will. Thus, incorporation by reference is valid.

In sum, University is entitled to $5,000 from Testator's estate, since the 2014 document is validly incorporated by reference in the will.

해설

난이도: 1(a)번 문제: 하
　　　　1(b)번 문제: 상
　　　　2번 문제: 중

핵심 단어 및 논점

- validity of will
- mental capacity
- extrinsic evidence
- mistaken belief
- dependent relative revocation doctrine (DRR)
- incorporation by reference

1. The municipality's actions with respect to Parcel 1 constitute a taking under the Constitution, since those were recognized as total regulatory taking.

Under the Fifth Amendment Taking Clause, the governmental taking of private property for public use is prohibited without just compensation. Taking Clause is also applicable to state and local governments through the Fourteenth Amendment.

There are two types of taking: physical and regulatory taking. Regulatory taking (non−physical taking) is recognized when: (1) the government denies all economic value of the private property (total regulatory taking), (2) several factors are considered and regulatory taking is recognized (Penn Central taking), (3) when an exaction was imposed by a government in exchange for a discretionary benefit conferred by the government (land−use exaction), or (4) the government authorizes a permanent physical occupation of property (Loretto taking).

Here, total regulatory taking is recognized. The the municipality rezoned Parcel 1 as exclusively residential. However, Parcel 1 was used as a landfill for solid waste disposed and, therefore, the construction of any single− or multifamily residence on the land that was previously used for solid waste disposal. In other words, all economic value of the property or all reasonable investment−backed expectations are denied. Thus, total regulatory taking is recognized.

In sum, the municipality's actions with respect to Parcel 1 constitute a taking under the Constitution, since those were recognized as total regulatory taking.

2. The municipality's actions with respect to Parcel 2 constitute a taking under the Constitution, since a permanent physical occupation is recognized.

As to Loretto taking, a permanent physical occupation of property authorized by the government is recognized as a taking. There is a taking without regard to whether the action achieves an important public benefit or has only minimal economic impact on the owner.

Here, the municipality authorized the utility to run electrical power lines diagonally across Parcel 2 and to erect towers supporting the lines on Parcel 2. The running of the power lines and erecting towers lead permanent physical occupation. The municipality could argue that the occupation is by another entity (the electrical utility company) and it is not governmental action. However, such fact does not change the conclusion.

In sum, the municipality's actions with respect to Parcel 2 constitute a taking under the Constitution, since a permanent physical occupation is recognized.

3. The municipality may seize Parcel 3 under the taking clause of the Fifth Amendment as incorporated by the Fourteenth Amendment, since it is for "public use."

Under the Fifth Amendment Taking Clause, governmental taking of private property for public use is prohibited without just compensation. Taking Clause is also applicable to state and local governments through the Fourteenth Amendment.

Here, the municipality announced its intent to seize the Parcel 3, meaning that the parcel will be physically taken by government. The physical taking is constitutional only when it occurs "for public use" and "with just compensation." Assuming that the municipality offers to pay just compensation, the main issue is whether the taking is for public use or not.

Public purpose is recognized when the issues are as to public safety and public health. Additionally, the government may transfer property from one private party to another if future use by the public is the purpose of the taking. In this case, the municipality will resell it to a private developer who will erect and operate a high—end shopping mall. It is to increase property—tax revenues to fund police and fire services and to stimulate cityside business development. Additionally, the mall will create leisure, recreational, and employment opportunities for residents. These are all within the police powers and are recognized as "public use." Thus, the physical taking in this case is constitutional taking.

In sum, the municipality may seize Parcel 3 under the taking clause of the Fifth Amendment as incorporated by the Fourteenth Amendment, since it is for "public use."

해설

난이도: 하

핵심 단어 및 논점

- Taking Clause (Fifth Amendment)
- physical taking
- regulatory taking
- total regulatory taking
- Loretto taking
- public use

1번, 2번 문제는 municipality의 행위가 'taking에 해당하는지' 그 여부를 판단하는 문제이고, 3번 문제는 taking을 할 수 있는지를 물어보는 문제로서, 'taking의 요건'이 충족되었는지 그 여부를 판단하는 문제이다. 1번, 2번의 경우 지문에서 municipality는 해당 parcel을 물리적으로(physically) take한 것이 아니고, zoning을 하거나 제3자에게 해당 토지를 사용할 수 있도록 허가하는 방식을 취했다. 즉 각 행위가 regulatory taking에 해당하는지를 판단해야 하는데, 네 유형의 regulatory taking 중 해당하는 유형의 요건에 관해 analysis한다. 3번의 경우, municipality가 "seize"함으로써 토지이용을 제한하고 있는 바, physical taking에 해당한다. 그러나 모든 physical taking이 가능한 것은 아니고, "for public use"한 목적을 가지고, 토지주에게 "just compensation"을 지급하는 경우에 한해 constitutional taking으로 인정된다. 3번 문제에서 just compensation의 지급을 가정하였으므로, 본 문제의 주된 논점은 "for public use"이다.

1번, 2번 문제

답안요령

> 1. Taking Clause
> 2. Regulatory taking 유형(×4)
> 3. Analysis + 결론

TIP Regulatory taking에 대해 논하기 전, Taking Clause에 대한 기본적인 설명을 해야 한다.

1. LLC was bound on the purchase agreement with the farm−supply store, since agency is created between Ben and the neighbor and the neighbor had actual authority in making the purchase.

The agency law is applicable in LLC. When LLC's operating agreement fails to specify the type of LLC, the LLC is presumed to be member−managed, unless the member's operating agreement specifies how the LLC is to be managed.

Here, the operating agreement is silent, LLC is presumed to be member−managed. Thus, each member has authority to bind the LLC and Ben has authority to carry out the business, the purchase of the hole digger in this case.

Agency arises when: (1) there is a formal or informal agreement between the principal and the agent, (2) the agent's conduct on behalf of the principal primarily benefits the principal, and (3) the principal has the right to control the agent.

Here, when Ben asked the neighbor to buy the hole digger for LLC, the neighbor said, "No problem." It shows the neighbor's assent. The written agreement is not required. Second, the neighbor's purchase was on behalf of Ben, who is a member of LLC. Third, the neighbor is under the Ben's control, since he made the purchase following Ben's request. Moreover, compensation for the purchase is not required for the creation of the agency.

An agent has actual authority when contracting on behalf of his principal if: (1) the principal explicitly told the agent so to act or (2) the agent reasonably believes that the principal wishes the agent so to act based on the principal's manifestations to the agent.

Here, there is no fact indicating that Ben explicitly told the neighbor how to act. However, it is reasonable for the neighbor to believe that Ben wishes her to act. This is because the neighbor knew that Ben had a one−half interest in LLC and

Ben asked her to purchase the hold digger for LLC. Thus, LLC is bound by the purchase the neighbor made.

In sum, LLC was bound on the purchase agreement with the farm−supply store, since agency is created between Ben and the neighbor and the neighbor had actual authority in making the purchase.

2. LLC did not receive notice of the fallen tree, since the neighbor did not have authority to receive notification on behalf of LLC.

Under the agency law, notification given to an agent is effective as notification given to a principal. This rule applies only when the agent has either actual or apparent authority to receive those notification.

Here, as mentioned above, the neighbor is an agent of LLC. However, her authority is limited to make a purchase of a hole digger and she lacks authority to receive notification of the fallen tree. Thus, the fact that the neighbor received the notification from the man does not mean that LLC has notification.

In sum, LLC did not receive notice of the fallen tree, since the neighbor did not have authority to receive notification on behalf of LLC.

3. Adele's text message to Ben did not cause a dissolution of LLC, since member's dissociation does not cause dissolution of LLC.

An LLC member may dissociate from the LLC at any time by expressing her will to withdraw. However, it does not dissolve the LLC unless there is: (1) a consent of all members, (2) the occurrence of an event in operating agreement (OA) causing dissolution, (3) the passage of 90 consecutive days during LLC has no members, or (4) judicial involuntary dissolution (court order).

Here, Adele's text message shows her intent of withdrawing. However, the operating agreement for LLC does not mention member withdrawal, member buyout rights, or company dissolution, and therefore the text message does not cause a dissolution of LLC. Thus, Adele does not have a right to payment from LLC for her half interest in the company.

In sum, Adele's text message to Ben did not cause a dissolution of LLC, since member's dissociation does not cause dissolution of LLC.

해설

난이도: 1번 문제: 상
2번 문제: 하
3번 문제: 하

핵심 단어 및 논점

- agency creation
- actual authority
- dissociation (LLC)
- dissolution (LLC)

1번 문제

LLC의 member인 Ben이 neighbor에게 purchase를 부탁함. Neighbor가 purchase를 했고, 이에 대해 LLC는 책임이 있는가.

⇒ 이는 두 파트로 구분하여 판단해야 한다. 하나는 ① (LLC-Ben) 간의 agency이고, 다른 하나는 ② (Ben/LLC-neighbor) 간의 agency이다. 두 agency가 모두 유효하고, agent에게 authority가 있는 경우에만 LLC의 책임이 인정된다.

①의 agency에서는 LLC가 principal, Ben이 agent에 대응된다. Ben이 LLC의 agent로서, neighbor를 agent로 지정할 authority가 있어야 한다. ②의 agency를 더 명확히 설명하자면, Ben-neghbor 간의 agency가 아닌 LLC-neighbor 간의 agency이다. Ben을 위한 purchase를 하도록 한 약속이 아니고, LLC를 위한 purchase를 하도록 한 약속이었기 때문이다. 따라서 LLC가 principal, neighbor가 agent에 대응된다. Neighbor가 purchase를 할 수 있는 authority가 있어야 한다.

① Member-managed LLC에서는 모든 member가 LLC의 agent로서, 제3자를 LLC의 ordinary course of business를 수행할 agent로 지정할 authority를 가진다. ② LLC와 neighbor간 agency가 성립되었고(요건 3개), neighbor에게 actual authority가 있다. 따라서 neighbor의 행위(purchase)는 principal인 Ben이자 LLC를 bind한다. 즉 LLC는 본 계약에 대해 책임이 있다.

본 사안에서 principal의 status, 예컨대 partially disclosed principal인지 그 여부를 판단하는 것은 논점과 무관하다. Principal의 status는 agent의 책임유무를 판단하는 기준으로, 본 문제는 LLC의 책임유무, 즉 principal의 책임유무에 대한 것이기 때문이다.

2020Sep Contracts

1. The computer system does not conform to the store's contractual obligations, since the contract implies a warranty of fitness for a particular purpose.

A contract for the sale of goods is governed by UCC2. The term "goods" means movable things at the time of making a contract. Here, a contract between the father and the woman is to sell the computer, and it is governed by UCC2.

Under the UCC2, contracts for sale of goods include implied warranties of merchantability and fitness for a particular purpose. A contract implies a warranty of fitness for a particular purpose when: (1) the seller knows or has reason to know the particular purpose for which the goods are required and (2) that the buyer relies on the seller's skill or judgment to select or furnish suitable goods.

Here, the father told the woman that he wanted a computer system that would enable his son to play even the most advanced online computer games with ease. Additionally, he knew nothing about computers and needed the woman to pick the right system for him. He bought the system relying on the woman's recommendation. Thus, the contract between the father and the woman implies a warranty of fitness for a particular purpose.

The implied warranties may be excluded when (1) the disclaimer is in writing and is conspicuous or (2) there are expressions like "as is," "with all faults," or other language which in common understanding calls the buyer's attention to the exclusion of warranties and makes plain that there is no implied warranty. "Conspicuous" means so written, displayed, or presented that a reasonable person must have noticed it. Whether a term is conspicuous or not is determined by a court.

Here, the contract stated "Seller makes no warranties that extend beyond the description of the computer on the first page of this agreement." The woman could argue that this statement is the disclaimer. However, the purchase agreement contained a list of "Terms and Conditions" which consists of 16 numbered paragraphs printed in a very small typeface. The disclaimer was at the 12th paragraph. Additionally, nothing on the front of the agreement indicated that there was any text on the back, and there is no indication that the father turned over the agreement. Meanwhile, there is no fact indicating that there are expressions like "as is." Thus, the implied warranty should not be excluded in this case.

In sum, the computer system does not conform to the store's contractual obligations, since the contract implies a warranty of fitness for a particular purpose.

2. The father has the right to return the computer system to the store and get the purchase price back, since he justifiably revoked the acceptance.

When the seller breaches the implied warranty, the buyer can recover the price if the buyer either rightfully rejected the purchased goods or justifiably revoked acceptance of it. When the buyer accepted the goods, right to reject is precluded. Acceptance occurs when the buyer, after reasonable opportunity to inspect the goods, tells the seller that the goods conform to the contract or he will retain it despite nonconformity.

Here, the father went back to the computer store after a week of use. The father could argue that more than one week is reasonable time to inspect the computer system. However, the court could conclude that it became clear that the computer system was inadequate for the needs of online gaming after a week of use, but he did not immediately inform it to the woman. Thus, the father accepted the purchased goods.

Even if the court conclude that the father accepted the purchased goods, the father can recover the purchase price if he justifiably revoked the acceptance. A buyer may revoke acceptance if: (1) nonconformity of the goods occurs, (2) it substantially impairs the value of the goods to the buyer, and (3) the buyer accepted the goods either: on the reasonable assumption that a nonconformity would be cured; without discovery of a nonconformity if acceptance was induced by either difficulty of discovery before acceptance; or the seller's assurance.

Here, the father justifiably revoked the acceptance. First, as mentioned above, the computer system the father purchased does not conform his needs. Second, the unsuitable computer system for the purpose substantially impairs the value to the father. Third, the father accepted the system because of the woman's assurance. Moreover, it is difficult to discover the nonconformity of computer system.

In sum, the father has the right to return the computer system to the store and get the purchase price back, since he justifiably revoked the acceptance.

3. The father has the right to $700 in addition to the purchase price. He would also be entitled to incidental and consequential damages.

When the buyer justifiably revoked the acceptance, he/she is entitled to the purchase price and the difference between the contract price and the market price of the goods. Additionally, the buyer is entitled to incidental and consequential damages.

Here, the contract price of the computer system was $2,500 and the market price is $3,200 according to the expert. Thus, the father is entitled to $700 in addition to the purchase price ($2,500). There is no fact indicating incidental and consequential damage the father suffered.

In sum, the father has the right to $700 in addition to the purchase price. He would also be entitled to incidental and consequential damages.

해설

난이도: 하

핵심 단어 및 논점

- implied warranties of fitness for a particular purpose
- acceptance (UCC2)
- revocation of acceptance (UCC2)
- damages ($ 계산)

1. The supermarket had a duty to preserve the video recording, since the litigation was anticipated when the video recording was destructed.

The duty to preserve information exists when the party who destroyed or altered evidence has notice that the evidence is relevant to litigation or should have known that the evidence may be relevant to future litigation. This rule also applies to ESI evidence. A dispute alone does not raise the duty to preserve, and a future litigation should be probable and specific. The party must take reasonable steps to preserve the information and the duty exists even if such destruction occurs in the regular course of business.

Here, the woman's attorney mailed the supermarket's owner a letter informing him that the woman intended to sue the supermarket for her injuries. Moreover, the letter demanded the supermarket preserve all relevant information. Thus, the litigation was reasonably anticipated. Even if there is the record—retention policy, those information should have been preserved.

In sum, the supermarket had a duty to preserve the video recording, since the litigation was anticipated when the video recording was destructed.

2(a). The court would consider various factors in making decision on sanctions, such as whether information is retrievable, whether the other party is prejudiced, and whether the spoliating party acted with bad intent.

Sanctions are authorized only if the information cannot be restored or replaced through additional discover. When the other party is prejudiced by the failure to preserve information, the court may consider, on its discretion,: (1) the level of culpability of the spoliating party and (2) the degree of prejudice the loss of evidence has caused the other party. As to certain sanctions, the court would consider whether the spoliating party acted with bad intent to deprive another party of the information's use in litigation. If bad intent is recognized, a presumption that the lost information was unfavorable to the sanctioned party would be made or default judgment would be entered against the spoliating party.

In sum, the court would consider various factors in making decision on sanctions, such as whether information is retrievable, whether the other party is prejudiced, and whether the spoliating party acted with bad intent.

2(b). The court would allow the parties to submit the other evidence, presuming that the destructed recording was favorable to the woman.

Here, the video recording of the peach—display incident and the woman's fall has been deleted and it could not be recovered. Thus, sanctions are authorized.

As to the woman's prejudice, the destruction by the supermarket is highly prejudicial to the woman since the owner ordered to delete the video recording after reviewed it. Only the owner knows the favorable part or unfavorable part of the video recording. Additionally, the woman would offer other evidence as to the incident but it may less persuasive than the video recording.

As to the defendant's intent, it is highly likely for the court to conclude that the owner had bad intent. The owner instructed the supermarket's employees to comply with the policy and to delete all recordings after he learned that the recording is available on a hard drive in the supermarket's possession. Moreover, the instruction was made after the owner received the attorney's letter.

With these analyses, the court is likely to grant the motion for an adverse inference instruction, but not the motion for a default judgment. Even if the other evidence is less persuasive than the video recording, it is not impossible for the parties to reconstruct the incident.

In sum, the court would allow the parties to submit the other evidence, presuming that the destructed recording was favorable to the woman.

해설

난이도: 하

핵심 단어 및 논점

- duty to preserve (discovery)
- poliation of evidence
- sanction

2번 문제

2(a) 문제는 court가 sanction에 관해 고려해야 하는 사항이 무엇인지 묻고 있고, 2(b) 문제는 court가 내리게 될 판결을 예측하도록 한다. 즉 sanction이라는 issue에 대해 2(a)는 rules를 작성하고, 2(b)는 그에(2(a)) 대한 analysis를 하도록 구분되어 출제된 것이다. 따라서 수험자는 2(b)를 '2(a)에 작성한 내용을 바탕으로' 작성해야 할 것이다.

2020Oct Trusts

1. Amy is not entitled to receive a distribution from the Friends' Trust, since the Trust is invalid trust without definite beneficiaries.

To be a valid trust, there must be definite one or more beneficiaries. A trust with indefinite beneficiaries is invalid.

Here, the Friends' Trust includes the provision stating "to distribute the income annually among my friends in equal shares." The term "my friends" is indefinite since specific people in the class cannot be recognized. Thus, the trustee has no duty under the Friends' Trust.

In sum, Amy is not entitled to receive a distribution from the Friends' Trust, since the Trust is invalid trust without definite beneficiaries.

2. In modern law, Bob validly appointed the assets of the Child's Trust into a new trust that could pay its income to David for his life, since a donee of a special power of appointment may exercise through a new trust and may create more limited interests than the addressed interest by the donor.

In the past, a donee of a special power is not allowed to make a distribution that is not specifically directed by a donor. However, in modern law, such restrictions are not adopted. When a donee has a special power to appoint trust principal outright, the donee can create more limited interests to the objects of the power.

Here, under the Child's Trust, the trustee was directed "to distribute the principal, during Bob's life or upon his death, to any or all of his issue as he appoints by a deed of appointment or will." Even though the trustee is required to distribute the principal to Bob's son, David, he distributed "income" to David only "for life." It could be invalid in the past, but, in modern law, creating more limited interests (life estate) than the addressed interest (in fee simple) is allowed. This is because Bob has a power to appoint trust principal.

In sum, in modern law, Bob validly appointed the assets of the Child's Trust into a new trust that could pay its income to David for his life, since a donee of a special power of appointment may exercise through a new trust and may create more limited interests than the addressed interest by the donor.

3. Charity does not have interests in that trust, since it is non−objects. University has interests in that trust as the taker in default of appointment.

A donee of a special power of appointment can only exercise the special power in the designated objects. If a donee exercise the power in non−objects, the appointment is ineffective and the property passes to the taker in default of appointment.

Here, Bob (donee of the power) is directed to distribute the trust principal to any or all of his issue under the Child's Trust. Thus, Bob's issues are designated objects. However, Bob appointed Charity as a beneficiary and the appointment is ineffective. The ineffectiveness of the appointments to the non−objects does not affect the appointments to the object. Therefore, Bob's exercise of his power is partially ineffective, and the appointment to David is permissible while the appointment to Charity is impermissible. As to impermissible appointment, University is entitled to the trust principal after David's life as a designated taker in default of appointment under the Child's Trust.

In sum, Charity does not have interests in that trust, since it is non−objects. University has interests in that trust as the taker in default of appointment.

해설

난이도: 1번 문제: 하
　　　　2번 문제: 중
　　　　3번 문제: 하

핵심 단어 및 논점

- validity of trust
- definite beneficiaries
- special power of appointment
- trust principal outright
- designated object
- taker-in-default of appointment

2번 문제

본 문제의 핵심 논점을 파악하기 위해서는 문제를 세분화하여 읽는 것이 중요하다.

"Did Bob validly appoint the assets of the Child's Trust into a new trust that could pay its income to David for his life? Explain."

① Bob이 David에게 'income'을 분배한 행위가 valid한가.

② Bob이 Daivd에게 'his life'에 한하는 권리, 즉 fee simple이 아닌 life estate를 appoint한 것이 valid한가.

1. The judge should allow the bartender to testify about what he overheard the owner saying on the phone. This is because it either is an admission by the opposing party or falls within hearsay exception of present state of mind.

To be admissible, evidence must be relevant. Relevant evidence is any evidence that tends to make the fact more or less probable than it would be without the evidence. Here, the statement may show that the person who fired the restaurant is the owner and it is relevant.

Hearsay is an out of court statement offered in evidence to prove the truth of the matter asserted. Hearsay is inadmissible. Here, the statement is hearsay. It was made in the restaurant, out−of−court, and it is offered to prove that the owner did fire his failing restaurant to get back some money. Thus, it is hearsay and inadmissible.

However, the statement is not hearsay and is admissible if: (1) the statement is offered against the opposing party and (2) the statement is made by the opposing party. Here, the bartender (prosecutor) offered the statement against the opposing party, the owner and the statement is made by the owner. Thus, it is admissible as officially nonhearsay.

Moreover, the statement also falls within the hearsay exception as a present state of mind. A present state of mind is a statement made by a declarant that conveys his then existing state of mind, such as present intent, motive, or plan. Here, the statement indicates the owner's plan to firing and it is admissible as a hearsay exception.

In sum, the judge should allow the bartender to testify about what he overheard the owner saying on the phone. This is because it either is an admission by the opposing party or falls within hearsay exception of present state of mind.

2. The judge should allow the bartender to testify about what he overheard the waiter saying to the owner. This is because it is either a statement against interest or an admission by co-conspirator.

The statement is relevant, since it shows that the fire was planned by the owner. However, it is hearsay. The statement was made by the waiters in the restaurant and it is offered to prove that the owner planned to burn his restaurant.

However, the testimony of a now unavailable declarant may be admissible if the statement was against the declarant's pecuniary, or penal interest when it was made. Here, the declarant is the waiter and he is unavailable because he fled overseas after learning that he was under investigation for arson. Additionally, the statement was against his interest since it shows his criminal liability. Thus, the statement falls within the hearsay exception as a statement against interest.

Moreover, the statement is admissible as an admission. It is not hearsay and is admissible if: (1) the statement is offered against the opposing party and (2) the statement is made by the opposing party. When the declarant and the party have agency or employment relationship, co-conspirators, or partners, the declarant's statement is admissible as a party admission. Admission of a co-conspirator is a statement that is made during the declarant was participating in furtherance of a conspiracy.

Here, the statement is made by the waiters and it is offered against the owner. The waiters are co-conspirators of the owner the statement was made during they was participating in furtherance of the firing. Thus, admission exception is also applicable in this case.

In sum, the judge should allow the bartender to testify about what he overheard the waiter saying to the owner. This is because it is either a statement against interest or an admission by co-conspirator.

3(a). The judge should not admit the certified arson investigation report, since it is hearsay and there is no applicable exception rule.

The report is hearsay. It is prepared by a police arson investigator and it would be offered to prove the truth of the contents.

However, public records are admissible under the hearsay exception. Public records are reports as to matters observed by law enforcement officer and factual findings from a legally authorized investigation.

Here, although the certified arson investigation report is public records, but the exception rule does not apply if the public records is offered by the prosecutor against the defendant in a criminal case. Thus, the report is hearsay and inadmissible.

In sum, the judge should not admit the certified arson investigation report, since it is hearsay and there is no applicable exception rule.

3(b). The judge should not admit the certified arson investigation report in light of the owner's constitutional objection. This is because admission violates confrontation clause under the Sixth Amendment.

The Confrontation Clause of the Sixth Amendment gives defendants the right to confront witnesses against them. The right is applicable, only if: (1) the statement was testimonial, (2) the declarant is unavailable to testify at trial, and (3) the defendant had no opportunity to cross−examine the witness before trial.

Here, the report is testimonial since it contains analysis that the declarant (investigator) would be provided at trial. The arson investigator is unavailable to testify at trial because he has died. Additionally, the owner (defendant) was arrested on July 1, before the report is written on August 1 and the prosecutor plans to provide testimony of an expert witness who did not participate in the arson investigation. Thus, there was no opportunity for the defendant to cross−examine the investigator before trial. Thus, the report violates the defendant's constitutional right.

In sum, the judge should not admit the certified arson investigation report in light of the owner's constitutional objection. This is because admission violates confrontation clause under the Sixth Amendment.

해설

1번, 2번 문제

답안요령

1. Relevance★
   + analysis
2. Hearsay 기본 rule: 정의 + inadmissible
   + analysis (hearsay에 해당한다)
3. However, [present state of mind] exception + rule
   + analysis

3번 문제

답안요령

1. Hearsay 여부 판단★
   ① Hearsay 기본 rule
   ② 그러나 hearsay exception에 해당하여 admissible 가능
   ③ Exception rule
   ④ Analysis
2. The Confrontation Clause
   ① Requirements
   ② "Testimonial"
   ③ "Primary purpose"
   ④ Analysis

TIP 본 답안요령은 문제가 세분화되어 있지 않고 '특정 statement의 admissibility를 판단하라'와 같이 해당 statement에 관한 '모든' 논점을 고려해야 하는 문제를 기준으로 작성되었다. 이 경우, Confrontation Clause뿐만 아니라 hearsay에 대한 내용을 서술하는 것이 고득점 포인트다. 한편, 본 기출(2020Oct)과 같이 hearsay 문제와 Confrontation Clause 문제로 구분되어 있다면, 답안 또한 각 논점으로 구분하여 서술한다. 즉 3(a)문제는 답안요령 1번을, 3(b)문제는 답안요령 2번을 서술한다. 3(b)문제는 요건 중 ②요건에 중점을 두고 analysis하는 것이 중요하다.

1(a). The partnership is bound on the purchase contract, since Aldo had apparent authority.

Under the general agency law, a principal is liable on the contract when a agent has either actual or apparent authority. Apparent authority arises when the transaction was for the ordinary course of business and the other party had no notice that an agent has no authority.

In our case, all—electric garbage trucks have become common in the trash collection business, and it shows that the purchasing the trucks is for the ordinary course of business. Additionally, Aldo purchased the truck in the partnership's name and the other party (truck dealership) had no notice of absent of authority. Thus, Aldo had apparent authority to make the purchase contract.

In sum, the partnership is bound on the purchase contract, since Aldo had apparent authority.

1(b). Assuming that the partnership is bound, Carlos is liable for the unpaid balance of the purchase prince, since Carlos is jointly and severally liable for it.

Partners are personally and jointly and severally liable for the partnership's debts. Here, it is assumed that the partnership is bound to the contract. Thus, Carlos (partner) is personally and jointly and severally liable for the contract.

In sum, Carlos is liable for the unapid balance of the purchase prince, since Carlos is jointly and severally liable for it.

1(c). Assuming that the partnership is bound, Aldo is entitled to reimbursement from the partnership for the down payment he made on the truck, since he made down payment for the ordinary course of partnership's business.

A partner has right for the reimbursement when a payment was made as a partner of the partnership, unless he breached his fiduciary duty.

Here, as mentioned above 1(a), the transaction was for the ordinary course of partnership's business and Aldo made down payment using his personal funds. Additionally, there is no fact indicating Aldo breached his fiduciary duty.

In sum, Aldo is entitled to reimbursement from the partnership for the down payment he made on the truck, since he made down payment for the ordinary course of partnership's business.

2. Aldo is not entitled to be paid for the value of his services to the partnership, since he has no right to receive compensation other than the share of profits.

Even though a partner shares profit, he has no right to receive compensation for services he made as a partner. A partner may receive compensation only in a winding up process or when there is consent of other partners.

In our case, Aldo has demanded that the partnership pay him for the value of his services and there is no express agreement regarding it. There are no facts indicating that the exception rules are applicable here.

In sum, Aldo is not entitled to be paid for the value of his services to the partnership, since he has no right to receive compensation other than the share of profits.

3. The partnership is not bound on the sales contract for the land, since Carlos had not agreed to the contract.

As to matters outside the ordinary course of business, there must be unanimous consent from the partners.

Here, the partnership operated its business only in State A and did not operate any business in State B. Thus, selling the land in State B is outside the ordinary course of business. However, Carlos had not agreed to the contract.

In sum, the partnership is not bound on the sales contract for the land, since Carlos had not agreed to the contract.

해설

난이도: 하

핵심 단어 및 논점

- general agency rule
- apparent authority
- ordinary course of business
- no notice
- personally liable
- jointly and severally liable
- reimbursement
- fiduciary duty
- compensation
- share profits
- unanimous consent

1(a)번 문제

논점: Apparent authority

답안요령

1. General agency rule
2. Principal's liability
   i. Actual authority
      + analysis
   ii. Apparent authority
      + analysis
3. 결론

1. The ordinance could be recognized as either a content—based restriction or a content—neutral restriction. It could be recognized as a content—based restriction since it treats signs differently based on the contents. However, it could also be recognized as a content—neutral restriction since it made a narrow exemption and put general manner prohibition.

In this case, the city ordinance treats signs differently based on the contents. Except for signs as to time and temperature information, all other signs are restricted. Thus, it is content—based restriction. Such restrictions are constitutional only when it satisfies the strict scrutiny test (SS test).

Alternatively, the city ordinance could also be recognized as a content—neutral restriction. This is because it imposes narrow exceptions only for signs as to time and temperature information. With the narrow exceptions, it is hard to say that the ordinance focuses on the content and imposes restriction based on the content, but it imposes general manner restriction. It bans from having flashing lights, lights of changing degree of intensity or color, or electronically scrolled messages. Content—neutral restriction is subject to intermediate scrutiny test (IR test) or rational basis test (RR test) which is less strict than the strict scrutiny test.

In sum, the ordinance could be recognized as either a content—based restriction or a content—neutral restriction. It could be recognized as a content—based restriction since it treats signs differently based on the contents. However, it could also be recognized as a content—neutral restriction since it made a narrow exemption and put general manner prohibition.

2. Assuming that the ordinance is content−based, it is unconstitutional since it is subject to the strict scrutiny test.

If the ordinance is a content−based restriction, it is constitutional only when it is narrowly tailored to City's compelling interest. The burden of proof is on City.

In this case, the purpose of the ordinance is to preserve the aesthetic beauty of City and to promote traffic safety. Aesthetic beauty of city and traffic safety could not be recognized as compelling interest.

Even though traffic safety could be recognized as compelling interest, the ordinance is consitutional only when it is narrowly tailored to achieve the compelling interest. However, the ordinance is not but over−inclusive. According to the studies presented by City's Commissioner of Traffic Safety, signs have only a small safety impact on the roadways with speed limits under 30 miles per hour. However, the ordinance imposes the restriction on all roadways, including roadways with speed limits under 30 miles per hour. Thus, the ordinance is not narrowly tailored to City's compelling interest, traffic safety.

Additionally, the ordinance is under−inclusive. According to the studies presented by City's Commissioner of Traffic Safety, signs with flashing, changing, or moving displays significantly increase the rate of accidents on roadways. To achieve traffic safety, City would need to restrict all such displays that disturb drivers. However, the ordinance imposes restriction only on flashing lights, lights of changing degree of intensity or color, and electronically scrolled messages. Thus, the ordinance is not narrowly tailored to City's compelling interest, traffic safety.

In sum, assuming that the ordinance is content−based, it is unconstitutional since it is subject to the strict scrutiny test.

3. Assuming that the ordinance is content−neutral, it is constitutional since it is subject to the time, place, manner test.

If the ordinance is a content−neutral restriction, it is constitutional only when: (1) the ordinance is narrowly tailored, (2) to serve an important government interest, and (3) leaves open alternative channels. The burden of proof is on City.

In this case, the aesthetic beauty of City and traffic safety are recognized as important interests and the second factor is satisfied.

As to the first factor, "narrowly tailored" factor, it is different from one used in content−based restriction case. While "narrowly tailored" factor used in content− based restriction case means that the ordinance does not over or under−inclusive, the factor in the content-neutral restriction case means that the governmental interest will be achieved less effectively absent the regulation. In this case, the ordinance bans presenting signs on the public property to preserve the aesthetic beauty of City with exceptions for time and temperature information. Narrow exceptions are narrowly tailored to achieve the interest. Additionally, although the ordinance over-inclusive, it can prevent additional accidents on the roadways with speed limits under 30 miles per hour. Thus, the governmental interest (traffic safety) will be achieved less effectively absent the regulation. The first factor is satisfied.

Thirdly, the ordinance must leave open alternative channels. Here, the ordinance bans only flashing lights, lights of changing degree of intensity or color, and electronically scrolled messages. There are many other methods that neighborhoods can communicate. The ordinance does not affect both quality and quantity of communication, and it satisfies the third factor.

In sum, assuming that the ordinance is content-neutral, it is constitutional since it is subject to the time, place, manner test.

해설

난이도: 상

핵심 단어 및 논점

- freedom of speech (First Amendment)
- content-based restriction
- content-neutral restriction
- "narrowly tailored" 해석
- SS test
- IR test

1. State B is required to enforce the State A child support order, since it has full faith and credit in any states.

Child support order judgment from a state has full faith and credit in any other states.

Here, the child support order was made in the divorce court in State A. Thus, this judgment has full faith and credit in State B.

In sum, State B is required to enforce the State A child support order, since it has full faith and credit in any states.

2. The State B court has not jurisdiction to modify the father's child support obligation, since State A has continuing and exclusive jurisdiction.

Original court has continuing and exclusive jurisdiction until: (1) any of the parties continues residence in the same and (2) all parties did not consent in writing other jurisdiction to modify the order.

Here, State A is the original court. (1) Following the divorce, the mother continued to live in State A with the children. (2) There is no fact indicating that the mother consented in writing State B to modify the order. Thus, State A is original court and it has exclusive and continuing jurisdiction.

In sum, the State B court has not jurisdiction to modify the father's child support obligation, since State A has continuing and exclusive jurisdiction.

3. A court should not reduce the child support obligation, since retroactive modification is not allowed and his change in circumstance is neither substantial nor continuing.

Federal law absolutely forbids retroactive modification of child support obligations. Prospective modification of a child support order is available only when the petitioner can show a continuing and substantial change in circumstances.

Here, as to the retroactive modification, the father asked that the reduction be made retroactive to the date he lost his job. It is not allowed. As to the prospective modification, father was terminated from his job, but received a lump sum severance payment of $75,000. It is hard to say the termination makes the support obligation unreasonable, and it is not a substantial change. Additionally, he has had several job interviews in State B, and market conditions make it likely that he will eventually find a job comparable to the one he had in State A. It shows that his change would not be continuing. Thus, prospective modification is not available.

In sum, a court should not reduce the child support obligation, since retroactive modification is not allowed under the federal law and his change in circumstance is neither substantial nor continuing.

4. A court should modify the amount of the spousal support, since there was substantial and continuous change. However, the period of the award is a close call.

Spousal support order may be modified only when there is substantial and continuing change in a party's circumstances. A change that is anticipated or voluntary or bad faith may not modify the support order.

Here, five months after the divorce, the mother had a heart attack, forcing her to cut back her work. Her annual pay was reduced to $7,000 and her doctor recommends that she not resume full−time work, because full−time work and caring for the children and the home would be too stressful. This change is substantial and continuing.

Courts consider various factors in determining the amount or period of the award: lack of self−support, marriage period, having/no children, and burdened person's ability to contribute to spouse's future.

Here, the mother was awarded the sole custody of the two children.The mother's expenses have not changed since the time of the divorce judgment. Thus, the court would increase the spousal support obligation. As to the period of the award, marriage period is 12 years, relatively short period. Her doctor recommends that she not resume full-time work, but there is no fact indicating that the mother lacks capacity to find a job permanently. Thus, it is a close call. In sum, a court should modify the amount of the spousal support, since there was substantial and continuous change. However, the period of the award is a close call.

해설

난이도: 하

핵심 단어 및 논점

- full faith and credit
- exclusive and continuing jurisdiction
- 'retroactive' modification of child support obligation
- 'prospective' modification of child support obligation

- substantial and continuing change
  → unreasonable
- modification of spousal support order
- amount
- period (extension)

1번 문제(추가 설명)

– 각 주마다 child support order를 내리는 기준에 대해 달리 규정하고 있어, collecting child support across state lines가 굉장히 어렵다. 이 문제를 해결하고자 Congress가 mandated all states to adopt UIFSA하였다. 타 주의 order가 full faith and credit을 가져야 한다는 논리를 뒷받침하는 Act(federal law)는 다양하다. 그중 Full Faith and Credit for Child Support Orders Act와 UIFSA가 대표적이다. 그 외에도 IV-D of the Social Security Act 등이 있다.

– UIFSA는 full faith and credit of the child support order를 인정하는 데 있어, 두 개에 대한 입증을 전제로 하고 있다. ① location of the offending parent와 ② paternity가 그것이다. ①은 지불의 의무가 있는 부모의 '지불능력'을 뜻하는 바, 국가는 이에 관련된 자료에 access할 수 있다.

2번 문제

Original court has exclusive and continuing jx.

① C/O/O 계속 거주(continues to live)

② no consent

동일한 의미, 다른 표현

Under UIFSA, original court has exclusive and continuing jurisdiction over child support order until:

ⅰ. Neither child, obligor, or obligee continues to live in the state; or

ⅱ. There is written consent by all parties to other jurisdiction to modify the order.

3번 문제

Spousal support의 금액과 기간을 구분하여 논하는 것이 고득점포인트다. 금액과 기간 모두 여러 상황을 종합적으로 고려하여 판단해야 하는데, spousal support의 목적, 즉 '이혼으로 인한 경제적 피해 방지'에 부합해야 하는 바, substantial and continuing change 유무가 핵심기준이다. 각 논점에 관해 어떤 상황을 고려해야 하는지 구분되어 있는 것은 아니나, 일반적으로 '금액'은 recipient의 경제상황에 있어 예상치 못한 변화가 있는 경우 금액인상이 인정될 가능성이 높다. 한편, '기간'은 spousal support의 유형을 선택하는 문제라고 할 수 있는데, 유형에는 permanent support, temporary support, rehabilitative support, reimbursement support, lump sum support 등이 있다. 그리고 support 지급기간의 '연장(extension)'은 original order상의 종료일까지 recipient가 경제적 생활을 하지 못할 가능성이 상당할 때 인정된다. 예컨대, recipient의 나이가 retirement age이거나, work experience가 전혀 없거나, educational level이 낮을 때, extension이 허용될 가능성이 높다.

	Permanent	Temporary	Rehabilitative	Lump sum	Reimbursement
Definition	일정 기간 동안(평생) 얼마씩 지급하라	divorce pending하는 동안 지급하라	[Recipient가 취업을 할 때까지] 지급하라 (self-sufficient 할 때까지)	총 얼마를 한꺼번에 지급하라	[Burdened person이 professional license를 취득했으니], 지급하라
Time period	Long term	Short term	Short term		

2021Feb
2021Feb Agency & Partnership

<u>1(a). The woman and the man are not partners in the food−truck business, since the man has no power to control or manage the business.</u>

A general partnership is created when two or more persons, as co−owners, carry on a business for profit. No written agreement or formalities are required. A general partnership is created when two or more persons, as co−owners, carry on a business for profit. Additionally, a person who receives a share of the profits of the partnership business is presumed to be a partner of the business.

Here, the woman and the man cooperated for the food−truck business and they promised that the man would receive 10% of the profits. Thus, it is presumed that the man is a partner of the business. However, the woman could rebut the presumption by showing that man does not have any power to control or manage the business just like the woman. The woman promised 10% of the profits to compensate the delivery service, not to appreciate his ultimate control of the business.

In sum, the woman and the man are not partners in the food−truck business, since the man has no power to control or manage the business.

<u>1(b). Assuming that the woman and the man are partners in the food−truck business, the woman would be liable to the farmer for the damage, since the man's negligence occurred in the ordinary course of the business.</u>

A partner is an agent of the partnership for the purpose of its business. When a partner's action appears to be in the ordinary course of the partnership's business, his wrongful act creates a partnership obligation.

Here, the man negligently ran his car into a farmer's stall while parking at the market. The damage occurred in the ordinary course of the business. Thus, his act creates a partnership obligation. Additionally, each partner is jointly and severally liable for the partnership obligation and, therefore, the woman is liable for the damage the man caused.

In sum, assuming that the woman and the man are partners in the food—truck business, the woman would be liable to the farmer for the damage, since the man's negligence occurred in the ordinary course of the business.

2(a). The man is not an employee of the woman, since the woman does not direct his performance in detail.

Agent is a person or entity that acts on behalf of another, the principal. In other words, the principal controls the agent.

Here, the man does the early morning produce shopping for the woman. Although the woman texts him each night indicating the type of produce to buy, the man makes his own decision in selecting and purchasing the requested produce. In other words, the man is not under the woman's control. Additionally, there are no factors indicating whether there is an employee—employer relationship, such as level of skills required and the length of the relationship. Thus, the man is not an employee.

In sum, the man is not an employee of the woman, since the woman does not direct his performance in detail.

2(b). Assuming that the man is an employee of the woman, the woman would be vicariously liable to the farmer, since the driving was within the scope of his employment.

Principal is vicariously liable for torts committed by the agent, if principal employed him as an employee. Additionally, principal will be liable for the agent's tortious conduct only if it occurred within the scope of his employment.

Here, the accident caused by the man occurred while the man was driving to make the purchases.

In sum, assuming that the man is an employee of the woman, the woman would be vicariously liable to the farmer, since the driving was within the scope of his employment.

3(a). The man is not an independent contractor for the woman, since he was not under the woman's control.

In determining whether an agent is an employee or independent contractor, the main considered factor is the principal's control over the agent's performance.

Here, as mentioned above, the man was not under the woman's control although he acted on behalf of the woman.

In sum, the man is not an independent contractor for the woman, since he was not under the woman's control.

3(b). Assuming that the man is an independent contractor for the woman, the woman would not be vicariously liable to the farmer for the damage since the man had no apparent authority.

A principal is not liable for torts committed by the agent, if principal employed him as an independent contractor. However, a principal would be vicariously liable when the third party relies upon the appearance of agency. In other words, when the independent contractor has apparent authority, the principal is liable.

Here, there is no fact indicating that the man has apparent authority.

In sum, assuming that the man is an independent contractor for the woman, the woman would not be vicariously liable to the farmer for the damage since the man had no apparent authority.

해설

난이도: 하

핵심 단어 및 논점

- agency rule
- partnership
- in the ordinary course of the business
- jointly and severally liable
- employee-employer relationship
- vicarious liability
- independent contractor
- principal's control
- within scope of the employment

1. The portrait of Testator's grandparents passes to Charles, since the original will executed on July 1, 2015 is revoked by the handwriting on the back of the will.

State A permits wills to be completely or partially revoked by the execution of a subsequent will or codicil, or by physical act or by cancellation when accompanied with an intent to revoke the will or codicil.

Here, there is neither physical act nor cancellation on the clause 1. However, words are on the back of the will in Testator's handwriting without signatures.

State A law provides that unsigned holographic wills or codicils are valid. Thus, the handwriting is a codicil and the original will would be partially or entirely revoked by it. The will is revoked only to the extent that it is inconsistent with the provisions of the holographic codicil.

Here, the holographic codicil is inconsistent to the extent that Testator wanted the portrait to go to his first cousin, Charles. Thus, except for the clause 1, no other provisions are revoked.

In sum, the portrait of Testator's grandparents passes to Charles, since the original will executed on July 1, 2015 is revoked by the handwriting on the back of the will.

2. Beth is not entitled to either the antique bookcase or the motorcycle, since the revocation is invalid and DRR is inapplicable.

Testator's intent to revoke is presumed when a will is marked with cancellation upon the word.

In clause 2 of the will, the phrase "antique bookcase" had been scratched out by Testator and immediately above it he had typed in the word "motorcycle." Thus, Testator's intent to revoke is presumed. However, the typing was neither signed nor witness nor in handwriting, and it is not a valid will.

Under the dependent relative revocation doctrine (DRR), if a testator revokes a will or codicil based on a mistake of fact or law, the revocation is ineffective if it appears that the testator would not have revoked but for the mistake.

Here, antique bookcase and motorcycle are not similar and the court would not apply DRR in this case.

In sum, Beth is not entitled to either the antique bookcase or the motorcycle, since the revocation is invalid and DRR is inapplicable.

3. Donna is entitled to the bookcase and the motorcycle, since the will is incorporated by reference.

Under either UPC or common law, incorporation by reference is valid if: (1) testator intended to incorporate, (2) A writing existed at the time or before the will was executed, and (3) the writing is substantially identified in the will.

Here, Testator specifically typed that he give all of his tangible personal property not otherwise effectively disposed of to the person he have named in a letter. It shows his intent to incorporate the letter into his will and the letter is substantially identified in the will. Moreover, the letter was dated June 15, 2015 and it existed before the will was executed on July 1, 2015. Thus, incorporation by reference is valid and Donna is entitled to all of Testator's tangible personal property not otherwise effectively disposed of, the bookcase and the motorcycle.

In sum, Donna is entitled to the bookcase and the motorcycle, since the will is incorporated by reference.

4. Adam and Beth are equally entitled to the bank account, following the typical intestacy laws of the states.

According to the typical intestacy laws of the states, absent descendants or a spouse, an intestate's property is distributed to (1) parents, (2) the descendants of the parents (that is, the intestate's siblings and their descendants), (3) more remote ancestors, and (4) the descendants of the more remote ancestors, in that order.

Here, in addition to the portrait of his grandparents, the antique bookcase, and the motorcycle, there was a bank account with a balance of $10,000. Bank account is not tangible personal property and it cannot be bequeathed by the letter. Thus, intestacy law applies. Adam and Beth are Testator's living relatives and they are equally entitled to the bank account.

In sum, Adam and Beth are equally entitled to the bank account, following the typical intestacy laws of the states.

해설

난이도: 하

핵심 단어 및 논점

- revocation
- physical act
- holographic will
- codicil
- intent to revoke
- dependent relative revocation doctrine (DRR)
- incorporation by reference
- intestacy law

1. The woman and the passenger are permitted to join their claims in a single lawsuit, since both claims is raised by the same occurrence and the man's negligence is a common question.

Two or more plaintiffs or defendants may join their claims in a single lawsuit whenever: (1) the claims to be joined are arising out of the same transactions or occurrence and (2) there is a question of law or fact common to all the parties.

Here, each claim brought by the woman and the passenger is raised by the highway accident. The man's negligence will be treated in both claims. Thus, two requirements are satisfied.

In sum, the woman and the passenger are permitted to join their claims in a single lawsuit, since both claims is raised by the same occurrence and the man's negligence is a common question.

2. The woman is precluded from bringing her claim since her claim should have raised her claim as a counterclaim but she failed to do so.

Defendant is required to bring his claim as a counterclaim against plaintiff if the counterclaim arises out of the same transaction or occurrence as the plaintiff's claim against the defendant and there is common question of law or fact. When a defendant failed to raise a compulsory counterclaim, he is barred from bringing a later independent action on the claim.

In some courts, a failed compulsory counterclaim is barred in the subsequent action because the defendant waived the claim. In some courts, a failed compulsory counterclaim is barred in the subsequent action by claim preclusion (res judicata).

Here, the woman's claim is based on the injures suffered in the highway accident and who has responsibility is the common question. Thus, the woman should have raised her claim as a counterclaim and she failed to do so.

In sum, the woman is precluded from bringing her claim since her claim should have raised her claim as a counterclaim but she failed to do so.

3(a). The man is precluded from denying that he was negligent, since issue preclusion arises.

Issue preclusion arises when: (1) earlier judgment is a valid final judgment on the merits, (2) issue was essential to the earlier judgment, (3) issue was actually litigated and determined, and (4) the party being precluded from re—litigating the issue was adequately represented in the previous action.

Here, issue preclusion arises. First, the fact indicated that the man did not appeal and the judgment became final three months ago. Second, in the original action raised by the man, man's negligence was necessary issue. Third, in the earlier case, the man alleged that he had exercised due care and auction at all times. Under the State B applicable law, the contributory negligence applies and the man would have to prove his lack of negligence. Fourth, the man brought the action himself and there is no fact indicating that the man was not adequately represented in the previous action.

In sum, the man is precluded from denying that he was negligent, since issue preclusion arises.

3(b). Whether the passenger can assert the issue preclusion depends on the statute adopted in State A.

Traditionally, issue preclusion required strict mutuality and both the party asserting issue preclusion and the party against whom issue preclusion was asserted were bound by the prior judgment. In most of modern courts, strict mutuality requirement is rejected. A party who was not a party in a previous case can use collateral estoppel offensively in a new case against the party who lost in the previous case, unless estoppel would be unfair.

Here, the first judgment is from a federal court sitting in diversity in State A, and State A governs the preclusion issue. However, State A does not clearly indicate whether it abandons mutuality requirement. If State A recognizes mutuality requirement, the passenger is precluded from using issue preclusion since he was not a party in the earlier judgment. If State A denies mutuality requirement, the passenger can use issue that the man was negligent offensively against the man.

In sum, whether the passenger can assert the issue preclusion depends on the statute adopted in State A.

해설

난이도: 2번 문제: 중
　　　　3(b)번 문제: 중
　　　　그 외 문제: 하

핵심 단어 및 논점

- claim preclusion
- compulsory counterclaim
- issue preclusion
- mutuality

3(b)번 문제

본 기출과 같이, mutuality 요건 인정여부가 명시되어 있지 않은 경우, 요건이 인정되는 경우와 그렇지 않은 경우를 구분하여 작성하는 것이 고득점 포인트다.

1. Secondbank and Thirdbank have enforceable security interests in the key-manufacturing machine. Firstbank does not have enforceable security interest in the machine, since its security agreement does not sufficiently describe the collateral.

A security interest attaches to collateral when: secured party gave value to debtor; debtor has rights in the collateral; and the debtor authenticated a security agreement.

As to Secondbank, Secondbank loaned $400,000 to KeyCo, KeyCo owns its equipment, key-manufacturing machine, and KeyCo signed the agreement. Thus, security interest of Secondbank is effective.

As to Thirdbank, Thirdbank loaned $600,000 to KeyCo, KeyCo owns its equipment, key-manufacturing machine, and KeyCo signed the agreement. Thus, security interest of Thirdbank is effective.

As to Firstbank, Firstbank loaned $200,000 to KeyCo and KeyCo owns its equipment, key-manufacturing machine. However, the third requirement is not satisfied. The security agreement must describes the collateral. Although the description is not required to be detailed, but it must reasonably identifies what is described. Here, the security agreement says that KeyCo granted Firstbank a security interest in "all of KeyCo's assets." The provision "all of KeyCo's assets" does not reasonably identify the collateral. Thus, the security interest of Firstbank is ineffective.

In sum, Secondbank and Thirdbank have enforceable security interests in the key-manufacturing machine. Firstbank does not have enforceable security interest in the machine, since its security agreement does not sufficiently describe the collateral.

2. The security interest of Firstbank cannot be perfected since it is ineffective. The security interest of Secondbank is not perfected, since it did not file a financing statement and did not possess the machine. Only Thirdbank has perfected security interest in the key−manufacturing machine by filing a financing statement.

As to Firstbank, a security interest cannot be perfected that does not attach. As mentioned above, the security interest of Firstbank is ineffective and, therefore, it cannot be perfected.

As to Secondbank and Thirdbank, there are many ways to perfect the security interest. The collateral can be perfected by filing a financing statement or taking possession of the collateral. There is no fact indicating that Secondbank either filed a financing statement or took possession of the machine. Thus, Secondbank does not have perfected security interest. Meanwhile, Thirdbank filed a properly completed financing statement in the appropriate filing office, listing KeyCo as the debtor and indicating the collateral as "all of KeyCo's assets." Even though the description is insufficient to satisfy the effectiveness of the security interest, it is sufficient to perfect the security interest. Thus, Thirdbank has perfected its security interest.

In sum, the security interest of Firstbank cannot be perfected since it is ineffective. The security interest of Secondbank is not perfected, since it did not file a financing statement and did not possess the machine. Only Thirdbank has perfected security interest in the key−manufacturing machine by filing a financing statement.

3(a). Thirdbank's security interest has priority over Secondbank's security interest.

A security interest cannot be perfected that does not attach. Firstbank's security interest is ineffective and, thus, cannobe be perfected.

Between an unperfected secured creditor and a perfected secured creditor, a perfected secured creditor has superior claim to the collateral.

Here, Thirdbank's security interest is perfected and it has priority over Secondbank's security interest. The fact that Thirdbank knew about KeyCo's transactions with Firstbank and Secondbank does not change the result.

In sum, Thirdbank's security interest has priority over Secondbank's security interest.

3(b). Secondbank's security interest is subordinate to the Supplier's lien, since it is unperfected. Thirdbank's security interest is superior to the Supplier's lien, since it is perfected before the lien is created.

Judgment lien creditors have priority over conflicting security interests if the person became a lien creditor before the conflicting security interest was perfected.

Secondbank's security interest is unperfected. An unperfected security interest is subordinate to a judicial lien in the same collateral. Thus, Secondbank's security interest is subordinate to the Supplier's lien.

Meanwhile, Thirdbank's security interest is perfected before the Supplier's lien is created. Thus, Thirdbank's security interest is superior to the lien.

In sum, Secondbank's security interest is subordinate to the Supplier's lien since it is unperfected and Thirdbank's security interest is superior to the Supplier's lien since it is perfected before the lien is created.

해설

난이도: 하

핵심 단어 및 논점

- effectiveness of security interest
- perfection
- description of the collateral
- judgment lien
- priority

3번 문제

- 세 개 이상의 security interests 간 priority를 판단하는 경우, rules를 중심으로 title을 세분화하여 서술하는 것이 좋다. 본 기출은 총 4개의 security interests 간 priority를 판단하는 문제로서, 3(a)는 "perfected security interest > unperfected security interest"라는 rule을 기준으로, 3(b)는 lien creditor와 perfection에 관한 rule을 기준으로 작성되었고, 각 rule에 따라 4개의 interests 간 순위를 판단한다.
- 3(a)의 경우, 사안에 "Thirdbank knew about KeyCo's transactions with Firstbank and Secondbank"라는 점이 명시되어 있는 바, priority를 판단할 때 actual notice는 무관하다는 점을 서술하는 것이 고득점 포인트다.

1. The friend had an implied easement from prior use over the man's 80 acres since the woman acquired it and it passed to the friend.

If the woman acquired an implied easement from prior use, the friend has interest on the easement. Implied easement from prior use is recognized when: (1) both parcels have been owned by the same person at the time when the prior use arises, (2) the prior use has benefited the other portion of the land, (3) the prior use has been apparent, (4) the prior use has been continuous, and (5) the prior use has been reasonably necessary for the use and enjoyment of the benefited property.

As to the first requirement, the 170−acre tract of farmland was purchased by the man and he conveyed the westernmost 90 acres to the woman. Thus, the first requirement is satisfied.

As to the second requirement, when the man owned the both parcels, the gravel road gave him two routes from his house to the small town. In other words, using the gravel road benefited the 90 acres, which was sold to the woman. Thus, the second requirement is satisfied.

As to the third requirement, the gravel road was visible at the time of conveyance. It is enough for the woman to know about the road. Thus, the third requirement is satisfied.

As to the fourth requirement, courts are divided in determining whether continuousness requirement is satisfied. In modern jurisdictions, the use that is not merely temporary or casual satisfies the requirement, while, in the past, the use should not be intermittent. Here, the man frequently used the road and the fourth requirement is satisfied.

As to the fifth requirement, in majority jurisdictions, requirement of reasonable necessity is satisfied when the owner of the dominant estate would be put to appreciable expense to provide a substitute for the claimed easement. Here, there is no other ways to access the county road which shorten the travel time. If there is no implied easement, significant expenditure of time or money should be paid to get shorter time. Thus, the fifth requirement is satisfied.

In sum, the friend had an implied easement from prior use over the man's 80 acres since the woman acquired it and it passed to the friend.

2. The builder took ownership of the 80 acres subject to the implied easement since he had inquiry notice of the prior use.

The builder could argue that the easement was unrecorded and it cannot be traceable in chain of title. Thus, the builder takes ownership free from the easement.

However, in some jurisdictions, the recording act does not apply to implied easements. This is because such easements are created by implication, not by the deed. Moreover, even if the implied easements are subject to the recording act, he had an inquiry notice of the easement since the grave road was visible. Thus, he is not a bona fide purchaser and is not protected under the recording act.

In sum, the builder took ownership of the 80 acres subject to the implied easement since he had inquiry notice of the prior use.

해설

난이도: 하

핵심 단어 및 논점

- implied easement from prior use
- recording act
- inquiry notice

1. UCC2 applies in this case, since the contract was for 100 shopping carts. And the parties both are merchants.

A contract for the sale of goods is governed by UCC2. The term "goods" means movable things at the time of making a contract.

Here, a contract between the grocer and the supplier is to sell the shopping carts, and it is governed by UCC2.

Merchant is a person who deals in goods of the kind at issue.

Here, the grocer opens a supermarket and the supplier is a shopping—cart supplier. Thus, both are merchants.

In sum, UCC2 applies in this case, since the contract was for 100 shopping carts. And the parties both are merchants.

2. An oral agreement for 100 shopping carts for $125 each is valid under UCC2, since under UCC2 a contract can be made in any manner.

Under UCC2, a contract for sale of goods may be made in any manner sufficient to show agreement including conduct by both parties which recognizes the existence of such a contract.

Here, the conversation between the grocer and the supplier is sufficient to show their agreement. The statements clearly shows that they agreed to buy or sell 100 of shopping carts by March 31. Thus, an oral agreement is made between them.

In sum, an oral agreement for 100 shopping carts for $125 each is valid under UCC2, since under UCC2 a contract can be made in any manner.

3. The envelope satisfies the statute of frauds (SOF) and it is enforceable only up to 60 shopping carts which is stated in the document.

Under UCC2, a contract for the sale of goods for the price of $500 or more is enforceable, only when there is a writing sufficient to show that a contract for sale has been made between the parties and signed by the party to be charged.

Here, the contract between the grocer and the supplier is for the price of $12,500, and therefore it is subject to SOF. The envelope the supplier sent states, "The 60 shopping carts you ordered... Please send us payment of $75,000 (60 carts x $125/cart)..." It is sufficient to show that the contract is made.

The term "signed" is broader than simply bearing a conventional signature. It includes using any symbol executed or adopted with present intention to adopt or accept a writing.

Here, the party to be charged is the supplier. The fact does not clearly indicate whether the supplier signed on it or not. However, the fact shows that the envelope was a document printed on the supplier's letterhead. It is highly likely for the court to conclude that the letterhead can constitute a signed writing.

Under the UCC2, the contract is not enforceable beyond the quantity of goods shown in such writing.

Here, the document states that "The 60 shopping carts you ordered..." and the grocer cannot enforce the supplier to sell 100 shopping carts.

In sum, the envelope satisfies the statute of frauds (SOF) and it is enforceable only up to 60 shopping carts which is stated in the document.

4. The note sent by the grocer to the supplier on March 2 does not satisfy SOF, since it has no signature of grocer (sender).

Merchants' confirmatory memo exception applies, when: (1) between merchants, (2) a sender confirms the agreement in writing and signed it, (3) the receiver has reason to know the contents of it, and (4) the receiver did not make any objection to its contents within 10 days after he received it.

Here, the grocer could argue that merchants' confirmatory memo rule applies and therefore the note sent on March 2 is valid. However, (2) the sender (grocer) did not sign the memo. Thus, the memo is not a valid contract.

In sum, the note sent by the grocer to the supplier on March 2 does not satisfy SOF, since it has no signature of grocer (sender).

In sum, there is no enforceable contract requiring the supplier to sell 100 shopping carts, but requiring to sell 60 shopping carts.

해설

난이도: 상

핵심 단어 및 논점

- CL? UCC2?
- formation of contract (UCC2)
- "in any manners"
- sufficient to show
- SOF
- in writing
- $500 or more
- signed by the party against whom the enforcement is sought
- merchant's confirmatory memo

본 지문에는 총 3개의 agreement가 존재한다. 따라서 이 agreement 간 관계를 잘 파악하고 각 agreement에 어떤 rule이 적용되어야 하는지 파악하는 것이 매우 중요하다. 답안의 로직은 다음과 같다. (첫 번째 문단을 A, 두 번째 문단을 B, 세 번째 문단을 C라고 칭한다.)

A   100개에 대해 oral로 합의함.
→ UCC2이므로, in any manners로 합의가 되면, valid contract으로 인정한다.
→ 그러나 $500을 초과하므로, SOF가 적용된다.

B   March 2, note
→ Writing이다. 그러나 the party against whom the enforcement is sought인 supplier의 서명이 없다.
→ SOF를 충족하지 못한다.
→ SOF의 예외에 해당하는가? (merchant's confirmatory memo)
→ Sender인 grocer의 서명이 없다. (handwritten note가 서명된 note를 의미하지는 않는다.)
→ SOF 예외도 적용될 수 없다.
→ <B> 부분은 invalid하다.

[C] March 31, envelope

→ Writing이다. 그리고 the party against whom the enforcement is sought인 supplier의 서명도 있다.

→ SOF를 충족한다.

→ 그러나 그 내용이 oral로 했던 100개가 아닌, 60개에 대한 writing이다.

→ 60개에 대한 부분만 valid하다.

→ 따라서 grocer가 breach했다.

※ 고득점 포인트 (arguable point)

Grocer는 merchant's confirmatory memo를 근거로 note가 valid하다고 주장할 것이다. 그러나 grocer의 서명이 없으므로, 예외의 rule이 적용될 수 없는 바, note is invalid.

예상질문

Q. 본 사안에서 perfect tender rule은 논점인가?

논점이 아니다. Perfect tender rule은 'breach 여부'를 판단하는 기준으로서, 유효한 계약이 있어야만 적용된다. 즉 계약이 유효해야만 그 내용에 따라 채권·채무가 정해지고, 당사자의 행위가 해당 채무를 제대로 이행했는지 그 여부(breach 여부)를 판단할 수 있다. Validity가 전제되어야만 breach 여부를 판단할 수 있다. 본 문제는 'enforceable contract' 유무에 대한 것으로서, validity를 판단하는 문제이다.

1. The facts are sufficient for a jury to find that the son acted negligently. This is because his visual impairment and mom's instructions are considered in this case.

In a negligence action, child's action is compared with the standard of other child who has similar age, intelligence, and experience. Additionally, physical characteristics are considered in measuring a reasonable standard of care.

In this case, the mother instructed her son to remain in her grasp. However, the son broke free of her grasp and ran toward a nearby candy display. Failure to follow parent's instruction can be recognized as negligence. Moreover, the son was visually impaired and knew that he was in crowding and jostling by other patrons. It is considered that son's actions are unreasonable and son is negligent.

In sum, the facts are sufficient for a jury to find that the son acted negligently. This is because his visual impairment and mom's instructions are considered in this case.

2. The facts are sufficient for a jury to find that the Big Box acted negligently. This is because Big Box owes duty of care to its customers (invitee).

An invitee is one who enters on the land with the landowner's express or implied invitation with the landowner or for the landowner's benefits. A landowner has a duty to warn of or to make safe dangerous condition that the landowner knows or has reason to know and which the plaintiff was not likely to discover. A landowner owes a duty to inspect for dangers.

In this case, son is a business visitor of Big Box and he is invitee. Big Box owes the son duty to warn and duty to inspect for dangers. Thus, Big Box should take reasonable steps to eliminate cheesecake that could cause accidents. Even though actual notice is absent, constructive notice of dangerous conditions is recognized when a reasonable time to discover is passed.

In this case, there is no fact indicating that Big Box has actual notice. Cheesecake was on the floor in the store's self−service dinning area and cheesecake displays had last been stocked several days before the accident. Thus, the possibility that the employee of Big Box dropped the cheesecake is very low. However, Big Box owes duty to inspect dangerous conditions for its customers. The fact that the cheesecake was flattened and dirty shows that a reasonable time period has already been passed. Even if Big Box has constructive notice on the dangerous condition (cheesecake) on the floor, it did not take reasonable steps to eliminate it. In other words, Big Box was negligent.

In sum, the facts are sufficient for a jury to find that the Big Box acted negligently. This is because Big Box owes duty of care to its customers (invitee).

3. The customer can be held liable for enhancing the son's injury, since the customer owes duty to aid to son.

Generally, there is no duty to come to the aid of another. However, once an actor undertook to assist someone, he/she owes duty to aid to the rescuee. The rescuer should exercise due care when providing assistance and he/she is liable for his negligence.

In this case, the customer attempted to help the son to stand and he owes duty to aid to son. The customer negligently twisted the son's arm and worsened the son's injury.

In sum, the customer can be held liable for enhancing the son's injury, since the customer owes duty to aid to son.

4. The son can recover the full amount of damages from Big Box only, since the rescue by the customer is proximately caused by the negligence by Big Box and both Big Box and the customer are jointly and severally liable.

Danger invites rescue. The wrong that imperils life is a wrong to his rescuer. Thus, rescue is not an intervening actors and a tortfeasor who negligently causes the initial injury is liable for any enhanced harm.

In this case, it is assumed that Big Box negligently caused the son's slip. Thus,

Big Box is liable for any enhanced harm that is caused from negligence by rescuer, the customer in this case.

If more than one defendant were negligent, those defendants would be jointly and severally liable for the damages. Each of those defendants is liable for the full amount of the plaintiff's damages from the negligence.

In this case, both Big Box and the customer are negligent and the son can recover from either Big Box or the customer for full amount of damages.

In sum, the son can recover the full amount of damages from Big Box only, since the rescue by the customer is proximately caused by the negligence by Big Box and both Big Box and the customer are jointly and severally liable.

해설

난이도: 하

핵심 단어 및 논점

- child (standard of care)
- invitee (standard of care)
- constructive notice
- duty to aid
- jointly and severally liable
- proximate causation

1번 문제

- NCBE 해설에서는 children이 행동해야 할 standard of care에 대해 age, intelligence, education을 고려하는 다수설뿐만 아니라 특정 나이를 기준으로 해당 나이 이하의 아이는 과실을 범할 수 없다는 rule을 고려하는 소수설에 대해서도 논하고 있다. 기준이 되는 나이는 각 재판권마다 달리 규정하고 있다. The Third Restatement에서는 5세 미만의 아이는 과실을 범할 수 없다고 간주한다. Children's standard of care를 다수설과 소수설로 구분하여 논하면 perfect한 답안이 되겠으나, NCBE 해설에서 다수설과 소수설로 구분하는 것에 대한 배점이 비교적 낮은 것(10%)을 감안하였을 때, 다수설만을 논하더라도 충분할 것으로 생각된다. 다만, analysis를 충분히 작성하는 것이 중요하다.

- 본 답안은 son이 negligent하다고 서술하였으나, 이 결론은 중요하지 않다. 주어진 사안을 logic하게 analysis한다면 결론이 다르다 하더라도 충분히 고득점 할 수 있다. 예컨대, 다음과 같은 logic으로 son이 negligent하지 않음을 주장할 수 있다. Son이 엄마의 주의를 따르지 않았으나 그가 6세임을 감안하면 candy display 쪽으로 달려간 것이 unreasonable하다고 보기는 어렵다. 또한 그의 visual impairment를 고려했을 때 cheesecake의 위험성(이것을 밟았을 때 미끄러질 수 있는 위험)에 대해 고려하지 않고 달린 행동은 unreasonable하지 않다. 따라서 그는 not negligent하다.

2번 문제

Landowner는 invitee에게 위험한 상황에 대해 duty to warn, duty to inspect을 지고 있다. 따라서 위험한 상황을 대비해 지속적으로 확인(inspect)하고 위험한 상황이 발견

될 경우 이를 해결하기 위해 합리적인 방법을 취해야 한다. 본 사안에서 바닥에 cheesecake이 떨어져 있었던 것은 위험한 상황이다. 그러나 cheesecake이 납작하고 더럽다는 사실을 통해 오랜 시간동안 Big Box 직원이 이를 인지하지 못했다는 것을 알 수 있다. 즉 직원의 행동은 duty to inspect에 부합하지 못하는 바, Big Box의 과실이 인정된다.

3번 문제
본 사안에서는 행위자의 'negligence'를 명시하였으므로 그의 행위가 undertaking to assist인지 그 여부에 대해 논할 필요가 없다. 따라서 아래 답안요령은 기출문제 2012July, 2015July에 적합하고, 본 문제에는 적합하지 않다. 이처럼 문제에서 중점을 두고 있는 논점을 파악하는 것이 가장 중요하다. 또한 문제에서 "Good Samaritan" statute에 대해 논하지 말라고 명시하였으므로, 이에 대해 작성하더라고 no credit이다.

답안요령

1. No duty to aid
2. Exception(duty가 인정되는 경우)

4번 문제
본 문제는 'duty to aid'와 'proximate causation' 논점에 대한 문제이다. 주어진 사안을 요약하면 다음과 같다. Big Box의 negligence로 인해 son이 다쳤고, 그런 son을 도와주려던 customer의 negligence로 인해 다쳤다. Big Box는 son의 injuries 모두에 대해 책임을 지는가. 이는 customer의 행위(rescue)가 Big Box의 negligence에 의해 proximately cause되었는지 그 여부를 판단하는 문제, 즉 customer의 행위가 intervening factor로 인정되는지 그 여부를 판단하는 문제이다. 일반적으로 rescue 행위는 최초 행위자(Big Box)가 행위 당시 충분히 예상가능한 행위로 인정되는 바, intervening factor로 인정되지 않고 Big Box의 행위에 의해 proximately cause되었다고 본다. 또한 son의 injuries에 대해 두 명(Big Box와 customer)의 negligence가 인정되는 바, 그들은 jointly and severally liable하므로 son은 그들 중 임의로 선택하여도 fully 배상받을 수 있다. 따라서 son은 Big Box로부터 모든 injuries에 대해 배상받을 수 있다.

1. Ethan cannot block the merger, since the merger voting rules adopted in State A should be satisfied. The votes of Carlos and Diana are enough.

A corporate merger is in which two corporations are combined into one surviving corporation. Two corporations which are incorporated in different states may be merged, following the requirements of the state in which it is incorporated.

Here, Winery Inc. is incorporated in State A and Organic Wines Corp. is incorporated in State B. The approval is of Winery Inc.'s merger and the requirements adopted in State A should be satisfied. State A has adopted the MBCA.

Under the MBCA, the plan of merger must be adopted by a majority of the board of directors and then by at least a majority of the shareholders who are entitled to be cast on the plan.

Here, Carlos, Diana, and Ethan are equal shareholders of the corporation and are the only members of board of directors in Winery Inc.. Carlos and Diana constitute a majority of the board of directors and two−thirds of the shares. Thus, the merger can be approved without Ethan's voting.

In sum, Ethan cannot block the merger, since the merger voting rules adopted in State A should be satisfied. The votes of Carlos and Diana are enough.

2. Ethan has a right to demand that he receive payment in cash equal to the fair value of his shares in Winery Inc., since shareholders have right to dissent, rather than shares of Organic Wines Corp.

Under the MBCA, shareholders have the right to dissent from fundamental corporate transactions and they are entitled to demand payment in cash for her shares from the corporation. Those demands would be made through either a negotiation with the corporation or a judicial appraisal. When a judicial appraisal is held, the shareholder receives payment in cash for the fair value of her shares. Here, merger of the corporation is a fundamental transaction, and Ethan has the right to dissent. Additionally, Winery Inc. is not a publicly traded corporation. Thus, Ethan is entitled to receive payment in cash for the fair value of her shares, rather than shares of Organic Wines Corp.

In sum, Ethan has a right to demand that he receive payment in cash equal to the fair value of his shares in Winery Inc., since shareholders have right to dissent.

3. Ethan could not successfully sue the Organic Wines Corp. directors in State A, since the directors actions are justified under the statute of State B.

Under the internal affairs doctrine, the internal affairs, including the duties of directors, are governed by the state of incorporation.

Here, Organic Wines Corp. is incorporated in State B and its business is primarily operated in State A. However, the claim is regarding the duties of directors, the laws of State B govern it. Under the statute of State B, directors are free from liability for claims that they did not seek to maximize shareholder profits if their decisions are consistent with the corporation's stated social or environmental purpose. Directors are required to advance the corporation's purpose even if at shareholder expense. Thus, the directors could justify promoting sustainable and organic practices at the expense of maximizing shareholder profits.

In sum, Ethan could not successfully sue the Organic Wines Corp. directors in State A, since the directors actions are justified under the statute of State B.

해설

난이도: 상

핵심 단어 및 논점

- corporate merger
- right to dissent
- right to demand payment in cash for shares
- voting
- publicly traded corporation
- closely held corporation
- market out exception
- internal affairs doctrine

1번 문제

본 문제는 'Ethan이 merge하는 것을 반대할 수 있는지' 그 여부를 파악하는 것이다. 즉 Winery Inc.가 merge를 진행할지 그 여부를 정하는데 있어, 누구의 투표(voting) 및 찬성이 필요한지에 대해 논해야 한다. 따라서 'Winery Inc.가' incorporated되어 있는 주 법을 따라야 하는 바, State A는 MBCA를 채택하고 있다.

2번 문제

본 문제는 핵심 논점을 파악하는 것이 중요한데, 그것은 문제를 잘 읽으면 쉽게 파악할 수 있다. "instead of receiving shares in Organic Wines Corp."라는 표현이 본 문제의 핵심이다. Ethan이 merge한 Organic Wines Corp.가 아닌, 기존의 Winery Inc.에서 자신이 소유하고 있던 shares만큼을 'cash(현금)로' 받기를 주장할 수 있는지 그 여부를 판단하는 문제이다.

3번 문제

Organic Wines Corp.의 shareholder가 Organic Wines Corp.의 director를 상대로 제기된 소송으로서, internal affairs에 대한 소송이다. 따라서 해당 회사가 incorporated된 주 법이 판단의 기준이 되는 바, State B의 statute가 기준이 된다.

2021July Family Law

1. State A's exercise of personal jurisdiction does not violate the woman's rights, since the woman's minimum contacts in State A are recognized.

The interstate enforcement and modification of child support are governed by the UIFSA. In determining the personal jurisdiction over a nonresident defendant, long−arm statute is adopted and the court use minimum contacts test as due process requirement. Due process requires that defendant's acts be a purposeful activity and it was foreseeable that he will be in the forum state.

Here, the woman voluntarily moved to State A and voluntarily involved in the sexual intercourse with the man. The child's birth was foreseeable and the state has strong interest in ensuring the paternity, care and support for the child. The woman could argue that her rights under the due process is violated, because the sexual intercourse happened 15 years ago and she left State A just after giving birth. However, the sexual activity are directly related to the basis for jurisdiction.

In sum, State A's exercise of personal jurisdiction does not violate the woman's rights, since the woman's minimum contacts in State A are recognized.

2(a). The court does not have subject−matter jurisdiction to award the man sole custody of the daughter, since State A is not the daughter's home state.

Child−custody is governed by PKPA and UCCJEA. Under both the Acts, a court has exclusive jurisdiction to issue an initial custody decree if the state: (1) is the child's home state on the date of commencement of the proceeding; or (2) was the child's home state within the past six months and the child is absent from the state, but a parent or person acting as a parent continues to live in the state. A "home state" is the state where the child has lived with a parent for at least six consecutive months immediately before the commencement of a child—custody proceeding.

Here, when the action was commenced, the daughter had lived in State A for only three weeks. Additionally, daughter had lived in State B for bout 14 years which she is now absent from and her mother continues to live State B. Thus, State A is not the daughter's home state.

In sum, the court does not have subject—matter jurisdiction to award the man sole custody of the daughter, since State A is not the daughter's home state.

2(b). The court has subject—matter jurisdiction to require the woman to pay the man child support, but the court may not order the woman to pay child support to the man, the noncustodial parent.

Child support is governed by UIFSA. Under the UIFSA, home state rule establishes priority among child support orders. Even after a pleading is filed in another state, a state court may exercise jurisdiction for a support order only if: (1) that state is the home state of the child or (2) the jurisdiction in the other state has been timely challenged.

Here, State A is not the home state of the daughter, but the State A court is not precluded from issuing a support order. This is because there was no petition held in State B. However, the woman has been a sole custodian of the daughter, and the court may not order her to pay child support to the man, the noncustodial parent.

In sum, the court has subject—matter jurisdiction to require the woman to pay the man child support, but the court may not order the woman to pay child support to the man, the noncustodial parent.

해설

난이도: 2(b)번 문제: 상
　　　 그 외 문제: 하

핵심 단어 및 논점

- personal jurisdiction
- minimum contact
- purposeful availment
- subject-matter jurisdiction
  (child custody)
- PKPA

- UCCJEA
- home state
- subject-matter jurisdiction
  (child support)
- UIFSA

본 기출문제의 핵심 논점은 'family law에 관한 소송의 jurisdiction'이다. 주 법원에서 소송을 청취할 때에는, 연방법원에서 진행되는 것과 마찬가지로 SMJ와 PJ를 판단하여야 한다. 1번 문제가 PJ에 대한 것이고, 2번 문제가 SMJ에 대한 것이다. 1번 문제의 경우, 2009Feb 기출문제를 함께 공부할 것을 추천한다.

2번 문제

UIFSA를 적용하면, State A는 child support에 대해 jurisdiction을 가진다. 따라서 본 소송을 청취할 수 있다. 그러나 문제는 구체적으로 'woman에게 child support를 지급하라고 명할 수 있는지' 그 여부에 대해 판단하도록 요구하고 있다. 'Man'에게 지급하라고 명하는 것이 아니고, 'woman'에게 지급하라고 명하는 것이다. 여기서 woman은 지금까지 아이를 양육해온 custodian이라는 것을 고려하는 것이 고득점 포인트다. 대개 noncustodian(본 사안에서는 man)에게 child support 지급을 명한다. 그러나 State A는 child custody에 대한 jurisdiction이 없으므로 이에 대해 청취할 수 없는 바, woman이 그대로 custodian으로서 인정된다. 따라서 State A가 woman에게 child support를 요구할 가능성은 매우 적다. 즉 A주 법원이 재판권(jurisdiction)은 가지나, custodian인 woamn에게 child support를 요구할 가능성은 매우 적다. 수험자는 UIFSA를 적용한 후, 재판 내용을 구체적으로 생각해 보아야 한다.

<u>1(a). The officer's warrantless seizure of the man did not violate the man's Fourth Amendment rights, since the hot pursuit warrant exception is applicable even though the arrest occurred in the man's house.</u>

The Fourth Amendment provides that people should be free from unreasonable searches and seizures. The Fourth Amendment applies to the states through the Fourteenth Amendment.

Generally, police may arrest a person without warrant when they have probable cause. Probable cause is recognized when the reasonable police would find a probability of the commission of a crime objectively.

Here, a teenager told him that the man knocked the woman and took her purse. Knocking down the woman can be interpreted as using force. Thus, under the totality of the circumstances, it is reasonable for the police officer to have probable cause that the man committed a robbery.

However, arresting a person in his own house require warrant, unless exception rules are applicable. Under the hot pursuit warrant exception, the warrant is not required. Hot pursuit occurs when an officer engages in immediate or continuous pursuit of the suspect from the scene of a crime.

Here, the chasing started just after the man took the purse and the police engaged in the pursuit from the scene to the home. There was no any delay in this pursuit. Additionally, the chase was for a robbery and a robbery is categorized as a felony in all jurisdictions. Since the underlying offense is serious, the exception rule is highly applicable in this case.

In sum, the officer's warrantless seizure of the man did not violate the man's Fourth Amendment rights, since the hot pursuit warrant exception is applicable even though the arrest occurred in the man's house.

1(b). The officer's warrantless seizure of the purse did not violate the man's Fourth Amendment rights, since the plain view doctrine is applicable.

Regardless of the result in 1(a) above, the police is not allowed to search the house (seizure the property in the house). However, the police can search without warrant, only when warrantless search exception is applicable.

Under the plain view doctrine, the police may do warrantless search if: (1) the police were lawfully present in a position, (2) the police discover evidence of crime or contraband, (3) the evidence is observed in plain view, and (4) probable cause exists to believe that the items are evidence, contraband of a crime.

As mentioned above, the police was lawfully present in the man's home under the hot pursuit exception. Additionally, the officer had chased the man from the scene. When the police kicked the door open, the man was out of breath and the pursue was on the floor near his feet. Under this circumstance, it is reasonable to think that the man stole the purse and the purse is from the woman. Thus, plain view doctrine applies in this case.

In sum, the officer's warrantless seizure of the purse did not violate the man's Fourth Amendment rights, since the plain view doctrine is applicable.

2. The trial court did not violate the man's constitutional due process rights, since there was no improper police influence on the identification.

The on−scene identifications and subsequent in−court identification from the same witness are inadmissible, if the process was so suggestive and there is improper police influence.

Here, the girl made an out−of−court identification when she saw the man handcuffed in the backseat of the squad car. The police involved in arresting the suspect and discussing the crime with the girl. However, these facts do not mean improper police influence on the identification. Additionally, the girl suddenly shouted and it was unanticipated by the police.

In sum, the trial court did not violate the man's constitutional due process rights, since there was no improper police influence on the identification.

해설

난이도: 1(a)번 문제: 상
1(b)번 문제: 중
2번 문제: 하

핵심 단어 및 논점

- searches and seizures
  (Fourth Amendment)
- warrant
- home arrest (warrant 필요함)
- hot pursuit warrant exception
- identification
- due process
  (Fourteenth Amendment)
- suggestive
- improper police influence

1(a)번 문제

답안작성 로직은 다음과 같다.

Arrest = Seizure of person → 수정헌법 4조, 14조(State) 적용 → 일반적으로 arrest에는 PC만 요구될 뿐, warrant는 요구되지 않는다. → 그러나 home arrest의 경우에는, warrant가 요구된다. → 그러나 warrantless search(seizure)에 해당된다면, warrant 없이도 arrest가 가능하다.

1(b)번 문제

답안작성 로직은 다음과 같다.

집에서 arrest하는 것이 합헌이라 할지라도, 이것이 집에서의 search가 허용된다는 것을 의미하지는 않는다. → 일반적으로 search에는 warrant가 요구된다. → 그러나 warrantless search(seizure)에 해당된다면, warrant 없이도 arrest가 가능하다.

> TIP "집에서 arrest하는 것이 합헌이라 할지라도, 이것이 집에서의 search가 허용된다는 것을 의미하지는 않는다."는 점을 명시하는 것이 고득점 포인트다.

1. Clause 3 of the testator's will determines who takes the share of a beneficiary who predeceased the testator.

State A's anti-lapse statute expressly provides that it applies "unless the decedent's will provides otherwise." Testator expressly provided in his will how to distribute the share of a beneficiary who predeceased the testator, to the heirs of that beneficiary.

In sum, Clause 3 determines who takes the share of a beneficiary who predeceased the testator.

2. Doris's nephew is entitled to the testator's house, since there is no survivorship requirement to the bequest to Doris's nephew and Doris's nephew is her sole heir.

Here, the bequest to Doris is different from the bequests made under Clause 2 and Clause 3. In comparison to the bequests made under Clause 2 and Clause 3, the bequest to Doris does not have survivorship requirement and the will expressly indicated that the share of a beneficiary who predeceased the testator is provided to the heirs of her. Since Doris predeceased the testator, Doris's heirs are entitled to the testator's house. In this case, Doris's sole heir is her nephew.

In sum, Doris's nephew is entitled to the testator's house, since there is no survivorship requirement to the bequest to Doris's nephew and Doris's nephew is her sole heir.

3. Under the common law, the residuary bequest to Bill lapses, while it does not lapse and Bill's heir, his daughter Alice, is entitled to the half of the residuary estate under UPC.

Under the common law, the residuary bequest to Bill lapses.

Here, the phrase in the will "if he survives me" shows survivorship requirement. Clause 3, regarding the distribution of the share of predeceased beneficiary, applies only when the will does not expressly provide otherwise. Thus, Clause 3 is inapplicable in this case in which the survivorship requirement is expressed in the will. Additionally, State A's anti−lapse statute cannot protect the share from the lapse since the will clearly shows the testator's intent that the bequest is effective only if the beneficiary survives him. Thus, the share to Bill lapses.

Under the UPC, the phrase in the will "if he survives me" itself does not prove the testator's intent that the bequest is effective only if the beneficiary survives him. Thus, following Clause 3, Bill's heir, his daughter Alice is entitled to the half of the residuary estate.

In sum, under the common law, the residuary bequest to Bill lapses, while it does not lapse and Bill's heir, his daughter Alice, is entitled to the half of the residuary estate under UPC.

4. Testator's sister is entitled to Bill's one−half share under the no residue of a residue rule, while Alice is entitled under the residue of a residue rule.

Regarding a residuary bequest which lapses, the distribution depends on the rule adopted by the jurisdiction, residue of a residue rule or no residue of a residue rule.

If the bequest to Bill, the residuary bequest, lapses, its disposition depends on the rules. If State A adopts the common law no residue of a residue rule, Bill's share passes to the testator's heir, the testator's sister. Thus, Alice and the testator's sister would take the bank account equally. If State A adopts the residue of a residue rule, Bill's share passes to the other surviving residuary beneficiary, Alice. Thus, Alice would take $250,000 entirely.

In sum, Testator's sister is entitled to Bill's one−half share under the no residue of a residue rule, while Alice is entitled under the residue of a residue rule.

5. Bill's daughter is entitled to Bill's one−half share if the bequest to Bill does not lapse.

As discussed above, if the bequest to Bill does not lapse, it passes to Bill's heir, his daughter. Thus, Alice and Bill's daughter share $250,000 equally.

In sum, Bill's daughter is entitled to Bill's one−half share if the bequest to Bill does not lapse.

해설

난이도: 3번 문제: 상
4번 문제: 상
그 외 문제: 하

핵심 단어 및 논점

- anti−lapse statute
- surviving contingency
- common law v. UPC

- surviving contingency
- no residue of a residue rule
- residue of a residue rule

3번 문제

문제에서 명시적으로 Clause 2를 고려하여 답하도록 요구하고 있으나, State A의 anti−lapse statute를 Clause 2와 비교분석하여 작성하는 것이 고득점 포인트다. 3번 문제의 주된 논점이 survivorship requirement이며, 이에 관한 rules는 State A의 anti−lapse statute와 Clause 2이기 때문이다.

4번 문제

Common law와 UPC를 적용하였을 때 다른 결과가 도출된다는 점을 강조하는 것이 고득점 포인트다. 따라서 단락을 나누어 각 rule에 대한 analysis를 하여, 수험자(작성자)가 common law와 UPC를 비교분석할 수 있음을 어필해야 할 것이다.

2021July Civil Procedure

1. The federal court should not grant the attorney's motion to dismiss, since the supplemental jurisdiction can be exercised.

Federal courts have original jurisdiction over all civil actions arising under the federal laws or Constitution. Here, the woman's defamation claim against the attorney is based on state law.

The district courts have original jurisdiction over the civil actions when there is complete diversity of citizenship between the parties and the amount in controversy exceeds $75,000. Here, the attorney and the woman are both citizens and domiciliaries of State A. Thus, there is no diversity.

Under the supplemental jurisdiction statute, district courts may hear claims that could not be heard, if those claims that are part of the same or controversy under Article III, if they derive from common nucleus of operative fact.

Here, the woman's age discrimination claim is based on federal law, ADEA, and the federal court may exercise the supplemental jurisdiction (SPJ) if her defamation claim and the age discrimination claim derive from common nucleus of operative fact. Both claims arise out of the treatment by her attorney and both claims are about issues in the firm the woman had worked. Both claims are about the reason why the woman has been fired. Thus, both claims arise out of common nucleus of operative fact.

The district court has discretion to decline to exercise SPJ in three situations: (1) there are complex issue on state claim, (2) state claim predominates federal claim, (3) federal court dismissed all claims that it had original jurisdiction, or (4) there are other compelling reasons.

Here, there is no fact indicating any possibility that the court may refuse to exercise SPJ.

In sum, the federal court should not grant the attorney's motion to dismiss, since the supplemental jurisdiction can be exercised.

2. The federal court should not grant the attorney's motion to dismiss the woman's defamation claim as required by State A, since the Federal Rules of Civil Procedure govern this issue.

Under State A pleading rules, a plaintiff's defamation claim is required to allege the time and place where the allegedly false statement was made, the persons to whom it was made, and the particular words constituting defamation. Here, the woman's claim failed to satisfy the requirement.

However, regarding practice and procedure in federal courts, the Federal Rules of Civil Procedure govern all civil actions and proceedings in federal court, unless those rules do not abridge, enlarge, or modify any substantive right.

Here, the issue is regarding the pleading of claims and, under FRCP, there is no requirement for specification in detail. A pleading containing a short and plain statement of the claim is adequate. This rule prevails any special state—law rules regarding the pleadings.

In sum, the federal court should not grant the attorney's motion to dismiss the woman's defamation claim as required by State A, since the Federal Rules of Civil Procedure govern this issue.

해설

난이도: 중

핵심 단어 및 논점

- federal−question jurisdiction (FQJ)
- diversity jurisdiction
- supplemental jurisdiction (SPJ)
- Erie doctrine
- pleading (FRCP 8(a))

본 사안에서 원고가 제기한 소송(claim)은 총 두 개로, ① age discrimination을 근거로 한 소송과 ② discrimination을 근거로 한 소송이 그것이다. 원고가 제기한 소송이 두 개 이상인 경우, 문제를 읽을 때 어떤 소송에 대한 문제인지 파악해야 한다. 본 기출문제는 모두 ②에 대한 것임에 유의하여야 한다.

1번 문제

답안요령

1. SPJ에 대한 기본 rule
2. Considering factors (×4)
   + analysis
3. Court's discretion (×3)
   + analysis
4. 결론

TIP1 │ 본 답안요령은 주어진 사안에 대해 법원이 SPJ를 가지는지 그 여부를 논하는 모든 경우에 사용될 수 있는 바, joinder 또는 intervention이 jurisdiction 측면에서 허용가능한지 판단할 때에도 본 답안요령의 형식 안에서 작성한다.

TIP2 │ SPJ에 대한 답안은 analysis, 특히 2번에 대한 analysis를 최대한 자세히 논하는 것이 고득점 포인트다. Logical−relationship test를 적용하는 경우가 많다.

TIP3 │ 위 3번에 해당하는 사안이 없는 경우: There is no fact indicating any possibility that the court may refuse to exercise SPJ.

TIP4 ① Counterclaim과 ② cross-claim 제기 가능성 여부를 판단하는 경우, res judicata 가능성 여부를 함께 고려하는 것이 고득점 포인트다. ①은 첫 번째 원고 갑·피고 을 간 소송에서 을이 갑을 상대로 별도로 두 번째 소송을 제기할 수 있는지 그 여부를 판단하는 경우로서, 을이 제기한 두 번째 소송이 compulsory counterclaim이라면 res judicata가 적용되어 두 번째 소송(을이 제기한 소송)은 진행할 수 없다. ②는 원고 갑이 피고 을, 병, 정을 상대로 소송을 제기했고, 그 이후 을이 정을 상대로 cross-claim을 제기한 후 정이 을을 상대로 한 별도의 cross-claim을 제기한 경우, 정의 cross-claim에 res judicata가 적용되면 정의 cross-claim은 불가하다.

2번 문제
본 문제의 핵심은 pleading에 관해 'State A와 FRCP 중 어떤 rules를 적용해야 하는지' 판단하는 것이다. Pleading은 civil procedure에 관한 것이므로 FRCP 8(a)가 적용되며, 본 조항은 State A와 같이 구체적인 진술을 요구하지 않는다. 따라서 woman의 pleading은 적합하며, 법원은 이를 기각(dismiss)해서는 아니된다. 한편, 본 문제는 FRCP 8(a)의 내용 및 이에 대한 analysis를 물어보는 문제가 아니다. 따라서 woman이 제출한 pleading의 내용이 구체적으로 FRCP 8(a)의 내용에 부합하는지 그 여부에 대해서는 서술할 필요가 없다.

1. The bank does not have an enforceable security interest in the portable welding machine, since the man does not have right on it.

A security interest is enforceable when: (1) debtor authenticated a security agreement, (2) debtor has rights in the collateral, and (3) secured party gave money to secured party.

Here, equipment is goods other than inventory, farm products, or consumer goods. The portable welding machine is equipment. Additionally, (1) the man signed a loan agreement and (3) the local bank gave the man $50,000 business loan. However, the man does not have right in the portable welding machine. The bank has right in all of the man's equipment. However, the mother made it clear that the man could use the barn but not her welding machine. Thus, the security interest is unenforceable.

In sum, the bank does not have an enforceable security interest in the portable welding machine, since the man does not have right on it.

2(a). The bank has an enforceable security interest in the diesel−engine repair tools, since these tools are after−acquired collateral and all three requirements for the effectiveness of security agreement are satisfied.

Here, the man bought the tools after he made security agreement on June 1. The agreement contained a provision pursuant to which the man granted the bank a security interest "in all my equipment, including equipment hereafter acquired," which means security interest in after−acquired collateral. Additionally, (1) the man signed a loan agreement, (2) the man bought the tools, and (3) the bank gave the man $50,000 business loan.

In sum, the bank has an enforceable security interest in the diesel−engine repair tools, since these tools are after−acquired collateral and all three requirements for the effectiveness of security agreement are satisfied.

2(b). The tool seller has an enforceable security interest in the tools, since all three requirements for the effectiveness of security agreement are satisfied.

(1) The man signed a written agreement on June 10, (2) the man bought the tools, and (3) the tool seller allowed the man to pay the remaining $13,500 in monthly installments over a two-year period.

In sum, the tools seller has an enforceable security interest in the tools, since all three requirements for the effectiveness of security agreement are satisfied.

2(c). The tool seller's interest has priority, since his security interest is PMSI and perfected within 20 days.

A security interest can be perfected when it is attached to the collateral.

Assuming that both the bank and the tool seller have such security interests in these tools, those interests can be perfected by filing, possessing, or controlling.

Here, the local bank properly filed the financing statement on June 1. The tool seller also filed the financing statement on June 11.

Between perfected security interests, the first to file or perfect rule applies. Under the rule, the security interest that was the earlier to be either perfected or the subject of a filed financing statement has priority. Here, the bank filed the statement on June 1 and the seller on June 11. Thus, the bank has priority.

However, PMSI in nonconsumer goods has priority over conflicting interests on the same collateral when the interest is perfected when the debtor receives possession of the collateral or within 20 days thereafter.

Here, the seller has a security interest in the tools and it secures the monthly installments for the tools. Thus, the seller's interest is PMSI in nonconsumer goods. The seller filed the statement next day, and the seller has priority over the bank.

In sum, the tool seller's interest has priority, since his security interest is PMSI and perfected within 20 days.

해설

난이도: 2(c)번 문제: 중
　　　　그 외 문제: 하

핵심 단어 및 논점

- security interest
- equipment
- rights in the collateral
- after−acquired collateral

- priority
- perfection
- first−to−file or perfect rule
- purchase money security interest (PMSI)

<u>**1(a). The woman did not commit armed robbery of the $100 cash, since neither elements are satisfied.**</u>

Theft is the unlawful taking and carrying away of property from the person.

Here, the homeowner pulled $100 from her purse and held the cash out toward the woman. The woman's act does not meet the element. Additionally, the woman went to homeonwer to collect an overdue payment from a homeowner and it cannot be recognized as unlawful taking.

Armed robbery requires the intent of theft.

Theft requires the intent to permanently deprive the owner of the property.

Here, as mentioned above, the homeonwer voluntarily gave the cash to the woman. Thus, the intent requirement is not satisfied.

Armed robbery requires carrying a dangerous weapon. "Dangerous weapon" is regulated under the State A statute.

Here, the woman was holding the pruning shears and it is not (1) firearm. (2) It is not designed to use as a weapon and it is not a thing that is reasonably recognized capable of producing death or great bodily harm. Additionally, the woman hold it pointing toward the ground. Thus, it does not fall under (3).

As to the (1) requirement, using force violence, or assault, there is no fact indicating that the woman's action satisfies it. As to the (2) requirement, putting the victim in fear of serious injury, there is no fact indicating that the woman tried to put the homeowner in fear although the homeowner was frightened.

In sum, the woman did not commit armed robbery of the $100 cash, since neither elements are satisfied.

1(b). The woman committed theft of the figurine, since all elements under State A statute are satisfied.

Under State A statute, the woman committed theft.

Here, there is no fact indicating that the woman is entitled to any tips for delayed payment. Additionally, the fact that the woman glanced to make sure the homeowner wasn't looking shows she acted without consent. Thus, the woman's action constitutes unlawful taking.

As to intent, the woman sold the figurine just right after she took it from the front lawn and it shows she had intent to permanently deprive it.

In sum, the woman committed theft of the figurine, since all elements under State A statute are satisfied.

1(c). The woman committed criminal possession of the figurine as stolen property, since all elements under State A statute are satisfied.

Under State A statute, woman committed the crime.

Here, woman stole figurine and hold it (until selling it). Additionally, she sold it and it shows the intent to benefit the woman other than homeonwner.

In sum, the woman committed criminal possession of the figurine as stolen property, since all elements under State A statute are satisfied.

2. The woman's assistant committed criminal possession of stolen property, since all elements under State A statute are satisfied.

Under State A statute, woman's assistant committed the crime.

Here, the woman told her "Just don't ask where I got it" and the assistant noticed a $200 price tag attached to the figurine. The woman offered to sell it for $10 and it is significantly lower than the amount on the tag. These facts show that the assistant reasonably should know that it is a stolen property. As to intent requirement, the assistant said "I can sell it for a hefty profit" and it shows she hold the figurine to benefit himself.

In sum, the woman's assistant committed criminal possession of stolen property, since all elements under State A statute are satisfied.

해설

난이도: 중

본 문제는 죄책을 정의한 statute를 '해석'하는데 초점을 두고 있는 바, 모든 요건에 대해 빠짐없이 작성하는 것이 가장 중요하다. 난이도가 높지는 않으나 시간이 오래 걸리는 문제이다.

핵심 단어 및 논점

- theft
- armed robbery
- dangerous weapon
- act
- intent (mens rea)

1(a)번 문제

- Theft와 armed robbery의 관계를 파악하여, armed robbery에 theft의 성립요건이 포함된다는 점을 서술하는 것이 고득점 포인트다. 이는 MPT에서 조문을 읽을 때에도 꼭 필요한 리딩 스킬이다.
- Armed robbery의 성립유무를 4개의 요소(파트)로 구분하여 각 요소를 analysis해야 한다. 4개의 요소는 theft의 act, theft의 intent, armed robbery의 dangerous weapon, armed robbery의 (1)과 (2)이다. 문제에서 "all elements"라고 명시하였으므로, woman이 첫 번째 요소를 충족하지 못했다 할지라도, 나머지 요소의 성립 여부를 모두 작성해야 한다.

1(c)번 문제

Woman이 figurine을 훔쳐 타인에게 판매한 행위는 theft와 criminal possession of stolen property, 이 두 죄책에 모두 해당한다. 따라서 본 문제의 결론은, woman은 criminal possession of stolen property를 'commit했다'이다.

Q. "Commit했다"는 결론은 Double Jeopardy Clause에 위배되는 바, 답이 될 수 없지 않은가?

위배되는 것은 맞다. 즉 대부분의 주에서 헌법상 Double Jeopardy Clause를 근거로 woman의 행동(하나의 행동)에 대해 두 개의 죄책을 인정하지는 않을 것이다. 그러나 이는 최종판결선고 시 고려되는 헌법상 제한으로, 단순히 woman의 행위가 criminal possession of stolen property의 모든 요건을 충족했는지 그 여부를 판단'하는 본 문제와는 무관하다. 즉 본 문제는 죄책유무를 판단하는 문제이고, Double Jeopardy Clause는 그다음에 논할 문제다.

1. Amy and Bill have the authority as members of the board to vote to approve their trip to Belgium at corporate expense, since there was the affirmative vote of a majority of directors.

Board of directors (BOD) make decisions for the corporation. Their decision is valid when there is the affirmative vote of a majority of directors.

Here, Amy, Bill, and Sharon are directors. All three were in the board meeting and Amy and Bill (majority of BOD) voted to approve their trip to Belgium at corporate expense. Thus, the decision is valid.

In sum, Amy and Bill have the authority as members of the board to vote to approve their trip to Belgium at corporate expense, since there was the affirmative vote of a majority of directors.

2. Amy and Bill violated the duty of loyalty, but they are protected under the fairness test since the trip to Belgium is mainly for the corporation.

When directors make a conflicting interest transaction, duty of loyalty is violated.
Here, Amy and Bill can take in nearby museums and historic sites which are unrelated with the business. This is personal interest of Ann and Bill and it has conflicting interest against the corporation. Thus, having the corporation pay for their Belgium trip is violation of duty of loyalty.

However, safe harbor rule protects a director who breaches his duty of loyalty. Safe harbor rule applies when: (1) there is an approval by disinterested directors or shareholders, (2) a director fully disclosed all relevant information, and (3) a director played no part in the disinterested directors' vote directly or indirectly.
Here, Amy and Bill are 'interested directors (and shareholders),' but only Sharon is 'disinterested director (and shareholder).' Amy and Bill participated in the vote

and the requirement (1) was not satisfied. Thus, safe harbor rule does not protect Amy and Bill.

When directors make a conflicting interest transaction, fairness test can be used. Generally, the directors have the burden to show that the transaction was fair.

Here, taking in nearby museums and historic sites were just small part of the trip. The trip to Belgium is mainly for the corporation, getting new ideas about ingredients and brewing techniques. Additionally, there is no fact showing the payment is unfair price and unfair dealing. Thus, it is fair.

In sum, Amy and Bill violated the duty of loyalty, but they are protected under the fairness test since the trip to Belgium is mainly for the corporation.

3. Sharon cannot personally recover from Amy and Bill all the expenses for that trip paid by BC, since Sharon may bring derivative suit against them.

A derivative suit is one regarding fiduciary breach by directors or challenging allegedly illegal action by management. If a claim is for shareholder's rights, it is a direct suit.

Assuming that Amy and Bill violated the duty of loyalty, Sharon may bring derivative suit against them. In derivative suit, any remedies are turned to the corporation, not the directors or shareholders.

In sum, Sharon cannot personally recover from Amy and Bill all the expenses for that trip paid by BC, since Sharon may bring derivative suit against them.

4. Sharon cannot bring a derivative claim to recover from Amy and Bill the expenses paid by BC that related to third prior trips to Germany, since Sharon was not a shareholder at the time the expenses were made.

A derivative suit can be raised only by a shareholder who is a shareholder at the time of the act.

Here, Sharon was elected as the third director of BC after BC paid expenses to prior trips to Germany. Thus, Sharon cannot bring a derivative suit as to the trips to Germany.

In sum, Sharon cannot bring a derivative claim to recover from Amy and Bill the expenses paid by BC that related to third prior trips to Germany, since Sharon was not a shareholder at the time the expenses were made.

해설

난이도: 2번 문제: 상
　　　　3번 문제: 중
　　　　그 외 문제: 하

핵심 단어 및 논점

- make decisions for the corporation
- affirmative vote
- majority of directors
- duty of loyalty
- conflicting interest transaction (self-dealing)
- personal interest
- conflicting interest against the corporation
- safe harbor rule
- disinterested directors or shareholders
- fairness (test)
- fair price
- fair dealing
- derivative suit
- direct suit
- remedies are turned to the corporation
- at the time of the act

2번 문제

- 본 답안에는 'conflicting interest transaction' 표현이 사용되었으나, 이 대신 'self-dealing' 표현을 사용해도 무방하다. 여기서 중요한 것은 Belgium trip을 위해 회삿돈을 사용하는 것이 conflicting interest transaction인지 그 여부에 대한 로직을 상세하게 작성하는 것이다. 즉 왜 conflicting interest transaction으로 인정되는지 (혹은 되지 않는지), 그 판단과정을 상세히 analysis해야 한다. 어떤 표현을 사용했는지는 점수에 영향을 미치지 않는다.

- 세 개의 논점, 즉 conflicting interest transaction 여부, safe harbor rule 적용여부, fairness 적용여부에 대해 모두 서술해야 한다. 본 답안은 이 세 논점을 별도의 넘버링 없이 작성하였으나, 각 논점을 별도의 title로 구분하여 작성하는 것도 좋은 방법이다.

- 'Amy와 Bill이 회삿돈으로 museums와 historic sites를 가는 것이 fair한지' 그 여부에 대해 자세히 analysis해야만 고득점 할 수 있다. Fair하다 혹은 fair하지 않다는 결론은 점수에 영향을 미치지 않는다.

3번 문제

본 문제에서 핵심 문구는 'personally recover'이다. 소송을 통해 Sharon이 직접 Amy 와 Bill로부터 손해배상을 청구할 수 있는지 그 여부를 판단하는 문제로서, derivative suit(claim)의 기본 성격에 대한 문제이다.

4번 문제

본 문제에서 핵심 문구는 'prior trips to Germany'이다. Trips to Germany와 trips to Belgium의 차이점을 비교할 수 있는지를 시험하는 문제였다. 어렵지 않은 문제였으나, 문제를 꼼꼼히 읽지 않으면 틀리기 쉽다.

2022Feb Agency

<u>1(a). As to the yellow chairs, Peter is not bound by the contract signed by Angela with the furniture store, since Angela had neither actual nor apparent authority.</u>

Under general agency rule, a principal is liable to the contract made by an agent when the agent had either actual or apparent authority. Actual authority arises when the principal expressly told the agent to do so or agent reasonably believes that the principal wishes him to do so.

Here, Peter clearly told Angela that he want Angela to buy 50 red chairs. Additionally, Angela responded, "I fully understand. Agreed." and it shows she clearly knew that she has no authority to purchase the yellow chairs. Thus, Angela had no actual authority.

Apparent authority arises when (1) a third party reasonably believes that the actor is authorized, (2) that belief is from the principal's manifestation, and (3) the third party has no notice.

Here, there is no fact indicating Peter's manifestation as to the contract. Thus, Angela had no apparent authority.

In sum, as to the yellow chairs, Peter is not bound by the contract signed by Angela with the furniture store, since Angela had neither actual nor apparent authority.

<u>1(b). Angela is bound by the contract she signed with the furniture store, since Peter was an undisclosed principal and Angela is a party to the contract.</u>

An undisclosed principal exists when a third party did not know the existence of principal and the identity of principal.

Here, Angela did not mention to the salesperson that she was buying the chairs for someone other than herself or that she had authority to buy only red chairs. Thus, Peter is an undisclosed principal.

When there is an undisclosed principal, the opposing party assumes that the party with whom it contracts will be bound by the contract. Thus, when the contract is breached Angela is liable for the breach of contract.
In sum, Angela is bound by the contract she signed with the furniture store, since Peter was an undisclosed principal and Angela is a party to the contract.

2. As to the used cargo bike, Angela cannot recoup from Peter the $8,000 under the Second Restatement of Agency, since Peter cannot ratify the contract. Under the Third Restatement of Agency, Angela can recoup since Peter can ratify the contract.

Ratification relates back to the time of the transaction.
Here, Angela had no authority to purchase the used cargo bike, since Peter told her to buy a new electric bicycle. However, after trying out the cargo bike, Peter called Angela and said that he would keep the bike.

Under the Second Restatement of Agency, ratification requires the agent to act purport to be acting for the principal.
Here, as mentioned above, Peter is an undisclosed principal and "purporting" requirement cannot be satisfied. Thus, Peter cannot ratify the contract.

Under the Third Restatement of Agency, either purporting or acting is required. Thus, Peter can ratify the contract and he needs to indemnify Angela for the contract. Principal should indemnify the agent for the purchase when (1) the agent acted within the actual authority or (2) it is beneficial to the principal.
Here, ratification occurred and it is treated as if the transaction was authorized at the time of the transaction. Thus, Angela can recoup.

In sum, as to the used cargo bike, Angela cannot recoup from Peter the $8,000 under the Second Restatement of Agency, since Peter cannot ratify the contract. Under the Third Restatement of Agency, Angela can recoup since Peter can ratify the contract.

3. As to the pizza oven, Peter is bound by the contract signed by Angela, since Angela had apparent authority.

Here, it is reasonable for the owner to believe Angela's authority, since Peter told the owner "I have asked my sister Angela to come to your store to purchase a pizza oven on my behalf for the pizza parlor." Additionally, the owner had no notice Angela was exceeding her authority.

In sum, as to the pizza oven, Peter is bound by the contract signed by Angela, since Angela had apparent authority.

해설

난이도: 2번 문제: 상
　　　　그 외 문제: 하

핵심 단어 및 논점

- general agency rule
- actual authority
- expressly
- agent reasonably believes
- apparent authority
- third party reasonably believes
- traceable to the principal's manifestation
- undisclosed principal
- ratification
- Second Restatement of Agency
- Third Restatement of Agency
- indemnify

2번 문제

본 문제는 ① ratification 존재여부와 ② ratification이 인정될 경우 principal과 agent 간의 관계, 이 두 논점에 대한 것이다.

① Ratification 존재여부의 경우, 기본적으로 ratification의 세 요건을 모두 충족했는지를 기준으로 판단한다. 특히 이번 기출문제는 undisclosed principal의 사안으로 출제된 바, ratification의 요건 중 첫 번째 요건(the agent acted or purported to act as an agent on the person's behalf)에 중점을 두고 답안을 작성해야 하는데, Second Restatement of Agency와 Third Restatement의 내용을 구분하여 그 결론을 도출하는 것이 핵심이다.

② Ratification이 인정되면, agent가 해당 계약을 체결할 당시 actual authority를 가지

고 있었던 것과 같이 취급된다. 즉 대리권을 가지고 체결한 계약이므로, agent가 해당 계약에 의거해 상대방에게 지불한 대금이 있다면 principal로부터 indemnify 받을 수 있다. 이는 'ratification이 인정된다 할지라도 agent is still liable to the third party'라는 rule과 구별되는 내용이다. Agent is still liable하다는 것은, 제3자가 해당 계약이 제대로 이행되지 않아 'agent를 상대로 소송을 제기하면' agent가 패소한다는 의미로, agent가 완벽한 대리권을 행사하지 않았다는 것이다. 즉 (1) agent가 actual 또는 apparent authority를 가지고 (2) 제3자에게 principal의 존재를 명확히 언급해야 하는데, 그렇지 못한 경우 해당 계약에 책임을 져야 한다. Ratification이 인정되면 agent가 해당 계약을 체결할 당시 actual authority를 가지고 있었던 것과 같이 취급되는 바, (1)요건은 충족된다. 그러나 partially disclosed principal 또는 undisclosed principal인 경우에는, (2)요건이 충족될 수 없다. 즉 제3자가 자신의 계약상대방이 principal이 아닌 agent로 인지했으므로, agent가 해당 계약에 대해 책임을 지는 것이다. 정리하자면, ratification이 인정된 후의 (a) agent-principal 간의 관계와 (b) agent-third party 간의 관계, 이 두 관계를 구분해야 한다. (a)관계는 'ratification의 효과'에 따라 agent의 actual authority가 인정되는 바, principal은 agent에게 대금을 지급해야 한다. 한편, (b)관계는 'agent의 완벽한 대리권유무'를 기준으로 판단하는 바, partially disclosed principal 또는 undisclosed principal일 때 agent는 해당 계약에 대해 책임을 진다.

1. The bank may not reach Bob's interest in present and future distributions of trust income, since there is spendthrift clause in the trust instrument.

Under the spendthrift clause, creditors of a trust beneficiary is not entitled to trust assets until trust assets are distributed to the beneficiary.

Here, the second clause of the trust instrument is a spendthrift clause which restricts alignment or assignment of trust interest. Thus, the bank, beneficiary's creditor, cannot reach Bob's interest.

In sum, the bank may not reach Bob's interest in present and future distributions of trust income, since there is spendthrift clause in the trust instrument.

2. Bob's former wife may reach Bob's interest in present and future distributions of trust income, since the exception rule applies.

Even with a spendthrift clause, claims against a beneficiary for unpaid child support can be enforced against the trust.

Here, Bob's former wife seeks to enforce a $30,000 judgment against Bob for unpaid child support. Thus, exception rule applies.

In sum, Bob's former wife may reach Bob's interest in present and future distributions of trust income, since the exception rule applies.

3(a). Daughter's power of appointment is special power or appointment.

There are two types of power of appointment: general power and special power. A general power allows the appointee to exercise the power as she likes. A donee of a special power of appointment can only exercise the special power in the permissible objects.

Here, the trust instrument requires Settlor's friend to distribute trust income to

Daughter, Ann, and Bob and principal to Daughter's heirs at law. Thus, it is special power.

In sum, daughter's power of appointment is special power or appointment.

3(b). An appointment of trust principal by Daughter to Settlor's twins would be ineffective, since twins would not be "heirs at law" of Daughter.

If a donee exercise the power in nonobjects, the appointment is ineffective and the property passes to the taker in default of appointment.

Here, under the trust instrument, trust principal should be distributed following Daughter's death as she may appoint by her will among her heirs at law. "Heirs at law" means persons who are entitled to the share of the estate under the intestacy law. When there is a surviving descendant of decedent, siblings are not entitled to the intestate share of estate. Ann and Bob are Daughter's descendant and twins are siblings of Daughter. "Heirs" are determined when Daughter died, and it is likely that Ann and Bob survive Daughter. Thus, twins, siblings of Daughter, would be not entitled to the intestate share.

In sum, an appointment of trust principal by Daughter to Settlor's twins would be ineffective, since twins would not be "heirs at law" of Daughter.

3(c). The trust principal would pass to Daughter's descendants upon her death, since they are permissible objects and two requirements would be satisfied at the time of Daughter's death.

If a donee exercise the power in nonobjects, the appointment is ineffective and the property passes to the taker in default of appointment. When the taker in default is not specified in the trust, permissible objects take the share when (1) they are defined and limited class and (2) donor specified that permissible objects may take the share only if the donee elected them.

Here, permissible objects are Daughter's heirs. At the time of Daughter's death, those will be defined and limited class. Additionally, there is no fact indicating Daughter must elect permissible objects. Thus, if Daughter fails to exercise her power, Daughter's heirs (may be Ann and Bob) would take the trust principal.

In sum, the trust principal would pass to Daughter's descendants upon her death, since they are permissible objects and two requirements would be satisfied at the time of Daughter's death.

해설

난이도: 2번 문제: 중
   3(b)번 문제: 상
   3(c)번 문제: 중
   그 외 문제: 하

핵심 단어 및 논점

- spendthrift clause
- child support (예외)
- power of appointment
- special power of appointment
- permissible object
- heirs at law
- siblings
- descendant

2번 문제

본 문제는 spendthrift clause가 적용되지 않는 예외의 경우에 대한 것이다. 1번과 2번 문제는 '주체'만 달리하고 동일한 논점(Bob's interest에 reach할 수 있는지 그 여부)에 대한 것으로, bank와 former wife의 '상황'에 따라 다른 rule이 적용될 수 있다는 것을 예상할 수 있다.

3(a)번 문제

본 문제는 Daughter가 가진 권한의 '유형(classification)'을 묻고 있다. 따라서 power of appointment의 모든 유형, 즉 general power와 special power를 모두 언급하는 것이 좋다. 한편, power of appoint를 가진 자(appointee)가 행한 '행위의 적합성'에 대해 논하는 문제의 경우에는 해당하는 power의 유형만 언급해도 충분하다(2020Oct 기출).

3(b)번 문제

답안 로직은 다음과 같다.

Power of appointment의 유효성은 twins가 permissible objects인지 그 여부를 기준으로 판단한다.

→ Twins는 "heirs of Daughter"가 맞는가?

→ "Heirs of law"는 누구를 의미하는가?

→ 고인(Daughter)의 직계비속(Ann and Bob)이 생존할 확률이 높다. 따라서 고인의 형제(twins)는 Daughter의 유산에 대해 intestate share가 없다.

1. There is an enforceable contract, since the agreement is made under UCC2 and SOF does not apply here because there is a merchant's confirmatory memo.

A contract for the sale of goods is governed by UCC2. "Goods" means movable things at the time of making a contract.

Here, a contract between Buyer and Seller is to sell silk, and it is governed by UCC2.

Under UCC2, a contract for sale of goods may be made in any manner sufficient to show agreement, including conduct by both parties which recognizes the existence of such a contract.

Here, on January 9, Buyer and Seller clearly agreed in a telephone call that Buyer would buy 10,000 yards of silk. Seller stated "I'm glad that we were able to reach agreement" and it is sufficient to show the agreement between them.

Under the statute of frauds (SOF), a contract for the sale of goods for the price of $500 or more is not enforceable unless there is some writing sufficient to indicate that a contract for sale has been made between the parties and signed by the party to be charged. Under UCC2, writing must contain quantity of goods. Here, the contract price was $100,000 and it is subject to this rule. Buyer sent a signed note to Seller and the note states that the deal is "for the 10,000." However, the note is signed by Buyer but the party to be charged is Seller. Thus, SOF is unsatisfied.

However, When a writing is a merchant's confirmatory memo, the writing is not required. A writing is a merchant's confirmatory memo when: (1) the contract is made between merchants; (2) the sender makes the writing in confirmation of the contract within a reasonable time, (3) the writing is received and the receiving party has reason to know its contents, and (4) the receiving party does not make objection to its contents within 10 days after it is received.

Here, (1) both Buyer and Seller are merchants who deal in goods of the kind. (2) Buyer sent the memo next morning after the agreement has been made. (3) Seller received the note and Seller agreed in a telephone call. (4) Seller did not respond to it in any way. Thus, the writing is not required.

In sum, there is an enforceable contract, since the agreement is made under UCC2 and SOF does not apply here because there is a merchant's confirmatory memo.

2. The contract requires Seller to deliver the silk to Buyer's place of business because of the prior course of dealing.

When the contract does not specify the delivery obligations, gap−filling provision applies and a seller does not have delivery obligation. However, the course of dealing should be considered.

Here, the January 9 agreement does not clearly indicate the delivery obligations. However, in each of the earlier transactions, Seller delivered the silk to Buyer at no extra charge. Thus, Seller had an obligation.

In sum, the contract requires Seller to deliver the silk to Buyer's place of business because of the prior course of dealing.

3. Buyer is entitled to damages of $20,000 as cover damages ($2*10,000 yards).

When a seller breached the contract, a buyer is entitled to cover damages which are measured by the difference between the contract price and the cover price.

Here, Buyer made a good−faith and commercially reasonable purchase of 10,000 yards of silk at a price of $12 per yard. Contract price was $10 per yard. Thus, Buyer is entitled to $20,000 ($2*10,000 yards).

In sum, Buyer is entitled to damages of $20,000 as cover damages.

해설

난이도: 1번 문제: 상
2번 문제: 상
3번 문제: 하

핵심 단어 및 논점

- UCC2
- goods
- in any manner
- statute of frauds (SOF)
- signed by the party to be charged
- quantity of goods
- merchant's confirmatory memo
- gap-filling
- course of dealing
- cover damages

1번 문제

본 문제에는 세 개의 논점이 있다. 각 답안에 대한 답안 로직은 다음과 같다.

① Agreement가 존재하는가?

→ UCC2에서는 any manner를 인정한다. 따라서 telephone call로 통화한 내용은 agreement로 인정된다.

② Agreement의 validity에 대해 defense가 적용되는가? (SOF가 적용되는가?)

→ 대금이 $500을 초과하는 바, SOF가 적용된다. Memo가 존재하나, '서명'요건(계약성립을 부정하는 자, 즉 본 사안에서는 Seller가 서명해야 함)을 충족하지 못하였으므로 SOF를 충족하지 못한다.

③ SOF의 예외가 적용되는가?

→ Merchant's confirmatory memo가 적용된다. 따라서 해당 계약은 valid하다.

상기 논점②에서 SOF에서 요구하는 writing의 내용 및 구성을 꼼꼼히 analysis하는 것이 중요하다. SOF는 writing을 요구하는 단순한 룰이 아니다. 즉 누가 서명해야 하는지와 writing 내용에는 무엇이 있어야 하는지를 구체적으로 요구하는 룰이다. Writing에는 계약성립에 대한 intent가 명시되어 있고, UCC2가 적용되는 계약의 경우 writing에 반드시 quantity가 명시되어 있어야 하며, 계약성립을 부정하는 자(본 사안에서는 Seller)의 서명이 존재해야만 SOF를 충족하는 writing으로 인정된다. 최근 기출문제는 하나의 논점에 대해 '모든' 요건을 꼼꼼히 analysis하거나, 해석의 여지가 있는 표현들에 대해 상세하게 analysis해야 하는 스타일로 출제되고 있다. 따라서 답안지에 단순히 결과만 작성하면 안 되고, 반드시 그 결과가 도출된 로직을 상세히 analysis해야 할 것이다.

2번 문제

본 문제는 'gap—filling'과 'course of dealing'이 두 개념 중 어떤 것이 우선 적용되는지 판단하는 것이 핵심이다. Gap—filling이란, 계약서상 계약당사자 간 의무(place of delivery, time for delivery, notice of termination)가 명시되어 있지 않은 경우 UCC2에서 제공하는 기본 rule(§2—308(a))이다. 그러나 본 rule은 'unless otherwise agreed'한 경우, 즉 별도로 정해진 바가 없는 경우에 한해서만 적용되는 것으로, 계약당사자들 간의 course of dealing이 있다면 그것이 우선 적용되어야 한다.

__1. The court should deny the Defense counsel's motion as to the detective's anticipated testimony about gang identification, since all four elements to be an expert witness are satisfied.__

Expert opinion is admitted when (1) the expert's scientific, technical, or other specialized knowledge will help the trier of fact to understand the evidence or to determine a fact in issue, (2) the testimony is based on sufficient facts or data, (3) the testimony is the product of reliable principles and methods, and (4) the expert has reliably applied the principles and methods to the facts of the case.

Here, (1) the detective has specialized knowledge on the gang, since he has been a detective for six years and, throughout that time, his primary assignment has been to investigate gangs and criminal activity in City. Additionally, the fact in issue is about the gang and his experience will help the jury to understand the nature of the gang. (2) Detective was a corrections officer and did interviewing, investigating, and identifying gang members and he have attended training sessions. (3) and (4) His testimony is based on his experience and he said he is quite familiar with "The Lions." Thus, all four elements to be an expert witness are satisfied.

In sum, the court should deny the Defense counsel's motion as to the detective's anticipated testimony about gang identification, since all four elements to be an expert witness are satisfied.

__2. Defense counsel's motion as to the photograph of Defendant's tattoo and the former gang leader's anticipated testimony should be granted if it is to show the defendant acted in conformity with the gang member's character trait. By contrast, the motion should be overruled if it is to prove motive.__

Generally, character evidence is not admissible to prove that a person acted in conformity with the particular character trait. Some rules as to character evidence are subject to FRE 403: if a probative value is substantially outweighed by the danger of prejudice, confusion, or misleading the jury, the relevant evidence is not admissible. By contrast, evidence of crimes or other acts may be admissible for another purpose, such as motive, intent, absence of mistake, identity, or lack of accident.

Here, the evidences are proving that Defendant is a member of The Lions gang. If those evidences are submitted to prove that Defendant committed attempted murder in conformity with the gang member's particular character trait, they are inadmissible. Its probative value is substantially outweighed by danger of prejudice. However, if those evidences are submitted to prove the motive, it is admissible. If those are used to prove the reason why Defendant shoot Victim, it is admissible.

In sum, Defense counsel's motion as to the photograph of Defendant's tattoo and the former gang leader's anticipated testimony should be granted if it is to show the defendant acted in conformity with the gang member's character trait. By contrast, the motion should be overruled if it is to prove motive.

3. Defense counsel's motion as to Victim's anticipated testimony should be overruled, since it makes the fact more probable and it is as to motive.

Evidence is relevant if it has tendency to make a fact more or less probable than it would be without the evidence and the fact is important in determining the action.

Here, Victim's anticipated testimony is as to the motive of the action, the shooting. This makes whether the defendant's shooting was the result of a gang dispute more probable. Additionally, the testimony shows why the dispute occurred (Victim said she would not participate in an attack that was planned on another gang). This is important in determining the shooting. Here, the fact in issue is whether Defendant has committed attempted murder.

In sum, Defense counsel's motion as to Victim's anticipated testimony should be overruled, since it makes the fact more probable and it is as to motive.

해설

난이도: 1번 문제: 중
    2번 문제: 상
    3번 문제: 하

핵심 단어 및 논점

- expert opinion
- character evidence
- FRE 403
- MIMIC (예외 룰)
- relevant

1번 문제

Detective가 expert witness에 해당하는지 그 여부를 판단하는 문제이다. Expert witness 인정요건을 꼼꼼히 analysis하는 것이 핵심이다. 이때 사안 내용 중 'directive 가 제공한 정보'들을 각 요건에 매칭하는 것이 고득점 포인트다.

2번 문제

- Character evidence의 admissible 여부는 그것을 제출한 '목적'을 기준으로 판단한 다. 그런데 주어진 사안에는 각 evidence들의 제출 목적이 명시되어 있지 않은 바, 제출 목적을 구분하여 admissible 여부를 판단하는 것이 고득점 포인트다.
- Character evidence 논점에 관한 문제가 출제되면, 그 예외(MIMIC)의 경우를 반드 시 함께 논해야 한다.

3번 문제

본 문제는 해당 evidence가 relevant한지 그 여부를 묻고 있다. 따라서 해당 evidence 가 '본 재판과' relevant한(혹은 하지 않은) 논거를 상세히 언급해야 할 것이다.

1. Whether Seller's and Buyer's oral agreement is enforceable is a close call, since no integration or merger clause is not determinative and there is no fact indicating whether the omission is natural in such type of contract between Seller and Buyer.

Under the parol evidence rule, the terms of oral agreement that predate a written agreement is inadmissible, when a contract has been reduced to a completely integrated writing. In determining whether the writing is completely or partially integrated, the court considers various factors.

Here, Seller and Buyer orally agreed that if Seller sold the winery to Buyer, he would continue to use the label for as long as he sold red wines. Buyer and Seller entered into and signed a lengthy written agreement. The agreement did not include any provision about future use of the red wine label with Seller's picture. The agreement did not include the provision as to the picture but it is not inconsistent with the oral agreement. Thus, the oral agreement is enforceable if the writing is not complete integrated.

The written agreement is integrated, since it includes how Buyer would pay Seller after several oral agreements. However, whether it is completely integrated is a close call. The written agreement did not contain an integration or merger clause. It supports the written agreement is not completely integrated, but it is not determinative. The fact that the written agreement is lengthy and the parties signed on it supports the written agreement is completely integrated. An agreement is not completely integrated if there is no terms which are naturally omitted from the writing. However, there is not fact indicating whether the terms as to using the label is naturally omitted from the writing.

In sum, whether Seller's and Buyer's oral agreement is enforceable is a close call, since no integration or merger clause is not determinative and there is no fact indicating whether the omission is natural in such type of contract between Seller and Buyer.

2. Seller could introduce evidence of the negotiations, since the term in the contract is vague.

Extrinsic evidence is admissible when the terms in contract is vague.

Here, Buyer and Seller did not agree on the precise share of the first−year profits that Buyer must pay to Seller. The term "fair share of the winery's profits" is vague and ambiguous. Seller tries to introduce evidence of the negotiations to help explain the meaning, and it is admissible.

In sum, Seller could introduce evidence of the negotiations, since the term in the contract is vague.

3. Buyer would not prevail on a claim that Seller breached her obligations under the agreement by opening her new winery, since the provision violates public policy.

A promise is unenforceable when it violates public policy. If the restraint is greater than one that is required to achieve a party's business interest, it violates public policy and unenforceable.

Here, the written agreement stated that Seller was not permitted to own or operate a winery anywhere in the United States for 10 years after the closing. This provision restricts Seller not to compete Buyer's business. Buyer's business may be protected under the provision, but this restriction is too broad and unreasonable.

The provision is restricting anywhere in U.S., not specified regions. Additionally, 10−year restriction is also unreasonable for protecting Buyer's business.

In sum, Buyer would not prevail on a claim that Seller breached her obligations under the agreement by opening her new winery, since the provision violates public policy.

해설

난이도: 1번 문제: 상
2번 문제: 중
3번 문제: 하

핵심 단어 및 논점

- parol evidence rule
- "completely integrated" 해석
- final expression
- extrinsic evidence
- vague
- public policy
- covenant not to compete
- unreasonable

1번 문제

논점: Parol evidence rule 중 "completely integrated" 표현에 대한 해석

"Completely integrated" 표현 해석에 대한 절대적인 기준이 없기 때문에 결론보다는 논거와 로직이 매우 중요하며, close call임을 내세워 열린 결론을 맺어도 좋다.

2번 문제

본 문제는 "introduce evidence"할 수 있는지 그 여부를 판단하는 문제로서, term을 해석하는 데 있어 외부증거를 제출할 수 있는지에 대한 것이다.

예상질문

Q. 2번 문제의 논점은 parol evidence rule이 아닌가?

아니다. Parol evidence rule은 written agreement 이전에 존재했던 agreement의 내용을 증거로 제출할 수 있는지 그 여부에 대한 rule이다. 2번 문제의 논점과 parol evidence rule은 term을 해석하는데 증거 제출여부를 판단한다는 점에서 비슷하나, 엄격히 구분하자면 2번 문제는 extrinsic evidence에 대한 것이고, parol evidence rule에 대한 것이 아니다.

3번 문제

- "covenant not to compete"라는 표현을 익혀두도록 하자.
- 5년 미만의 경우, reasonable하다고 본다.
- Covenant(제한)가 unreasonable하다고 하여 unenforceable한 것은 아니다. Covenant가 계약당사자의 이익을 위해 필요하다고 판단되는 경우에는 enforceable하다. 원고의 confidential information이 제공됨으로써 피고(party sought to be bound)가 상당한 advantage를 가지는 경우가 그러하다. Confidential information에는 계약당사자의 operations, trade secrets, 민감한 정보(customer list, business practices, upcoming products(출시 전 상품), marketing plans 등)가 포함된다.

  "When the party sought to be bound might gain a competitive advantage by exploiting confidential information about the other party's operations or trade secrets, or use of sensitive proprietary information such as customer lists, business practices, upcoming products, and marketing plans."

2022July Corporations & Agency

<u>1. The corporation is bound by the land−sale agreement with the bank signed by Carol, since, even though Carol had neither actual nor apparent authority, BOD ratified the agreement.</u>

Under general agency rule, a principal is liable to the contract made by an agent when the agent had either actual or apparent authority. Actual authority arises when the principal expressly told the agent to do so or agent reasonably believes that the principal wishes him to do so.

Here, the board unanimously authorized Danielle to hire Carol and Danielle asked Carol to act on behalf of the corporation to obtain the loans, and Carol agreed to do so. Thus, agency between the board and Carol has been made. The corporation asked Carol to purchase a parcel of land for $5 million, but Carol made the contract for $6 million. Carol had no actual authority to the contract. Additionally, there is no fact indicating it is reasonable for the bank to believe Carol has authority. Thus, there was no apparent authority.

Ratification relates back to the time of the transaction. However, agent is still liable to the third party on the transaction.

Here, Even though there was neither actual nor apparent authority to Carol, Carol described to the board the terms of the agreement and all directors participated in the vote of the special meeting. Danielle and third director voted to approve the land sale and quorum existed and majority of BOD approved it. Thus, ratification existed and the corporation is bound by the agreement.

In sum, the corporation is bound by the land−sale agreement with the bank signed by Carol, since, even though Carol had neither actual nor apparent authority, BOD ratified the agreement.

2. The bonus payment made to Danielle was not proper, since it is a conflicting interest transaction and both safe harbor rule and fairness test do not protect Danielle.

Conflicting interest transaction is a transaction that the director had knowledge and a material financial interest. It is called as self−dealing in common law.

Here, the bonus payment made to Danielle is beneficial to Danielle and it is financially conflicting with the corporation's interest. Thus, it is a conflicting interest transaction.

Safe harbor rule protects a director who breaches his duty of loyalty. First of all, a director's conflicting interest transaction is protected under the safe harbor, when: (1) there is an approval by disinterested directors or shareholders, (2) a director fully disclosed all relevant information, and (3) a director played no part in the disinterested directors' vote directly or indirectly.

Here, Danielle and the third director voted to distribute all the sale proceeds to Danielle. Danielle is an interested directors and the first requirement is unsatisfied. Thus, safe harbor rule is inapplicable here.

When directors make a conflicting interest transaction, fairness test can be used. Generally, the directors have the burden to show that the transaction as a whole was fair in terms of fair price and fair dealing.

Here, there is no fact indicating that the payment to Danielle is beneficial to the corporation or fair.

In sum, the bonus payment made to Danielle was not proper, since it is a conflicting interest transaction and both safe harbor rule and fairness test do not protect Danielle.

3. Brain has sufficient grounds to seek the judicial dissolution of the corporation based on oppression doctrine.

There are two types of dissolution: voluntary and involuntary. There could be an involuntary dissolution, when a member's action is oppressive and directly harmful to other members. Under the oppression doctrine, courts can order to close corporation when actions by controlling shareholders violate the reasonable expectations of non−controlling shareholders.

Here, Danielle and the third director (controlling shareholders) voted to approve the land sale. However, it violates the reasonable expectation of Brain since the board unanimously approved a parcel of land for $5 million. Second, controlling shareholders voted to distribute all the slae proceeds to Danieele as a bonus payment. It also violates the reasonable expectation, since the baord setted a reasonable salary for Brain and Danielle is responsible for securing the financing. Third, Brain requested to see all accounting records, but the board refused it. It is another violation of the reasonable expectation. Thus, oppression doctrine applies. In sum, Brain has sufficient grounds to seek the judicial dissolution of the corporation based on oppression doctrine.

해설

난이도: 1번 문제: 상
        2번 문제: 하
        3번 문제: 중

핵심 단어 및 논점

- general agency rule
- actual authority
- apparent authority
- ratification
- quorum
- conflicting interest transaction
- self−dealing
- safe harbor rule
- disinterested director (qualified director)
- fairness
- involuntary dissolution
- oppression doctrine
- controlling shareholders (majority shareholders)
- reasonable expectations

1번 문제

본 문제는 agency와 corporation 과목이 혼합된 것이다. 답안의 로직은 다음과 같다.

Carol과 corporation 간 agency가 형성되어 있다.

→ Carol은 actual authority 및 apparent authority가 없었다. 따라서 corporation은 책임이 없다(General agency rule이 적용되지 않는다).

→ General agency rule이 적용되지 않는다 할지라도, ratification이 이루어졌다면 corporation은 해당 계약에 대해 책임이 있다.

→ Corporation, 즉 BOD는 특정 안건을 approve하기 위해서는 quorum이 충족되어 야 한다. 본 사안에서 directors 모두(총 세 명) 투표에 참여했고, 그중 두 명이 찬 성했으므로 해당 안건은 approve된다(Carol이 체결한 계약을 ratify한다).

→ Corporation은 ratify했으므로, 해당 계약에 대해 책임이 있다.

3번 문제
논점: judicial dissolution의 근거 중 oppression doctrine

Danielle과 the third director(BOD)가 결정한 사안과 Brain의 생각(expectation)이 충돌 하는 부분은 세 개다. 그런데 이 내용들은, 이전 BOD 회의에서 결정한 바(reasonable expectation)와 차이가 큰 바, Brian은 oppression doctrine을 근거로 judicial dissolution 을 구할 수 있다.

1(a). The AD Trust is validly created when Arlene bought the bonds and revised Schedule A to list them as assets of the trust, since the asset is not required to be transferred to the trust at the same time when the trust is created.

To be a valid trust, there must be testator's intent, capacity, definite beneficiary, trustee, and property. The same person should not be sole trustee and sole beneficiary.

Here, even though Arlene Doe is sole trustee, but is not a sole beneficiary. As to the property, a trust is created when the any assets are transferred to the trust. However, this requirement does not mean that the transfer should be made at the same time when the trust is created. Thus, the trust is created when Arlene bought the bonds and revised Schedule A to list them as assets of the trust.

In sum, the AD Trust is validly created when Arlene bought the bonds and revised Schedule A to list them as assets of the trust, since the asset is not required to be transferred to the trust at the same time when the trust is created.

1(b). The AD Trust was effectively revoked, since it is revocable.

A trust is revocable unless stated otherwise. A power to revoke includes the power to amend. Revocation is valid when there is testator's intent.

Here, the trust instrument had no provision regarding whether it was revocable or irrevocable. Thus, it is presumed as revocable trust and there is no fact indicating that there is no intent.

In sum, the AD Trust was effectively revoked, since it is revocable.

2. The trust for the benefit of Donna was valid, since clear and convincing evidence establishes the trust.

No writing is required for a valid trust. However, a trust orally created is valid only when there is clear and convincing evidence.

In our case, Arlene gave her friend the package and said "I revoked the AD Trust because I decided that I want my niece Donna to have everything ..." The fired said, "Okay." This clearly shows Arlene's intent to create a trust and intent to make a gift to Donna.

In sum, the trust for the benefit of Donna was valid, since clear and convincing evidence establishes the trust.

3. The testamentary trust for the benefit of the Political Party was not valid, since it is not a charitable trust and is subject to RAP.

According to the terms of the trust for the Political Party, it lasts in perpetuity. However, any trust is subject to RAP except for charitable trust. The rule against perpetuities (RAP) does not apply to charitable trust. A charitable trust is a trust that is beneficial to the community.

Here, the trust is to benefit Political Party, a particular political party. Additionally, the Political Party's exclusive mission is to support candidates for public office 'who accept its political views.' Thus, the trust is not public in nature.

In sum, the testamentary trust for the benefit of the Political Party was not valid, since it is not a charitable trust and is subject to RAP.

4. Bob is entitled to 1/3 of the bank account, Fred is entitled to other 1/3, and three nieces share the other 1/3.

Here, Bob, Fred, and three nieces Carla, Donna, and Edna survive Arlene. According to per stirpes method, 1/3 of the bank account is entitled to Bob and other 1/3 of the bank account is entitled to Fred. Three nieces Carla, Donna, and Edna share the other 1/3 (each is entitled to 1/9 of the bank account).

해설

난이도: 하

핵심 단어 및 논점

- validity (시점)
- property
- revocation
- inter vivos trust
- orally
- clear and convincing evidence
- no writing requirement
- RAP exception
- last in perpetuity
- charitable trust
- beneficial to the community
- per stirpes

1. Developer is a person required to be joined if feasible to the Builder v. Lender action under FRCP 19(a), since the absence of Developer may impair its ability to protect its interest as a practical matter and it places Lender being subject to substantial risk.

Under FRCP 19(a), the party is required to be joined (is a compulsory joinder) when: (1) accord and complete relief cannot be granted without the person or (2) the person's interest is so relating to the subject of the action that the absence of the party may impair or impede the person's ability to protect the interest, as a practical matter, or make the existing party be subject to a substantial risk of incurring double, multiple, or otherwise inconsistent duty.

Here, Developer entered into a written construction contract with Builder Co., and the loan agreement between Developer and Lender provided that any funds disbursed by Lender under the loan agreement. If the court finds for Builder, Lender should make the payment of $100,000 and Developer should repay for it. Thus, the absence of Developer may impair its ability to protect its interest as a practical matter.

Additionally, if Developer does not join in this case, Lender is placed in a substantial risk both on paying for $100,000 and on being sued by Developer for withholding the payment.

In sum, Developer is a person required to be joined if feasible to the Builder v. Lender action under FRCP 19(a), since the absence of Developer may impair its ability to protect its interest as a practical matter and it places Lender being subject to substantial risk.

2. Joinder of Developer would deprive the court of SMJ, since supplemental jurisdiction cannot be applied in compulsory joinder case.

When (1) the case is based on diversity jurisdiction and (2) the party joins the case under Rule 19 (as a compulsory joinder), complete diversity is required and supplemental jurisdiction cannot be applied.

Here, (1) the Builder v. Lender action is held in federal district court in State A, invoking the court's diversity jurisdiction. (2) As mentioned above in 1, Developer is a compulsory joinder. However, joinder of Developer does not have its own jurisdiction. Developer is LLC and its only members are Amy, a domiciliary of State a, and Barbara, a domiciliary of State B. Thus, it is domiciled in State A and State B. Builder is a State B corporation and Lender is incorporated in State A with its PPB in State A.

In sum, joinder of Developer would deprive the court of SMJ, since supplemental jurisdiction cannot be applied in compulsory joinder case.

3. The court should grant the motion to dismiss, since Lender or Builder could raise action in State courts.

When the joinder is not feasible, the court may, in equity and good conscience, dismiss the case or proceed the action. The court consider many factors, such as: (1) whether the absence of joinder creates substantial risks of prejudice to the existing party and (2) whether the plaintiff has alternative adequate remedy.

Here, as mentioned above, the absence of Developer creates substantial risks of prejudice to Lender. However, Lender could raise action in state courts and it has remedy even without the joinder. Additionally, Builder may sue both Developer and Lender in State B and no facts indicating any obstruction preventing Builder from suing them in State B. Thus, the court should dismiss the action.

In sum, the court should grant the motion to dismiss, since Lender or Builder could raise action in State courts.

해설

난이도: 상

핵심 단어 및 논점

- compulsory joinder
- supplemental jurisdiction
- diversity jurisdiction
- LLC domiciliary-member
- PPB, be incorporated
- alternative adequate remedy

- 본 기출은 Rule 19가 compulsory joinder라는 점, compulsory joinder에 SPJ가 적용되지 않는 경우, compulsory joinder가 join할 수 없을 때 법원의 판단기준, 이 세 개의 논점에 대한 것이다.
- 각 논점에 따라 동일한 사안이 다르게 해석될 수 있다. 즉 1번과 3번에서 언급된 사안은 공통되나(analysis 부분), 그것이 ① Rule 19 적용여부를 판단할 때와 ② compulsory joinder가 join할 수 없을 때 법원이 어떻게 판단해야 하는지, 각 논점을 논할 때 달리 해석된다.

1. Wanda is obligated to pay the property taxes on the family home, since she is a life tenant.

Life tenant has both the right to use the estate and the duty to pay all ordinary expenses (e.g., taxes) during the lifetime.

Under the Oscar's will, Wanda is a life tenant, while Adele is vested remainder. Adele left her entire estate to Frank. Thus, Frank has future interest on the building. Between a life tenant and a future interest holder, life tenant is obligated to pay the taxes. However, this duty is limited to the extent of the gross income or fair value of the property. Here, rental income is more than enough to pay the property tax.

In sum, Wanda is obligated to pay the property taxes on the family home, since she is a life tenant.

2. Oscar has possibility of reverter with the term "so long as" and the interest is valid since RAP does not apply here.

Here, the conveyance is valid "so long as at least four apartments in the apartment building are rented to families ...." Frank has fee simple determinable on the building, while Oscar (grantor) has possibility of reverter and the right automatically reverts to Oscar when the condition is breached.

Rule against perpetuities (RAP) applies to particular interests. Possibility of reverter is not the one subject to RAP. Thus, Oscar's interest is valid.

In sum, Oscar has possibility of reverter with the term "so long as" and the interest is valid since RAP does not apply here.

3. Wanda has possibility of reverter (reversionary interest) and it is valid.

As mentioned above, Oscar has possibility of reverter (reversionary interest) and it is devisable. Thus, upon Oscar's death, his right passes to Wanda under his will. Wanda's interest has same features with Oscar's interest. Thus, Wanda has reversionary interest. As mentioned above, RAP does not apply to reversionary interest.

In sum, Wanda has possibility of reverter (reversionary interest) and it is valid.

4. After February 1, 2021, Wanda owns the apartment building, since Frank's interest is automatically terminated.

As mentioned above, Frank's interest is fee simple determinable. Beginning Feb 1, 2021, no apartments in the building were being rented to below−median−income families. It means the condition is breached. Thus, Wanda who has reversionary interest automatically owns the building.

In sum, after February 1, 2021, Wanda owns the apartment building, since Frank's interest is automatically terminated.

해설

난이도: 1번 문제: 상
3번 문제: 중
그 외 문제: 하

핵심 단어 및 논점

- life tenant
- duty to pay taxes
- fee simple determinable
- possibility of reverter (reversionary interest)
- RAP

<연도별 기출정리표>

	A & P	Corp.	UCC9	Family	Wills	Trusts	RP	K	Civil	Torts	Con Law	E	Crimes
2024 Feb	○				○		○	○				○	○
2023 July		○	○		○				○	○			○
2023 Feb			○		○		○	○	○			○	○
2022 July	○	○			○	○	○	○	○			○	
2022 Feb	○	○	○			○		○					○
2021 July	○	○		○	○		○			○			
2021 Feb			○		○			○	○				○
2020 Oct	○			○		○			○		○	○	
2020 Sep	○	○		○	○		○	○			○		○
2020 July	○	○	○	○	○	○	○			○	○	○	
2020 Feb	○		○				○	○	○			○	○
2019 July		○		○	○	○	○	○	○			○	○
2019 Feb	○					○			○	○	○		○
2018 July		○	○				○	○				○	
2018 Feb	○			○			○	○	○				○
2017 July	○		○	○	○	○	○	○	○	○	○	○	○
2017 Feb	○	○	○	○		○	○	○					
2016 July		○	○	○	○				○	○		○	○
2016 Feb		○	○				○	○	○	○	○	○	
2015 July	○		○		○	○		○	○	○			○
2015 Feb		○		○	○		○	○	○	○	○		
2014 July		○							○		○	○	○
2014 Feb	○		○			○			○		○		○

	A & P	Corp.	UCC9	Family	Wills	Trusts	RP	K	Civil	Torts	Con Law	E	Crimes
2013 July	○				○			○	○	○		○	
2013 Feb	○					○	○	○	○		○	○	
2012 July	○				○	○			○	○	○		○
2012 Feb		○			○		○	○	○	○		○	
2011 July				○		○	○		○				○
2011 Feb	○	○		○	○	○			○				
2010 July				○	○			○	○		○		
2010 Feb	○	○		○		○	○		○	○		○	
2009 July			○	○		○					○		○
2009 Feb	○	○		○	○		○		○	○		○	
2008 July	○					○	○	○	○		○		
2008 Feb		○	○		○	○			○	○		○	○
출제된 횟수	18	17	14	14	20	18	18	19	27	13	15	18	19

저자 약력

백 희 영

서울 출생

중국KISQ고등학교 졸업

미국미주리주립대 경영학과 졸업

경영학, 법학, 컴퓨터공학 전공

미국변호사(워싱턴DC)

중국텐진화씨엔법률사무소 파트너 변호사

강 좌

백희영 미국변호사 강좌   www.BHYbar.com

 − MEE실전반

 − PT실전반

 − 룰정리/암기반

 − 객관식기본이론

 − 객관식기본문풀(NCBE 공식문제)

 − 객관식파이널 etc.

저 서

「미국변호사법①─MEE편」

「미국변호사법②─CEE편」

「미국변호사법③─객관식편」

미국 변호사법 ❹ MEE 기출문제 해설집

초판발행	2024년 8월 30일
지은이	백희영
펴낸이	안종만 · 안상준
편 집	장유나
기획/마케팅	장규식
표지디자인	BEN STORY
제 작	고철민 · 김원표
펴낸곳	㈜ **박영사**
	서울특별시 금천구 가산디지털2로 53, 210호(가산동, 한라시그마밸리)
	등록 1959. 3. 11. 제300-1959-1호(倫)
전 화	02)733-6771
f a x	02)736-4818
e-mail	pys@pybook.co.kr
homepage	www.pybook.co.kr
ISBN	979-11-303-4775-2 13360

copyright©백희영, 2024, Printed in Korea

* 파본은 구입하신 곳에서 교환해 드립니다. 본서의 무단복제행위를 금합니다.

정가   45,000원